AF839020

PAROLE FUTURES

Does parole have a future? If it does, can we begin to imagine a different path? Is progressive penal reform possible, or has the time come to consider more radical alternatives in a context where there is little, if any, consensus on the underlying aims and techniques of contemporary prison release? What does this all mean for the prisoners, families, victims and publics upon whose confidence the parole system ultimately depends?

This book brings together a world-leading panel of 27 experts who draw upon insights from law, sociology, criminology and political science to explore these pressing questions. At a time when many parole systems are experiencing considerable strain, the aims of this collection are twofold: first, to encourage systematic and critical reflection on the rationalities, institutions and practices of parole. Second, to think big, and pose ambitious 'what if' questions about the possible futures of parole and prison release.

Offering novel insights from Asia, Australia, Europe, North America and South America, this collection builds the case for, and then showcases, a 'way of doing' parole research that is global in outlook, interdisciplinary in approach and unapologetically normative in character.

Oñati International Series in Law and Society

A SERIES PUBLISHED FOR THE OÑATI INSTITUTE
FOR THE SOCIOLOGY OF LAW

General Editors
Rosemary Hunter David Nelken

Founding Editors
William L F Felstiner Eve Darian-Smith

Editorial Board
Carlos Lugo, Hostos Law School, Puerto Rico
Jacek Kurczewski, Warsaw University, Poland
Marie-Claire Foblets, Max Planck Institute for
Social Anthropology in Halle, Germany
Ulrike Schultz, Fern Universität, Germany

Recent titles in this series

The Legacies of Institutionalisation: Disability, Law and Policy in the 'Deinstitutionalised' Community
Edited by Claire Spivakovsky, Linda Steele and Penelope Weller

Gender and Careers in the Legal Academy
Edited by Ulrike Schultz, Gisela Shaw, Margaret Thornton and Rosemary Auchmuty

Contesting Austerity: A Socio-Legal Inquiry
Edited by Anuscheh Farahat and Xabier Arzoz

The Right to the Continuous Improvement of Living Conditions: Responding to Complex Global Challenges
Edited by Jessie Hohmann and Beth Goldblatt

Supporting Legal Capacity in Socio-Legal Context
Edited by Mary Donnelly, Rosie Harding and Ezgi Tascioglu

What Is a Family Justice System For?
Edited by Mavis Maclean, Rachel Treloar and Bregje Dijksterhuis

Combining the Legal and the Social in Sociology of Law: An Homage to Reza Banakar
Edited by Håkan Hydén, Roger Cotterrell, David Nelken and Ulrike Schultz

Criminal Justice and The Ideal Defendant in the Making of Remorse and Responsibility
Edited by Stewart Field and Cyrus Tata

Socio-Legal Trajectories Across Europe: Comparative Perspectives
Edited by Christian Boulanger, Naomi Creutzfeldt and Jennifer Hendry

Parole Futures: Rationalities, Institutions and Practices
Edited by Harry Annison, Nicola Carr and Thomas Guiney

For the complete list of titles in this series
see www.bloomsbury.com/uk/series/oñati-international-series-in-law-and-society

Parole Futures

Rationalities, Institutions and Practices

Edited by
Harry Annison
Nicola Carr
and
Thomas Guiney

Oñati International Series in Law and Society

A SERIES PUBLISHED FOR THE OÑATI INSTITUTE FOR THE SOCIOLOGY OF LAW

•HART•
OXFORD • LONDON • NEW YORK • NEW DELHI • SYDNEY

HART PUBLISHING

Bloomsbury Publishing Plc

Kemp House, Chawley Park, Cumnor Hill, Oxford, OX2 9PH, UK

1385 Broadway, New York, NY 10018, USA

Bloomsbury Publishing Ireland Limited, 29 Earlsfort Terrace, Dublin 2, D02 AY28, Ireland

HART PUBLISHING, the Hart/Stag logo, BLOOMSBURY and the Diana logo are trademarks of Bloomsbury Publishing Plc

First published in Great Britain 2025

Copyright © The editors and contributors severally 2025

The editors and contributors have asserted their right under the Copyright, Designs and Patents Act 1988 to be identified as Authors of this work.

All rights reserved. No part of this publication may be: i) reproduced or transmitted in any form, electronic or mechanical, including photocopying, recording or by means of any information storage or retrieval system without prior permission in writing from the publishers; or ii) used or reproduced in any way for the training, development or operation of artificial intelligence (AI) technologies, including generative AI technologies. The rights holders expressly reserve this publication from the text and data mining exception as per Article 4(3) of the Digital Single Market Directive (EU) 2019/790.

While every care has been taken to ensure the accuracy of this work, no responsibility for loss or damage occasioned to any person acting or refraining from action as a result of any statement in it can be accepted by the authors, editors or publishers.

All UK Government legislation and other public sector information used in the work is Crown Copyright ©. All House of Lords and House of Commons information used in the work is Parliamentary Copyright ©. This information is reused under the terms of the Open Government Licence v3.0 (http //www.nationalarchives.gov.uk/doc/open-government-licence/version/3) except where otherwise stated.

All Eur-lex material used in the work is © European Union, http://eur-lex.europa.eu/, 1998–2025.

A catalogue record for this book is available from the British Library.

A catalogue record for this book is available from the Library of Congress.

ISBN: HB: 978-1-50998-217-2
ePDF: 978-1-50998-219-6
ePub: 978-1-50998-218-9

Typeset by Compuscript Ltd, Shannon

For product safety related questions contact productsafety@bloomsbury.com

To find out more about our authors and books visit www.hartpublishing.co.uk. Here you will find extracts, author information, details of forthcoming events and the option to sign up for our newsletters.

For Jenny, for making everything possible – HA

For JBR – NC

With thanks to my wonderful parents, Pauline and Dennis – TG

Acknowledgements

The editors would like to extend their sincere thanks to the Oñati International Institute for the Sociology of Law for hosting the workshop, The Future of Parole: Ideas, Institutions and Practices. We are also grateful to Nahikari Borda Zumeta, Ombudsman for the Basque Country, Ciairín de Buis, Chief Executive Officer, Parole Board of Ireland, and Professor Nick Hardwick, Royal Holloway and Former Chair of the Parole Board of England & Wales, for sharing their reflections and providing a much welcome practitioners' perspective. Our thanks are due to the Hart Bloomsbury team for their help and support during the preparation of this edited collection. Finally, we would like to express our gratitude to each of the contributing authors for going on this journey with us. This was not an easy brief, and we continue to be inspired by your passion, creativity and intellectual curiosity. The workshop underpinning this book received financial support from a Southampton Law School Strategic Research Fund award and the University of Nottingham's Research Support Fund, for which we are grateful.

Contents

List of Contributors

Mikel Anderez Belategi, Criminal Law Lecturer at the University of the Basque Country/Euskal Herriko Unibertsitatea

Harry Annison, Professor of Criminal Justice at the University of Southampton Law School

Jasmina Arnež, Research Associate at the Institute of Criminology at the Faculty of Law, University of Ljubljana

Lorana Bartels, Professor of Criminology at the Australian National University

Kristel Beyens, Professor of Criminology and Penology at Vrije Universiteit Brussel

Lars Breuls, Professor of Penology at Vrije Universiteit Brussels

Nicola Carr, Professor of Social Work and Social Policy at Trinity College Dublin

Mary Corcoran, Professor of Criminology at Keele University

Netanel Dagan, Assistant Professor at the Hebrew University of Jerusalem

Catalina Droppelmann, Lecturer at the Pontificia Universidad Católica in Chile

Sergio Faúndez, PhD student at the Universitat Pompeu Fabra Barcelona

Arie Freiberg, Emeritus Professor of Law at Monash University

Thomas Guiney, Assistant Professor of Criminology at the University of Nottingham

Fergus McNeill, Professor of Criminology and Social Work at the University of Glasgow

Delaney Mosca, PhD student at the University of California, Irvine

Nicola Padfield, Emeritus Professor of Criminal and Penal Justice at the University of Cambridge

Mojca M Plesničar, Assistant Professor in Criminology and Criminal Law at the University of Ljubljana

Rosemary Ricciardelli, Professor of Sociology and Criminology at the Memorial University of Newfoundland

Ebony Ruhland, Associate Professor of Criminal Justice at Rutgers University Newark

Doris Schartmueller, Associate Professor at the California State University

Chris Seeds, Assistant Professor of Criminology, Law and Society at the University of California, Irvine

Micheal P Taylor, Research Assistant at the Memorial University of Newfoundland

Saori Toda, PhD student at Hitostubashi University

Marion Vannier, Senior Lecturer in Criminology at the University of Manchester

Dirk van Zyl Smit, Emeritus Professor of Comparative and International Penal Law at the University of Nottingham

Carolina Villagra, Assistant Professor at Universidad de Chile

Beth Weaver, Professor of Criminal and Social Justice at the University of Strathclyde

1

Editors Introduction: Does Parole have a Future?

HARRY ANNISON, NICOLA CARR AND THOMAS GUINEY

I. INTRODUCTION: NAVIGATING PAROLE'S MORAL COMPLEXITIES

SIMON (1993) HAS argued that the emergence, and subsequent realignment, of parole in many jurisdictions has tracked the shifting contours of penal (late) modernism. While sharing much in common with historic penal developments such as remission, the ticket of leave and the marks system (Bottomley 1990), parole is defined by a broad constellation of legal and administrative mechanisms which allow the custodial element of a sentence to be varied with the remainder served either in the community under licence or terminated unconditionally (West 1972). For these reasons, parole has become one of the most recognisable features of the contemporary penal policy landscape and a site of intense political contestation. These bureaucratic procedures are a defining feature of the carceral experience for many prisoners, and significant resources continue to be invested by nation states in their operation.

The changes in the rationalities, institutions and practices of parole across time are marked (see, eg Shute 2003), and considerable variation can be viewed internationally (Padfield et al 2012; Armstrong and Durnescu 2017; van Zyl Smit and Corda 2018). However, what continues to unite these diverse penal practices is a demonstrable impact upon the scale, scope and reach of the penal system. These penal practices require ongoing moral justification (Duff and Garland 1994), not least because of their uneven impact on groups within society and the values that they do (or do not) reflect (Carvalho and Chamberlen 2023).

Parole's operation blurs the boundaries between parliament, judiciary and executive, and poses important questions for the constitutional separation of powers as a foundational principle of liberal democratic thought (Guiney 2023). Moreover, as Dagan (2022; 2023) and others have noted, parole is defined by a unique temporality where the past, present and possible futures of punishment frequently collide. Not only does parole amplify long-standing philosophical tensions between retributivist and consequentialist justifications for punishment, it operates as a sphere of symbolic moral communication that speaks directly to prisoners, victims and the general public (Aviram 2020).

For many prisoners, parole is the primary pathway out of custodial settings that in many jurisdictions have become more punitive, exclusionary and characterised by regimes of greater depth, weight and tightness (Crewe 2011). The prospect of release remains a powerful motivator for prisoners, but in recent years the distinction between prison and the community has been further complicated by the growth of the carceral state and the emergence of new and malign expressions of mass supervision (McNeill 2019; Phelps and Ruhland 2022).

In many jurisdictions, parole is characterised by net-widening, mesh-thinning and extended periods of supervision with the possibility of recall to prison for the breach of a panoply of licence conditions (Harding et al 2022). While parole is commonly associated, at least aspirationally, with resettlement, the restoration of liberty and democratic citizenship, there are indications that it is often experienced by impacted people as little more than a transition from one system of disciplinary control to another.

Parole's embodiment of motivating ideologies and cultural dynamics in a particular locale (see Loader and Sparks 2016; Brangan 2022) makes it an ideal locus for debates about desirable alternative futures. At the same time, its recurring tendency to be grafted onto, and become symbiotic with, pre-existing systems of punishment complicates matters considerably. For those desiring a long term-process of de-carceration for example, does a reformist approach to parole improve short-term prospects or merely further embed carceral logics? Paroling authorities have in some localities acted as potential allies for campaigners with a unique institutional vantage point on sentence progression and the importance of rehabilitation, but do such collaborations risk perpetuating systems of punishment that are unjust, ineffective and inhumane? Can parole be reformed from within, or should these systems be dismantled in favour of more radical models of social justice? As will become apparent, these questions require a well-crafted ethical position that confronts the relative merits of pragmatic and idealistic approaches, and their grounding in specific cultural contexts.

In some respects, these complex moral dilemmas have been 'baked in' since the first systems of parole were established in the early twentieth century. Early advocates of parole would no doubt recognise many of the debates that continue to define prison release in contemporary liberal democracies, even though we have seen the dramatic amplification of some concerns, especially as many nations have experienced the 'heating up' of public and political debate surrounding penal policy (Pratt 2007; Loader and Sparks 2011): public confidence in the parole system (Fitzgerald et al 2022), the independence and legal status of parole boards (Padfield 2020), the voice and role of victims in the parole process (Morgan and Smith 2005; Caplan 2012; Hail-Jares 2019) and the moral justifications for punishment that connect front-end sentencing decisions to back-end prison release policy and practice (Dagan 2022).

Contemporary penal developments, especially seen in international scope, resist neat compartmentalisation into narratives of 'progress' or 'decline'. One can observe in the European context that the greater procedural reliability in prison release decision-making and the evolving jurisprudence of both the European Court of Human Rights (ECtHR) and common law appellate courts have done much to safeguard the right to a fair trial (see van Zyl Smit and Snacken 2009). (By contrast, we can note considerable concerns about the politicisation of parole in the USA: Aviram 2020; Reitz and Rhine 2020.) From our vantage point in England and Wales at least, recent developments in parole mean these decision-making structures are notably less secretive and more transparent, with greater efforts being made to improve the diversity of Parole Board members (JUSTICE 2022). However, do 'innovations' such as increased transparency come at a cost, requiring involved parties to revisit the scene of the crime in a renewed public glare?

While at the same time, one can also observe the impact of an ascendant 'parole populism', associated with increased media and political interest in the decision to release, and a rhetorical foregrounding of victims' perspectives as a central concern of parole proceedings, which has eroded the rights of prisoners and promoted an all-encompassing emphasis on 'public protection' (Fitzgerald et al 2022). On such an account, 'hard cases' capture the popular imagination and motivate political decision-making, with moments of crisis and scandal operating as major drivers of penal policy (Annison and Guiney 2022). Parole boards are firmly established within a broader apparatus of risk management, community supervision and control (Simon 1993; Annison 2020). The extraordinary growth of indeterminate sentencing in many countries has seen the locus of sentencing discretion move 'downstream' from the criminal courts and an expanding cohort of recalled prisoners has renewed long-standing concerns about executive overreach and the limits of the liberal democratic state (Rhine et al 2017).

For all these reasons, prospects for parole systems that administer the release of prisoners in a fair, consistent and efficient manner are under increasing strain (Carr and Blay 2019; Guiney 2022). Does parole have a future? If it does, what should that future look like? Is progressive penal reform possible in a context where there is little if any consensus on the underpinning penal philosophies, aims and techniques of parole? What does this all mean for policy-makers and the criminal justice practitioners that work within the penal system or the prisoners, families, victims and members of the general public upon whose confidence the parole system ultimately depends?

In seeking to encourage new directions in this field, our introduction to the collection begins to set the scene for the contributions that follow: first, we reflect upon a number of objections to contemporary parole policy and practice that continue to disrupt the status quo. Second, we expand on what it means to speak of contemporary crises of parole. Third, we review a rich intellectual tradition of thinking normatively about the future of parole and, fourth, begin to sketch out an approach to the study of parole that we hope will open up new vistas for scholarship in this field. In the fifth and final section of this introduction, we sketch out the plan of this book, summarising the contributions.

II. DISRUPTING THE STATUS QUO: FOUR CRITIQUES OF PAROLE POLICY AND PRACTICE

Throughout its history, parole has proved problematic for liberal conceptions of penality. The rehabilitative ideal did, at least for a period of time, provide a partial answer to liberal concerns about its expansive dangers (see Loader 2006). More recently, notions of rehabilitation have taken on a distinctly late-modern character (Robinson 2008), even as populist punitive dynamics have taken greater hold (Pratt 2007). We summarise the following concerns and critiques here, not to capture nostalgia for a lost *status quo ante*, but to identify resources (many of which appear in subsequent chapters) by which new possibilities might emerge (Dzur et al 2016).

A. The Liberal Critique

As we have alluded to above, parole sits uncomfortably within liberal traditions of political thought that emphasise individual rights, the rule of law, the constitutional separation of powers and parsimony in the use of state punishment. For this reason, many of the most persuasive liberal critiques of parole have centred upon the growing influence of unaccountable parole boards. In their landmark book, *The Question of Parole*, von Hirsch and Hanrahan (1979) presented a wide-ranging critique of the entire edifice of parole in the USA and called for a phased shift towards a more determinate sentencing framework premised upon a just-deserts sentencing philosophy.

Similar arguments were made contemporaneously by Roger Hood (1979) in his proposals for a system of automatic parole, but more recently the liberal gaze has centred upon the actuarial and risk-based modalities of the new penology (Simon and Feeley 1992). For example, in a perceptive analysis of parole reform in Canada, Brodeur (1990) predicted the 'slow attrition of parole' as it morphs from a system of early release into one of release at the latest possible point. Ashworth and Zedner's (2014) *Preventive Justice* stands as a leading normative examination of the appropriate limits of penal measures justified on the basis of risk and future harm. They identify crucial issues, including the considerable ethical perils posed by false positives and false negatives, and question the extent to which detention in a *penal* setting for those serving preventive sentences can be justified. In a recent contribution to debates regarding parole decision-making in England and Wales, Barry (2023) has argued that 'future dangerousness has begun to colonize our theories of punishment', concluding that, if taken to its logical conclusion, 'it could be argued that the prison population in the future will comprise such high risk and persistent offenders as to make parole unsustainable as a risk management tool'.

B. The Populist Objection

Successive governments have seized upon the symbolic power of parole to demonstrate 'toughness' with respect to violent and sexual offending, to express solidarity with the victims of crime and to reaffirm a populist credo that purportedly stands in opposition to an unaccountable and out-of-touch penal elite (Fitzgerald et al 2022; Annison and Guiney 2025). Over time, this trend towards a performative style of penal politics has seen the official embrace of crime control practices that 'allow a certain view of public opinion to take precedence over its penal effectiveness' (Roberts et al 2003: 5). It is often emotive, appealing to the symbolism of 'ideal victims' and 'folk devils' for political advantage. It stands in contrast to the 'cooler', evidence-based logics of epistemic crime control often advocated by academics and criminal justice campaigners (Loader and Sparks 2017: 106).

Reflecting on recent developments in Victoria, Australia since the death of Jill Meagher in September 2012 by a person who had been subject to release on parole, Moffatt et al (2019) argued that a model of 'parole populism' has emerged that strips prisoners and parolees of significant rights, hampers rehabilitation efforts and fails to deliver on the promises made to the electorate. More generally, Pratt (2008) draws attention to the way in which populist slogans such as 'truth in sentencing' and 'life means life' have permeated parole policy in practice in ways intended to break the monopoly of criminal justice experts and restore popular common sense in decision-making.

C. The Abolitionist Critique

In their early consideration of the question of whether parole should be abolished, von Hirsch and Hanrahan (1978) observed that abolition was favoured by many across 'a wide spectrum of political and philosophical viewpoints' (1978: iii). In their survey of these arguments, they concluded that parole should not be continued in its present form, arguing instead that release decisions should be informed by 'just deserts' principles and should be determined at a much earlier stage (at or shortly after sentencing); that instead of allowing revocations for new criminal activity, such allegations should be subject to ordinary criminal processes; and that post-release supervision should be eliminated entirely.

Their rationale for the last recommendation reflected concerns regarding net-widening mentioned above, as well as the perceived utility of supervision for parolees. Ultimately, von Hirsch and Hanrahan (1978) fell short of recommending the outright abolition of parole. They even supported the idea of retaining vestigial authority in parole boards, who they envisaged would oversee the changes they proposed.

Their arrived position reflects some of the inherent tensions between reformist and abolitionist perspectives (Mathiesen 1974). A more purist abolitionist critique would require more fundamental questioning of the penal rationales and logics that sustain parole systems as well as engagement with wider questions about how criminal justice and carceral responses have, in many contexts, become the default answer to social harms (Coyle and Scott 2021). Clearly, critiques of parole cannot be unyoked from broader concerns regarding the criminal justice system and the use of imprisonment in particular (Ryan and Sim 2007). Abolitionist perspectives are also informed by grass-roots perspectives and community activism which aim to link different areas of struggle. Prominent examples include abolitionist debates in the USA which draw direct lines between racial injustice and carcerality (Davis 2003). A further important dimension of abolitionism involves moving from rarified theoretical debate towards direct engagement with and by those most impacted. An abolitionist critique in the context of parole would therefore link to wider prison abolitionism as well as a broadening out of the range of voices and perspectives that are typically included in these debates.

D. The Forgotten Critique? Recentring Prisoner Agency

As a burgeoning 'convict criminology' has argued, the voice of prisoners has not been adequately acknowledged in academic scholarship, policy-related research and penal reform (Earle 2017). While there have been some welcome attempts to improve engagement with criminal justice-impacted people (and communities) through the use of prison councils and other participatory democratic strategies (Weaver 2019), the opportunities for co-production in the parole sphere has remained limited.

A consistent body of research has drawn attention to the importance of prisoner agency, resistance and voluntary rule compliance in prison settings. Parole requires considerable narrative labour (Warr 2020), whereby prisoners present themselves – and their journey from 'dangerousness' to 'safety' – in a manner that is deemed acceptable by power holders. This faces considerable challenges, including that 'progression' may not be well understood or hold agreed meanings for prisoners and parole decision-makers (Jarman and Vince 2022); that the prisoners' identity is ultimately externally imposed by powerholders, rather than being of their own agency (Warr 2020); and that racialised dynamics impose additional burdens for racially minoritised prisoners (Warr 2023).

From the perspective of institutional leaders, these issues have considerable practical implications (see generally Crewe and Liebling 2023). For example, Kelly et al (2020) noted in their qualitative study of prisoners in Scotland that many did not have a clear understanding of parole or feel fully engaged in the process:

> Further consideration needs to be given to how prisoners' effective participation in the parole process can be increased. This is particularly important as a means of promoting perceptions of procedural justice – prisoners' perceptions that they have been listened to and treated fairly by justice practitioners – which in turn may enhance the perceived legitimacy of Parole Board decisions and prisoners' willingness to comply with the licence conditions imposed upon them to manage their behaviour when they are released. (Kelly et al 2020: 327)

Where legitimacy breaks down, the overall effectiveness of parole decision-making is jeopardised. In Belgium, Beyens et al (2022) have documented how prisoners frequently 'max out' their sentences in order to avoid the pains of temporal indeterminacy. More recently, in a systematic review of research on parole waiver, Dodd and Sydes (2024) found that a notable cohort of prisoners are now opting out of parole consideration due to perceptions of onerousness, fear of parole denial and re-entry barriers.

III. A LESS CERTAIN FUTURE: THE CRISES OF CONTEMPORARY PRISON RELEASE

Crises – those 'moments of truth', where there is the possibility to bear witness to a new time or epoch – play a critical role in the penal policy-making cycle (Annison and Guiney 2025). Building on our own research (Guiney 2018; Carr and Blay 2019; Annison 2020), we argue here that the past, present and possible futures of parole continue to be shaped by three long-standing and interconnected 'penal crises' that have undermined public trust, weakened human rights protections and promoted populist reforms that prioritise the electoral success of a policy over its penal effectiveness.

A. A Crisis of Administration

In recent decades, the administrative demands of a large and increasingly complex prison population – the practice of parole, by and within relevant institutions – has presented huge challenges to state decision-makers. In part, this reflects the basic challenge of administering a penal system at scale at a time when criminal justice budgets have failed to keep pace with significant prison expansionism. However, the crisis of administration also reflects the growing complexity of contemporary sentencing frameworks and 'hyperactivity' in the penal field that has seen an almost constant cycle of policy change, including initiatives on victims' rights, new forms of dangerousness legislation and changes to the computation of parole eligibility.

For example, in France, Herzog-Evans (2019) has shown how attempts to fast-track the prison release process to alleviate pressure on the prison population have led to a 'McDonaldisation' of procedures which, as a consequence, lack the necessary legitimacy in the eyes of both the penal actors (judiciary, lawyers, probation officers) and the prisoners who were its subjects. She has shown how the policy intention was usurped by the lack of attention given to meaning and materiality of the process, not least the fact that prisoners opting to participate in the new and 'quicker' system were not afforded necessary resettlement supports.

Moreover, the SPACE data – data on the numbers of people imprisoned and subject to supervision in the community across Council of Europe member states – reveals a widening of the nets of penal control, and that post-release supervision is part of this (Aebi et al 2019). Increased attention towards the lived experience of supervision and the contingency of life at liberty but subject to restrictions points towards the need for a greater focus on the weight, breadth and tightness of these conditions following release from prison (McNeill 2019). This is particularly important in the contexts in which the range of controls within the community have expanded, evidenced in part by the growth in the use of technology such as electronic monitoring (Hucklesby et al 2021). At the same time, the changing contours of conditional release and post-custodial supervision reflect different and sometimes oscillating rationalities.

B. A Crisis of Legitimacy

Parole boards now suffer from a serious legitimacy crisis. This includes a lack of clarity about how discretion is exercised in decision-making and, by extension, what prisoners, prisoner families, victims and the general public can legitimately expect from this process. In this context, parole is being pulled in different directions by the requirements of public protection, risk management and procedural justice. On the one hand, parole boards have often sought to legitimise their work by appealing to their decision-making *performance*. On the other hand, a series of hard-won legal, political and social movements have compelled parole boards, with varying degrees of success, to reframe their work in ways that better reflect the competing legitimacy claims of *procedural* justice.

In recent years, there has been an unprecedented amount of law making in most Australian states and territories, often spurred on by high-profile murders or other violent offences committed by parolees (see Freiberg et al 2018). A series of legislative initiatives have restricted the discretion afforded to state-level parole boards, promoted the use of 'no body, no release' clauses and, in some cases, resulted in the use of emergency legislation to prevent the release of certain named individuals (Moffa et al 2019). Freiberg and colleagues argue that, while some of the proposed changes may be positive (eg efforts to increase the diversity of parole boards), the developments are driven by an 'underlying political response that shows an aversion to risk, coupled with a desire to give succour to victims and appease a presumed public concern about parole' (Freiberg et al 2018: 214).

In Belgium, Beyens et al (2022) have reported how prisoners in the former category frequently 'max out' their sentences in order to avoid the pains of temporal indeterminacy linked to the decision-making involved with gradual discretionary release. Meanwhile, a pertinent development in the ECtHR has been the sighting of an emerging jurisprudence of a 'right to hope' (Vannier 2016) for life-sentenced prisoners. This has tended to be interpreted as requiring a realistic prospect of release (Ashworth and Zedner 2019). This clearly directly question engages both prisoner progression and the systems and processes – and basic availability – of appropriate systems of parole.

C. A Crisis of Ideas

As crime control has emerged as a less certain field (Garland 2001), penal policy-makers have struggled to articulate a clear strategic vision outlining the purpose(s) and function of prison release. Parole, as originally conceived, was justified on the basis of a 'recognisable peak' in an individual's rehabilitation where the interests of the community were better served by the careful reform and reintegration of the offender in the community rather than their continued incarceration (Shute 2003). However, the crises outlined above have stripped penal policy-making of its early optimism and inhibited the formulation of a clear strategic vision that connects everyday policy and practice with broader penological ideas. As Guiney (2023: 629) has argued:

> In this less certain climate, the decision to release has become imbued with all the anxieties and contradictions of late-modern penality; the management of risk; fear of dangerous 'others'; the disruptive influence of penal populism and the challenge of reconciling parole with a retributivist sentencing philosophy premised upon moral 'desert', proportionality and truth in sentencing.

For example, in the context of England and Wales, Padfield (2019) has argued that one can discern three broad historical phases in the history of parole. An early focus on rehabilitation and penal pragmatism (1967–91) shifted to a subsequent concern on the control of risky offenders (1991–2003), and more recently has mutated into a form of management of delayed released for an increasing number of prisoners (2003–onwards). At the time of writing, the parole system in England and Wales sees itself buffeted by febrile wider cultural dynamics that place it at the centre of challenging questions about public safety, recognition of (often historically downplayed) forms of serious harm, competing views on the nature and relevance of expertise, and pressures for greater transparency (Annison 2020). As the contributions to this edited collection make clear, similar challenges are being posed in many other national contexts. Equally importantly, Padfield's observation that parole's three core potential priorities – public protection, rehabilitation and prisoner rights – are not only contested but often fudged even as activity surrounding parole policy increases (Padfield 2020) can be applied beyond her focus on England and Wales.

Notions of 'crisis' and 'normality' are inherently culturally constructed (see Annison and Guiney 2025). While these can be understood through the lens of overarching concepts such as late modernity, globalisation and neo-liberalism, we should exercise caution in anticipating how specific political, economic and cultural dynamics may play out in specific contexts (Brangan 2022). Parole is inherently tied to time and place: to specific political cultures, institutional logics and community expectations. It interrelates with wider questions about the purposes of punishment, such as long-standing questions about the balance between different rationalities, including rehabilitation, retribution, reparation and public protection.

IV. REIMAGINING THE FUTURE OF PAROLE: RATIONALITIES, INSTITUTIONS AND PRACTICES

Given these considerations, it is perhaps unsurprising that the future of parole has always been of equal, if not greater, interest to punishment scholars as its present-day effects.

Writing in 1915, BW Brown declared confidently that parole was 'an institution of the future'. While still a relatively new penal innovation at the turn of the twentieth century, systems of parole had been implemented in more than 30 American states and the momentum for reform was building in Canada, New Zealand, Australia, France, Belgium and Prussia. The next step was to standardise these gains, and Brown argued that the careful implementation of parole on the basis of rigorous scientific study of the causes of delinquency could drive a revolution in the aims and techniques of penal policy:

> To every candid observer it must be evident that the parole system, just coming into its own as an organic entity in harmony with the most advanced ideas on the social treatment of crime, offers both to society and the criminal hope for the future which prison walls can never afford. What other institution, new to criminology or any other social field, can sustain the claim that it has produced better results for less than one-fifth the cost of its predecessor? (Brown 1915: 72)

Parole would arrive later in England and Wales, but the dust had barely settled on the Criminal Justice Act 1967 before its future became the subject of intense scholarly attention. Published more than half a century ago, West's (1972) edited collection *The Future of Parole* represented an early attempt to think systematically about the 'principles, problems and possibilities that now apply to parole systems globally'. Writing in the foreword, Lord Hunt, the first Chair of the Parole Board in England and Wales, would capture the mood and optimism of the times:

> There was the infectious hope that it [parole reform] contained the seeds of significant social advance. There was, and will remain, the need to develop a special skill, compounded of a wide conspectus of experience and sound judgement, in making assessments on the issue of releasing into the community, at the optimal point in time … (Hunt 1972: 8)

In reality, these lofty principles provided cover for more prosaic concerns, such as cost-saving, prison overcrowding and order control (Shute 2003). It is nonetheless striking how differently the future is imagined in contemporary discourse. Elements of this ideational shift were observed by Bottomley (1990) in his comparative study of the origins, developments and prospects for parole. Reflecting on the evolving roles and purposes of parole release in the USA, Canada, and England and Wales, Bottomley observed a 'chameleon-like capacity' to adapt to changing social, political and penal environments (Bottomley 1990: 364). In the future, parole would continue to drift still further away from its original spirit and ethos as governments responded to a growing accountability agenda and public concerns about crime. For these reasons, Bottomley predicted that parole may disappear as we know it, but expressed hope that the gradual democratisation of parole would contribute to a fairer, more humane and effective penal system:

> We might thus, at best, envisage parole systems of greater fairness and accountability for prisoners, with an increased professional input for the assessment and management of risk, and a depoliticization of operational responsibility within prison systems that can manage to control themselves. (Bottomley 1990: 368)

With the benefit of hindsight, Bottomley's review captures a moment in time when the old was dying but the new had not yet been born. Just over a decade later in a provocative lecture entitled 'Thoughts on the Future of Parole' delivered at The Vera Institute of Justice in 2002, Travis would proclaim that 'It's time to end parole as we know it'. Starting with a clean slate and inviting his audience to imagine different ways of doing the work of justice, Travis argued that: (i) as a matter of principle, the executive branch of government should not decide the length of a prison term; and (ii) America's century long experiment with parole boards had proved conclusively that their decisions were simply too susceptible to organisational manipulation and arbitrary exercises of discretionary power to provide an 'effective pillar for a coherent system of justice':

> My heretical proposition is that we assign this oversight role to two entities – sentencing commissions and sentencing judges. In this new world, sentencing commissions would take on the task of developing standards for the re-entry process, and holding

> departments of corrections accountable for meeting those standards. Sentencing judges would be expected to create and review re-entry plans for each person sent to prison, just as they now approve supervision plans for those on probation.

From a different starting point, Maruna et al (2012) argued that the history of bail bonds in the USA – and the injection of free-market principles into the penal system – might portend a different, and dystopian, future for parole. At the time of writing, several US states had enacted the Conditional Post-Conviction Release Bond Act, with the implication that certain categories of prisoner could secure early release by posting 'post-conviction bail'. As with pre-trial bail, prisoners would pay a percentage of a bond to secure their release under the contractual responsibility of a commercial bail agency. If release conditions were breached, bounty hunters were then legally empowered to seize and return the parolee to prison. Maruna et al (2012) predicted that once privatisation had been introduced into the parole equation, it was likely to grow in influence, fundamentally reshaping the nature of prison release.

Not all contemporary accounts have been so pessimistic. In perhaps the most influential recent contribution to these debates, Rhine et al (2017) present a 10-point plan for the 'revitalisation' of parole release in the USA that is said to offer both a comprehensive and aspirational model for the future. Guided by a punishment theory the authors characterise as an application of 'limiting retributivism' or 'modified just deserts', Rhine et al (2017: 295) present a comprehensive account of how changes in institutional structure, grounds for release, the operation of risk management tools, the selective use of supervision and so on could help to recentre the basic liberal democratic principle that 'the greater the authority concentrated in the prison release decision, the greater the need for procedural regularity'.

> A plan for revitalization of parole release should lay out a comprehensive and aspirational model for the future. It must address the institutional structure of parole boards, how much release discretion they are given, the substantive grounds for release decisions, the use of risk assessments in the decisional process, decision-making tools such as parole release guidelines, the requirements of fair and reliable procedures, victims' rights at parole hearings, the need for parole supervision in some but not all cases, the intensity of parole conditions, and the length of parole supervision.

Rhine et al (2017) offer a powerful call for international scholars seeking to think systematically about the future and present a comprehensive, principled and realistic programme of reform. But as the authors themselves recognise, this vision is grounded within the American experience of mass incarceration and adopts a pragmatic strategy that seeks 'evolutionary changes to existing institutions rather than a "ground-up" building of new infrastructures' (Rhine et al 2017: 287).

In pursuing ambitious thinking about parole futures – whether critical, reformist or abolitionist (or otherwise) in orientation – comparative analysis can be a powerful first step in exercising the criminological imagination: it invites reflexivity and encourages greater sensitivity to our individual assumptions, beliefs and biases about the world (Brangan 2022). It challenges ethnocentrism and confronts us with counter-evidence that disrupts the belief 'that what we do, our way of thinking about and responding to crime, is universally shared or, at least, that it would be right for everyone else' (Nelken 2009). It emphasises contingency and reminds us that there is nothing inevitable about the way things are; it draws attention to the importance of policy transfer and allows us to explore how ideas about crime and criminal justice might be borrowed, adapted and embedded in an increasingly global and interconnected world.

V. OUR APPROACH: THE PROMISE (AND PITFALLS) OF NORMATIVE THEORISING

When taken as a whole, the varied bodies of work discussed here represent a range of means by which to locate parole policy and practice within broader normative and political perspectives. They allow us to step back from current arrangements, to recognise the contingency of the present as a 'former future' (Levitas 1991) and critique those ways of thinking that concede too much in their acceptance of existing power relationships and forms of knowledge production. This can be a daunting prospect, but recent criminological scholarship has made considerable strides in thinking about the future in ways that are ambitious, systematic and conceptually consistent, that distil the foundational principles that should underpin parole or its alternatives and that articulate a coherent and persuasive roadmap for how such change could be brought about.

Reacting to a long-standing disciplinary pessimism that has often seen criminologists retreat into penal nostalgia (Dzur et al 2016), in recent years there has been a renewed interest in normative theorising. For example, Durnescu (2013) has predicted the future of probation in European is likely to be defined by greater harmonisation. In the US context, Harding et al (2022: 12) have been applauded for their efforts to 'redirect conversation about community supervision from its emphasis on crime prevention and risk reduction towards a new paradigm focused on social integration and economic justice'. Similarly, Burke et al (2022) have sought to sketch out 'a comprehensive and positive reimagining' of probation practice in England and Wales, one which is better able to support the personal, social, moral and legal rehabilitation of individuals who have been subject to criminal sanction.

Building upon and working within this intellectual tradition, an international community of academic researchers were invited to discuss the future of parole at a three-day conference at the Oñati International Institute for the Sociology of Law. Contributing authors were asked to reflect upon the development of parole and prison release from a range of disciplinary perspectives and articulate a normative vision for the future. Reflecting the principles of realistic utopian thought (Loader 1998; Copson 2014), we encouraged our collaborators to think big and pose ambitious questions about the rationalities, institutions and practices of parole; to ground their chapters in the past and present, but also return to first principles and think imaginatively about possible futures; to move beyond 'what is' and think about 'what could be'. Authors were encouraged to move beyond the parochial (albeit recognising the importance of locality: Nelken 2009), encouraging an exploration of the broader, cross-cutting theoretical implications of research – in other words, to think normatively about what parole, or indeed alternative systems of prison release, might look like.

Of course, there are no right answers to these questions. All systems of thought require difficult trade-offs and force us to confront the potentially undesirable consequences of a more coherent or 'principled' approach to prison release. Where possible, authors have been afforded the space to explore these tensions between idealism and realism, between radicalism and pragmatism, and between abstract principles and grounded dynamics. In this way, this edited collection contributes to an emerging research agenda, a way of 'doing' parole research, that is premised upon the following foundational principles.

1. **An international perspective:** The proposed edited collection has been designed to facilitate exchange between an international community of researchers working on parole and prison release policy and practice. Our workshop explored the rationalities, institutions and practices shaping parole and prison release from a range of different perspectives and included contributions from researchers based in Australia, Belgium, Canada, Chile, England & Wales, Israel, Japan, Scotland, Slovenia, Spain, United States and South Africa. As well as presentations from practice perspectives from Ireland, England and Wales and the Basque Region.
2. **An interdisciplinary perspective:** A key strength of this collection is its socio-legal approach. It moves beyond doctrinal accounts of prison release, instead placing these issues within their broader sociological, political, cultural and economic contexts. In so doing, this edited collection brings together a world leading panel of twenty-seven experts who draw on insights from law, sociology, criminology and political science to explore these pressing questions.
3. **A multi-stakeholder perspective:** Each chapter draws on original research to consider parole and prisoner release from a range of perspectives, including from the point of view of decision-makers, policy-makers, prisoners and the wider public. This multifocal approach greatly enhances our understanding and provide fertile grounds for rich debate.
4. **A normative perspective:** A key strength of this collection is a focus on encouraging new ideas and fresh perspectives on parole and prison release. Contributing authors have been encouraged to think big, to ask 'what if?', to pose difficult questions and to provide thought-provoking and proactive answers that move the debate forward.

VI. OUTLINE OF THE EDITED COLLECTION

Working within this tradition of structured normative theorising, the chapters presented here are split into three sections and organised around the cross-cutting themes of rationalities, institutions and practices. Part I reflects upon the evolving aims, purposes and rationalities of parole and contemporary prison release. It seeks to understand what parole is for, how it is understood by the general public and the role it plays in effective sentencing progression.

The opening chapter, from Bartels and Freiberg, reflects upon public attitudes towards parole board decision-making. They outline findings from an innovative attitudinal study where members of the public were asked to reflect upon a number of hypothetical parole board cases. The authors identify a worrying disconnect between the views of parole board members and the public. They explore how a series of public engagement strategies could help to (re)build trust in the system.

In Chapter Three, Schartmueller explores the as yet untapped potential of procedural justice to strengthen both the interior and exterior legitimacy of the parole system. Through a systematic review of the procedural justice literature, Schartmueller identifies international best practice and demonstrates how this could be applied to parole law, policy and procedure. In a similar vein, in chapter Four, Ruhland draws attention to a problematic lack of transparency in American parole board decision-making and sets out recommendations to improve the composition of parole board membership and improve decision-making accountability.

Chapter Five examines the moral basis of parole in a rapidly changing social context, confronting the challenge faced by many nations of an ageing prison population. Vannier argues that the future-orientated logic of many parole systems is fundamentally challenged by an ageing prison population. While prison release has frequently been justified as a 'temporal privilege' that is justified by the human capacity to change, Vannier demonstrates that the ageing process is creating new and conflicting temporalities that demand fundamentally new ways of conceptualising parole.

In the final chapter of Part I, Dagan offers a radical rethinking of parole as a form of symbolic closure to the penal dialogue between the community and the imprisoned individual. He argues that a sharper focus on the moral purpose of parole help insulate the system from discriminatory, risk-obsessed, punitive and populist critiques. Further, Dagan argues that it also creates important opportunities to envision a more optimistic future for parole by bringing 'what parole is' closer to 'what parole can be'.

In Part II of this collection, the focus turns to the institutional arrangements that have developed globally to administer prison release decision-making in a fair, consistent and defensible manner. Collectively, the chapters examine the formal legal basis of current prison release arrangements and the compromises, tensions and conflicts that underpin these arrangements.

van Zyl Smit opens this section by reflecting upon recent high-profile judgments of the South African Constitutional Court and begins to situate these controversies within a contemporary history of parole for life-sentence prisoners. He argues that creating a fair release system will require not only a return to the ideals of the 1990s, but also an acceptance that such a release system needs impartial decision-makers and carefully targeted resources to support them.

Reflecting on a period of significant parole reform in the UK, and England and Wales in particular, Padfield in chapter Eight explores the broader pressures to which parole is subject, not least a legacy of penal populism and austerity that has left the prison system and probation services in parlous states. She sets out principled reasons for progressive reform, while also identifying a number of significant barriers which should temper our hopes. Ultimately, Padfield emphasises that, as one cog in a wider system, to consider parole reform is to confront foundational challenges regarding the penal system as a whole.

In Chapter Nine, Beyens and Breuls review recent penal developments in the Belgium parole system. Reflecting on the 'principle of relative autonomy' between sentencing and sentence implementation, the authors argue that the current parole framework has created a number of unforeseen issues that have undermined its state goals. They set out proposals for a new system of semi-automatic release, which would help to close the gap between stated rehabilitative ideals and structural constraints within the Belgian penal system.

In Chapter Ten, Arnež and Plesničar describe developments of parole in the context of Slovakia. This is often described as an 'exceptional' nation, with its low imprisonment rates and resistance to penal populism drawing parallels with Scandinavian nations. They describe, in this context, how long-standing institutional arrangements have rarely been questioned or subject to sustained academic research. This has led to little collective understanding of its aims, governance or decision-making, which this chapter begins to address.

Similar themes are identified in Chapter Eleven by Anderez Belategi, who argues that conditional release in Spain must be understood as a part of a broader framework of 'scientific individualisation' established by the General Prison Law. Recent reforms have disrupted this long-established process of sentencing progression, and this chapter builds the case for greater decision-making consistency anchored in the constitutional aim of reintegration.

In Part III of the collection, we explore the everyday practices of prison release as they are experienced by prisoners, prison staff, probation and social workers and healthcare professionals with a stake in the penal system. The chapters explore the unique challenges and pressures created by current prison release arrangements and how practitioners seek to navigate these changes.

In Chapter Twelve, Seeds and Mosca examine the implications of a rapid increase in the number of incarcerated people aged 55 or older in the USA. Many American prisons are now facing a 'perfect storm' of chronic illness and skyrocketing mortality rates, but current prison release pathways remain unresponsive to questions of medical treatment and care. In this context, the authors review existing approaches to prison release that centre upon medical treatment, setting out a number of proposals for reform.

In Chapter Thirteen, Toda explores the paradox of parole in Japan. She examines how recent initiatives in social welfare services and aftercare for offenders aimed at preventing recidivism interact uncomfortably with a system of prison release that affords parole decision-makers broad discretion, releasing only 'safe' prisoners for short periods on licence during which they are rarely recalled. Highlighting the importance of parole as a transitional support mechanism towards resettlement, Toda critically evaluates the benefits and limitations of the current practices. She argues for a fundamental rebalancing of parole functions to ensure more effective coordination between social welfare services and aftercare for offenders.

This focus on the importance of public opinion finds parallels in the work of Villagra, Droppelmann and Faúndez presented in Chapter Fourteen. Tracing key moments of parole reform in Chile, the authors argue that parole has diverged significantly from its original purpose as a reintegration tool. Rather, over time, it is argued to have become highly sensitive to crime management policies and public opinion. While many of the dynamics identified are common across many national contexts, Villagra et al argue for the adoption of a Southern Criminology perspective, which would in part prioritise examination of structural social justice over managerialist concerns.

In Chapter Fifteen, drawing on a major study with Canadian federal parole officers in Ontario, Canada, Ricciardelli and Taylor build the case for a therapeutic alliance model of working. They argue that workplace relationships are central to good practice, including improving the 'responsivity' aspect of the influential risk–needs–responsivity (RNR) model. The authors explore the barriers to an effective working alliance between practitioners and prisoners, arguing that improvements in this regard can aid parolee rehabilitation and improve staff wellness.

In the final chapter of this collection, Corcoran, McNeill and Weaver (Chapter Sixteen) provide a valuable provocation to the state-oriented thinking that often predominates in debates regarding parole. By contrast, they build a case for an approach they term 'generative justice'. The chapter discusses empirical research conducted into Italian Social Cooperative through-the-gate projects, in order to draw out key underlying principles of epistemic justice and lived experience. The authors use the conceptual resources they compile to explore the potential for new responses to crime and punishment that are better placed to build social solidarity, recognition, reciprocity and inclusion.

VII. CONCLUSION

The coverage of debates reflects existing scholarship and ways of thinking about parole that have an established history. Our invitation to contributors to push the boundaries of thinking about parole has yielded important insights about possibilities for the future(s) of parole in different contexts. While we have achieved a good range of geographical and disciplinary diversity, we are conscious of the fact that edited collections of this nature are limited by structural and social factors, including research resourcing, publication practices and linguistic barriers, to name but a few. We recognise these limitations. Our hope is that this edited collection will be the start of a conversation and prompt wider debates and discussion about the possible future(s) of parole.

REFERENCES

Aebi MF, Hashimoto YZ and Tiago MM (2019) 'Probation and Prisons in Europe, 2018: Key Findings of the SPACE Reports' (Strasbourg, Council of Europe) http://wp.unil.ch/space/files/2019/05/Key-Findings_SPACE-II_190520-1.pdf.

Annison, H (2020) 'Re-examining Risk and Blame in Penal Controversies: Parole in England and Wales' in J Pratt and J Anderson (eds), *Criminal Justice, Risk and the Revolt Against Uncertainty* (Basingstoke, Palgrave Macmillan) 139–63.

Annison, H and Guiney, T (2022) 'Populism, Conservatism and the Politics of Parole in England and Wales' 93(3) *The Political Quarterly* 416.

—— (2025) 'Crisis and Penal Policymaking in England and Wales: Concepts, Theories and Future Directions' in A Corda (ed), *Research Handbook on Penal Policy* (London, Edward Elgar).

Armstrong, R and Durnescu, I (eds) (2017) *Parole and Beyond. International Experiences of Life Prison* (London, Palgrave Macmillan).

Ashworth, A and Zedner, L (2014) *Preventive Justice* (Oxford, Oxford University Press).

—— (2019) 'Some Dilemmas of Indeterminate Sentences: Risk and Uncertainty, Dignity and Hope' in JW de Keijser, JV Roberts and J Ryberg (eds), *Predictive Sentencing: Normative and Empirical Perspectives* (London, Bloomsbury) 107–27.

Aviram, H (2020). *Yesterday's Monsters: The Manson Family Cases and the Illusion of Parole* (Oakland, CA, University of California Press).

Barry, M (2021) 'Walking on Ice': The Future of Parole in a Risk-Obsessed Society' 25(2) *Theoretical Criminology* 325.

Beyens, K, Breuls, L and Gilbert, E (2022) 'The "Reintegration Paradox": Working Towards the Future While Standing Still' in N Carr and G Robinson (eds), *Time and Punishment. New Contexts and Perspectives* (Basingstoke, Palgrave Macmillan).

Brangan, L (2022) *The Politics of Punishment: A Comparative Study of Imprisonment and Political Culture* (Abingdon, Routledge).

Brodeur, JP (1990) 'The Attrition of Parole' 32(3) *Canadian Journal of Criminology* 503.

Brown, BW (1915) 'Parole an Institution of the Future' 6(1) *Journal of the American Institute of Criminal Law and Criminology* 65.

Bottomley, AK (1990) 'Parole in Transition: Comparative Study of Origins, Developments, and Prospects for the 1990s' 12 *Crime and Justice: Review of Research* 319.

Burke, L, Carr, N, Cluley, E, Collett, S and McNeill, F (eds) (2022) *Reimagining Probation Practice. Reforming Rehabilitation in an Age of Penal Excess* (London, Routledge).

Caplan, JM (2012) 'Protection Parole Board Legitimacy in the Twenty-First Century: The Role of Victims' Rights and Influences' 7(1) *Victims & Offenders* 53.

Carr, N and Blay, E (2019) 'Parole and Prisoner Release: Exploring Rationalities Across Time and Place' 11(3) *European Journal of Probation* 119.

Carvahlo, H and Chamberlen, A (2023) *Questioning Punishment* (London, Routledge).

Copson, L (2014) 'Penal Populism and the Problem of Mass Incarceration: The Promise of Utopian Thinking' 23(1) *The Good Society* 55.

Coyle, MJ and Scott, D (2023) *The Routledge International Handbook of Penal Abolition* (New York, Routledge).

Crewe, B (2011) 'Depth, Weight, Tightness: Revisiting the Pains of Imprisonment' 13(5) *Punishment & Society* 509.

Crewe, B and Liebling, A (2023) 'Reconfiguring and Reimagining Penal Power' in A Liebling, S Maruna and L McAara (eds), *Oxford Handbook of Criminology* (Oxford, Oxford University Press).

Dagan, N (2022) 'Overcoming Penal Boundaries: Exploring the Evolution of Retributive Time Through Parole Decision-Making' 62(1) *British Journal of Criminology* 37.

Davis, A (2003) *Abolition Democracy* (New York, Seven Sisters Press).

Dodd, S and Sydes, M (2024) 'Freedom Waived: A Systematic Review of Research on People in Prison Who Forgo the Opportunity for Release on Parole' *European Journal of Criminal Policy Research* https://doi.org/10.1007/s10610-024-09596-8.

Durnescu, I (2013) 'The Future of Probation in Europe: Common in the Middle and Diverse at the Edge' 60(3) *Probation Journal* 316.

Dzur, AW, Loader, I and Sparks, R (eds) (2016) *Democratic Theory and Mass Incarceration* (Oxford, Oxford University Press).

Earle, R (2016) *Convict Criminology: Inside and Out* (Bristol, Policy Press).

Feeley, M and Simon, J (1992) 'The New Penology: Notes on the Emerging Strategy of Corrections and Its Implications' 30 *Criminology* 449.

Fitzgerald R, Dodd, S, Freiberg, A and Bartels, L (2022) *Parole on Probation: Public Opinion, Public Confidence and Parole Decision-Making* (Basingstoke, Palgrave Macmillan).

Garland, D (2001) *The Culture of Control: Crime and Social Order in Contemporary Society* (Oxford, Oxford University Press).

Guiney, T (2018) *Getting Out: Early Release in England and Wales, 1960–1995* (Oxford, Oxford University Press).

—— (2023) 'Parole, Parole Boards and the Institutional Dilemmas of Contemporary Prison Release' 25(3) *Punishment & Society* 621.

Hail-Jares, K (2019) 'Weighing Words: The Impact of Non-victim Correspondence on Parole Board Decisions' 38(4) *Justice Quarterly* 678.

Harding, DJ, Western, B and Sandelson, JA (2022) 'From Supervision to Opportunity: Reimagining Probation and Parole' 701(1) *Annals of the American Academy of Political and Social Science* 8.

Herzog-Evans, M (2019) 'French Early Release: McProcedures and McRe-entry' 11(3) *European Journal of Probation* 188.

Hood, R (1974) *Tolerance and the Tariff: Some Reflections on Fixing the Time Prisoners Serve in Custody*, NACRO Reprint No 11 (London, NACRO).
Hucklesby, A, Beyens, K and Boone, M (2021) 'Comparing Electronic Monitoring Regimes: Length, Breadth, Depth and Weight Equals Tightness' 23(1) *Punishment & Society* 88.
Hunt, L (1972) 'Foreword' in D West (ed), *The Future of Parole* (London, Duckworth).
Jarman, B and Vince, C (2022) *Making Progress?* (London, Prison Reform Trust).
JUSTICE (2022) *A Parole System Fit for Purpose* (London, JUSTICE) https://files.justice.org.uk/wp-content/uploads/2022/03/22164155/JUSTICE-A-Parole-System-fit-for-Purpose-20-Jan-2022.pdf.
Kelly, L, McIvor, G and Richard, K (2020) 'Prisoners' Understanding and Experiences of Parole' 30 *Criminal Behaviour and Mental Health* 321.
Levitas, R (1990) *The Concept of Utopia* (Bern, Peter Lang).
Loader, I (1998) 'Criminology and the Public Sphere: Arguments for Utopian Realism' in P Walton and J Young (eds), *The New Criminology Revisited* (London, Palgrave Macmillan).
—— (2006) 'Fall of the "Platonic Guardians": Liberalism, Criminology and Political Responses to Crime in England and Wales' 46 *British Journal of Criminology* 561.
Loader, I and Sparks, R (2011) *Public Criminology?* (London, Routledge).
—— (2016) 'Ideologies and Crime: Political Ideas and the Dynamics of Crime Control' 17 *Global Crime* 314.
McNeill, F (2019) *Pervasive Punishment: Making Sense of Mass Supervision* (Bingley, Emerald).
Maruna, S, Dabney, D and Topalli, V (2012) 'Putting a Price on Prisoner Release: The History of Bail and a Possible Future of Parole' 14(3) *Punishment & Society* 315.
Mathiesen, T (1974) *The Politics of Abolition* (Oxford, Martin Robertson).
Moffa, M, Stratton, G and Ruyters, M (2019) 'Parole Populism: The Politicisation of Parole in Victoria' 31(1) *Current Issues in Criminal Justice* 75.
Morgan, K and Smith, BL (2005) 'Victims, Punishment, and Parole: The Effect of Victim Participation on Parole Hearings' 4(2) *Criminology & Public Policy* 333.
Nelken, D (2009) 'Comparative Criminal Justice' 6(4) *European Journal of Criminology* 291.
Padfield, N (2019) 'Giving and Getting Parole: The Changing Characteristics of Parole in England and Wales' 11(3) *European Journal of Probation* 153.
Padfield, N (2020) 'The Function of the Parole Board – Avoiding Failure or Promoting Success?' (July) *Public Law* 468.
Padfield, N and Maruna, S (2006) 'The Revolving Door at the Prison Gate: Exploring the Dramatic Increase in Recalls to Prison' 6(3) *Criminology & Criminal Justice* 329.
Padfield, N, van Zyl Smit, D and Dunkel, F (2012) *Release from Prison: European Policy and Practice* (London, Routledge).
Phelps, MS and Ruhland, EL (2022) 'Governing Marginality: Coercion and Care in Probation' 69(3) *Social Problems* 799.
Pratt, J (2007) *Penal Populism* (London, Routledge).
—— (2021) *Law, Insecurity and Risk Control* (London, Palgrave).
Reitz, KR and Rhine, EE (2020) 'Parole Release and Supervision: Critical Drivers of American Prison Policy' 3 *Annual Review of Criminology* 281.

Rhine, EE, Petersilia, J and Reitz, KR (2017) 'The Future of Parole Release' 46(1) *Crime and Justice* 279.
Roberts, JV, Stalans, LJ, Hough, M and Indermaur, D (2003) *Penal Populism and Public Opinion Lessons from Five Countries* (Oxford, Oxford University Press).
Robinson, G (2008) 'Late-Modern Rehabilitation: The Evolution of a Penal Strategy' 10 *Punishment & Society* 429.
Ryan, M and Sim, J (2012) 'Campaigning For and Campaigning Against Prisons: Excavating and Reaffirming the Case for Prison Abolition' in Y Jewkes (ed), *Handbook on Prisons*, 1st edn (London, Routledge).
Shute, S (2003) 'The Development of Parole and the Role of Research in Its Reform' in L Zedner and A Ashworth (eds), *The Criminological Foundations of Penal Policy: Essays in Honour of Roger Hood* (Oxford, Oxford University Press) 377–439.
Simon, J (1993) *Poor Discipline: Parole and the Social Control of the Underclass 1890–1990* (Chicago, University of Chicago Press).
Vannier, M (2016) 'A Right to Hope? Life Imprisonment in France' in D van Zyl Smit and C Appleton (eds), *Life Imprisonment and Human Rights* (Oxford, Hart Publishing).
van Zyl Smit, D and Snacken, S (2009) *Principles of European Prison Law and Policy: Penology and Human Rights* (Oxford, Oxford University Press).
van Zyl Smit, D and Corda, A (2018) 'American Exceptionalism in Parole Release and Supervision: A European Perspective' in KR Reitz (ed), *American Exceptionalism in Crime and Punishment* (New York, Oxford University Press) 410–86.
von Hirsch, A and Hanrahan, KJ (1978) *Abolish Parole?* (Washington, DC, National Institute of Law Enforcement and Criminal Justice).
—— (1979) *The Question of Parole – Retention, Reform and Abolition?* (Cambridge, MA, Ballinger).
Warr, J (2020) 'Always Gotta Be Two Mans': Lifers, Risk, Rehabilitation, and Narrative Labour' 22 *Punishment & Society* 28.
—— (2023) 'Whitening Black Men: Narrative Labour and the Scriptural Economics of Risk and Rehabilitation' 63 *British Journal of Criminology* 1091.
West, D (ed) (1972) *The Future of Parole* (London, Duckworth).

Part I

Rationalities

2

You be a Parole Board Member: Public Attitudes and Mock Parole Board Decision-Making

ARIE FREIBERG AND LORANA BARTELS*

I. INTRODUCTION

PAROLE TENDS ONLY to come to sustained public attention when a parolee commits a serious offence while at liberty. This happened in Victoria, Australia in 2012, when Adrian Bayley, who was on parole for a series of sex offences, raped and murdered a well-known journalist (Bartels 2013). This event led to extensive parole reforms, not only in the state in which this offence took place, and a shift in attitudes towards parole more broadly (Freiberg et al 2018).

In recent years, a form of 'parole populism' has emerged, which has further politicised parole decision-making, restricted the discretion of parole authorities (Moffa et al 2019), seen parole abolished in some jurisdictions in the United States of America (USA) and seen fewer prisoners either being eligible for parole or granted release (Fitzgerald et al 2023). Numerous reviews of parole systems in Australia, Canada, Scotland, and England and Wales have produced significant changes in parole, including the prioritisation of community protection over rehabilitation, the elevation of victims' rights and the reservation of powers for political officers over some decisions, especially in relation to high-risk sexual and violent offenders (Annison and Guiney 2022; Fitzgerald et al 2023).

Given the salience of public opinion in the development of public policy (Turner 2018), studies of the public's attitudes to criminal justice generally, and parole in particular, can provide an insight into the degree of public confidence in some of the institutions of justice and trust in governments more broadly. Public opinion in relation to these issues can be gauged in many ways: through polling and interviewing juries who have entered a verdict in a trial, representative

* This study was partly funded by Australian Research Council grant DP150100569. The authors acknowledge the contribution of Robin Fitzgerald and Shannon Dodd to this project. We thank them, the editors and Professor Julian Roberts for their comments on earlier drafts of this chapter.

surveys, deliberative polls, focus groups and citizens' juries, among others (Bartels et al 2018).

Against this highly charged backdrop, this chapter presents some findings from novel public opinion research we conducted on Australian attitudes to parole. The first phase involved a nationally representative survey with 1200 people and aimed to measure public attitudes to parole, as well as the factors that may account for differences in those attitudes (see Fitzgerald et al 2016; 2020). We also attempted to gauge parole authorities' views of the public, regarding such relations as bidirectional (Fitzgerald et al 2023). Our study found mixed support for parole (Fitzgerald et al 2016; 2023). We explored these issues in more detail through in-depth follow-up interviews with a subsample of 30 respondents, seeking to gain insight into public attitudes to parole by means of a 'You be the parole board' exercise. This involved providing respondents with hypothetical scenarios, placing them in the role of a parole board member.[1]

In this chapter, we argue that the expansion of parole board membership to include victims of crime, community members and others who do not necessarily have professional criminal justice experience calls for research to determine whether, and if so how, their views may differ from those who have traditionally comprised parole boards and the criminal justice professionals who advise them. If differences emerge, how should parole authorities respond?

II. FACTORS THAT INFLUENCE PAROLE DECISION-MAKING IN AUSTRALIA

Each Australian state and territory has an independent parole authority (generally a 'board': see Fitzgerald et al 2023). In most jurisdictions, the factors an authority considers in determining whether to grant parole are set out in legislation, with 'protection of the community' generally the paramount consideration. Other factors include:

- the nature and circumstances of the offence;
- the offender's:
  - prior criminal history;
  - previous history of supervision in the community;
  - release plans;
  - conduct in custody;
  - participation in programmes in custody;
  - likelihood of complying with parole;
- comments by the sentencing court;

[1] We acknowledge that parole boards make decisions as a collective. Future research could explore the dynamics of collective decision-making by giving individual mock board members vignettes, then facilitating group decision-making. Unfortunately, this was beyond the scope of the present project.

- the risk to the community/risk of reoffending;
- reports/recommendations by psychologists, community corrections, etc; and
- submissions by the victim(s)/their family and/or impact on the victim(s)/their family (Bartels 2013).

III. 'YOU BE THE DECISION-MAKER' EXERCISES

One method of gauging attitudes on issues of this nature is to place a member of the public in the shoes of a decision-maker by providing them with a hypothetical scenario and asking them to decide the outcome and the reasons for their decision. Vignette studies such as 'You be the judge' exercises are commonly used to educate the public about the difficulties and complexities of decision-making in emotionally charged contexts, such as family violence and sentencing (Horstman et al 2019; Cheah et al 2022). They are also used by sentencing advisory councils (SACs) in Australia (see Byles and Gill 2014; Queensland SAC 2023; Victorian SAC 2023).

Compared to the use of hypothetical cases in sentencing, the use of such cases involving mock parole board members in relation to parole decision-making is less common. For example, Lindsay and Miller (2011) used 120 college students to study release decision-making, to compare their views with those of real parole board members presented with the same scenarios. Miller et al (2014) also used university undergraduate students to study whether religious conversions/secular lifestyle changes and race affected mock parole board members' release decisions, emotions and perceptions. ElBassiouney et al (2022) used 720 participants to explore how an incarcerated person's race/ethnicity, mental health status and the type of conversion/lifestyle change experienced in prison would impact a mock parole board member's decisions, perceptions and emotional reactions. Yelderman et al's (2021) study with 1317 participants examined the 'actor observer effect', that is, the difference between making a release decision as a mock parole board member and reading about the same decision and outcome as a member of the public.

Studies of lay members of parole boards, or potential lay members, are important because, unlike sentencing in Australia, which is undertaken by a legally trained judicial officer,[2] parole boards generally include at least one member of the community, together with lawyers and experts, such as psychologists and social workers (see Fitzgerald et al 2023: Table 2.1). Public attitudes are therefore likely to be more immediately transferable to actual instances of decision-making. In addition, unlike court hearings, which are open to the public, parole hearings usually take place behind closed doors, so the public generally has little insight into what takes place in such settings (see Fitzgerald et al 2023).

[2] *cf* some European jurisdictions, where lay people are involved in sentencing decisions.

IV. THE CURRENT STUDY

A. Participants

As parole board membership diversifies, the views and attitudes of the lay public become more important, as does our need to understand them. In particular, we wanted to better understand why members of the public made certain parole decisions, when provided with information similar to actual parole board members. The interviews therefore aimed to explore their reasoning. We selected 30 participants from the sample of 1200 who had indicated their willingness to be contacted for further research. The sample was generally representative in terms of age and gender, but there were no Indigenous respondents or participants from the two jurisdictions with the smallest populations (see Table 2.1 for demographic details).

Table 2.1 Participant demographics

Gender	Male: 53% Female: 47%
Age	Average: 52 Range: 19–69
Education	High school: 30% Diploma: 7% Bachelor's degree: 32% Post-graduate degree: 13% Other: 17%
Employment	Full-time: 37% Part-time: 17% Retired: 33% Other: 13%

B. Materials

Five vignettes were created. In devising these, our aim was to construct hypothetical scenarios, including the type of information typically considered by parole authorities in their release decision-making. The word count was 500–600 words and each provided brief information about the offence(s) and sentence; the circumstances of the offence(s) and victim(s); and the offender's prior criminal history, behaviour in prison and participation in programmes, release plan and risk assessment. We held the correctional service recommendation for release constant; in each case, they 'recommended release'. Appendix 2.1 summarises the scenarios.

C. Procedure

Each participant was randomly sent two scenarios, before being interviewed. They were informed in advance that they would need to make a release decision in relation to each vignette. They also received supplementary information (including that parole 'allows for the supervised release of offenders from prison back to the community before the end of their full term of imprisonment').[3]

Participants were asked:

- Would you grant or deny parole for this offender?
- What is the most important purpose that will be achieved from granting/denying parole to this particular offender?
- What were the most important factors that influenced your decision to grant/deny parole to this offender?
- You indicated that you were (very/not very) confident in the offender's chances of successfully completing parole without reoffending. Why is this the case?

Those that recommended parole were also asked:

- What do you think will be the biggest obstacles to this offender's success while on parole?
- What types of parole conditions would you impose on this offender?

Participants who denied parole were asked:

- Would you recommend that parole be considered for this offender at a later date and, if so, how long until you think parole should be reconsidered?
- What information would you want to see in the offender's case file before you would feel confident in granting parole to this offender?
- Would there be any parole conditions that, if imposed on this offender, might increase your willingness to grant parole?

The interviews were conducted by telephone by the Social Research Centre in 2015 and the project had ethics approval from the University of Queensland. The interviews were professionally transcribed and analysed by the researchers. We summarise the responses thematically, supported by quotes from the transcripts.

[3] Study materials available from the authors on request.

V. FINDINGS

A. Parole Determinations

There were 12 respondents for each scenario. As set out in Table 2.2, overall, respondents granted parole in 52 per cent of cases and denied parole in 47 per cent of cases. However, there were clear differences, on the basis of offence type. In both the sex and family violence cases, only 25 per cent granted parole. In the armed robbery cases, the reverse obtained, with 75 per cent granting parole, regardless of whether the offender was Indigenous.[4] In the remaining case (involving a female property offender), seven respondents (58 per cent) granted parole and five (42 per cent) denied it. It is not clear to what extent this was influenced by this being the only case involving a female and/or the only one not involving violence.

In this chapter, we focus on the respondents' comments in the sex and family violence cases. Although they provide a notable exception to the majority outcome, where respondents were prepared to grant parole, these cases invoked the strongest responses and we therefore regard them as providing particularly important insights into the public's attitudes to parole and, as will emerge, sentencing and the justice system more broadly.

Table 2.2 Parole decision, by case type

	Grant	Deny	Undecided
Sex	25%	75%	0%
Family violence	25%	75%	0%
Robbery – non-Indigenous	75%	17%	8%
Robbery – Indigenous	75%	25%	0%
Property – female	58%	42%	0%
Total	52%	47%	2%

B. General Views of Parole

Generally, the principal objective of parole in Australia is 'to reduce reoffending, by providing for an offender's supervised reintegration into the community' (New South Wales Law Reform Commission 2015: 50; see also Freiberg et al 2018). Respondents generally agreed with this approach, observing that parole provided an opportunity for the prisoner to rehabilitate and change

[4] As we note below, Indigenous people are significantly overrepresented in Australian prisons. This research was intended to explore whether decision-makers' attitudes towards the offender's Indigenous status affected their decisions.

their behaviour, and gave them some hope. A number saw parole as providing a person with a 'second chance' to prove themselves, to give them the benefit of the doubt and redeem themselves, so that they did not have to pay for the crime for the rest of their lives (see further below; Fitzgerald et al 2020).

Some also saw parole as not being just for the benefit of the prisoner, but as a means of increasing their commitment to the legal system, reducing the risk of them becoming 'bitter and twisted' and being better for society generally. One participant pragmatically noted that parole relieved overcrowded prisons. Some participants had a pessimistic view of prison as an institution, due to its abnormal environment, which was not conducive to change or rehabilitation, but was in fact possibly criminogenic. Accordingly, parole was effectively seen as the lesser of two evils. Our survey (Fitzgerald et al 2016) found mixed support for parole: 46 per cent agreed that prisoners should be released to serve the last part of their sentence under supervision, while 59 per cent agreed that prisoners should serve their entire sentence in custody – a contradictory and ambivalent finding. In addition, 27 per cent did not believe offenders should ever be granted parole. The interviews revealed that some respondents identified that one of the major strengths of parole was the fact that the offender was released into the community under supervision, being monitored and with some support. The level of support was regarded as crucial to lessening the risk of reoffending, even though the respondents recognised the risk inherent in the parole system generally.

Parole in Australia is seen as a privilege, not a right. For example, the website of the Prisoners Review Board of Western Australia states: 'Parole is a privilege and is only given to prisoners who comply with prison rules, are truly committed to maintaining a positive lifestyle and becoming a contributing member of the community' (2020: np; see also Bartels 2013; Fitzgerald et al 2023; New South Wales Law Reform Commission 2015). Some of our interviewees saw parole as a reward; no one regarded it as a right. Respondents who were not supportive of parole regarded it a sending a 'wrong message to the community', arguing that a 'harder line' was necessary. Those who believed that prisoners should serve their entire sentence in custody had different reasons for doing so. Some simply did not believe in parole as an institution and felt that the sentence imposed by the court should be the sentence served. As one respondent stated in the context of the family violence case: 'I don't think I believe in it [parole]. I just think a sentence is a sentence' (PA7, female, deny). 'Truth in sentencing' has long been an issue in sentencing, with parole (as well as remissions, or good behaviour time) being viewed as undermining the sentence imposed by the court and making the sentence 'appear to be a joke' (Freiberg 1992). A range of recent reforms in Australia have purported to respond to this (see Freiberg et al 2018).

Several respondents also rejected the concept of rehabilitation and preferred that the full term be served for the purpose of retribution. A number regarded incapacitation as being more important than rehabilitation, implicitly providing more safety for the community (see Callinan 2013). Those who responded in this way may have been unaware that prisoners released at the expiration of their sentence are released into the community without any supervision, despite being provided with a statement at the outset of the research that explained this. Nor were they probably aware that parole reduces reoffending rates.

Some considered that granting parole lessened the message that general deterrence is intended to send. Another common perspective was that rehabilitation would be more likely to occur in prison, especially for the female offender, who had problems with substance abuse. Unfortunately, this is not supported by the research, with few Australian custodial programmes subject to robust research and/or showing limited effectiveness (see, eg Halstead and Poynton 2016; Day 2020).

C. Key Factors Relevant to Respondents' Decision-Making

(i) Community Safety and Risk

Most Australian jurisdictions have legislation that requires parole authorities to give paramount consideration to the safety and protection of the community in deciding whether to grant, vary, revoke or cancel a parole order (Bartels 2013; Freiberg et al 2018). In our survey (Fitzgerald et al 2016), 77 per cent indicated that community safety should be a priority, higher than rehabilitation. The interviews reflected this finding, with many articulating the difficulties of balancing the risk of reoffending against the benefits of release on parole. Respondents' decisions were very much coloured by their perceptions of risk for particular offences.

As discussed above, the sex offender was assessed as being of moderate risk of offending but recommended for release. Nevertheless, 75 per cent of respondents denied parole, primarily because they regarded him as a risk to society in general, with some believing that sex offenders have a high likelihood of reoffending. For example, PA20 (female, deny) asserted: 'sex offenders generally can't help themselves, it's sad to say', while PA7 (female, deny) said 'I just don't think that they can be rehabilitated'. This is consistent with research showing that the public believes that sex offenders cannot be rehabilitated and are irredeemable recidivists (see, eg Freiberg et al 2015). However, this view runs counter to the empirical research, especially in relation to subsequent sex offending (eg Hanson et al 2018; Dowling et al 2021).

In the present case, the offender was regarded by some as still posing a threat to his children, with one respondent observing that it was preferable to keep him in custody for the full term, so that the victims would be adults on his release. Even when respondents considered that the risk of reoffending was low to moderate, they were not willing to take the risk, though the three respondents who would have granted parole were prepared to 'take a chance'.

The risk-averse nature of the responses in the context of sex offences is captured in the following comments:

> Am I willing to take that risk, that he could go out and do this again with other young children? He may never have that opportunity, but I just don't know. I couldn't … I just think, given the opportunity to repeat again, to offend again, I think they would, so why take that risk? Why put our children in harm's way? (PA16, male, deny)
>
> We have to put community safety first … and foremost … I do feel sometimes that it's a joke, it's not taken into consideration. (PA7, female, deny)

Similarly, in the family violence case, many referred to risk generally and recognised that, while there may be a relatively low risk to the offender's partner, the man might pose a danger to future partners. One noted the dangers of family violence escalating to murder. Conversely, the three who would have granted parole were of the view that he was generally at low risk of reoffending. Paradoxically, perhaps, respondents were more willing to grant parole in the substance-affected armed robbery scenarios, despite the evidence showing substance abuse is a risk factor for reoffending (see, eg Dowden and Brown 2002; Link and Hamilton 2017).

Public perception of risk of reoffending is less likely to be based on empirical studies than media reporting of crime and the salience of those reports, including beliefs that crime rates are rising (see, eg Moore 2020). In this context, several respondents referred to media reports of offences committed on parole, parole failures and the prevalence of family violence offences. Critically, we found that more respondents who commented on media stories denied parole than those who granted it.

(ii) The Nature and Circumstances of the Offence

In theory, it is the role of the court to impose a sentence that reflects the nature and gravity of the offence and for parole authorities to exercise their discretion within the boundaries set by the court (see *Power v R* (1974) 131 CLR 623). Although parole authorities can consider the nature and circumstances of the offence and comments by the sentencing court (Bartels 2013), it is not generally their role to effectively resentence the offender, if they believe the sentencer has erred (generally, by being too lenient).

A notable feature of the interviews was the very strong view that, in the sex and family violence cases, the courts did not reflect the serious nature of the offences (as evidenced by the sentence given) and, consequently, it was the respondents' responsibility to redress this error by denying parole. A number described these offences as 'serious', 'very serious' or 'abhorrent', and considered both the non-parole periods and maximum terms too short. A few considered that, in relation to the sex offences, the sentence 'per victim' was too short. In this context, we note that the respondents would not have had any understanding of the sentencing principle of totality. The perception that the courts had been too lenient in the sex offender case is reflected in the following quotes:

> I think he should do his time and then face whatever's going to come to him in the future ... The crime has been committed. Now you pay the time, and I still think six years is not enough, especially when it was his own two children. For one-and-a-half years for each child, this man can get parole? No. Absolutely not. Let him do his full time. Don't give him the chance to come out and say to other people or to even think to himself, 'ooh I did three years and got away with that'. (PA11, female, deny)

> Let him serve out the full sentence. You've got to remember there were two victims there as well and seven years is only three-and-half each. (PA21, male, deny)

> For sexually assaulting your two little girls, I'd have given him 10 years ... I think that's horrible. (PA26, male, grant)

Australian studies with jurors have revealed that they generally suggest more lenient sentences than those imposed by the judge in the case in which they were involved. Furthermore, around 87–90 per cent of jurors considered the sentence imposed appropriate (Warner et al 2011; 2017). However, they were less likely to be satisfied with the sentences imposed for sex offences, especially those involving child victims, than other offence types (see Tasmanian SAC 2013; Warner et al 2017). Our survey (Fitzgerald et al 2016) found that only 8 per cent of respondents supported parole for hypothetical offenders serving sentences for child sex offences and 15 per cent supported it for murder, compared with 66 per cent for burglary and fraud. The comments below reveal the visceral and emotional responses from some of the interviews:

> I think it's beyond a parent's reckoning ... it just choked me ... I know it's barbaric ... [but] I think they should be tattooed, so the public can see what they are. I also think males, if they do this, they should be sterilised. (PA11, female, deny)

> I find it very frustrating that they're allowed to integrate, especially sexual offenders, are allowed to integrate back into society ... and seem to have access to see children and go out and mingle amongst the community. It makes me sick to my stomach that I could be at a park playing with my children and there could be a repeat offender paedophile sitting in the park, and it's like Christmas for them, isn't it? (PA7, female, deny)

> I'm a mother ... This is abhorrent to me. I'd quite like to remove his testicles. (PA28 (female, deny)

(iii) Prior Offending and Breaches of Parole

In our survey, 27 per cent of respondents identified prior criminal history as an important factor and 75 per cent felt that past parole violators should never be granted parole (Fitzgerald et al 2016). Prior criminal history and breaches of parole may indicate that the offender is more likely to offend again and/or breach or contravene the order in other ways, having been unresponsive to previous court orders or, in the case of prior offences, suggest that the instant offences are more serious. Participants' views of this factor were mixed and varied, depending on the offence. In relation to the sex offence, despite the lack of prior convictions, some respondents disregarded this factor, in view of the seriousness of the offence. Some were also sceptical that he had not committed such offences previously. Australian courts are not permitted to sentence someone for offences they have not been convicted of (*R v De Simoni* (1981) 147 CLR 383). Nevertheless, two respondents did not believe this was his first offence, even if he did not have a criminal record. Instead, they felt he had probably 'got away with it' previously:

> I know he has got no other history, but that doesn't mean he's – this is only the first time he's ever been caught, really. You don't know if he's been looking at things online ... but there's probably generally some other behaviour there that would be a little bit – oh, there's some alarm bells there. (PA20, female, deny)

> That really upsets me when someone says 'oh, look, he doesn't have any previous history of sexual assault'. Well, maybe that's because he hasn't been caught, so how do we know that he hasn't sexually abused someone else previously? I know that you should treat someone as innocent until proven guilty and you shouldn't perhaps go on the assumption that they have offended, if there's no proof that they have, but how can we go on the assumption that he hasn't? (PA7, female, deny)

The nature of the offence also appeared relevant in the family violence case, where the offender's past history of violence against a woman was important to several who denied parole and indicated some degree of escalation. Even one respondent who granted parole found the prior assault 'concerning' (PA5, male, grant). The fact that the offender had a record of prior offending and parole breaches also weighed heavily on respondents' minds in relation to the female offender burglary case, where the offending itself was less serious. Many of those who denied parole noted both her prior offending and especially her history of parole breaches. Reflecting the 'forfeiture' theory of repeat offending (Fitzgerald et al 2020), one respondent noted that she had had 'enough chances' and did not warrant any more. As she said:

> [S]he had breached ... parole previously twice. So, as a community member, you'd go, oh how could that happen? How could they lie? You know, so she'd been given the opportunity before and she'd abused it – twice. So, it's great that she's working through her stuff and she should continue to do that, but she doesn't get the privilege of receiving parole again ... it has to be earned and the fact that you've breached it previously twice ... you've had enough chances, in terms of trying to be integrated ... so people have tried to assist you twice before and you haven't made the most of your opportunities then. So, people are going to try to continue to assist you whilst you're in prison, but you just need to serve out the rest of your whole sentence – you don't get that second chance again. She did the wrong thing three times. We've tried to help her, and she's thrown it back in our face, you know. Shows that we're compassionate, but ... she's mistaken our kindness for weakness. (PA4, female, deny)

In contrast, in the two armed-robbery cases, most respondents were prepared to grant parole despite noting the relevance of the offender's past history, including terms of imprisonment, and describing it as a 'concern' or a 'problem'. One respondent noted that the prior history had been taken into account in the imposition of a long sentence, thereby implicitly acknowledging that it was not the role of the parole authority to resentence the offender, but to consider the risk to the community and the offender's prospects of rehabilitation. This respondent thereby appropriately acknowledged the limited role of a parole authority, in contrast with our findings in relation to the sex case, where respondents appeared to want the parole authority to function as a de facto resentencing body.

(iv) Rehabilitation and Prison Programmes

In our survey (Fitzgerald et al 2016), 25 per cent of respondents indicated that completion of rehabilitation programmes was an important factor and 77 per cent felt that desistance was possible for most offenders under the right circumstances. For parole authorities, an offender's participation in programmes while in custody is important; in some cases, failure to participate is a bar to release, even if this is due to the programme being unavailable (which may be due to resource issues and is clearly beyond the offender's control). In both armed robbery cases, most who granted parole placed considerable weight on this factor, seeing it as a positive development, desire to rehabilitate, 'turning point', second chance, sign of redemption and signal that the offender was responding to the court's orders. However, one participant reflected her ambivalence (like many) towards rehabilitation:

> I think rehabilitation is possible, so I think … people can be redeemed and I believe strongly in a second chance, given that opportunity but it's not a carte blanche thing, so you get one, you take it, you use it and … if you don't treat it with the respect it requires, then you've lost that and maybe you've lost it forever … justice still needs to be served, so there is a consequence for every action. (PA4, female, deny; see also Fitzgerald et al 2020)

Those who would have denied parole were sceptical of the likelihood of rehabilitation and the programmes themselves. This scepticism about the genuineness of the offender's commitment to rehabilitation emerged strongly in the comments about the sex offender case. They were also sceptical about rehabilitation generally, and thought that he could not be rehabilitated and that his participation was 'token', as the following comments illustrate:

> I don't know how sincere he is about it. And the bit when, you know, 'found God', I'm just like, oh please! [Laughs] (PA1, female, deny)

> The more I read of this case the more I sort of looked at the person and went, he's playing the system. That's the way it came across to me, he seems to be just doing what he has to, to get out. He knows what the parole system is, he's doing the bits and pieces. (PA16, male, deny)

By contrast, the minority who granted parole saw this offender's involvement in prison programmes as important and positive.

(v) The Causes of Crime

The public's views of the value, or likelihood, of rehabilitation are embedded in the broader question of their views of the causes of crime. If they believe that offending is the result of considered choices, they are more likely to hold the offender personally responsible for their actions and be less sympathetic to any factors that may mitigate the penalty and explain the offender's behaviour.

Our survey found that 48 per cent of respondents agreed that crime resulted from an offender's rational decision-making process, rather than their social circumstances. In relation to the non-Indigenous armed robbery, one respondent was ambivalent, asking 'who is really responsible – the offender or the state?', before deciding to deny parole (PA1, female). Another respondent (PA28) felt that 'the system' had failed this man, whom she granted parole. Indigenous Australians are much more likely to be incarcerated than non-Indigenous people, although the reasons for this are complex (Australian Law Reform Commission 2017). Our scenarios sought to determine whether an offender's Indigenous status affected decision-making. We found that 75 per cent of participants would grant parole in both scenarios. Nevertheless, the participants were aware of, and sensitive to, the Indigenous offender's cultural background.

Once again, the strongest views on this issue were expressed in relation to the sex offender:

> I'm sick and tired of, you know, these sex offenders – oh they were abused as children … – well, a lot of people have hard, you know, you just get on with it and … get on with your life. What? You want to dwell on sorrow and misery for the rest of your life? Well, if you want to be a victim, then you will be a victim … [It's] everyone else's fault but mine. Again, blaming everything else but himself and I just, I have no time for that … [there are] too many excuses to, you know, to put a label on something and blaming, blaming everything. You feel like saying – what about some personal responsibility? (PA1, female, deny)

> My understanding is that sexual offenders, especially against children in families, by and large tend to have a history of undergoing a similar abuse themselves.[5] The whole thing about personal responsibility. It is very easy to go – 'life's tough, life's hard' or 'I'm a victim' or 'poor me' and whether a way out of that might be alcohol, to escape problems or it might be gambling to escape the economic issues. You need to stop and look at yourself and say, 'I've got a problem'. Using that as an excuse … that's really becoming unconscionable behaviour (PA13, male, deny)

Those who denied parole placed little weight on the mitigating factors mentioned in the sex offence case, ie his marital issues, increased stress at work, alcohol abuse and depression. On the other hand, in the burglary, domestic

[5] This view is supported by research: see, eg Ogloff et al (2012).

violence and robbery cases – where problems of addiction, alcohol or substance abuse, prior experiences of sexual abuse and the lack of skill, jobs or education were identified – those who would have granted parole took these factors into account.

(vi) Victims

Since the 1960s, victims have played a larger role in the criminal justice system, including in sentencing and parole. In sentencing, victims can submit a victim impact statement (VIS) and the common law principle to take the harm to the victim into account (*Siganto v R* (1998) 194 CLR 656) has arguably gained greater prominence in recent years. Victims or those involved in victims' organisations now sit on parole authorities and victims may sometimes make submissions in relation to parole release or the conditions of such release (Bartels 2013). Our survey (Fitzgerald et al 2016) found that 70 per cent of respondents agreed that victims should have more say in the decision to release.

Our interviews did not canvass this issue, but respondents expressed strong views about the impact on the victims, especially in relation to the sex offender case, where it was noted that the victims were young, suffered harm and needed protection. Where applicable, the VIS was variously received: some found them important; some found them useful to understand the effect of the crime on the victim; some 'noted' them but felt they were not significant in their decision-making; and one was sceptical about their findings. One participant observed that a VIS was relevant in sentencing, but less so in parole decision-making. In respect of the family violence case, which also elicited strong and unfavourable views of the offence and offender, the effect of the crime on the victim and her safety were relevant factors, reflecting some public ambivalence about family violence. In this context, however, there were elements of victim-blaming, suggesting that the victim was 'neurotic' or there may have been some provocation by the victim. These views were expressed by the minority, who granted parole.

In the robbery cases, those who granted parole noted that the harm to the victim was not a dominant factor and was not that serious, and the victim's trauma was 'uncertain'. Another view was that, while harm to the victim was a relevant factor, the focus in the parole context is on offenders and their rehabilitation. In general, these respondents' inclination to support the offender's rehabilitation saw them downplay the harm to the victim, although we consider it possible to recognise both aspects and structure justice responses that seek to achieve this. One respondent noted that keeping the offender in prison did not help the victim. This stood in contrast to the sex and family violence cases, where some considered that incapacitation, by keeping the offender in custody, was of benefit to the victim.

VI. CONCLUSION

The erosion of trust in parole boards, as evidenced by the restrictions of their powers in many jurisdictions, requires them to reconsider their traditional relationships to the communities that they serve and explore ways to rebuild confidence in their work and restore their legitimacy. This research has shown a significant degree of scepticism by interviewees about the people and processes involved in parole decision-making. Both those who granted and denied parole were suspicious about parole generally, the people who prepared reports for the decision-makers, rehabilitation, the benefits of correctional programmes, offenders' commitment to – and compliance with – programmes, and the genuineness of expressions of remorse and promises made about future behaviour, including commitments to change, career promises, release plans and sever ties with anti-social friends.

Several participants showed little empathy with the offenders, particularly the sex offender. This aligns with jury research, indicating that the public favours retribution over other purposes of sentencing (Warner et al 2019). Where there was empathy, it was with the victim, especially for two participants who were themselves victims of family and sexual violence, although the latter did not consider that this influenced her decision (PA22, female, deny).

The scepticism, or possibly even cynicism, of the value of parole expressed by many of the participants in this study reflects the ambivalent feelings about parole of members of the public generally (Fitzgerald et al 2016; 2020) and captures the challenges faced by parole authorities in many jurisdictions, particularly following tragic and very public failures. Our research with mock parole board members provides a better understanding of public attitudes to parole and how they may differ from parole decision-makers themselves. The disparity between these views suggests two possible futures for parole, which are congruent, rather than being in conflict.

The first is to recognise and accept the salience of public attitudes and the pluralistic nature of community views. This requires a greater role for public deliberation, in the development of criminal justice policies. This already occurs with bodies such as sentencing commissions or councils. It also requires that parole boards address the demographic deficit, to increase the range of views that have traditionally been represented on parole boards. As Fitzgerald et al noted (2023: 97): 'The significant expansion of parole board membership to become more diverse and representative of the community … represent[s] an important step in bridging the gap between public understandings of parole and actual parole practices.'

The second is to address the lack of understanding about the purposes of parole and the way it operates, which this study has demonstrated. Despite our instructions, many respondents probably did not understand that release without parole meant release without supervision or support. Why would one expect that respondents would understand parole, given its relatively unseen role in the sentencing process (unseen, that is, until revealed in the media, when it fails)? Providing the public with more information is a strategy that focuses on changing the public's views. Research on public opinion and sentencing shows that the more information members of the public have about sentencing practices, the less punitive they become (for a recent review of the research, see Jeffs et al 2023). Analysis of the data on the Victorian SAC's 'You be the judge' sentencing exercises reveals that providing people with more information about the purposes and operation of sentencing, or the criminal justice system more generally, results in a closer alignment between members of the public and actual sentencing practices (Byles and Gill 2014).

Public education may redress this cognitive deficit, but this is a challenging task (Fitzgerald et al 2023). We found that most respondents granted parole, but this varied on the basis of offence type, with strong support for parole in the robbery cases, modest support in the burglary case and little support in the sex and family violence cases. Despite recommendations for release by the correctional authorities in every case, their advice was often rejected. These emotional responses overrode the legal factors authorities are required to take into consideration. Ultimately, parole, like sentencing, is a human process (Hogarth 1971).

Other strategies adopted by Australian parole authorities strive for better communication with the public. These include websites that contain information about parole generally, including its benefits, and the composition and membership of parole boards; information for victims; frequently asked questions; media releases; publications; and links to relevant government sources. They also include holding public hearings and publishing decisions, to increase the transparency of parole decision-making; public presentations by board at conferences, seminars and with strategic stakeholders; deliberative forums or other forms of participatory engagement; using social media; participating in documentaries about parole; producing or participating in podcasts; and responding to media stories about parole, particularly when crises occur (Fitzgerald et al 2023).Whether any of these strategies actually increase the public's understanding of confidence in parole is yet to be determined. And, as history has shown, when catastrophic failures occur, trust and confidence are easily shaken. However, with more lay members on parole boards, even better insight may be gained from exploring how lay members of parole authorities approach their task. Future research should also consider the effects of collective decision-making on changing attitudes and approaches to parole, among both traditional parole board and lay members.

REFERENCES

Annison, H and Guiney, T (2022) 'Populism, Conservatism and the Politics of Parole in England and Wales' 93(3) *The Political Quarterly* 416.

Australian Law Reform Commission (2017) *Pathways to Justice – Inquiry into the Incarceration Rate of Aboriginal and Torres Strait Islander Peoples*.

Bartels, L (2013) 'Parole and Parole Authorities in Australia: A System in Crisis?' 37 *Criminal Law Journal* 357.

Bartels, L, Fitzgerald, R and Freiberg, A (2018) 'Public Opinion on Sentencing and Parole' 65(3) *Probation Journal* 269.

Byles, D and Gill, C (2014) 'Citizen Judges' 88(12) *Law Institute Journal* 52.

Callinan, I (2013) *Review of the Parole System in Victoria* (Corrections Victoria).

Cheah, C and Koay, K (2022) 'Knowing the Unknown: Application of Qualitative Vignette Method in the Social-Political Sensitive Business Environment' *International Journal of Qualitative Methods* https://doi.org/10.1177/16094069221074495.

Day, A (2020) 'At a Crossroads? Offender Rehabilitation in Australian Prisons' 27 *Psychiatry, Psychology and Law* 939.

Dowden, C and Brown, S (2002) 'The Role of Substance Abuse Factors in Predicting Recidivism: A Meta-analysis' 8 *Psychology, Crime and Law* 243.

Dowling, C, Boxall, H, Pooley, K, Long, C and Franks, C (2021) *Patterns and Predictors of Reoffending Among Child Sexual Offenders: A Rapid Evidence Assessment* (Australian Institute of Criminology).

ElBassiouney, A, Ayala, R and Sircy, K (2021) 'Factors Influencing Mock Parole Board Members: The Impact of an Incarcerated Person's Race/Ethnicity, Conversion While in Prison, and Mental Health Status' 22 *Analysis of Social Issues and Public Policy* 286.

Fitzgerald, R, Bartels, L, Freiberg, A, Cherney, A and Buglar, S (2016) 'How Does the Australian Public View Parole? Results from a National Survey on Public Attitudes Towards Parole and Re-entry' 40 *Criminal Law Journal* 307.

Fitzgerald, R, Freiberg, A and Bartels, L (2020) 'Redemption or Forfeiture? Understanding Diversity in Australians' Attitudes to Parole' 20 *Criminology and Criminal Justice* 169.

Fitzgerald, R, Freiberg, A, Dodd, S and Bartels, L (2022) 'Building Public Confidence in Parole Boards: Findings from a Four-Country Study' 66 *British Journal of Criminology* 1395.

Fitzgerald, R, Dodd, S, Freiberg, A and Bartels, L (2023) *Parole on Probation: Public Opinion, Public Confidence and Parole Decision-Making* (Palgrave Macmillan).

Freiberg, A (1992) 'Truth in Sentencing? The Abolition of Remissions in Victoria' 16 *Criminal Law Journal* 165.

Freiberg, A, Donnelly, H and Gelb, K (2015) *Sentencing for Child Sexual Abuse in Institutional Contexts* (Royal Commission into Institution Child Sexual Abuse).

Freiberg, A, Bartels, L, Fitzgerald, R and Dodd, S (2018) 'Parole, Politics and Penal Policy' 18 *Queensland University of Technology Law Review* 191.

Halstead, I and Poynton, S (2016) 'The NSW Intensive Drug and Alcohol Treatment Program (IDATP) and Recidivism: An Early Look at Outcomes for Referrals' (New South Wales Bureau of Crime Statistics and Research).

Hanson, R, Harris, A, Letourneau, E, Helmus, L and Thornton, D (2018) 'Reductions in Risk Based on Time Offense Free in the Community: Once a Sex Offender, Not Always a Sex Offender' 24 *Psychology, Public Policy, and Law* 48.

Hogarth, J (1971) *Sentencing as a Human Process* (Toronto, University of Toronto Press).

Horstman, N, Bond, C and Eriksson, L (2019) 'Sentencing Domestic Violence Offenders: A Vignette Study of Public Perceptions' 36 *Journal of Interpersonal Violence* NP11916.

Jeffs, S, Allen, S, Klambauer, E and Hidderley, L (2023) *Understanding of Sentencing: Community Knowledge of Sentencing Terms and Outcome* (Queensland SAC).

Lindsey, S and Miller, M (2011) 'Discretionary Release Decisions of Actual and Mock Parole Board Members: Implications for Community Sentiment and Parole Decision-Making' 18 *Psychiatry, Psychology and Law* 498.

Link, N and Hamilton, L (2017) 'The Reciprocal Lagged Effects of Substance Use and Recidivism in a Prisoner Reentry Context' *Health Justice* https://doi.org/10.1186/s40352-017-0053-2.

Miller, S, Lindsey, S and Kaufman, J (2014) 'The Religious Conversion and Race of a Prisoner: Mock Parole Board Members' Decisions, Perception, and Emotions' 19 *Legal and Criminological Psychology* 104.

Moffa, M, Stratton, G and Ruyters, M (2019) 'Parole Populism: The Politicisation of Parole in Victoria' 31(1) *Current Issues in Criminal Justice* 75.

Moore, E (2020) 'Public Confidence in the New South Wales Criminal Justice System: 2019 Update' (New South Wales Bureau of Crime Statistics and Research).

New South Wales Law Reform Commission (2015) *Parole*.

Ogloff, J, Cutajar, M, Mann, E and Mullen, P (2012) 'Child Sexual Abuse and Subsequent Offending and Victimisation: A 45 Year Follow-Up Study' (Australian Institute of Criminology).

Prisoners Review Board of Western Australia (2020) 'What Is Parole?' www.prisonersreviewboard.wa.gov.au/W/what_is_parole.aspx.

Queensland SAC (2023) 'Judge for Yourself' www.sentencingcouncil.qld.gov.au/education/judge-for-yourself.

Tasmanian SAC (2013) 'Sex Offence Sentencing' Research Paper.

Turner, E (2018) *Public Confidence in Criminal Justice: A History and Critique* (Springer).

Victorian SAC (2023) 'Education' www.sentencingcouncil.vic.gov.au/education.

Warner, K, Davis, J, Walter, M, Bradfield, R and Vermey, R (2011) 'Public Judgement on Sentencing: Final Results from the Tasmanian Jury Sentencing Study' (Australian Institute of Criminology).

Warner, K, Davis, J Spiranovic, C, Cockburn, H and Freiberg, A (2017) 'Measuring Jurors' Views on Sentencing: Results from the Second Australian Jury Sentencing Study' 19 *Punishment and Society* 180.

Yelderman, L, Lawrence, T, Lyons, C and DeVault, A (2021) 'Actor–Observer Asymmetry in Perceptions of Parole Board Release Decisions' 28 *Psychiatry, Psychology and Law* 623.

Appendix 2.1 Summary of scenarios provided to participants

#	Age	Gender	Offence/s	Sentence length	Risk level	Context
1	37	Male	Sexual assaults	6y, 3y served	Moderate	Sexual assaults against offender's daughters, aged 12 and 13, over three years. Offences took place while he was experiencing marital issues and increased work stress. He was increasingly depressed and using alcohol to cope with his emotions. After the offences came to light, the offender and his wife separated. The daughters' VIS described feelings of betrayal and disappointment. He had no prior criminal history. He had one minor incident in prison, when he attempted to send his daughters a letter. He said he was writing to ask for their forgiveness. The letter was written as part of an assignment in his sex offender programme, but he was not expected to mail the letter. He participated actively in the sex offender programme, with reasonably positive reports. He attended Alcoholics Anonymous sessions and had renewed his religious faith. He had good employment prospects and was planning to live 100 kilometres from his ex-wife and daughters.
2	34	Male	Armed robbery	7y, 4½y served	Moderate	Offender entered a liquor store late at night with a knife, threatened employee and fled premises with approximately $200 cash. The motive appeared to be financial. At the time of offence, he had no job skills, was unemployed and using alcohol and drugs daily. The VIS indicated that the employee was physically unharmed, but still experienced trauma-related symptoms, including nightmares and anxiety. The offender had served two prior prison sentences for assault causing bodily harm and drink-driving. He did not receive parole for those sentences, because he refused to participate in prison-based programmes. During the current sentence, he initially refused to participate in programmes, but then completed some. Early on, he had several institutional charges (including being under the influence of alcohol and fighting with other prisoners). He had offers of employment and accommodation on release.

(continued)

Appendix 2.1 *(Continued)*

#	Age	Gender	Offence/s	Sentence length	Risk level	Context
2A						As above, but offender was Aboriginal. He agreed to participate in programmes 'through the encouragement of an Aboriginal Elder who works in the prison'. He 'gained a great deal through his involvement in Aboriginal-specific programming' and planned to 'continue an Aboriginal substance abuse program in the community'.
3	36	Male	Assault and harassment	4½y, 2¾y served	Low overall, moderate for spousal violence	Offender had a volatile relationship with then-girlfriend, with the police called regularly. She moved to a women's shelter and he harassed her with phone calls, saying she had provoked him. She remained fearful he would try to find her, if released, so she changed her name and moved to an undisclosed location. He had two prior arrests for drink-driving and two incidents of assault against a previous partner. In prison, he initially had a couple of minor verbal incidents with other offenders, but these did not persist. He completed programmes for substance abuse and family violence. He had good employment prospects and a confirmed place of residence.
4	34	Female	Burglary, theft, possession of stolen credit card information	1y, 2y served	Moderate	Offender was arrested following a complaint of a burglary in progress at a shop. She had $500 cash and three stolen credit cards from an earlier theft. She pleaded guilty and cooperated with police. She had served two previous prison sentences for fraud and theft over $5000 and two breaches of previous parole orders. During the first six months of her sentence, she was in trouble twice (for refusing a direct order from a corrections officer and fighting with another prisoner), but her behaviour then improved. She had a serious drug problem, most recently addiction to 'ice'. In prison, she actively participated in and completed a substance abuse programme and attended psychological counselling to deal with the sexual abuse she experienced as a teenager. She was a single mother, with a six-year-old daughter in foster care since the age of 12 months. She wanted to try to re-establish contact, once her life is straightened out. She has confirmed accommodation and plans to continue Narcotics Anonymous upon release.

3

Applying Procedural Justice Principles to the Life-Sentence-Release Decision-Making Process

DORIS SCHARTMUELLER

I. INTRODUCTION

A LIFE PRISON sentence is a penal option in most countries (van Zyl Smit and Appleton 2019). In jurisdictions without the death penalty, this constitutes the ultimate form of punishment. At the same time, life sentences do not function the same in all jurisdictions in which they are imposed. They come in many different forms and variations. While some persons sentenced to life in prison have the possibility of being released after having served a minimum number of years, which is often either statutorily prescribed or set discretionarily upon sentencing, other life sentences involve being imprisoned permanently. A common feature of life sentences, however, is that the exact date of release from prison is uncertain and dependent on the decision of an authorised institution.

The decision to conditionally release[1] a life-sentenced person from prison is sensitive and complicated. The forces of 'penal populism' – public discourse that emphasises the 'undeservingness' of people who commit crimes – have devalued criminal justice experts' opinions and have led to more politicisation of penal policies (Pratt 2007). A life sentence is prone to becoming a scapegoat of penal failures in populist environments due to the nature of the sentence – typically a longer prison sentence of at least a decade given for a violent or habitual offence – and the societal responses to this sentence, triggered by public outrage, about the harm caused by the crime and the possibility of the convicted person jeopardising public safety upon release (Anderson 2019).

[1] In this chapter, I use the term 'conditional release' to refer to the early release from prison under specific conditions that must be obeyed. In some jurisdictions, the term 'parole release' is preferred.

Tensions between retribution and rehabilitation as penal objectives run high in life-sentence-release decisions. While the focus of rehabilitation is on who a person is and what he or she has done, especially since being convicted, retribution prioritises the seriousness of a committed offence and the person's culpability (Herbert 2019; Ruhland 2020; Kokkalera and Singer 2023). The two objectives are difficult to balance in life-sentence cases. Consequently, decision-makers have foregrounded risk and public protection considerations over concerns about due process and the incarcerated person's rights, and many life-sentence-release processes have become 'shrouded in obfuscation and mystery' (van Zyl Smit and Appleton 2019: 234; Guiney 2023). However, opaque and inconsistent decisions not only negatively affect imprisoned people, who often do not understand the expectations and rationale behind such decisions, but also impact other stakeholders, such as family members, victims' families and the wider society, contributing to a crisis of legitimacy for prison release decision-makers in many jurisdictions (see chapter one in this volume).

In this chapter, I examine life-sentence-release decision-making in depth, with particular reference to how jurisdictions deal with these complicated cases. Despite the uncertainty behind the exact time of conditional release, life-imprisoned individuals should still be met with a clear set of procedural safeguards in the review process. This has become increasingly important given that life-imprisoned populations have grown in many jurisdictions in recent decades and decisions to release them have to be made more routinely (van Zyl Smit and Appleton 2019). I therefore discuss how procedural justice principles – well tested in the context of police and courtroom decision-making, as well as probation and parole – can assist with increasing the legitimacy of these discretionary processes. This application aims to invite readers to consider and critically assess the use of the principles of fairness in life-release decisions in their jurisdictions.

II. THE ORGANISING FRAMEWORK: PROCEDURAL JUSTICE

Procedural justice is a theory that emphasises the importance of fair decision-making processes to enhance legitimacy (Tyler 2003; Tyler and Lind 2004; Jackson et al 2010; Tyler 2010). Whereas distributive justice is primarily concerned with outcomes, procedural justice derives fairness from how authority is exercised in the process that leads to outcomes. In the criminal legal field, procedural justice theory has mostly been applied to police and court procedures (Sunshine and Tyler 2003; Tyler 2003),[2] but it has also been used to assess

[2] These are only two of the most prominent study examples.

correctional practices (eg Robinson and McNeill 2008; Jackson et al 2010; Tyler 2010).[3]

The procedural justice framework rests on four pillars that help build legitimacy through the careful and consistent exercise of authority (Tyler 2003; 2010; Jackson et al 2010). The first pillar emphasises voice, which refers to establishing mechanisms (formal and informal) to allow people affected by a decision to be heard (Tyler 2010). People are encouraged to address any concerns they might have about the process. As they can state their cases, they are lifted to the level of stakeholders, with their input becoming an essential ingredient in the decision-making process.

The second pillar concerns neutrality (Tyler 2003; Jackson et al 2010). This refers to the principle of decision-making in an unbiased, consistent and transparent manner. While a decision-maker's personal background and values, professional experience and daily conditions may limit his or her ability to be objective, the consistent application of clear, concise rules can allow a decision-maker to approach neutrality. Furthermore, frequently referencing the established rules can convey neutrality during the criminal legal process (Tyler 2010).

The third pillar concerns respectful treatment. In the correctional system specifically, not only have those incarcerated lost their liberty, but a criminal conviction also comes with stigma and the loss of certain rights. Regardless of their status, the idea is that the incarcerated population must be treated with respect and dignity at any decision point in the 'correctional continuum' (Mathews et al 2020: 207). Persons directly affected by decisions must be met with respect for their inherent rights as human beings.

The fourth pillar is the expression of honest concern for the people involved as a key element in achieving legitimacy. If decision-makers manage to communicate that they are working in the best interests of everybody involved and that every decision is made with this principle in mind, they contribute to establishing trust in authorities (Tyler 2003; Jackson et al 2010). For example, they can build trust by openly communicating the reasoning behind their decisions and the process followed to reach them (Tyler 2010). Trustworthiness is especially important in the criminal legal setting, where any decision must be made with the public good in mind.

These four pillars have been found to build a fairer process in different settings. The level of procedural justice that people going through the process subjectively experience, as well as how the functioning of the process is communicated to the public, can establish trust and confidence in the system. As Tyler and Lind (2004: 74) stressed, 'The key to successful functioning is to make

[3] A multitude of studies have recently been conducted on procedural justice and legitimacy in prisons. For a review of extant empirical literature on this topic, see Ryan and Bergin (2022).

decisions in ways that are viewed by those affected as fair'. A perception of fair rules can then also lead to voluntary rule compliance and more positive interactions with authorities (Jackson et al 2010).

I will utilise the four pillars of procedural justice to review what is known about life-release decision-making processes. This application is not based on an empirical test, but a survey of scholarly research conducted in different jurisdictions. While not a systematic review, this chapter offers a close examination of the qualitative and quantitative international bodies of work on this topic.

III. LIFE-SENTENCE-RELEASE DECISION-MAKING AND PROCEDURAL JUSTICE

As with any aspect of penal systems, life-sentence review mechanisms are derived from a jurisdiction's unique cultural, political and economic context.[4] In their book *Life Imprisonment: A Global Human Rights Analysis*, van Zyl Smit and Appleton (2019) attempted to categorise different life-release decision-making mechanisms into four groups. While judicial bodies are mandated to review life cases in much of continental Europe and some Latin American countries, non-executive committees, often in the form of parole boards, serve as the ultimate decision-makers in common law countries, such as England and Wales, the USA and Australia. Other jurisdictions, especially in Africa, rely on the executive branch to review life-sentence cases. In some jurisdictions, release from a life sentence is possible only through clemency, typically granted by the head of state. For example, those serving life without parole (LWOP) in a US state would first have to get their sentence commuted (ie reduced) by a governor before any parole board would decide on a conditional release.[5]

While prison release mechanisms have become more routinised and bureaucratised in many jurisdictions to deal with the rising demands of growing prison populations in recent decades, van Zyl Smit and Appleton's categorisation shows that life-sentence-release decision-making remains largely discretionary. This is important given the complexity behind life sentences and the need to engage such cases holistically. However, discretionary decision-making processes can create fertile ground for arbitrariness and bias. An application of the four pillars of procedural justice can invite a discussion on how life-release decision-making could be reimagined with a focus on the process rather than outcomes to enhance legitimacy and fairness for all. Table 3.1 summarises this application.

[4] van Zyl Smit and Appleton (2019) provide more details on the global comparison. Kokkalera and Singer (2019) offer a more detailed comparison between all US states.

[5] The Sentencing Project recorded that in 2020, 34.6% of all persons with a life sentence were serving its LWOP version (Nellis 2021).

Table 3.1 Procedural justice and a life-sentence-release decision

Pillars	Pillar I: Voice	Pillar II: Neutrality	Pillar III: Respect	Pillar IV: Trust
Definition	Direct involvement in the decision-making process	Consistent, transparent and unbiased application of rules	Fair and dignified treatment over the course of the process	Expression of honest concern for decisions made
Examples	Offering a realistic prospect of release The right to an oral hearing The right to appeal	Nature of the decision-making body Composition of the decision-making body Seeking input into the release decision	Hearing focus: revisiting of governing offence as opposed to post-conviction path	Open communication about the process Sharing of reasons for decision

A. The First Pillar: Voice

(i) A Prospect of Release

In some jurisdictions, life sentences do not come with the prospect of release, and there are no processes in which such sentences are routinely reviewed. The European Court of Human Rights has determined that every person serving life should have the realistic possibility of having his or her sentence reviewed (*Vinter and Others v United Kingdom* App nos 66069/09, 130/10 and 3896/10 (ECtHR 17 January 2012); Rogan 2018). Excluding a segment of the prison population from even having the prospect of release runs counter to the rehabilitative mission under which many penal systems operate. It also reduces people to their crimes and eliminates their redemptive potential.

Apart from simply offering a meaningful chance of conditional release, the timing of such a review should also be clearly stated (Hatheway 2017; van Zyl Smit and Reichstein 2018). Prison administrations are encouraged to provide the incarcerated population with feasible and timely opportunities so they can work towards their release – the rehabilitative mission again emphasised in the 2017 case of *Hutchinson v United Kingdom* (GC No 57592/08, 17 January 2017; Rogan 2018). To make the expectations about conditional release clearer, the minimum time to be served before a review should be specified in statute and repeated at regular, clearly articulated intervals in cases where conditional release is denied.

In the USA, where about one-third of life-imprisoned persons do not have any prospect of release, conversations about extending the prospect of release to all life sentences have been limited to juveniles (Hatheway 2017; Rogan 2018).[6] This can be problematic from a procedural justice perspective, because the adult population is outrightly left out of reform considerations. To highlight this concern, Hatheway (2017: 11) noted that 'failing to acknowledge the brokenness of the system in general risks legitimising it for non-juvenile lifers'. At the same time, LWOP has long operated in the shadows of the death penalty and has been advertised as a more humane alternative. As such, the public has come to accept this form of punishment without ever questioning its actual severity (Vannier 2021). With LWOP conversations being tied closely to the death penalty, retributive considerations have also overshadowed consequentialist release considerations. This explains why the sentence continues to be embraced, while its value from a crime-preventative standpoint has been consistently debunked. Recent studies and data have pointed to the rehabilitative activities of people serving LWOP and their redemptive potential (Herbert 2019; Schartmueller 2024), the lack of a deterrent effect of LWOP (Kleinstuber et al 2022) and its empty incapacitative promises (Anderson 2019; California Department of Corrections and Rehabilitation 2023).[7]

(ii) Oral Hearing

For those with the prospect of release, different review mechanisms have been established. For example, a candidate could be invited to an oral hearing, where he or she has the right to speak and make a personal statement (Kokkalera and Singer 2019). For life-imprisoned individuals who typically have served quite some time in prison before an initial decision is made, such a hearing might be the first in a long time to provide an opportunity to speak up (Murray 2014). In the UK, Padfield et al (2000) found that, from the perspective of an imprisoned person, oral hearings increased their sense of fairness.

On the downside, oral hearings have also been found to create disadvantages for some. Padfield et al (2012) pointed out that some candidates might not be as articulate as others. Some might have difficulty expressing themselves, especially if they are non-native speakers. While these concerns could be mitigated with the assistance of legal counsel and a translator, Shammas (2019) raised concerns about the performative requirements that life-imprisoned persons in particular

[6] *Miller v Alabama* 567 US 460 (2012) prohibited mandatory LWOP sentences for juveniles.

[7] A comparative meta-analysis on the issue of life sentence recidivism (ie receiving new convictions upon release) has shown that reoffending in this population is extremely rare (Anderson 2019). Furthermore, the California Department of Corrections and Rehabilitation (CDCR) has kept track of persons released from life sentences in the past few years, and the latest available official statistics reveal that 1.9% of persons conditionally released from life in fiscal year 2017/18 were again convicted within three years. In comparison, 44.9% of those released from a determinate prison term were reconvicted within the same period (CDCR 2023).

encounter during hearings. He highlighted the racial, ethnic and socioeconomic marginalisation of most life-imprisoned persons in California, all of whom are tasked with offering causal explanations of their criminality, a task that even a social scientist well versed in the subject would have difficulty doing. Similarly, Warr (2020) observed in England that those serving indeterminate sentences are expected to adopt a compliant self-identity in prison and any narratives outside this norm are dismissed or might even be seen as indicating a 'problem'. Given the inherent power dynamics, hearings can thus be further stigmatising and suppressing of individual voice.

(iii) Right to Appeal

The candidate's position in the decision-making process can also be strengthened by extending to them the right to appeal a release decision (Kokkalera and Singer 2019; Seah et al 2022; Hirtenlehner et al 2023). This opportunity would also create a check on the decision-making authorities (Seah et al 2022). For example, in Austria, every life-imprisoned person undergoes a statutorily prescribed court review of their life sentence after having served 15 years in prison. The life-imprisoned person can then reapply every year if denied, and each decision can be appealed to a higher court (Austrian Act on the Enforcement of Penal Sanctions, Strafvollzugsgesetz, StVG, section 152, paragraph 2). While the review at the 15-year mark is automatic, any appeals or additional reviews depend on the initiative of the life-imprisoned person or a local prosecutor. Whereas few candidates appeal or apply again within a year after having been denied, many wait longer between applications (Hirtenlehner et al 2023). These delays could suggest that some candidates feel discouraged by the process, especially if they have been denied in the past.

B. The Second Pillar: Neutrality

(i) Nature of the Decision-Making Body

The principle of neutrality requires us to consider decision-makers. Studies have revealed that there exists substantial variation in what type of decision-making body is mandated when reviewing life sentences. For member states of the Council of Europe, interest in the nature of a decision-making body was sparked by the case of *Thynne, Wilson, and Gunnell v The United Kingdom* 1990 [13 EHRR 666], which centred on the question of whether a life-sentence-release decision should be made by a judicial or political body. The case originated in the UK, where the Home Secretary, a political entity, was responsible for granting a release. The court reasoned that those serving life sentences should have access to regular reviews of their life terms so they can demonstrate any changes, with a body independent of the executive ideally conducting that review.

Following that court decision, discretionary lifer panels were introduced in England and Wales in 1992, and Padfield et al (2000; 2003) were the first to observationally study the panels. These comprised three members, with a judge serving as the chair. The decisions were made at oral hearings, which the incarcerated person was entitled to attend with legal representation. However, Padfield et al (2000) described judges' roles as chairs as being more 'symbolic', with them tasked primarily with representing the public's interests in a decision.

Some European countries rely on courts to review life-sentence cases. Denmark, Finland and Sweden transferred the life-release decision-making power from an executive to a judicial body following the *Thynne* decision. The court process was found to generate greater transparency and uniformity in decision-making (Schartmueller 2015; 2019). This was observed most in Finland and Sweden, where a single court – the District Court of the City of Örebro in Sweden and the Helsinki Court of Appeals in Finland – has been mandated to review all life-sentence cases.

In France, a panel of three professional judges is tasked with reviewing life-sentence cases after a set minimum time of incarceration. This review is conducted by a specialised court (geared towards increasing formality and consistency in the decision-making process), and appeals and further reviews are possible (van Zyl Smit and Appleton 2019)

As a final example of jurisdictions that have recently changed their processes, Belgium switched from using a parole board to a sentencing-implementation court consisting of a judge and two penal experts – one from the prison system and one from a reintegration entity – in 2007 to depoliticise the review process (see chapter nine in this volume). A life-imprisoned person is represented legally and can present his or her case to the specialised court (van Zyl Smit and Appleton 2019).

While the involvement of judicial bodies is beneficial from a procedural justice perspective, van Zyl Smit (2024; chapter seven in this volume) observed in South Africa that abolishing the death penalty led to an increase in life sentences. The Constitutional Court, which was mandated to review life cases, has had to deal with many high-profile – often political – cases. Although the Court has traditionally enjoyed legitimacy, these cases have harmed it and led to a reconsideration of the efficiency of the current process. To divert attention away from a single court, van Zyl Smit recommends mandating the sentencing court with reviewing the life term (van Zyl Smit 2024).

Countering these trends of expanding court involvement, Ireland relied on the country's Minister of Justice to ultimately decide on a release. This process has been described as casual, political and lacking in transparency (Griffin and O'Donnell 2012; Griffin 2015). It was only with the implementation of the Parole Act in 2019 that a parole board – comprised of different criminal justice professionals, including judges and mental health experts – was mandated to review and decide upon life-sentence cases to enhance due process and procedural safeguards for the incarcerated population (Griffin 2020).

Turning to Australia, where the life-sentence-release process varies among states and territories, Seah et al (2022) showcased Western Australia, where a governor serves as the final decision-maker in life-sentence-release cases. As Griffin and O'Donnell (2012) and Griffin (2015) had observed about Ireland, Seah et al (2022) described the penal decision-making process as highly politicised, dependent on public opinion and lacking in formality and transparency. Upon comparing the process in Western Australia with other jurisdictions in the country, Seah et al (2022) proposed removing ministerial involvement to avoid decisions falling hostage to penal populism and to increase procedural safeguards.

(ii) Composition of a Decision-Making Body

Apart from the nature of a decision-making body, some consideration must be given to who specifically comprises a decision-making body or who, at least, is allowed to provide input in a decision (Schwartzapfel 2015). For example, a non-executive committee, such as a parole board, could comprise a diverse pool of members in terms of their educational backgrounds and professional expertise (Paparozzi and Caplan 2009; Rhine et al 2015). To avoid convening a decision-making body that is only comprised of criminal justice practitioners tasked with maintaining public protection at all costs, some jurisdictions statutorily require the membership of a social worker, a mental health expert or a substance abuse counsellor.[8]

Those of these professional backgrounds contribute by asking questions geared more towards including a conversation about an incarcerated person's rehabilitative and reintegrative needs (Ruhland 2020). Each member prioritises certain factors over others, and even if some will control the process more than others, different voices are heard (Maguire et al 1984). For example, Padfield et al (2012) noticed in England and Wales that board members prepared questions for an oral hearing based on their professional expertise, which led to different questions being asked at each oral hearing.

Similarly, in a qualitative study assessing the release philosophies of parole board members in the USA, Ruhland (2020) observed that board members often posed questions influenced by their educational and professional experiences. Especially in life-sentence cases, it can thus be suggested that a decision-making

[8] To offer some examples, the US state of Oklahoma requires that at least two members of the Pardon and Parole Board have a minimum of five years of training or experience in mental health services, substance abuse services or social work (57 OK Stat § 57-332.1B (2019)). Similarly in West Virginia, at least three of the nine board members appointed after 1 July 2021 must have a minimum of five years of work experience in the fields of mental health, social work or inmate re-entry services (West Virginia Code §62-12-12(d)).

body comprised of individuals with diverse personal and professional experiences would lead to more probing questions and allow such a body to more thoroughly assess a candidate's background and path towards release.

(iii) Seeking Input Regarding a Release Decision

While some jurisdictions invite different types of practitioners to be members of the decision-making body, others simply seek input from specific actors as part of a decision-making process. Input can range from a recommendation for a release decision, either with or without specifying reasons, to obtaining a detailed report to allow the body to make a more informed decision. Such input can be either statutorily prescribed or optional (eg sought in only the most difficult cases).

Some jurisdictions seek the input of correctional personnel most familiar with a candidate. For example, a unique life-sentence-release decision-making process was adopted in the US state of Minnesota. The process involves the commissioner of corrections and an advisory panel of Department of Corrections representatives, including the warden of the prison where a life-imprisoned person is housed. Three years before the end of a mandatory minimum life term, the panel is tasked with reviewing the case and collecting information from the community of the sentencing county and from the prison facility employees with whom the life-imprisoned person regularly interacts (Minnesota Administrative Rules).

In Austria, executive courts are required to obtain a statement from a life-sentenced person, the local prosecutor's office and the prison warden or a designee (StVG, section 152, paragraph 2). If it appears useful to predict the candidate's community adjustment, a court may commission a medical, psychotherapeutic or psychological expert to conduct an assessment (StVG, section 152a, paragraph 2). Research has found that prisons and clinical experts have provided the courts with detailed rationales for their recommendations in written form, which is useful to the courts during the decision-making process. From a procedural justice perspective, however, the optional retrieval of expert reports could lead to inconsistency, as a court will not have the same type of detailed material to review for each case (Hirtenlehner et al 2023).[9]

In England and Wales, the release recommendations of psychiatrists, prison psychologists and probation officers were observed to affect decision outcomes (Padfield et al 2000). Likewise, Forde (2014) concluded that expert opinions, especially those of external probation officers, influenced a decision. The recommendations of other experts, a prison psychologist and a prison

[9] Of the 511 conditional release decisions reviewed, the court granted conditional release in 21% of the cases. Prisons and clinical experts were much more supportive of a release, recommending release in 37% and 39% of the cases, respectively. In contrast, a prosecutor was opposed to conditional release in 83% of the reviewed cases (Hirtenlehner et al 2023).

probation officer also mattered, with a combined measure of all these experts predicting the outcome in 84 per cent of the reviewed life-sentence parole cases. In domestic violence cases, psychologists were found to be especially influential with their recommendations in the decision outcome (Dyke et al 2024).

In Sweden, life-sentence cases are reviewed by a team of forensic experts from the independent National Board of Forensic Medicine, who are mandated to conduct a risk assessment before a review. These reports have been found to influence the court in its decision-making process (Sturup et al 2016).

In short, expert opinions – whether mandated or optional – have been shown to influence review decisions. Researchers, however, have cautioned against overreliance on expert opinions and risk assessments. While standardised risk assessments are used by experts in many jurisdictions nowadays to increase consistency in the decision-making process and to limit bias (Padfield et al 2003; Ruhland 2020), these tools do not get rid of subjectivity. Risk, such as any category in the behavioural sciences, is a socially constructed term, and standardised risk assessments are not a panacea of bias (Rhine et al 2015; Kokkalera and Singer 2023). Young and Pearlman's (2022) study about the striking racial disparities in life parole hearings in California revealed that seemingly 'neutral' professional evaluations, such as risk assessments and prison disciplinary records, consistently rate Black candidates lower and thus significantly contribute to racially differential outcomes in life parole cases. Unsurprisingly, even penal experts with much experience admit that assessments are difficult to complete and involve subjective interpretations (Padfield et al 2000). While penal experts can offer additional insight into a candidate's background, a short-sighted reliance on individual opinions and seemingly 'objective' assessments can further perpetuate bias and undermine neutrality.

(iv) The Unique Role of Prosecutors

While in several studies prosecutors were found to play a key role in the review process, their participation was consistently found to counter the principle of neutrality (Aviram 2020; Murcia 2022; Young and Pearlman 2022; Hirtenlehner et al 2023; Dagan 2024). Bell (2019), Kokkalera et al (2022) and Amalfi Wronski and Kokkkalera (2023) found that prosecutor objections significantly reduced the likelihood of release for life parole candidates in different US states. This is concerning given that Murcia (2022) estimated that prosecutors oppose parole for life-imprisoned persons in more than 80 per cent of cases by introducing questionable evidence. Young and Pearlman (2022) demonstrated that the racially disparate outcomes in California life parole decisions originated from expert opinions and prosecutorial recommendations. Further estimates of the significant role prosecutors play come from Austria (Hirtenlehner et al 2023), where their opposition to conditional release was voiced in 83 per cent of life cases, often without providing any explanation for their recommendations.

Prosecutors often find themselves responsible for excavating memories of a committed offence. For example, Aviram (2020) observed the strong role of prosecutors in California, who spoke on behalf of victims and emphasised retributive considerations while neglecting a balanced presentation of the purposes of continued incarceration. In Israel, Dagan (2024) demonstrated that attorney-general counsellors dominated life-sentence review hearings and shaped master narratives by implanting mistrust and doubt about a person under review. As they are professionally more oriented towards crime fighting, they can 'reconstruct [conditional release] as reinforcing condemnation' (Dagan 2024: 236) and make a release decision-maker become a 'resentencing authority' (Dagan 2023: 1235) rather than a person tasked with examining the merits of each case.

Other than finding themselves responsible for revisiting the committed offence and speaking on behalf of a victim, prosecutors' significant role in the life-sentence-release decision-making process raises concerns, as they often do not have the mandate, time or resources to engage in a detailed review of an entire complex case file, thus often defaulting to a denial of conditional release out of pure caution (Schwartzapfel 2015; Hirtenlehner et al 2023).

(v) Seeking Input from a Victim/Relatives of Victims

Crimes that result in a life-term prison sentence can alter the life trajectories of victims or their relatives in profound and complex ways. As victim's rights movements grew in the last two decades of the twentieth century, many jurisdictions, especially in common law countries, have created opportunities for them to participate in review proceedings in some way (van Zyl Smit and Appleton 2019). Such participation can range from notification about upcoming review proceedings to the possibility of submitting a written or oral statement as part of the process.

European countries with a civil law tradition have treated the issue of victim input with caution (Griffin and O'Donnell 2012). They worry that victim input could erode the objective criteria required to make an informed decision (Griffin 2018). Indeed, it is important to remember that the task of release decision-making is not to retry a case (Rhine et al 2015; Reitz and Rhine 2020). The heavy presence of victims' voices can take away from the process and must, therefore, be balanced carefully against other stakeholders' participation.

C. The Third Pillar: Respectful Treatment

While the first pillar (voice) calls for the right to be heard, the exact way hearings are conducted must also be assessed. While providing opportunities to be heard on different levels can enhance legitimacy, empirical studies that have thoroughly engaged with life-sentence review hearings have revealed that the way hearings are conducted can be perceived as negative. In California,

Bell (2019) uncovered that legitimate rehabilitation measures – successful programme participation and compliance with institutional rules – were applied inconsistently and sometimes even neglected in juvenile life parole cases. In the US state of Washington, Herbert (2024) analysed the audio transcripts of 42 juvenile parole board hearings, many of which involved people sentenced to life as youths, which were held from 2016 to 2019. The review board frequently dismissed redemptive narratives while shifting its focus of attention to the committed offence and any other past criminality. As such, the board was found to use hearings to reinforce the mark of a criminal past and further degrade and stigmatise a life-imprisoned person.

Speaking from personal experience with his first parole hearing in New York, Rodriguez (2019: 35) shared, 'I had no idea what to expect. I was anxious and nervous but also confident in the changes I had made in my life.' Yet, he soon realised that the decision-making body was only interested in discussing his offence, so he soon knew that he was 'denied for the same reason I was convicted' (Rodriguez 2019: 36). Finally, Shammas (2019: 156) concluded in an ethnographic study of California's life parole process that hearings took place 'without listening' but served the purpose of demoralising life-imprisoned people in an environment that automatically treated them with suspicion and outright hostility.

These examples illustrate that, even though the opportunity to be heard might exist, it does not guarantee that the same standards will be applied to each case. It does not assure that the candidates will be listened to and that their unique situations – an immediate history of years of incarceration – are sufficiently considered. If the task is to assess candidates' risk of reoffending, ample space should be given to them to address what matters most in their redemptive journey rather than spending the majority of a hearing reassessing a crime that led to a life sentence.

D. The Fourth Pillar: Trustworthiness

Life-release decision-making bodies face challenging tasks. In their review of complex cases, however, the fact that their work is done in the public's best interests is often overlooked. When, in exceptional cases, a person conditionally released from a life sentence reoffends, it catches the media's attention and can cost a decision-maker his or her career, even when 99 of the 100 decisions they made did not result in tragic recidivism (Anderson 2019). Considering this, how can we build trust in authorities and help increase the legitimacy of the decision-making process?

(i) Keeping the Mission Straight: Balancing Ideas

The fourth principle of the procedural justice framework can be incorporated into the life-release decision-making process by, for example, encouraging decision-makers to regularly refer to their mission. They should remind themselves of the origins of the discretionary release process, which is tasked with the evaluation of risk *and* rehabilitation (Caplan 2012). Reitz and Rhine (2020: 292) noted that 'the judicial minimum sentence is enough to satisfy purposes of punishment or desert so that continued incarceration must be justified by recidivism risk'. Although their assessment is not specifically about life sentences, this argument still applies, as most life sentences come with a minimum term to be served. In this respect, continued incarceration beyond that minimum must only be justified by consequentialist, forward-looking principles.

Sure, an offence can be revisited to determine the amends a life-imprisoned person has made – a consequentialist approach – but it should not be revisited solely to provide another opportunity to work through certain facts or details from the past – the retributive approach. By keeping the mission straight, it can be seen that a life-sentence-release process without procedural safeguards does not make anyone safer.

(ii) Written Procedures and Decisions

Apart from examining the nature of decision-makers, some scholars have highlighted the importance of written procedures for guiding operational processes of the life-sentence-release process (Rhine et al 2015; Rodriguez 2019). Trust in authorities can be enhanced via detailed explanations of decisions in both oral and written forms (Kokkalera and Singer 2019). If a decision-maker follows a matrix, applies it consistently to every decision and addresses all specified items in both oral and written explanations, this practice can lead to more consistency despite the complex and unique nature of each case. It can also communicate to all affected parties that each decision was handled with similar care.[10]

Finally, a summary of the reasons for a life-sentence-release decision could be made available to the public to demystify the life-sentence-release process and increase awareness about how the decisions were made in the interest of public safety. Two US states with one of the highest percentages of life-imprisoned persons in their total prison populations, Massachusetts and California, have incorporated this element in different ways. While Massachusetts publishes brief rationales for all life-sentence decisions on its parole board's website, California publishes only a list of names with a decision outcome. Meanwhile, the California governor's office shares brief rationales for all granted pardons and commutations on its official website and publishes parole reversal decisions

[10] Kokkalera and Singer (2019) surveyed the discretionary release practices for juveniles serving life sentences in all US states. While they found that many US states now share their decisions in written forms, several states do not.

on life sentences.[11] However, the state does not publish parole, pardon and commutation denials, which are most common. It can therefore be assumed that a governor plays 'politically much safer' by denying any requests, as he or she is not obligated to give reasons (Novak 2016: 160).

IV. DISCUSSION

In many jurisdictions, procedural justice principles – voice, neutrality, respectful treatment and trustworthiness – have been incorporated in life-release decision-making. It has even been observed in some jurisdictions that a life-imprisoned population enjoys more procedural protection than others who seek release from prison (Young and Pearlman 2022). This comparative overview highlights several important points about life-release decision-making processes. First, I discovered wide variations in the existing review mechanisms in selected jurisdictions. While the life-sentence-release decision-making process involves the discretionary decision of an authorised institution, such decisions are either made by judicial bodies or non-executive committees or involve political players. In some jurisdictions, the growing politicisation of the process has given rise to the replacement of non-executive committees or political decision-makers with judicial bodies, as the latter has largely been found to be more successfully insulated from the political process in the studied jurisdictions.

By their very nature, judicial processes allow for the swift incorporation of more procedural safeguards (eg the right to legal counsel and appeal). However, judicial bodies do not necessarily depoliticise the process in every jurisdiction. For example, van Zyl Smit (2024) showed that South Africa's Constitutional Court has lost legitimacy following a review of many high-profile life cases. Furthermore, even lower-court judges are not necessarily insulated from the political process. For example, superior court judges in the USA are typically elected and are thus directly accountable to the population. Mandating these courts to make the life-sentence-release decision could reignite memories of the committed offence and make it difficult for judges to review such cases objectively.

At the same time, life-sentence cases are highly complex, which explains why some jurisdictions mandate specialised courts to review these cases or invite expert opinions to help with a review. As I have discussed, many decision-makers rely on additional bodies to share specific insight, and these bodies are either mandated or available upon request. Overall, the input of several different voices – psychologists, psychiatrists, correctional personnel, social workers and victim advocates – in the life-sentence review process allows a decision-maker

[11] In California, the governor has the power to reverse a parole board grant decision in cases of indeterminate sentences given for murder (California Constitution, Art V § 8).

to become more informed about these cases and to make a more well-informed decision.

Still, life-sentence decisions, even when made by specialised bodies or based on a variety of opinions, have been shown to exacerbate certain systemic problems in penal systems. While intended to achieve consistency and impartiality in decision-making, heavy reliance on risk assessment tools and expert opinions in many jurisdictions has been shown to deepen racial or ethnic disparities. If there is too much focus on fixing the decision-making process, the creation of disparate outcomes might be neglected or overlooked. Additionally, this review has shown that increased opportunities for giving voice (eg through oral hearings, appeals) might be well intended and increase procedural safeguards, but they might not actually lead to more perceived fairness due to the power dynamics inherent in the process.

Finally, one could argue that the incorporation of procedural justice principles does not attempt to solve a problem at its root. As prison populations have grown, so has the life-imprisoned population in many jurisdictions. While efforts to reduce prison populations in recent years tend to focus on those serving shorter, determinate sentences, those serving life are often neglected. Consequently, decision-makers remain busy reviewing cases, and many have seen increasing workloads. Involving more experts and reviewing cases in more detail adds to this. The implementation of procedural justice principles could hence be seen as a quick cosmetic solution to a massive problem that many jurisdictions have dealt with for a while. We must therefore also ask ourselves whether a life sentence is really needed in the first place to meet different penal objectives or whether alternative sentences that do not involve life-long imprisonment and the discretion of a reviewing body could still serve communities well or even better.

V. CONCLUSION

Procedural justice theory is based on the premise that if a decision-making process is characterised by consistency, objectivity and respectful interpersonal treatment, decision outcomes will be perceived as fair and trust in authorities will be increased. As decision-makers involved in life-sentence review decisions have been faced with a particularly challenging task at a time of more politicisation of penal political issues and general distrust in criminal justice institutions, the procedural justice lens can offer a unique approach to dealing with these complex cases.

The value of incorporating procedural justice principles into a life-sentence review and a decision to grant conditional release lies behind the increased legitimacy of the process. Procedural justice can help make the process more transparent so that people are more well informed, which could lead to a demystification of the process and the destigmatisation of life-sentence cases. A concern for procedural justice in these cases is necessary to show that decisions are made on behalf of – and in the best interests of – everyone.

However, important questions must still be answered empirically. For instance, are judicial bodies perceived as more legitimate by those incarcerated for life, the victims and their relatives and the public or by non-executive committees? Or are jurisdictions that engage in particularly transparent practices, such as the sharing of detailed decision summaries with a life-imprisoned person and the public, met with more trust? Additional research is needed to study the value of incorporating more procedural justice principles into the unique decision-making processes that exist in different parts of the world.

REFERENCES

Amalfi Wronski, B and Kokkalera, SS (2023) 'Who Gets to Go Home? Examining the Correlates of Parole Release for the Elderly and Non-elderly' 46(5) *Journal of Crime and Justice* 682.

Anderson, JL (2019) 'Recidivism of Paroled Murderers as a Factor in the Utility of Life Imprisonment' 31(2) *Current Issues in Criminal Justice* 255.

Aviram, H (2020) *Yesterday's Monsters: The Manson Family Cases and the Illusion of Parole* (Oakland, CA, University of California Press).

Bell, K (2019) 'A Stone of Hope: Legal and Empirical Analysis of California Juvenile Lifer Parole Decisions' 54 *Harvard Civil Rights–Civil Liberties Law Review* 455.

California Department of Corrections and Rehabilitation (2023) 'Recidivism Report for Offenders Released from the California Department of Corrections and Rehabilitation in Fiscal Year 2017–18' www.cdcr.ca.gov/research/wp-content/uploads/sites/174/2023/04/Recidivism-Report-for-Offenders-Released-in-Fiscal-Year-2017-18.pdf.

Caplan, JM (2012) 'Protection Parole Board Legitimacy in the Twenty-First Century: The Role of Victims' Rights and Influences' 7(1) *Victims & Offenders* 53.

Dagan, N (2023) 'Parole as Resentencing: Exploring the Punitive Accounts of Parole Decision-Making Through the Comparative Case Study of Israel' 20(4) *European Journal of Criminology* 1231.

—— (2024) 'Parole as a Boxing Match: Lifers, Prosecution and the Adversarial Making of Parole Hearings' 26(2) *Punishment & Society* 223.

Dyke, C, Rivas, C and Schucan Bird, K (2024) 'Parole Decisions About Perpetrators of Domestic Violence in England and Wales' 63(2) *The Howard Journal of Crime and Justice* 142.

Griffin, D (2015) 'The Release and Recall of Life Sentence Prisoners: Policy, Practice and Politics' 53 *Irish Jurist* 1.

—— (2018) 'Settling the Weight of Victim Input on Parole Decisions' (6 April) *Law Society Gazette of Ireland* www.lawsociety.ie/gazette/in-depth/reform-of-parole.

—— (2020) 'Life Imprisonment and the Parole Act 2019: Assessing the Potential Impact on Parole Decision-Making' 4(1) *Irish Judicial Studies Journal* 25.

Griffin, D and O'Donnell, I (2012) 'The Life Sentence and Parole' 52(3) *British Journal of Criminology* 611.

Guiney, TC (2023) 'Parole, Parole Boards and the Institutional Dilemmas of Contemporary Prison Release' 25(3) *Punishment & Society* 621.

Hatheway, K (2017) 'Creating a Meaningful Opportunity for Review: Challenging the Politicization of Parole for Life-Sentenced Prisoners' 54 *American Criminal Law Review* 601.

Herbert, S (2019) *Too Easy to Keep: Life-Sentenced Prisoners and the Future of Mass Incarceration* (Oakland, CA, University of California Press).

—— (2024) 'Degradation or Redemption? A Parole Board Polices a Moral Boundary' 49(1) *Law & Social Inquiry* 308.

Hirtenlehner, H, Schmollmueller, L, Birklbauer, A and Schartmueller, D (2023) '"Life Is Life!" Oder doch nicht? Die Praxis der Entlassung aus lebenslangen Freiheitsstrafen in Österreich' ['"Life Is Life!" Or Is It? The Practice of Release from Life Imprisonment in Austria'] 145 *Juristische Blätter* 281.

Jackson, J, Tyler, TR, Bradford, B, Taylor, D and Shiner, M (2010) 'Legitimacy and Procedural Justice in Prisons' 191 *Prison Service Journal* 4.

Kleinstuber, R, Coldsmith, J, Leigey, ME and Joy, S (2022) *Life Without Parole: Worse Than Death?* (Abingdon, Routledge).

Kokkalera, SS and Singer, SI (2019) 'Discretionary Release Practices for Juveniles Facing Life: A Review of State Parole and Resentencing Procedures' in C Spohn and P Brennan (eds), *Handbook on Sentencing Policies and Practices in the 21st Century* (New York, Routledge) 129–50.

—— (2023) 'Now with the Possibility of Parole: Enabling a juvenile lifer's meaningful review' 63(1) *British Journal of Criminology* 115.

Maguire, M, Pinter, F and Collis, C (1984) 'Dangerousness and the Tariff: The Decision-Making Process in Release from Life Sentences' 24(3) *British Journal of Criminology* 250.

Mathews, B, Walker, A and Rhine, EE (2020) 'Awakening the Sleeping Giant: The Future of Paroling Authorities in America' 5(3) *Corrections: Policy, Practice and Research* 206.

Minnesota Administrative Rules, Corrections Department (2003) Ch 2940, Part 2940.1800 www.revisor.mn.gov/rules/2940.1800.

Murcia, EA (2022) 'Prosecutors, Parole, and Evidence: Why Excluding Prosecutors from Parole Hearings Will Improve California's Parole Process' 55 *Loyola of Los Angeles Law Review* 441.

Murray, P (2014) 'Procedural Fairness, Human Rights, and the Parole Board' 73(1) *CLJ* 5.

Nellis, A (2021) 'No End in Sight: America's Enduring Reliance on Life Imprisonment' (Washington, DC, The Sentencing Project) www.sentencingproject.org/publications/no-end-in-sight-americas-enduring-reliance-on-life-imprisonment.

Novak, A (2016) *Comparative Executive Clemency: The Constitutional Pardon Power and the Prerogative of Mercy in Global Perspective* (London, Routledge).

Padfield, N, Liebling, A and Arnold, H (2000) *An Exploration of Decision-making at Discretionary Lifer Panels*, Home Office Study 213 (Home Office Research, Development and Statistics Directorate) www.researchgate.net/profile/Alison-Liebling/publication/268259295_An_exploration_of_decision-making_at_discretionary_lifer_panels/links/54bcead30cf24e50e940b7c0/An-exploration-of-decision-making-at-discretionary-lifer-panels.pdf.

—— (2003) 'Discretion and the Release of Life Sentence Prisoners' in L Gelthorpe and N Padfield (eds), *Exercising Discretion: Decision-Making in the Criminal Justice System and Beyond* (London, Routledge) 97–124.

Paparozzi, MA and Caplan, JM (2009) 'A Profile of Paroling Authorities in America: The Strange Bedfellows of Politics and Professionalism' 89(4) *The Prison Journal* 401.

Pratt, J (2007) *Penal Populism* (London, Routledge).

Reitz, KR and Rhine, EE (2020) 'Parole Release and Supervision: Critical Drivers of American Prison Policy' 3 *Annual Review of Criminology* 281.

Rhine, EE, Petersilia, J and Reitz, KR (2015) 'Improving Parole Release in America' 28 *Federal Sentencing Reporter* 96.

Robinson, G and McNeill, F (2008) 'Exploring the Dynamics of Compliance with Community Penalties' 12(4) *Theoretical Criminology* 431.

Rodriguez, A (2019) 'The Obscure Legacy of Mass Incarceration: Parole Board Abuses of People Serving Parole Eligible Life Sentences' 22 *The City University of New York Law Review Footnote Forum* 33.

Rogan, M (2018) 'Discerning Penal Values and Judicial Decision Making: The Case of Whole Life Sentencing in Europe and the United States of America' 57(3) *The Howard Journal of Crime and Justice* 321.

Ruhland, EL (2020) 'Philosophies and Decision Making in Parole Board Members' 100(5) *The Prison Journal* 640.

Ryan, C and Bergin, M (2022) 'Procedural Justice and Legitimacy in Prisons: A Review of Extant Empirical Literature' 49(2) *Criminal Justice and Behavior* 143.

Schartmueller, D (2015) 'Life Imprisonment in Scandinavia: The Ultimate Punishment in the Penal Environments of Denmark, Finland, and Sweden' (PhD diss, Northern Arizona University).

—— (2019) 'How Long Is Life? Comparing the Processes of Release for Life-Imprisoned Offenders in Denmark, Finland, and Sweden' 25(4) *European Journal on Criminal Policy and Research* 391.

—— (2024) 'Between Redemption and Retribution: Justifying Commutations for Life-without-parole Sentences in California' 43(1) *Criminal Justice Ethics* 57.

Schwartzapfel, B (2015) 'Parole Boards: Problems and Promise' 28 *Federal Sentencing Reporter* 79.

Seah, G, Bartels, L, Tubex, H and Gately, N (2022) 'When Life Means What the Minister Says It Means: The Need to Reform Parole Laws for Prisoners Serving Life Sentences in Western Australia' 49 *University of Western Australia Law Review* 273.

Shammas, VL (2019) 'The Perils of Parole Hearings: California Lifers, Performative Disadvantage, and the Ideology of Insight' 42(1) *PoLAR: Political and Legal Anthropology Review* 142.

Sunshine, J and Tyler, TR (2003) 'The Role of Procedural Justice and Legitimacy in Shaping Public Support for Policing' 37(3) *Law & Society Review* 513.

Tyler, TR (2003) 'Procedural Justice, Legitimacy, and the Effective Rule of Law' 30 *Crime and Justice* 283.

—— (2010) 'Legitimacy in Corrections: Policy Implications' 9 *Criminology & Public Policy* 127.

Vannier, M (2021) *Normalizing Extreme Imprisonment: The Case of Life Without Parole in California* (Oxford, Oxford University Press).

van Zyl Smit, D and Reichstein, A (2018) 'Lebenslange Freiheitsstrafe in Europa: ein Überblick von Praxis und Recht' ['Life Imprisonment in Europe: An Overview of Practice and Law'] in S Schaede, G Koop and W Wirth (eds), *Für und Wider der lebenslangen Freiheitsstrafe? Eine lange Diskussion …* (Wiesbaden, Gesellschaft für Fortbildung der Strafvollzugsbediensteten eV) 1–22 https://ueaeprints.uea.ac.uk/id/eprint/69330/1/Chapter.pdf.

van Zyl Smit, D, Weatherby, P and Creighton, S (2014) 'Whole Life Sentences and the Tide of European Human Rights Jurisprudence: What Is To Be Done?' 14(1) *Human Rights Law Review* 59.

van Zyl Smit, D and C Appleton (2019) *Life Imprisonment: A Global Human Rights Analysis* (Cambridge, MA, Harvard University Press).

Warr, J (2020) '"Always Gotta Be Two Mans": Lifers, Risk, Rehabilitation, and Narrative Labour' 22 *Punishment & Society* 28.

Young, KM and Pearlman, J (2022) 'Racial Disparities in Lifer Parole Outcomes: The Hidden Role of Professional Evaluations' 47(3) *Law & Social Inquiry* 783.

4

Transparency and Legitimacy in the Future of Parole Release

EBONY L RUHLAND

I. INTRODUCTION

THE CRIMINAL LEGAL system in the USA comprises a federal system and a state system. Crime and convictions that are contained within a single state fall to that state to administer the process. As such, the criminal legal system in the USA, including the prison release process, is dependent on each state's laws and statutes. The USA has two primary sentencing structures – indeterminate and determinate (Reitz 2012). Determinate is a set sentence, whereas in indeterminate structures, an individual's release from prison is determined by a parole board or paroling authority (Tonry 1999; Zhang et al 2014). For example, an individual with an assault conviction may be given 15–20 years. The parole board then determines if the individual is released at the minimum 15-year mark, at the maximum 20 years or somewhere in-between. Most states in the USA have indeterminate sentencing systems (34 out of 50 states). The federal system is also indeterminate. Sixteen states operate determinate systems. Some determinate sentencing states may have an indeterminate function for old cases that were previously under an indeterminate system before switching to a determinate system (Rhine et al 2018).

The structure and nature of parole release are dependent upon each state. The members of the board, their qualifications and terms of service and the types of cases for which the boards are responsible also vary by state. Some parole boards are responsible for decisions beyond prison release, which could include setting conditions for those released or revoking the freedom of those who violate their conditions. Some state boards may also make compassionate release and clemency decisions. Consistent across parole boards are that members have discretion to make release decisions, and they commonly have a wide variety of information to consult to inform their decisions. But this wide discretion and availability of information that board members may consult can cause confusion on what specific factors or details matter to boards in their decision-making. Because the process is so broad, decisions are criticised for their lack of transparency

(Schwartzapfel 2015). The lack of transparent decision-making leads parole boards to be further criticised for both releasing dangerous individuals who are not ready to be released and for keeping individuals incarcerated who should be released (Cullen and Gendreau 2000). On both sides, these viewpoints call into question the legitimacy of the parole boards and their ability to make sound decisions. More research is needed to explore parole board members and how they go about making release decisions. This research will serve to illuminate a process that has been seen as closed off. A better understanding of the board's process, including what informs their decision-making, could increase the confidence of the public, as well as of incarcerated individuals who go before the board, in the board's ability to make sound and evidence-based decisions. The hypothesis is that a more transparent process could improve the legitimacy of parole boards. Additionally, society cannot afford to not understand the board process as they make critical decisions each day. One could argue that parole boards make life and death decisions, like the medical profession. To release unprepared individuals puts public safety at risk, yet to deny a prepared individual denies them their liberty. These decisions must be informed by using the evidence and science available, rather than weighing heavily on the board members' personal judgement. Further, board members should be educated and experienced, just as we require of the medical profession. Finally, the policies and procedures should be transparent, so that the public understands what guides their decision.

Scholars have focused extensively on mass incarceration, yet scrutiny of the decision-making of parole boards has largely been left of out of this conversation. Parole board members are legitimate decision-makers in reducing or solving the problem of mass incarceration. Exploring the transparency of parole boards, including who make up the boards and what informs their decisions, could further the legitimacy of parole boards. Exploring this issue could also improve the parole release process by ensuring boards members are using evidence-based factors in their release decisions. This is critical for the legitimacy of parole boards and to comprehensively address mass incarceration in the USA.

This chapter will explore the role of transparency in parole decisions. It will also illustrate the connection between transparency and legitimacy, including the factors that are important to achieving both constructs. Using survey findings, I present research that sheds light on how transparent (or not) parole boards are in the USA. Further, in relation to transparency, the public and those who are incarcerated know little about the members who make up the parole board, including their educational and professional backgrounds. I present findings on how parole board members are appointed, how their appointments may be terminated and the educational qualifications required to serve on the board. These factors are important in exploring transparency as they provide information about factors that might inform or influence member's decisions.

Finally, I use interview findings from incarcerated individuals who have been denied parole to understand their views of transparency and legitimacy during the parole process. In the conclusion of this chapter, I provide a discussion on recommendations to increase transparency in parole boards.

II. PURPOSE OF PAROLE BOARDS IN THE USA

The underpinning rationale of an indeterminate sentencing model was to release people once they were believed to be rehabilitated (Tonry 1999). Today, rehabilitation continues to be a focus in the decision-making process, but parole boards are also commonly concerned with the nature and severity of the current offence to determine if the person has served 'enough' time for their offending (Caplan 2007; Cotton 2008; Ruhland et al 2016) – an approach more aligned with the correctional goal of retribution. Parole boards are therefore frequently concerned with individuals serving ample time depending on the circumstances of the offence committed (Scott 1974; Cotton 2008). A primary purpose for many parole board members in their decision-making is to not compromise public safety in their release decisions (Ruhland 2020). Thus, parole boards aim to release individuals from prison who are not considered threats to public safety. However, overly weighing the current offence in the decision to release or not tells the board member little about the person's risk for recidivating or how they have used their time while incarcerated to rehabilitate themselves.

III. INFORMATION USED TO INFORM PAROLE BOARD DECISION-MAKING

Parole board members are generally allowed broad discretion to consider the factors that are important to them to make their decision and wide discretion on what information to consult to inform their decisions (Schwartzapfel 2015). Parole board members frequently consult prison institutional records, pre-sentence investigations, previous police reports, victim impact statements, input from the individual incarcerated, input from the sentencing judge, prosecutors or others, the individual's plan to re-enter society and so on (Ruhland et al 2016). How this information is used and weighed by each parole member may vary. There is scant research on how parole board members weigh each factor in their final parole decisions and how these vary amongst members on the same board. For example, a qualitative study exploring parole member decision-making found that for some board members the seriousness of the current offence was important as well as input from the victims. However, for other members within the same board, this same information mattered little on their decision to release or not (Ruhland 2020). While the study did not examine how this affected the actual outcomes with regard to release, it is plausible that decisions to release or not could be somewhat dependent on who one's parole board member is.

With the creation of risk–needs–responsivity (RNR) instruments, we have a better understanding of what increases one's likelihood to recidivate as well as what criminogenic needs to be focused on to reduce risk (Bonta et al 2008). However, RNR assessments are not without their concerns. RNR assessments frequently analyse the relationship between criminal history and conviction history to determine one's likelihood to recidivate (Starr 2014). Like the board's focus on the current offence, focusing heavily on one's criminal history tells us nothing about current rehabilitation efforts. There are also concerns that other variables in the RNR assessment to evaluate the risk of recidivation have disparate racial and class impacts (Eijk 2020). While there are some valid criticisms of RNR assessments, they are often better at predicting recidivism than personal judgements (Latessa and Lovins 2019). However, parole board decisions in the USA are largely subjective decisions made by the individuals who make up the board.

IV. TRANSPARENT PAROLE DECISION-MAKING

Parole boards have been criticised for their lack of transparency by the public and by individuals incarcerated (Schwartzapfel 2015). Without greater transparency around their decision-making, it is difficult to explain why some individuals are released from prison whereas other, similarly situated cases are denied release. These criticisms are not new. In the 1970s and 1980s, parole board decision-making in the USA was criticised by both conservatives and liberals. For conservatives, there was a belief that dangerous individuals were being released from prison 'early', without being fully rehabilitated. From the liberal viewpoint, it was believed that individuals were being denied a realistic prospect of release as their parole applications could always be dismissed on the grounds of insufficient evidence of rehabilitation (Cullen 2017). An additional complaint is that some incarcerated individuals believed that parole board members had already made their decision to deny parole before the individual was able to present their case for release at their parole hearing. Thus, the parole hearing is seen by some individuals as a performance or having a 'ceremonial function' rather than being an actual forum for individuals to make their case (Conley and Zimmerman 1982; Ruhland and Laskorunsky 2023). The limited transparency in decision-making may also lead to attitudes by the public and by candidates up for parole that decisions are rooted in bias or unfair conclusions by the parole board members (Carroll and Mondrick 1978; Hritz 2021). The limited transparency and a belief that decisions are rooted in bias may erode the legitimacy of parole boards and their decision-making authority.

Transparency and legitimacy are interconnected. If individuals see institutions, in this case parole boards, as legitimate, they are more likely to accept the authority's decision-making outcomes and more likely to report that they would comply with the laws or policies of the institution as well as accept the authority's decision even if they may not agree with it (Sunshine and Tyler 2003). Key to this compliance, however, are fair procedures and fair decision-making (Tyler 2010). One could argue that incarcerated individuals have no choice but to accept the decision of the parole board members – a denial of release means the person remains incarcerated. However, if individuals give up on the parole process because they do not believe it is legitimate, they could stop enrolling in classes or programming that could aid in their rehabilitation or prepare them for release. Additionally, individuals may engage in misconduct or commit other infractions if they are no longer trying to appeal to the parole board because they believe their chances for release are slim and decisions are biased (Ruhland and Laskorunsky 2023), thus putting the safety of the overall institution at risk.

Legitimacy of parole boards also matters for the public. In a few states, parole board members as well as whole boards have been terminated because an individual they released later committed another serious criminal offence. Some of these terminations may be political, as a way to demonstrate that there is a level of accountability for parole members' decisions. Yet, if parole board members are making sound decisions rooted in evidence, then those members should not be fired when an individual released from prison ends up committing another crime. If there is a possibility of being terminated for their decision- making, it may lead boards members to become risk averse or avoid releasing anyone from prison because that is the 'easier' or 'safer' route. The need to insulate board members and allow them to make their decisions without fear of repercussions further highlights the importance of transparent decision-making. Transparent decision-making could protect board members and their authority. It would also serve to legitimatise them or maintain their legitimacy because how decisions are made would be understood and presumably there would be more consistent decision-making among board members.

V. TRANSPARENCY AND LEGITIMACY OF PAROLE BOARDS

Parole board members regularly have complete discretion on which information and factors to utilise in deciding to release or not. Parole board members' goals in this decision-making is to make sure the individual up for parole is no longer a threat to public safety and to assess if they are rehabilitated (Ruhland 2020). The evidence-based literature on 'what works' in corrections supports elements that should be considered when evaluating risk for reoffending and rehabilitation (MacKenzie 2006). In particular, RNR assessments can predict recidivism and target services to reduce recidivism based on one's risk level (Bonta et al 2008). Members of parole boards consider risk assessment scores, but such scores often do not heavily influence their ultimate decision to release or not, as other factors (eg current offence, criminal history, prison conduct) commonly weigh more heavily. Some parole board members use the risk assessment scores just to confirm their decisions. For instance, if a parole board member decides not to release an individual and they look at their score and it is high risk, they feel even more confident in their decision to deny release. But the risk assessment can present a further decisional challenge if a parole board member is unsure whether to release an individual or not and, when they consult the risk assessment, the individual is assessed at medium risk. Parole board members prefer to use their personal expertise or judgement having examined the other pieces of information like criminal history, listed above rather than rely solely on risk assessments (Ruhland 2020).

Limited utilisation of risk assessments to inform practice is not uncommon with correctional personnel (Miller and Maloney 2013; Viglione et al 2015). Correctional officials do not fully trust risk assessments because they see them as biased or unreliable, or feel their professional experience outweighs what any instrument can prove (Viglione et al 2015). While there is room for improvement in risk assessment and cause for concern in overly relying on these instruments, risk assessment instruments are better tools for transparent decision-making as opposed to going with one's gut feeling or, as Latessa and Lovins write, 'so called expert opinion' (2019).

Professional discretion is important for parole board members to make decisions. However, guided discretion may allow more transparency as well as consistency in decisions among parole board members. Narrowing factors considered and weighing factors that evaluate rehabilitation would be one way discretion could be guided. Discretion should also be guided to prevent biased decision-making and to prevent release decisions being made based on a parole board member's background and/or what they consider to be important. Further, while all information may be consulted in release decisions, there is some information or factors that may warrant more weight in the final decisions than other factors. The lack of understanding and consistency in the current process erodes legitimacy. However, using procedural justice and the principles under this framework may serve to increase the transparency and legitimacy of the parole process.

VI. PROCEDURAL JUSTICE AND LEGITIMACY

Incarcerated individuals who have been denied release have little choice but to accept the decision of the parole board. Due to the broad discretion and the authority of the board, there are few opportunities for individuals to appeal the board's decision. Rather, individuals are commonly forced to just wait until their next hearing to again plead their case for released. That is, they must remain in prison even if they believe the decision of the board is unfair or even unlawful. Prisons are special environments in that there is more control over individuals than in any other criminal justice context and thus individual compliance may be gained through force more so than in other places (Jackson et al 2010). However, studies show that prisons cannot properly function through the reliance on force alone and that correctional officers and administrators rely heavily on the voluntary compliance of those they supervise to keep order (Irwin 1980; Bottoms and Tankebe 2012). Thus, it is important that the experiences of individuals in prison, such as their interactions with parole board members, do not undermine their willingness to follow institutional rules.

Research shows that increased use of procedural justice principles in the criminal justice system can enhance perceived legitimacy and compliance with rules (Murphy et al 2016). Individuals are more likely to follow the rules of an institution when they believe they are legitimate (Tyler 2004). In the case of parole, individuals who view the parole release process as fair may be more likely to accept the outcome of the decision as legitimate. Thus, they may be more likely to continue engaging in rehabilitative activities and avoid misconduct after an initial parole denial. The premise of legitimacy within procedural justice is that if fair procedures are used by legal authorities, it leads to voluntary compliance as well as an acceptance of decisions even if the outcome is not desirable (Jackson et al 2010).

Tyler (1988; 2006a; 2006b), a leading scholar on procedural justice and legitimacy, identifies six main factors that influence procedural justice (building from the work of Thibaut and Walker 1975; Leventhal 1980). These factors may serve to inform how individuals evaluate the legitimacy of the parole release process. The six factors are: (i) control and representation: the degree to which individuals feel they have influence regarding the decision being made and the degree to which individuals can share their side of the story; (ii) consistency: outcomes of decisions by authority figures across time, as well as comparing outcomes with the outcomes of other individuals; (iii) impartiality: the authorities having honest, unbiased consideration in their decision-making; (iv) accuracy of the decision: the authorities having the information they need to make an informed decision and transparency of how the decision was made; (v) correctability: having other authorities available to appeal decisions/outcomes; and (vi) ethicality: the authorities being courteous in their interactions and considering the rights of the individual (Tyler 1988). The degree to which individuals see these factors in the authority figures charged with decision-making impacts the degree to which individuals view the process as fair and legitimate.

Increased procedural justice strengthens motivations to follow the rules and support the goals of the institution (Jackson 2018). Bottoms and Tankebe (2012: 169) argue for a 'dialogic understanding of legitimacy' that considers the power holder's legitimacy and the audience of the power holder. In the context of this chapter, I ask: do incarcerated individuals and the public (the audiences) see parole board members (the power holders) as legitimate and, by extension, is the parole release process legitimate? If board members use a process that is fair and objective and embodies facets of procedural justice, incarcerated individuals and the public may be more likely to view the parole boards as legitimate, and then they may be more likely to accept an unfavourable outcome of the board's decision. On the other hand, a lack of procedural justice may lead individuals who have been denied parole to view the decision as unfair and the entire process as illegitimate. Society could view parole boards as illegitimate if they do not agree with the decisions (to release or not) because they do not understand how the decisions are made. Transparent decision-making and transparency of the parole board decision-making process can be used to assess the six factors needed for procedural justice. Achieving procedural justice may increase legitimacy.

VII. CURRENT WORK

Next, I will illustrate findings from two studies I conducted in partnership with and under the direction of the Robina Institute of Criminal Law and Criminal Justice (Robina Institute). The first set of findings comes from a national survey of paroling authorities. Findings from this survey will be used to highlight the role of transparency in parole decisions and how the inclusion of transparency may increase legitimacy. Associated with transparent process and legitimacy of parole boards is an examination of the individuals who serve on parole boards, including their educational background and level of experience. The second set of findings are generated from qualitative interviews with incarcerated individuals who were denied parole. The findings from this data will illuminate how individuals who have gone through the parole process and been denied parole experience the process, including their perceptions of fairness.

VIII. METHODS

For brevity, I will describe the methods briefly. However, see Ruhland et al (2016) for details on the Robina Institute Survey and Ruhland and Laskorunsky (2023) for the qualitative interview methods.

A. Parole Survey

The Robina Institute's Parole Survey was conducted in March 2015, and was distributed to all 50 states and the US Parole Commission. This expansive survey was endorsed by the Association of Paroling Authorities International. The survey covered many parts of the parole process, which were divided into sections and comprised: (i) the structure and administration of parole; (ii) information systems and statistical information; and (iii) issues and future challenges facing paroling authorities. In total, 45 of the 50 states, together with the US

Parole Commission, completed at least some portions of the survey. Maine, North Carolina, Tennessee, Vermont and Wisconsin did not complete any parts of the survey. The response rates for some questions vary as some questions did not apply to some respondents or the respondents otherwise skipped them. The survey was electronically administered using Qualtrics and analysed using Statistical Package for Social Sciences.

B. Interviews with Individuals Denied Parole

Participants who had a parole hearing but were denied parole were interviewed as part of a larger study that sought to examine parole release in individuals who were assessed as at medium risk. The parole agency that the Robina Institute was collaborating with wanted to know how to make better release decisions for individuals who were considered medium risk. The parole board in this Eastern state thought it was easier to make release decisions for low-risk individuals and denial decisions for high-risk individuals, but struggled with decisions for individuals who were evaluated in-between. The board members believed the low-risk individuals had a minimal likelihood of reoffending and thus mainly felt comfortable primarily releasing them. With individuals in the high-risk category, parole board members assumed the risk to offend was too great, and thus the safer to decision was to deny parole until a later date. Within the medium-risk category, the parole board members felt that the possibility of further offending was much less clear. The purpose of conducting interviews with people in this category was to understand their perspective in the parole process and hearing, with the hope that this would better inform the parole board members' decision-making. The interviews asked a broad range of questions on incarcerated individuals' perceptions and experiences with the parole process. A total of 66 individuals participated in the study at two male prison facilities and one female prison. Findings for this chapter will focus on the interview participants' views on the transparency, fairness and legitimacy of the parole process. All interviews were audio-recorded and transcribed. The transcripts were analysed by a team of two researchers, who used NVivo to organise the analysis.

IX. RESULTS

A. Board Appointment

Boards in the USA may require their members to have certain educational achievements or some other qualification, such as requiring a certain background (eg victim services, law enforcement). Just over half of the respondents (25 states) in the Robina Institute Survey reported that they have statutory requirements for parole board members. However, 19 states and the US Parole Commission have no statutory requirements. The qualification requirements for the 25 states varied. For 10 states a college degree is required, but the field of study is unspecified. One additional state required a degree, but this could be an associate degree. Fourteen states required a set number of years working in criminal justice or related fields rather than specifying educational requirements. Some states required board members to have both educational qualifications and experience working in the area. For two states, if individuals did not have an educational degree, they could still be on the parole board but had to have additional years of experience working in the field. While the educational requirements of the boards vary, it is important to note that the survey respondents reported that almost 90 per cent of the board members across the states had obtained a bachelor's degree or higher. Thus, despite the limited educational requirements in some states, parole board members were still highly educated.

In the USA, parole boards can be seen as political. This is perhaps not surprising when one considers how the majority of the states appoint individuals to the board. Thirty-seven of the survey participants said that the state governor had the sole authority to appoint members to the board. For the US Parole Commission, it is the president who has the authority to appoint members to the board. Further, there are multiple reasons why parole board terms may be terminated, including any reason given by the governor or other authority, which was the case in 14 states. In seven states, there could be a removal due to a change in the governor. Table 4.1 identifies the reasons why a member could be removed from the parole board.

Table 4.1 Reasons for parole board member removal

Reason for removal	Number of states
Malfeasance and misfeasance	23
Criminal conduct	18
Ethics law violations	15
Removal for any reason or no reason by governor or other appointed authority	14
Change in governor	7
Other	9

B. Board Transparency in Decision Making

Having information publicly available, including how decisions are made, the instruments used to make decisions and the goals/mission of the institution can increase the transparency of parole boards (see chapter two in this volume). Many releasing authorities (88 per cent) who responded to the Robina Institute

Survey reported that they publish information on how the parole process works. Twenty-five of the respondents reported that information on the parole board is published in administrative rules (commonly rules located within the government agency or department) and 22 respondents said it was available in statute. Nineteen respondents reported having information on the parole process on their agency website or in agency policies (17). Only six respondents said their agency published annual reports. Many (86 per cent) of the respondents stated that their parole boards had mission statements. Mission statements are important for transparency because they can translate to the individuals on parole and the public the purpose of the board and what the board is trying to achieve. Fewer (44 per cent) parole boards in the survey reported having vision statements, and even fewer (27 per cent) reported having values or principle statements.

However, it is not enough just to have mission and vision statements: they need to be actively utilised for them to be effective. They ought to inform decision-making. Of the Robina Institute Survey respondents, three-quarters (75 per cent) said they used these statements to guide their decision-making. However, with 25 per cent of respondents not using the statements in their decision-making, there is room for improvement in their use. Risk assessments and parole guidelines can also assist in decision-making. Most of the parole boards (90 per cent) said they used risk assessments, with the other 10 per cent saying they did not. The majority (75 per cent) of the parole boards that used them also said the risk assessments would be available to the public or researchers. Fewer parole boards (44 per cent) used release guidelines or sequential models. Parole release guidelines can 'govern consideration of offenders for release' (Rhine et al 2017: 283). Even though parole boards may have risk assessment and parole release guidelines, they still may not rank high in the parole board member release deliberations. Of the chairs' top release factors considered, risk assessments were ranked number five. Ahead of this factor were: (1) nature of present offence; (2) severity of current offence; (3) prior criminal record; and (4) inmate's disciplinary record.

C. Prisoners' Perception of Fairness

It is perhaps not surprising that most of the individuals interviewed who received a release denial felt that the process was unfair. Only three individuals out of 66 research participants reported that they thought the process was fair when asked questions on the subject. Individuals who are denied parole are plausibly more likely than those released to feel the process was unfair simply because the parole board denied their release. However, for several of the research participants, their reasons for why they felt it was unfair had less to do with the actual denial decision and more to do with the process and their lack of understanding of it. For many, they did think the process, including what factors were considered important by the board, was transparent. Additionally, many of the responses used factors that were consistent for achieving procedural justice in how they saw the process as unfair. They did not use the phrase 'procedural justice', but the concepts for why they saw the process as unfair interconnected with those under the procedural justice framework (ie control, consistency, ethicality). The limited transparency of the process left research participants feeling unsure what they could do to actually obtain a positive release decision. This unsureness commonly stemmed from interviewees' belief that they had done everything right to make their case for release and yet were still denied. One male participant illustrates this point:

> In my case … you have positive housing. You got a job. You got a positive job. You're getting jail recommendation that's telling you that he's doing something inside this institution that's correct. He's not getting into no trouble. He's not doing drugs, whatever it is, fighting, arguing with COs [correctional officers], none of that … I would ask them to take a look at that. Look at a person's institutional behaviour and record. I don't think they do that too often. I don't think that really matters.

This individual was not sure what information the board used to make their decisions because from their perspective they had a good file for release. The interview participant wanted the board to look more into their institutional casefile and see that they were doing a good job within prison. Another male interviewee thought the process was fair for him but not so much for others. He said that parole boards treat all crimes the same way and do not examine release decisions on a 'one-to-one' basis. He also felt boards did not evaluate how individuals have changed since being locked up in prison. This interviewee stated:

> Make it more just on a one-on-one basis and not just a blanket indictment or something like, 'You got a robbery. Okay. Yeah. Well, we know what you going to do. You've been locked up how many times? Yeah, the book says this. No.' What has this person been through since he's been locked up? Because sometimes experiences make a person … it forces a person to mature and to change, to look for growth and development. Do he have a job lined up? Can we investigate his job? Can we go to the site and check the job out? What's your family connections out there, your support network?

Another male participant also believed that parole board members just go off the convicted offence rather than reviewing and assessing if the person has been rehabilitated. From his perception, it does not matter what one has done to reform oneself while in prison because the board only cares about the convicted offence. This research participant said: 'It doesn't matter, but I would say what case you got … I guess whatever kind of case you got, it's like they go off that, how much trouble you got in.'

There were perceptions among the interviewees that no matter what they did to improve their lives, including what the board tells them to do, they would still be denied parole. One male interviewee said:

> I think that it's not fair in the sense of when they ask you to do everything you're supposed to do, and you do everything, exactly what they want you to do and stay

> out of trouble, and you still don't get to go, when you don't get a chance, I think that's unfair.

Another male participant had a hopeless response about the whole process and said, 'ain't nothing I can change. Ain't nothing I can change. That's the only thing I can say.' He felt like other interviewees, in that it did not matter how much an individual had changed and further it did not matter what one said in the hearing: the outcome was most likely going to be a denial. A female interviewee said she was not going to prepare for her hearing because she did not know how to prepare. She did not know what the parole board would ask or considered, so in her mind she did not know even how to prepare. She felt she was prepared for release and was not sure what more she could do to show she was ready. She said:

> Honestly, I don't know, because I've done everything humanely possible, I can do here. There's nothing mor e for me to do, except follow what the guards say, and follow – I'm going to go back to GED, and I'm not going to be able to get my GED for a long time, because– but they want me just to participate in that, so I'm going to go to my self-helps. I'm just going to do what I'm doing until I leave, until I see him again. I mean, we can– I'm not saying you and me– but I can sit all day in a room all day with somebody that's trying to prepare me for a hearing, but what good is that when we don't know what he's going to say?

Many of the interview participants believed the parole board members had already made their minds up to deny release before they even looked at their comprehensive file or met them in the hearing. This belief was because the interviewee perceived that the board members put a strong emphasis on the criminal offence. For other interviewees, they had no idea what factors were important to the board, and this led some to believe ultimately that decisions were dependent on who the board member was and what mattered to them. This lack of transparency in knowing what factors mattered and in how to prepare led many to feel hopelessness about the process and about the prospects for being released from prison (Ruhland and Laskorunsky 2023). For many interviewees, when they got their denial forms, there was little information or explanation as to why they were denied parole. Some forms would say 'lack of remorse shown' or 'lack of institutional programming'. This perplexed some individuals especially when they had remorse for their behaviour or had participated in programming. Some individuals desired more explanation of the reasons why they were denied parole so they could work to improve themselves.

Parole boards across the USA hear thousands of cases each year to determine if an individual is eligible for release. That involves hearing several cases in a single day. Thus, board members may use short hands or consider the same factors for each case to expedite their decision-making. Prior research along with findings from the Robina Institute Survey have shown that the top factors determining release are the nature and severity of one's current offence (Cotton 2008). Individuals who were incarcerated and denied release were frustrated by this because it left them little room to show that they had been rehabilitated. Further, they were not sure other than the criminal offence what else mattered in the board's decision-making. They felt the entire process lacked transparency right down to the reason the individual was denied parole. The research participants reported that they were given little information as to why they were denied parole or were provided with little information as to what they could do to increase their chances of release. Many of the individuals interviewed found the parole release process unfair and not solely because they were denied release from prison but because they did not understand the factors that board members used in the decision.

X. DISCUSSION AND IMPLICATIONS

Most parole boards report that information about the board is available to the public. Yet, incarcerated individuals may not have easy access to these materials as most boards report that information is located in statutes or in administrative policies. The public may not know where to access this information. Few parole boards that participated in the Robina Institute Survey reported posting information on their websites. It is recommended that more boards utilise websites to post information about their board members, including their members' biographies. This would show the public who is on the board and their qualifications and experience. Despite the variations in qualifications required across boards in the USA, most board members are qualified by both education and years of experience to serve on boards. Examining and ensuring qualifications are also important since many board members gain access to the board through political appointments. Further, posting information on agency websites would help in the transparency of the process to post information on how decisions are made and what information is considered.

Individuals going up for parole should not be kept or feel like they are in the dark (Schwartzapfel 2015) as to how decisions are made or what factors are important to boards. It benefits public safety when incarcerated individuals know what steps they need to complete in order to successfully gain release. Incentivising individuals to take classes, develop an adequate re-entry plan and avoid infractions in prisons benefits the individuals but also serves to rehabilitate the individual and prepare them for release. Individuals must believe there is a fair opportunity to plead their case for release to see legitimacy in the parole process. What would also help in this process is if more information could be shared on the reasons for the denial. The research participants were left confused about why they were denied parole, and this was partly because of the limited information provided on their denial sheets. However, it might be challenging or time consuming to provide more information since members hear several cases a week. Yet, at the same time, including more information could increase transparency.

Parole boards need better protections to make their decisions. As the Robina Institute Survey demonstrated, many members could be terminated for any reason, including at the whims of the governor. The problem with this is that it can create risk aversion among board members. They may fear releasing individuals because if the individual commits a serious offence, they are concerned not only about being terminated, but also about being publicly stigmatised for their decision. Thus, better protections to insulate the board from being hastily fired would allow them space to make better decisions. However, this increased protection from termination due to political reasons needs to come with increased transparency in their decision-making as well as the increased use of evidence-based decision-making. By board members being more transparent about what factors influenced their decisions versus what factors only informed their decisions, we can study if these factors are grounded in evidence-based practices and what we know about what contributes to the risk of reoffending. Using evidence-based and transparent practices could also serve to protect the board from being terminated if a release decision goes askew.

Discretion in parole release is important for evaluating when an individual is rehabilitated and ready to be released. Parole boards in the USA should be focused more on the correctional goal of rehabilitation and less on retribution. A non-utilitarian sentencing structure is primarily concerned with retribution, whereas indeterminate decision-making should weigh factors that address rehabilitation (Frase 2005). A key function identified by parole board members in their mission and decision-making is to not compromise public safety by releasing people who are risk for recidivating (Ruhland and Mitchell 2024). Weighing historical factors, such as current offence, is not useful for assessing who an individual is today. For legitimacy and transparency, parole boards must follow their missions and values in how they carry out their release decisions.

The mission, values and factors considered and weighed for release should all be aligned. This will increase the transparency of the process as well as ensure that decision-making is consistent across board members. The legitimacy of parole boards is threatened if decisions are overly dependent upon the individual board member's beliefs and concerns rather than in step with the organisational policies and evidence-based practices. Discretion could be maintained, but guided by release guidelines that highlight the mission and values, and state which factors should be weighted more than others. Further, the role of RNR assessments should be incorporated into the process more. At a minimum, boards should review how RNR assessments could be included more into the parole release process. The concerns with RNR assessments (van Eijk 2020) are warranted; more work should be completed to improve them. Yet, individual, subjective decision-making is also concerning (Latessa and Lovins 2019). There is more to do to reach a balance between using individual discretion and implementing RNR assessments with guidelines. Future research is needed to fully examine this issue.

More research is needed to examine parole boards' decision-making. This research will increase transparency. It could also identify areas where more training is needed or where more evidence-based practices or policies are needed. Mass incarceration has slightly reduced from its peak (Ghandnoosh 2023). However, to have a greater impact, we will need to focus on the back-end mechanism of parole boards' role in prison release.

REFERENCES

Bonta, J, Rugge, T, Scott, TL, Bourgon, G and Yessine, AK (2008) 'Exploring the Black Box of Community Supervision' 47(1) *Journal of Offender Rehabilitation* 248.

Bottoms, A and Tankebe, J (2012) 'Beyond Procedural Justice: A Dialogic Approach to Legitimacy in Criminal Justice' 102(1) *Journal of Criminal and Criminology* 119.

Caplan, JM (2007) 'What Factors Affect Parole: A Review of Empirical Research' 71(1) *Federal Probation* 16.

Carroll, L, and Mondrick, ME (1976) 'Racial Bias in the Decision to Grant Parole' 11(1) *Law & Society Review* 93.

Carroll, JS, Weiner, R, Coates, D, Galegher, J and Alibrio, JJ (1982) 'Evaluation, Diagnosis, and Prediction in Parole Decision Making' 11 *Law and Society Review* 1193.

Conley, JA and Zimmerman, SWE (1982) 'Decision Making by a Part-Time Parole Board: An Observational and Empirical Study' 9(4) *Criminal Justice and Behavior* 396.

Cotton, RF (2008) 'Time to Move On: The California Parole Board's Fixation with the Original Sentence' 27(1) *Law & Policy Review* 239.

Cullen, FT (2017) 'Correctional Rehabilitation' 4 *Academy for Justice* 235.

Cullen, FT and Gendreau, P (2000) 'Assessing Correctional Rehabilitation: Policy, Practice, and Prospects' 3(1) *Criminal Justice* 299.

Frase, R (2005) 'Punishment Purposes' 58(67) *Stanford Law Review* 67.

Ghandnoosh, N (2023) 'Ending 50 Years of Mass Incarceration: Urgent Reform Needed to Protect Future Generations' (Washington, DC, The Sentencing Project) www.sentencingproject.org/policy-brief/ending-50-years-of-mass-incarceration-urgent-reform-needed-to-protect-future-generations/.

Hritz, AC (2021) 'Parole Board Decision Making and Constitutional Rights' 17 *Annual Review of Law and Social Science* 335.

Irwin, J (1980) *Prisons in Turmoil* (Boston, MA, Little & Brown).

Jackson, J (2018) 'Norms, Normativity and the Legitimacy of Justice Institutions: International Perspectives' 14 *Annual Review of Law and Social Science* 145.

Latessa, E and Lovins, B (2019) *Corrections in the Community*, 7th edn (New York, Routledge).

Leventhal, GS (1980) 'What Should be Done with Equity Theory?' in KJ Gergen, MS Greenberg and RH Willis (eds), *Social Exchange: Advances in Theory and Research* (New York, Plenum Press) 27–55.

MacKenzie, DL (2006) *What Works in Corrections: Reducing the Criminal Activities of Offenders and Delinquents*, Cambridge Studies in Criminology (Cambridge, Cambridge University Press).

Miller, J and Maloney, C (2013) 'Practitioner Compliance with Risk/Needs Assessment Tools: A Theoretical and Empirical Assessment' 40(7) *Criminal Justice and Behavior* 716 https://doi.org/10.1177/0093854812468883.

Murphy, K, Bradford, B and Jackson, J (2016) 'Motivating Compliance Behavior Among Offenders: Procedural justice or deterrence?' 43(1) *Criminal Justice and Behavior* 102.

Reitz, KR (2012) 'The "Traditional" Indeterminate Sentencing Model' in *The Oxford Handbook of Sentencing and Corrections* 270.

Reisig, MD and Mesko, G (2009) 'Procedural Justice, Legitimacy, and Prisoner Misconduct' 15(1) *Psychology, Crime & Law* 41.

Reitz, K (2015) *The Oxford Handbook of Sentencing and Corrections* (Oxford, Oxford University Press).

Rhine, EE, Petersilia, J and Reitz, KR (2017) 'The Future of Parole Release' 46(1) *Crime and Justice* 279.

Rhine, EE, Watts, A and Reitz, KR (2018) 'Parole Boards Within Indeterminate and Determinate Sentencing Structures' (Robina Institute of Criminal Law and Criminal Justice) https://robinainstitute.umn.edu/articles/parole-boards-within-indeterminate-and-determinate-sentencing-structures.

Ruhland, EL (2020) 'Philosophies and Decision Making in Parole Board Members' 100(5) *The Prison Journal* 640.

Ruhland, EL and Laskorunsky, J (2023) 'The Hearing Is Just a Formality: You're Never Getting Out' *Crime & Delinquency* https://doi.org/10.1177/00111287231180097.

Ruhland, EL and Mitchell, KL (2024) 'Parole Condition Setting in Connecticut' (Robina Institute of Criminal Law and Criminal Justice) https://robinainstitute.umn.edu/sites/robinainstitute.umn.edu/files/2024-02/parole_condition_setting_in_connecticut.pdf.

Ruhland, EL, Rhine, EE, Robey, JP and Mitchell, KL (2016) 'The Continuing Leverage of Releasing Authorities: Findings from a National Survey' (Robina Institute of Criminal Law and Criminal Justice) https://robinainstitute.umn.edu/publications/continuing-leverage-releasing-authorities-findings-national-survey.

Scott, JE (1974) 'The Use of Discretion in Determining the Severity of Punishment for Incarcerated Offenders' 65(2) *Journal of Criminal Law and Criminology* 214.

Schwartzapfel, B (2015) 'Parole Boards: Problems and Promise' 28 *Federal Sentencing Reporter* 79.

Starr, SB (2014) 'Evidence-Based Sentencing and the Scientific Rationalization of Discrimination' 66(4) *Stanford Law Review* 803.

Sunshine, J and Tyler, TR (2003) 'The Role of Procedural Justice and Legitimacy in Shaping Public Support for Policing' 37(3) *Law & Society Review* 513.

Thibaut, J and Walker, L (1975) *Procedural Justice: A Psychological Analysis* (Hillsdale, NJ, Erlbaum).

Tonry, M (1999) 'Reconsidering Indeterminate and Structured Sentencing' (Sentencing & Corrections, Issues for the 21st Century, Office of Justice Programs).

Tyler, TR (1988) 'What Is Procedural Justice?: Criteria Used by Citizens to Assess the Fairness of Legal Procedures' 22(1) *Law & Society Review* 103.

—— (2004) 'Enhancing Police Legitimacy' 593(1) *Annals of the American Academy of Political and Social Science* 84.

—— (2006a) *Why People Obey the Law* (Princeton, NJ, Princeton University Press).

—— (2006b) 'Restorative Justice and Procedural Justice: Dealing with Rule Breaking' 62(2) *Journal of Social Issues* 307.

—— (2010) 'Legitimacy in Corrections: Policy Implications' 9(1) *Criminology and Public Policy* 127.
van Eijk, G (2020) 'Inclusion and Exclusion Through Risk-Based Justice: Analysing Combinations of Risk Assessment From Pretrial Detention to Release' 60(4) British Journal of Criminology 1080 https://doi.org/10.1093/bjc/azaa012.
Viglione, J, Rudes, DS and Taxman, FS (2015) 'Misalignment in Supervision: Implementing Risk/Needs Assessment Instruments in Probation' 42(3) *Criminal Justice and Behavior* 263.
Zhang, Y, Zhang, L and Vaughn, MS (2014) 'Indeterminate and Determinate Sentencing Models: A State-Specific Analysis of Their Effects on Recidivism' 60(5) *Crime & Delinquency* 693.

5

Old Age and Parole in France: Conflicting Temporalities

MARION VANNIER

I. INTRODUCTION

THIS CHAPTER EXPLORES, from a right-based approach (see chapter one in this volume), how old age intersects with parole, using the case of France as an example. The specific question addressed is how old age in prison challenges the traditional, forward-looking temporality of parole. A rights-based approach to the study of parole centres on ensuring that the fundamental human rights of individuals – particularly those of prisoners and parolees – are respected, protected and fulfilled throughout the parole process. This approach prioritises human dignity, fairness and justice in the administration of parole, focusing on how the system can align with international human rights standards and national constitutional protections. Research has, however, exposed how parole, as an exercise of 'coercive state power' (see editors' introduction), raises a number of moral and legal challenges.

The modern prison was originally designed for the young and healthy in the late eighteenth century in Europe, but now faces the urgent challenge of an ageing prison population – a phenomenon that is not only rapid, but also spans across the world (Filinson 2016; Humblet 2021). Imprisonment stands in the way of life course transitions (London and Myers 2006) and speeds up phases of physical, mental and cognitive forms of decline and loss of agency (Maschi et al 2011). Old age shortens under the effect of imprisonment and speeds up the future that lies ahead. As a result, older men do 'harder time' and experience imprisonment more severely than their younger counterparts (Vannier and Nellis 2023; Wahidin and Tate 2005; Mann 2016). The enhanced pains and harms endured by older prisoners raise several questions in penal politics and open urgent and topical conversations on the scope and nature of the human rights protections afforded to those who are old in prison as human beings capable of change and transformation.

Despite the criticisms that portray parole as an extension of the penal apparatus beyond prison walls (Annison 2020; Zatz 2021), a release mechanism by which prisoners can regain freedom offers – at least in theory – an opportunity for new beginnings (see chapter six in this volume). Getting out of prison before the official end date of the sentence is not merely a temporal privilege that reduces the duration of confinement and allows the prisoner to regain 'free' time, it is a legal right grounded in the principles of justice, rehabilitation and human dignity. It recognises that individuals who have served a portion of their sentence, demonstrated rehabilitation and met established legal criteria are entitled to reintegration into society under conditions that respect their fundamental rights. In contrast to the temporality produced by old age in prison, parole is oriented towards what lies ahead; it is forward and future looking. From a rights-based perspective, this temporality endorses, recognises and protects the universal human capacity to change. When old age is brought into the equation, conflicting temporalities emerge, eclipsing older prisoners' human capacity to change and progress. Yet the human capacity to change (to self-develop, self-fulfil and self-realise) is a feature of dignity, which is a grounding and fundamental concept of human rights law (Trotter 2022).

Release mechanisms that account for old age are rare and are mainly grounded on ensuring that prisoners can die outside prison bars rather than enjoy new beginnings (see chapter twelve in this volume). For instance, England and Wales provides an early release mechanism grounded on poor health for prisoners serving sentences of four years or more (Criminal Justice Act 1991, section 36). Release on compassionate grounds is processed through a Parole Board recommendation to the Secretary of State for Justice. The conditions for granting release on medical grounds include likely death within three months, severe incapacitation or where prolonged imprisonment would endanger a prisoner's life or reduce their life expectancy. Compounding matters, the Justice Secretary needs to find that there is no longer any risk of reoffending and that appropriate measures have been taken to ensure the prisoner's care and treatment upon release (Criminal Justice Act 1991, section 36). Prison staff in England and Wales have complained that the criteria for release on compassionate grounds is too restrictive, resulting in distressing situations where prisoners have died in prison or in a hospital or hospice while still under surveillance, such as by prison escorts (HM Chief Inspector of Prisons 2004). An interesting example is offered by the case of France, which provides two release mechanisms that account for old age, one implicit and the other explicit. There is a medical version of parole that considers old age from a health standpoint, and a social form of early release that is explicitly justified by old age.

The argument this chapter makes is that when old age intersects with parole, in its social and medical forms, conflicting temporalities emerge, which together question the extent to which older parole applicants' human capacity to change is protected. This argument rests on three main claims. Firstly, old age fails to challenge some of the orthodoxies around risk, in particular when sex crimes are involved. Both social and medical parole highlight how criminal justice actors involved in processes of release remain fixated on the offenders' criminal past rather than acknowledging older applicants' human capacity to undergo deep physical and moral transformations. Secondly, with respect to medical parole specifically, release endorses a short-term approach. It is centred on applicants' dying bodies rather than on ageing as an illustration of their human capacity to progress. Thirdly, the social version of parole requires evidence of social utility which is particularly discriminating for older applicants. Even though France offers an interesting example of how parole can account for old age, much still needs to be improved. A rights-based approach to parole would recognise the fact of ageing as a feature of the human capacity to change in both parole criteria and processes.

The first section below offers a brief reflection on the temporality of parole, in particular its future-orientation. The chapter then provides an overview of the French law, highlighting the requirements for securing parole on grounds of old age. Section IV critically discusses how old age changes parole's future-looking temporality. The concluding thoughts return to the rights-based approached articulated in this edited collection to reflect on the legitimacy of parole when old age is taken account.

II. THE TEMPORALITY OF PAROLE

Located at the 'back-end' of the penal continuum, parole is a mechanism that is inherently tied to the future. While it is activated during incarceration (ie the possibility of parole is built into the sentence when the judge hands it down), it is implemented once the prisoner has left prison. Social reintegration further supposes new beginnings with family members, employment and housing (Rhine et al 2017). Prison release is thus best seen as a window onto a better future that is worth changing for.

From a rights-based approach, parole's future orientation is inherent to a shift from retribution (which is backwards looking) towards rehabilitative steps which are concerned with prisoners' transformation and meaningful reintegration into society (Roberts 2019). It also recognises and is grounded on prisoners' capacity to transform where transformation recognises a prisoner's human capacity or potential to change, to better themselves (Radzik 2011; O'Loughlin 2021). It is fundamental, from a human-rights perspective, that prisoners preserve that capacity to change as it is so tightly linked to the idea of dignity, which is a grounding principle of European human rights law (Trotter 2022).

In paving the way to what lies ahead, some argue that parole has the power to bring closure, to conclude incarceration (see chapter six in this volume). This contrasts with parole's capacity to produce a carceral continuum whereby the former prisoner continues to be monitored and disciplined by bureaucratic and geographical constraints (Penikett et al 2019). From this perspective, parole does not bring an end to prison time but rather prolongs the damaging carceral effects.

This chapter offers a different viewpoint from which to consider parole's temporality, in particular its future-orientation, and the implications it carries for the recognition of prisoners' human capacity to change by taking account of the fact of ageing. Prison populations are ageing across the world (Hayes 2017; Bor 2022; Contrôleur Général des Lieux de Privation de Liberté 2022). The problem of old age and ageing in prison is not *terra incognita* in policy, but has impelled very limited political action (Turner et al 2018). However, this phenomenon is placing new pressures on prison staff and budgets (Humblet 2021). And while old age is something that will happen to most of us, the phenomenon takes on an entirely new dimension inside prison (Humblet 2021; Vannier and Nellis 2023). The harms of old age are reportedly exacerbated under the effect of imprisonment (Mann 2016). The transformations and changes that older prisoners endure have a different pace, scope and intensity (Vannier and Nellis 2023). For instance, ageing speeds up in prison, shortening the future and the time left upon release.

In sum, the temporalities of parole and old age often seem to be at odds with one another. Parole operates on timelines that prioritise rehabilitation and reintegration, often measured by criteria that may not align with the realities of ageing and fail to recognise transformations and changes. Meanwhile, old age brings its own pace and set of changes – emotional, cognitive and physical – that do not always fit neatly within the conventional frameworks used to assess readiness for release. This tension highlights the need for a more nuanced and rights-based approach to parole that acknowledges and accommodates the distinct temporalities and transformations of ageing. The orientation of parole thus needs to be re-evaluated under the light of the carceral ageing phenomenon.

III. SOCIAL AND MEDICAL PAROLE IN FRANCE

On 30 June 2024, out of a total prison population of 77,201, there were 5360 individuals over 50 years old in French prisons, ie 7 per cent of the French prison population (Ministère de la Justice 2024: Table 3). In addition to global demographic trends, changes to penal policies have increased the length of certain sentences and toughened the criminalisation of historic sexual offences (Touraut and Désesquelles 2015). Some defendants are thus old at the time of their imprisonment whilst others become 'old' in prison because of the length of their sentence. In France, sentencing adjustments can be granted after having served half or three-quarters of the sentence, depending on the seriousness of the crime.[1] These early release mechanisms include parole, electronic supervision and external placement. Parole requires evidence of a prisoner's social

[1] Law no 2004-204, 9 March 2004.

reintegration through work, family, accommodation, etc.[2] Here, I explore two forms of sentence adjustments relevant to old age: social parole on grounds of old age and medical parole.

In France, there is no age limit for incarcerating a prisoner under the French Code of Criminal Procedure (CPP). Old age, unlike youth, is neither considered at the sentencing stage nor taken into account to adjust the sentence's implementation in prison. There is one provision that refers explicitly to prisoners' old age in matters of early release. Article 82 of the 2009 Penitentiary Act[3] provides that prisoners over 70 years old may be released on parole under specific conditions:

> Where the convicted person is over seventy years of age … parole may be granted if the convicted person's integration or reintegration is ensured, in particular if he or she receives care appropriate to his or her situation on leaving the prison or if he or she can prove that he or she has a place to live, except in the event of a serious risk of recidivism of the offence or if such release is likely to cause a serious disturbance to public order.

The legal provision ensures that detainees aged 70 and over can be released on parole under less restrictive conditions by the *judge de application des peines*, who is not a parole board but a representative of the judiciary. Evidence of social reintegration is nonetheless required and, as we shall see below, is extremely strenuous in practice for those who are old. The rationale for parole on grounds of old age is illuminative of perceptions of vulnerability, which are articulated around broader societal concerns for the health of older people and respect for their past experiences (Combalbert and Rothé 2017).

The 2009 law further stipulates that 'the prison administration shall guarantee to all detainees respect for their dignity and rights'.[4] Such rights can be subject to some restrictions, notably to prevent recidivism, but the law specifies that they include considerations for age, states of health, disabilities and individual prisoners' personalities.

Early release on medical grounds may also be requested by prisoners whose state of health no longer appears to be compatible with detention and is another means through which to consider parole through the prism of old age, this time *implicitly*.[5] The introduction of medical parole in France in the late 2000s signals a move towards preventing prisoners from dying in prison. While getting

[2] The law on parole provides that 'Convicted persons who have to serve one or more custodial sentences may be released on parole if they make serious efforts at social rehabilitation and if they can prove that: (1) They are engaged in a professional activity, an internship or a temporary job, or that they are attending a vocational education or training course; or their essential participation in the life of their family; (3) or their need to undergo medical treatment; (4) or their efforts to compensate their victims; (5) or their involvement in any other serious integration or rehabilitation project'.

[3] Law no 2009-1436, 24 November 2009 (Penitentiary Act); Art 729 CPP.

[4] Law no 2009-1436, Art 22.

[5] Medical sentence suspension was introduced in 2002 (Loi n° 2002-303, 4 March 2002) and authorises seriously ill prisoners to access adequate care outside prison. Suspensions are not the

out of prison for medical reasons remains controversial, dying in prison had also become increasingly contentious (Linder and Meyers 2007; Chassagne 2014; Lagarrigue et al 2014; Queloz 2014). Parole may be requested by prisoners whose health no longer appears to be compatible with detention and is another means by which to consider parole through the prism of old age, albeit implicitly. At any point during a sentence, a judge can authorise the early release of a prisoner suffering from a terminal illness, or whose health is incompatible with continued detention. In 2005, the French Court of Cassation specified that the individual is predicted to die in 'the short term'.[6]

In practice, prisoners who have been convicted of the most serious violent crimes such as murder are eligible to early medical parole regardless of the time they have already served. However, a judge can revoke the release decision if the parolee's conditions improve, and the prisoner can be returned to prison. In other words, if they recover, the prisoner will be returned to prison. Unlike other sentencing adjustment measures, medical parole is not restricted to social reintegration requirements, such as securing a job.[7] Yet, medical parole remains conditioned by the absence of a 'serious risk of repetition of the offence'.[8] The next section offers a critical evaluation of the place given to old age in French mechanisms of parole. Old age, it is argued, defies parole's temporality as something that is future oriented.

IV. OLD AGE AND PAROLE: CONFLICTING TEMPORALITIES

While French law pertaining to release measures recognises the problem of old age in the carceral environment, in practice, the facts of ageing are rarely decisive factors in parole decisions. Rather, risk-based judgements tied to the criminal's past, combined with an emphasis on prisoners' dying or deteriorating bodies and on their social utility, together relegate considerations of old age to the peripheries of parole decisions and erode deeper reflections on the inadequacy of prolonged incarceration for older prisoners.

A. Old Age versus Risk

Under both medical and social parole, old age and the transformations tied to ageing and becoming old are eclipsed by risk considerations by the actors involved in the process of parole. Those who are old are not exempt

primary release mechanisms and tend to be considered when no other sentence adjustment can be obtained (Chassagne and Godard-Marceau 2019).

[6] Criminal Court, 28 September 2005.

[7] Art 720-1-1 CPP.

[8] Arts 147-1 and 720-1-1 CPP.

from character-based constructions when parole opportunities arise. Character-based judgment refers to how criminality is treated as a personality trait that endures and justifies sentencing and punishment (Lacey 2016). As argued by Lacey (2016: 35), character responsibility 'invites us to condemn not merely the sin but also, and fundamentally, the sinner'. Character responsibility ranges from extreme essentialism, where someone's character is viewed as stable and determinant of conduct, to the belief that criminal conviction is not necessarily a feature of individual personality. In between, criminal conduct produces a presumption of bad character that varies in degree. Criminal justice actors hold several preconceived ideas about offenders and prisoners which are shaped by the type of crime or the length of the sentence. While Lacey situates her theory in a study of criminal law, others have extended its application to understandings of rehabilitation (O'Loughlin 2021). Here we apply the notion of character-based judgment to the context of French parole with respect to older prisoners.

Attitudes towards older prisoners vary across criminal justice actors. The appearance of the ageing prisoner could potentially challenge some of the orthodoxies around risk. From a medical standpoint, older individuals may be granted parole if their health deteriorates to a point where adequate care cannot be provided within the prison system. This pragmatic approach reflects an understanding that ageing can significantly affect one's health, which, in turn, impacts one's ability to serve out a sentence in a carceral facility. Nonetheless, despite pressing medical needs, parole decisions are not solely based on health concerns: the individual's past behaviour, perceived risk and potential for rehabilitation remain central to the decision-making process. Views on victims (Salas 2005), as well as concerns over dangerousness and public security (Touraut 2019), shape how old age is treated in parole decisions (Touraut 2019). Judges who decide parole cases rely on the risk of recidivism to reject parole applications. When evaluating medical parole requests, judges refer to the seriousness of the crime and rely on elements included in the applicant's criminal record and reports on their past behaviour in prison (Bouagga 2012). The length of the sentence is also treated as an essential indicator of a prisoner's dangerousness and is determinant in parole decisions (Chassagne and Godard-Marceau 2019).

Perceptions of dangerousness are enhanced when sex crimes are involved. In France (and globally: see Ievins (2023)), the older prison population is composed of two groups: (i) those who were young at conviction and have grown old as their long-term sentence unfolds and (ii) those who were sentenced at an older age. A large proportion of the latter group have committed a sex offence. In 2018, over 30 per cent of the prison population aged 50 and over were serving long sentences (ie more than 10 years) for a sexual offence (Touraut 2019: 16). Individuals convicted of such offences are frequently seen through a lens of heightened threat and untrustworthiness, which can overshadow any considerations of rehabilitation or age-related vulnerabilities (Touraut 2019).

Some prison officers place a greater emphasis than others on old age in shaping their views and attitudes towards older prisoners. They will seek to preserve prisoners' tranquillity and monitor their well-being; these officers are less worried about potential escapes or encountering violent behaviours (Touraut 2019: 43). For most, however, concerns about risk and security remain paramount when dealing with prisoners deemed dangerous due to their past crimes, overshadowing any empathic attitudes towards those who age while incarcerated (Rostaing 1998). Prison officers' views on the crimes, sentence length, victims and dangerousness also have a practical upstream impact on the use of social and medical parole (Touraut 2019). While prison officers do not have the final authority to grant release, their influence on the process is significant. Officers who are reluctant to support older prisoners can impact their chances of obtaining parole in several ways. For instance, if officers are hesitant to encourage older prisoners to apply for release, they may withhold crucial guidance or information needed to navigate the parole process. This reluctance can extend to not assisting in the preparation of their release applications, which often require detailed documentation and a thorough presentation of the prisoner's case. Moreover, officers' participation in the assessment process is essential. They can provide insights into the prisoner's behaviour, rehabilitation efforts and readiness for reintegration. When officers choose not to engage in these assessments or provide unfavourable evaluations, it can negatively affect the prisoner's application. Their lack of support can make it exceedingly difficult for older prisoners to prepare and complete their release requests successfully.

When risk concerns outweigh considerations of age-related changes, it reveals how officers and other criminal justice professionals apply their own normative views on ageing in the interpretation and enforcement of legal rules related to release. This normative reformulation dynamic recasts the older prisoner as an 'ordinary prisoner' who is 'a naturally dangerous individual, separate from the rest of society, who is the control of their body and holds specific sociability and morality' (Le Caisne 2000: 198). In this context, age is not seen as a unique factor that should warrant special consideration, but rather as a characteristic that should be treated no differently than other aspects of an inmate's profile. This leads to a flattening of the unique challenges and transformations associated with ageing in prison, resulting in older prisoners being evaluated and processed according to the same criteria applied to younger or less elderly inmates.

To depart from this image and normative framing, and for old age to matter, the older prisoner needs to meet a certain 'ideal' in Nils Christie's terminology (1986). This might involve displaying vulnerability or frailty associated with ageing, such as having significant health issues or showing physical decline. When older prisoners present themselves in ways that align with these stereotypes, they may be more likely to garner empathy and support from decision-makers. For old age to offset concerns about risk, the prisoner must be perceived as vulnerable and non-threatening, similar to the stereotypical image of a gentle grandparent (Chassagne and Godard-Marceau 2019). Those who are perceived as 'pleasant' are indeed more easily cast as patients in need of treatment, care and empathy, whereas those who come across as 'disagreeable' are labelled as prison-deserving applicants. For instance, in her work on ageing in prison, sociologist Caroline Touraut (2019) describes how the parole decision of an older sex offender had been evaluated through the prism of their personality. His unpleasant and grumpy personality was a determining factor in refusing his medical parole. By contrast, a prisoner with a sympathetic personality, pictured as the traditional 'granddad', was found eligible to 'a significant reduction in his sentence' (Chassagne and Godard-Marceau 2019: 60–61).

These findings reveal a persistent tension between recognising the vulnerability of older prisoners and perceptions of their dangerousness. On the one hand, there is a growing awareness of the physical and emotional fragility that often accompanies ageing, leading to a view that older prisoners are necessarily vulnerable individuals who may require special consideration and protection. This perspective acknowledges the unique challenges they face, such as health issues, reduced mobility and a general need for compassionate treatment due to their advanced age. This appreciation of old age, however, rests upon a set of stereotypical expectations that demand older individuals be perceived as inherently harmless, compliant and pleasant. This ageist stereotype paints a simplistic and idealised picture of elderly people as meek and unthreatening, which can influence how their cases are assessed within the criminal justice system. From this stance, older individuals are expected to conform to a normative image of ageing that emphasises passivity and docility in order to be eligible to compassion and release.

On the other hand, the perception of dangerousness, particularly for those convicted of serious or violent crimes, or sentenced to long prison terms, remains a formidable barrier to early release applications. When old age is viewed through the lens of risk and threat, the positive transformations and changes tied to ageing are overlooked. The narrative of risk overshadows the affirmative changes that ageing can bring, such as diminished aggression, increased self-reflection or a greater capacity for remorse and personal growth.

The ambivalence between vulnerability and risk illustrates a long-lasting difficulty in reconciling the need for humane treatment of ageing individuals capable of human transformation with the imperative of ensuring public safety. But the ambivalence itself is somewhat reductive and short-sighted, as older prisoners are necessarily classified either as 'vulnerable because old' or 'risky because not sufficiently old' and thus vulnerable. To fully address this reductive and limiting ambivalence requires stepping away from the conventional binary 'age and vulnerability'.

B. Old Age as Deteriorating and Dying Bodies: Evidencing Shorter Futures

Social and medical parole systems place significant emphasis on the physical condition of applicants, with the state of their body being a crucial factor in determining eligibility. The centrality given to the ageing body may be explained by the feelings of compassion or pity that emerge from witnessing others' suffering (Boltanski 2008). To some extent, the deteriorating or dying older body can also qualm risk-based fears as there is something reassuring about bodies who become less agile and strong (Touraut 2019:60). The older prisoner's body becomes in some way a social resource that generates enough compassion to shape the application of the law. It is important to note, however, that the ageing body can also be perceived as an additional load for prison staff. Touraut (2019: 60) found that prison officers 'consider that these diminished bodies do not fall within their sphere of competence, and their presence even generates a certain amount of annoyance in view of the constraints they induce'.

The focus on the state of the body is especially pronounced in the context of medical parole, where the applicant's health condition is scrutinised to assess whether early release from incarceration is warranted. Under French law, prisoners must either be terminally ill or their bodily state must have become incompatible with carceral conditions. The process typically involves detailed medical documentation, evaluations by healthcare professionals and testimonies from experts who can attest to the prisoner's deteriorating health and its impact on their quality of life (Chassagne 2014; 2022).

The carceral incompatibility requirement is grounded in the need to demonstrate that older prisoners' health issues are so severe that continued confinement could aggravate their condition. If the body is not sufficiently damaged, then the prison environment will not appear as sufficiently inappropriate to justify early release. Consequently, it is older prisoners' physical condition that exposes the shortcomings of the carceral environment. This arguably places undue emphasis on physical deterioration as the primary measure of inhumane conditions. The focus on the body can overlook other important factors, such as the prisoner's mental health, the adequacy of medical care and the overall treatment and quality of life within the prison. Prisoners who are not visibly or severely physically damaged might still experience profound suffering due to inadequate healthcare, poor living conditions or lack of proper medical treatment. By relying heavily on demonstrable and recognisable damage as a criterion for early release, the system risks perpetuating injustice for prisoners whose conditions are severe but not yet critical. The result is a potentially cruel delay in addressing older prisoners' needs and ensuring their well-being, which is contrary to principles of humane treatment and justice.

Albeit central and determinant to activating early release on medical grounds, concerns over security once again overshadow vulnerability-shaped perceptions. While there may be a consensus amongst criminal justice actors for using release mechanisms on medical grounds when the body is dying, positions are more ambivalent when it comes to considering the incompatibility of ageing bodies with detention as grounds for release. For judges and prison staff alike, the lack of physical autonomy is insufficient to justify medical parole (Mortet and Fourment 2007; Touraut 2019). As a result, release mechanisms on grounds of medical health are used somewhat restrictively in France (Chassagne and Godard-Marceau 2019).

In addition, beliefs around older prisoners' criminal past raise several doubts over their sincerity when requiring release on medical grounds. Many judges recount examples of claimants who had not died in the weeks or even months following their release from prison, displaying a form of distrust for illness claims to obtain release (Chassagne and Godard-Marceau 2019: 59). Prison-based healthcare professionals also treat medical claims with suspicion, and as a result become caught between their role of protecting individuals whose bodies are no longer adapted to the constraints of detention and their fear of being manipulated and misled. Furthermore, there are no timing requirements for applying for parole, but applications from prisoners who are near their official release date generally do not generate the same reservations as those who have just started their sentence (Chassagne and Godard-Marceau 2019). A person who requests early release due to their health just after their trial tend to be seen as trying to strategically reduce their sentence, whereas a person who has already served a significant amount of time is perceived as having legitimate grounds for requesting a suspension of the remainder of their sentence on medical grounds (Chassagne and Godard-Marceau 2019: 59).

From a rights-based approach, the centrality given to deteriorating and dying bodies to justify parole offers a reductive understanding of what it means to change and become old in prison. Old age is associated with a diminished future. French law and its implementation by criminal justice actors requires that older prisoners demonstrate (reassure even) that the future beyond release will be fleeting and short-lived. And if they were to recover upon release, the law provides that prisoners need to be returned to prison. In other words, if parolees were to survive and access an extended and brighter future, parole could be rescinded. The use of parole in the case of older prisoners therefore conflicts with the traditional view that portrays early-release parole as something that paves the way to new, forward-looking and open-ended beginnings.

C. Demonstrating Social and Professional Utility: The Illusion of Meaningful Futures

In France, social reintegration is primarily understood through the perspective of professional reintegration. The parole system relies heavily on employment, viewing it as the primary safeguard against recidivism, as it reflects a person's sense of responsibility (Baader and Shea 2007). Engaging in an activity is also seen as a means to ensure that individuals maintain at least a basic level of social connections (Berg and Huebner 2011). When judges assess release applications, for example, they closely review the reasons brought forward for not returning to work. They expect parolees to demonstrate, in the absence of a job, an activity showing that the prisoner will try to keep themselves busy (Chassagne and Godard-Marceau 2019; Touraut 2019). The release plan must therefore provide evidence that the older person will not be completely idle upon release, as idleness would be perceived very negatively (Touraut 2019: 204–05). Thus, a prisoner's social utility becomes a key criterion for granting parole.

Yet, engaging in activities that promote employability becomes arduous for older prisoners. In French prisons, those with various physical disabilities and impairments face significant challenges in moving around the facility and accessing the treatment and programme spaces essential for maintaining employability (Désesquelles 2005; Laplaud 2021). The design and architecture of these prisons furthers hinders access to the activities required for parole eligibility. Originally constructed for young, able-bodied men, these facilities are incompatible with the natural ageing process (Demonchy 2008). The French Prison Inspectorate found that for those with reduced mobility, 'access to workshops, courses, activities and library is not possible' (Contrôleur Général des Lieux de Privation de Liberté 2009). Prison activities aimed at education and employment training are also ill-adjusted to older prisoners (INED 2001). Caroline Touraut and Aline Désesquelles refer to the 'tyranny of age' to illustrate the discriminations and exclusions older prisoners face in terms of carceral activities (Touraut and Désesquelles 2015). As a result, older prisoners seeking parole are more likely to miss out on job opportunities, rehabilitative activities and programmes designed to reduce risk and to promote social rehabilitation.

The question of social utility, when reduced to employability, becomes all the more incongruous for those whose work prospects no longer make sense. Older prisoners are indeed the least likely to return to work (Guillemard 2010). Reports evidence discrimination in recruitment on the basis of old age (Prouet and Rousselon 2018), and when prisoners reach the age to retire, work is frequently no longer an option in the community. When social reintegration cannot be built around a professional activity, the plans for release required in the parole process are particularly complex to develop (Touraut 2019: 203).

Compounding matters, prisoners must evidence that they have maintained bonds with the outside world to demonstrate their social utility. Yet, the barriers to securing a job upon release have ripple effects. In France, it is particularly complicated to find housing without work (Touraut 2019: 212–19). Older prisoners thus struggle to find places in a retirement facility home, either because of the sometimes extremely long waiting lists or simply because these places refuse to house former prisoners. Release seems less problematic when family ties have been preserved. The family remains an essential support for detainees as it indicates a prisoner's utility as a family member (Touraut and Désesquelles 2015). However, a sentence's length and old age can jeopardise such ties, reducing the chances of release (Kensey and Désesquelles 2006). Parole becomes particularly arduous when older prisoners have become institutionalised and cannot fare alone. In addition to the barriers to finding employment and accommodation after years of living in prison, breaking prison habits and adjusting to a society that has changed dramatically can be particularly hard for those who are old (Marchetti 2014). Thus, preparing for the release of long-term prisoners requires anticipating a range of difficulties 'to address adequately … the different demands of free life' (Goethals 1980: 83) after years of incarceration. When prisoners' families are present, they are not always willing or able to take care of them when they leave prison. For example, an older prisoner may not be able to return to their family home due to serious health problems that require medical attention. In addition, conditions imposed by the judiciary may prevent prisoners from returning to their family, such as geographical restrictions where the crime occurred or where the victim's lives (Touraut 2019: 206).

These reintegration difficulties effectively stand in the way of securing parole (Bouagga 2015). The duration of the procedure, coupled with the practical impediments to demonstrating social utility, can also lead to dramatic situations where older prisoners have died in prison while waiting for conditional release (Lacroix 2022). Socialisation requirements for release are particularly discriminating for those who are old. The hurdles to evidencing social utility, either through employability or family responsibility, in effect turn parole into something illusive and prolong detention rather than bringing it to an end.

V. CONCLUSION: RETHINKING PAROLE TO ACCOUNT FOR THE FACT OF AGEING

The conflicting temporalities that arise when old age intersects with parole question the humanity of parole as a mechanism that recognises and protects the human capacity to change and transform. Though rife with challenges, conventional wisdom suggests that parole will open the door onto a 'new' life, one that is rife with opportunities and new beginnings (Greene and Dalke 2021). When parole is confronted with old age, however, it morphs into a process that emphasises endings, in biological and social forms. Weight is given to the offender's criminal past, and character-based stereotypes over the prisoner's crime and sentence duration stall parole procedures. Parole, under the effect of old age, becomes stuck in the past and supports short-term survival. Transformations caused by ageing are only considered when they affect the body. And the body must be dying or significantly deteriorating, to reveal prison conditions' inadequacy, to justify parole. Furthermore, the focus on employability and social utility gives emphasis to another form of death, that of elderly prisoners' social exclusion. The social requirements for release become discriminatory under the effect of old age, and reinforce reductive and ageist perceptions of older people's social and professional value.

Parole, when confronted with old age, is everything but future oriented. It is turned towards the past and supports short-term survival. Old age shifts parole's temporality backwards and the human capacity to change seems to follow a *logic of finality*: elderly prisoners are stained by their past, yet are expected to construct a socially meaningful present to regain freedom. They are also required to ensure or 'reassure' they will not live in the future for too long. Old age and ageing processes defy the future-oriented feature of parole and ultimately require careful rethinking of the humanitarian vocation that underpins parole.

To maintain the legitimacy of parole as a mechanism for concluding prison sentences, particularly in the context of an ageing inmate population, we must fundamentally rethink the legal criteria and processes for release. A rights-based approach to parole must be attuned to the realities of ageing, especially the capacity of older prisoners for transformation.

Firstly, the pathways of both medical and social parole should be reconfigured so as recognise that personal change among older inmates manifests in diverse forms and unfolds at varying paces. The medical release system should not be contingent solely on proving terminal illness in the applicant. Instead, it should function in a quasi-automatic manner as physical and medical signs of ageing appear and intensify. The degree of automatic processing would increase as these signs intensify, with the process becoming faster and more streamlined in severe cases. The burden of proof would then shift to the parole board, requiring them to justify any denial of medical release once such signs are evident. The parole pathway for fit and healthy adults (young or old) remains blind to the question of ageing. The conventional metrics to gauge rehabilitation – such as participation in prescribed programmes, displays of remorse or behavioural conformity – are often ill-adjusted to the case of older prisoners. They should be revised to reconsider what constitutes meaningful or purposeful activities, particularly for those who are retired. Additionally, the criteria for demonstrating rehabilitation and social resocialisation would acknowledge that the passage of time in prison, combined with ageing, alter perceptions of remorse and understandings of shifted societal norms and values since the crime was committed and the sentence was imposed. For this group of the prison population, transformation is more likely to be internalised, reflecting shifts in mindset, values and self-perception rather than overt actions. A parole system that fails to recognise these subtler forms of change risks perpetuating injustices on grounds of old age by overlooking the true extent of older prisoners' rehabilitation and social worth. In sum, there needs to be some exceptional quasi-mandatory release pathways, and the more universal parole pathway needs to be more finely attuned to the release of older prisons in their infinite variety.

Secondly, the legal framework governing parole must reconceptualise ageing not as a process of inevitable decline, but as one that can also yield positive developments. The prevailing narrative in parole assessments tends to equate ageing with physical and cognitive deterioration, which, in turn, reinforces a bias against the release of older prisoners. However, ageing, and the changes that underlie the phenomenon, often brings with it increased emotional resilience, deeper empathy and a heightened sense of life's complexities (Lavretsky 2014). These attributes, born of time and experience, should be integral to the parole calculus, recognising that older prisoners possess unique strengths that could enrich society upon their release.

Thirdly, the criteria for parole must move beyond traditional indicators, such as employment prospects and family support, which may be less relevant or attainable for older inmates. The focus should instead shift to the transferable skills and experiential knowledge that older prisoners have accumulated over their lives, both inside and outside prison. These skills – whether in mediation, mentorship or community engagement – are often undervalued in current parole assessments, yet they are crucial for the successful reintegration of older individuals into society. A parole system that privileges these qualities would offer a more equitable and realistic assessment of an older inmate's readiness for release. In sum, by adopting a rights-based approach that is sensitive to the fact of ageing, the parole system can better align itself with principles of justice and humanity. Such a reimagining of parole is not merely a procedural adjustment, but is a necessary evolution that ensures the system remains relevant and fair, particularly as it confronts the challenges posed by an ageing prison population.

REFERENCES

Annison, H (2020) 'Re-examining Risk and Blame in Penal Controversies: Parole in England and Wales' in J Pratt and J Anderson (eds), *Criminal Justice, Risk and the Revolt Against Uncertainty* (Basingstoke, Palgrave Macmillan) 139–63.

Boltanski, L (2008) *Distant Suffering: Morality, Media and Politics* (Cambridge, Cambridge University Press).

Bor, JS (2022) 'The Aging of the US Prison Population: A Public Health Crisis' 41(5) *Health Affairs (Project Hope)* 622.

Bouagga, Y (2012) 'Le métier de conseiller d'insertion et de probation: dans les coulisses de l'État pénal?' 54(3) *Sociologie du travail* 317.

—— (2015) *Humaniser la peine? Enquête en maison d'arrêt* (Rennes, Presses Universitaires de Rennes).

Chassagne, A (2014) 'Surveiller, soigner, accompagner' in C Chevandier, J-M Larralde and PV Tournier (eds), *Enfermements, justice et libertés: Aujourd'hui et hier, ici et ailleurs* (Paris, L'Harmattan) 227–39.

—— (2022) 'Prisons de vieux, droit commun' 17(3) *Délibérée* 29.

Chassagne, A and Godard-Marceau, A (2019) 'Le juge, le médecin et le détenu. Regard critique sur la suspension de peine pour raison médicale' 156 *Médecine & Droit* 55.

Christie, N (1986) 'The Ideal Victim' in EA Fattah (ed), *From Crime Policy to Victim Policy: Reorienting the Justice System* (London, Palgrave Macmillan) 17–30.

Combalbert, N and Rothé, S (eds) (2017) *Vieillissement, vulnérabilités et animation sociale* (Paris, L'Harmattan).

Contrôleur Général des Lieux de Privation de Liberté (2009) 'Rapport de visite de la maison d'arrêt de Mulhouse'.

—— (2022) 'Rapport d'activité 2021' www.cglpl.fr/2022/publication-du-rapport-dactivite-2021/.

Demonchy, C (2008) 'Histoire de l'architecture carcérale' https://criminocorpus.org/fr/bibliotheque/video/374/.

Désesquelles, A (2005) 'Le handicap en milieu carcéral en France. Quelles différences avec la situation en population générale?' 60(1–2) *Population* 71.

Filinson, R (2016) 'A Day in the Life: How Time is Spent Doing Time among Older Inmates' 40(2) *Activities Adaptation & Aging* 125.

Goethals, J (1980) 'Les effets psychosociaux des longues peines d'emprisonnement' 4(1) *Déviance et société* 81.

Greene, J and Dalke, I (2021) '"You're Still an Angry Man": Parole Boards and Logics of Criminalized Masculinity' 25(4) *Theoretical Criminology* 639.

Guillemard, A-M (2010) *Les défis du vieillissement: Âge, emploi, retraite : perspectives internationals*, 2nd edn (Paris, Armand Colin).

Hayes, AJ (2017) 'Aging Inside: Older Adults in Prison' in BS Elger, C Ritter and H Stöver (eds), *Emerging Issues in Prison Health* (Dordrecht: Springer Netherlands) 1–12.

HM Chief Inspector of Prisons (2004) '"No Problems – Old and Quiet": Older Prisoners in England and Wales'.

Humblet, D (2021) 'Surviving Prison in Old Age' in D Humblet (ed), *The Older Prisoner* Palgrave Studies in Prisons and Penology (Basingstoke, Palgrave Macmillan) 189–227.

Ievins, A (2023) *The Stains of Imprisonment: Moral Communication and Men Convicted of Sex Offenses* (Oakland, CA, University of California Press).

INED (2001) *Handicaps, incapacités, dépendance: personnes en milieu carcéral* (ADISP).

Kensey, A and Désesquelles, A (2006) 'Les détenus et leur famille: des liens presque toujours maintenus mais parfois très distendus' (Données sociales: La société française).

Lacey, N (2016) *In Search of Criminal Responsibility: Ideas, Interests, and Institutions* (Oxford, Oxford University Press).

Lacroix, T (2022) 'Comment les professionnels des établissements pénitentiaires se représentent-ils la présence et les conditions de vie des personnes âgées en prison ?'.

Lagarrigue, A et al (2014) 'Privation deliberté et fin de vie: mourir digne implique-t-il de mourir libre ?' 13(4) *MedPalliat* 200.

Laplaud, A (2021) 'L'adaptation de la répression de la délinquance au vieillissement. A-t-on peur de la fin de l'image fantasmée du "grand âge": celle de personnes fragiles, vulnérables, sans défense … ?' *Trayectorias Humanas Trascontinentales* 10.

Lavretsky, H (2014) *Resilience and Aging: Research and Practice* (Baltimore, MD, JHU Press).

Le Caisne, L (2000) *Prison: Une ethnologue en centrale* (Odile Jacob).

Linder, JF and Meyers, FJ (2007) 'Palliative Care for Prison Inmates: "Don't Let Me Die in Prison"' 298(8) *JAMA* 894.

London, AS and Myers, NA (2006) 'Race, Incarceration, and Health: A Life-Course Approach' 28 *Research on Aging* 409.

Mann, N (2016) *Doing Harder Time?: The Experiences of an Ageing Male Prison Population in England and Wales*, 1st edn (London, Routledge).
Marchetti, A-M (2014) *Perpétuités. Le temps infini des longues peines* (Plon).
Maschi, T et al (2011) 'Trauma and Life Event Stressors Among Young and Older Adult Prisoners' 17 *Journal of Correctional Health Care* 160.
Ministère de la Justice (2024) *Statistiques trimestrielles de milieu fermé au 30 juin 2024.*
Mortet, L and Fourment, F (2007) *La suspension médicale de peine* (Paris, L'Harmattan).
O'Loughlin, A (2021) 'Risk Reduction and Redemption: An Interpretive Account of the Right to Rehabilitation in the Jurisprudence of the European Court of Human Rights' 41(2) *Oxford Journal of Legal Studies* 510.
Penikett, J, Daly, C and Milton, E (2019) 'A Study of Mentors in Wales "Coming to Closure"' 45(3) *Professional Development in Education* 405.
Prouet, E and J Rousselon (2018) 'Les seniors, l'emploi et la retraite' (*France Stratégie*) www.vie-publique.fr/rapport/37681-les-seniors-lemploi-et-la-retraite.
Queloz, N (2014) 'Mourir en prison: entre punition supplémentaire et "choix" contraint' 3 *Revue internationale de criminologie et de police technique et scientifique* 373.
Radzik, L (2011) *Making Amends: Atonement in Morality, Law, and Politics* (New York, Oxford University Press).
Rhine, EE, Petersilia, J and Reitz, KR (2017) 'The Future of Parole Release' 46(1) *Crime and Justice* 279.
Roberts, JV (2019) 'The Time of Punishment: Proportionality and the Sentencing of Historical Crimes' in M Tonry (ed), *Of One-Eyed and Toothless Miscreants: Making the Punishment Fit the Crime?* (Oxford, Oxford University Press).
Rostaing, C (1998) *La relation carcérale. Identités et rapports sociaux dans les prisons pour femmes* (Paris, Presses Universitaires de France (Le lien social) 331.
Salas, D (2005) *La volonté de punir ; essai sur le populaisme pénal* (Paris, Dalloz Librairie).
Touraut, C (2019) *Vieillir en prison. Punition et compassion* (Nîmes, Champ Social).
Touraut, C and Désesquelles, A (2015) *La prison face au vieillissement Expériences individuelles et prise en charge institutionnelle des détenus 'âgés'* (GIP – Mission de recherche Droit et Justice and l'Institut National d'Etudes Démographiques).
Trotter, S (2022) 'Hope's Relations: A Theory of the "Right to Hope" in European Human Rights Law' 22(2) *Human Rights Law Review* ngac007.
Turner, M et al (2018) 'Ageing and Dying in the Contemporary Neoliberal Prison System: Exploring the "Double Burden" for Older Prisoners' 212 *Social Science & Medicine* 161.
Vannier, M and Nellis, A (2023) '"Time's Relentless Melt": The Severity of Life Imprisonment Through the Prism of Old Age' 25(5) *Punishment & Society* 1271.
Wahidin, A and Tate, S (2005) 'Prison (E)scapes and Body Tropes: Older Women in the Prison Time Machine' 11(2) *Body & Society* 59.
Zatz, ND (2021) 'The Carceral Labor Continuum: Beyond the Prison Labor/Free Labor Divide' in E Hatton (ed), *Labor and Punishment: Work In and Out of Prison* (Oakland, CA, University of California Press) 133–78.

6

Parole as Penal Closure

NETANEL DAGAN*

I. INTRODUCTION

DISCRETIONARY PAROLE – early release from prison – is a rather unusual penological phenomenon. The cumulative efforts of investigation, prosecution, trial and sentencing are often concluded in a – hopefully rightfully imposed and proportionate – term of imprisonment for the convicted individual. This imprisonment, especially in retributive sentencing systems, should reflect primarily the moral seriousness of the crime at its time of commission (von Hirsch 2017). In contrast, parole, at least in theory, reflects a very different penal philosophy, especially in indeterminate discretionary sentencing systems (Reitz 2017). Depending on the specific jurisdiction, decades of imprisonment and even life imprisonment may become two-thirds, half or even less of the imposed term. This penal change is an outcome of an often-quick decision, with the public knowing little about it, decided upon behind closed doors and based on broad discretion (Rhine et al 2017). Decided often years or even decades after the crime, parole reflects a transition from retribution to rehabilitation, from past to future and from judicial to administrative (or quasi-judicial) decision-making.[1] As such, it is not surprising that parole is a highly controversial concept. Contemporary accounts of parole are wrought with 'penal pessimism' and tend to view the future of parole, if it has a future, as rather dystopic (see chapter one in this volume).

This pessimism is based on several arguments. Parole is often viewed by the public, media and policy-makers as compromising public safety; undermining confidence in law, parity and proportionality; and negating victims' demands

* My thanks to Marion Vannier, Adiel Zimran and the participants of the Oñati Workshop for their comments on this chapter. Special thanks to the editors for their valuable suggestions.

[1] In *Dickson v United Kingdom* [2007] ECHR 44362/04 (4 December 2007), the European Court of Human Rights held that 'in the course of serving a sentence, a prisoner should move progressively through the prison system thereby moving from the early days of a sentence, when the emphasis may be on punishment and retribution, to the latter stages, when the emphasis should be on preparation for release'.

for justice (Singer 1979; von Hirsch and Hanrahan 1979(. For public support for parole, see Fitzgerald et al (2022). In several Western systems, there have been attempts in 'tough on crime' and 'zero tolerance' political atmospheres to minimise and even abolish parole. Scholars have also argued that contemporary policy-makers have seized upon the symbolic power of parole to express solidarity with crime victims and reaffirm a populist credo (Annison and Guiney 2022: 417). The legal status of parole has also been subject to criticism. Parole is often viewed as a privilege rather than a right (see chapter one in this volume), the process suffers from poor procedural standards compared to criminal trials (Padfield et al 2022) and its outcomes are 'almost unreviewable' by courts, despite its enormous impact (Medwed 2008: 493).

In this chapter, I will attempt to offer a less pessimistic picture of parole, bringing what parole *should be* together with what parole *is*. As Duff (2001: 201) argued, 'the task of justifying criminal punishment … is the task of so transforming the content and context of criminal punishment that it can become what it ought to be.' As Annison et al also suggested, 'the processes of reimagining are in part a response and a resistance, in the criminological context, to dystopian visions of the penal present'.

I will further argue that parole holds a rather unfulfilled moral potential for penal theorists and penologists. Namely, moral issues should be viewed as part of 'back-end' rather than solely 'front-end' sentencing (Dagan 2022). To show the moral significance of parole, going beyond its narrow instrumental meaning in crime reduction or reducing prison populations, I will suggest one moral function of parole: its provision of *symbolic closure* to the penal dialogue between the community and the incarcerated individuals and possibly other actors (eg the crime victims). As I will argue, parole can ideally contribute to a sense of 'ending' the penal dialogue in four ways: (i) stopping the prison 'clock'; (ii) enabling recognition of prisoners' full status as citizens; (iii) allowing prisoners to come to terms of with their past; and (iv) enabling all stakeholders to remember the crime. In conclusion, I will argue that recognising the role of parole as a kind of 'penal closure' has meaning for policy as well: parole policies should be viewed as achieving a symbolic ending instead of reinforcing and extending punitive logic, in a process that is more public and positive instead of secret and punitive, and in which the role of the parole process as marking an ending will be more openly recognised.

At the outset, it is important to note that, globally, there are many kinds of parole release mechanisms, varying in terms of sentencing (in)determinacy, discretion and professional expertise; the use and type of risk assessment tools; the hearing procedure (eg oral hearing, file-based decision, more adversarial or inquisitorial process); and more (Rhine et al 2017; Yelderman et al 2022). To avoid technical and legal distinctions and complexities, and at the risk of overgeneralisation, I will refer to the general elements of discretionary parole: a discretionary decision of a parole board to release prisoners from incarceration before the formal expiration of their sentence, on condition of sustained lawful behaviour that is subject to supervision in the community.

II. CONCEPTUALISING PAROLE AS PENAL CLOSURE

Closure is a term used in many disciplines, including philosophy, literary studies, organisational studies, psychology, social work, anthropology, sociology and law. Closure does not have a fixed, unchangeable definition because emotions themselves are not fixed, unchanging entities with measurable characteristics; rather, they are at least in part socially and culturally constructed (Bandes 2020). Literary scholars define closure as 'a sense of appropriate cessation. It announces and justifies the absence of further development; it reinforces the feeling of finality, completion, and composure' (Kanwar 2001: 215). In psychology, the 'need for closure' is defined as a personality characteristic and a cognitive style that describes an orientation towards structure, stability, order, decisiveness, unambiguity and an aversion to uncertainty. Closure connotes something more than just that things have come to an end. It implies a sense of harmonious completion, of balance and equilibrium restored, of tension reduced, and it allows the pursuit of new challenges and activities (Albert 1984: 159–60). Closure is essential to change. Failing to achieve closure may have an emotional price – it may produce feelings of anxiety and distress, difficulties in letting go of the past and moving on, an inability to heal and grow, and lingering feelings of anger and resentment (Albert 1984; Strupp and Binder 1984: 259; Webster and Kruglanski 1994). It has also been found that desistance narratives include a rupture with the previous criminal identity, the desire to end a stage of life associated with crime and the wish to develop a 'conventional' life (Orlando and Farrington 2023: 5).

Reaching closure also often suggests a *process*, a course of action that involves evaluating, acknowledging and celebrating the achievement of specific goals and the acceptance of losses. Such a process often involves reflection and an appreciation of the past, acknowledging who one is, making transitions, adapting, reorienting and realigning one's thoughts about the future (Penikett et al 2019). During the closure process, there is often a positive reappraisal of negative experiences and a better framing of narratives (Habermas and Berger 2011). Achieving closure often involves the use of symbols and rituals that represent the end of a significant event or period and help to create a sense of order, meaning and boundaries (Hamber and Wilson 2022). When closure is achieved, it is often described as a kind of catharsis, a purging of emotions and a feeling of satisfaction on the part of the actor, and possibly of other parties involved (Bandes 2020).

In the penal context, closure is associated with punitive methods that bring a sense of finality (in the most obvious sense of the word) to the sentenced individual. One such example is the death penalty, often justified by the need to satisfy emotive vengeance and provide an 'ending' (Kanwar 2001: 217; Berns 2009: 398). Prison sentences can also bring about this kind of violent closure, such as in cases of life sentences without the possibility of parole, which essentially amount to 'death by incarceration' and minimise the opportunity for a dignified death that would allow prisoners a sense of closure with their family or friends (Johnson and McGunigall-Smith 2008: 335; Liebling 2017). But closure does not need to be only punitive and lethal. In this chapter, I suggest that the concept of closure can serve as a theoretical framework for analysing and reimagining parole.

Prison experience, like other human experiences, has a temporal dimension; it has a beginning and an end, and possibly also temporal entrances, pauses, gaps and interruptions, as well as temporally ordered sequences of all kinds (Albert 1984; Armstrong and Weaver 2013). In the context of prison sentences, closure on both the individual and social fronts seems to be especially needed. Imprisonment can go on for years, even a lifetime. This is often a complex, volatile, emotional and highly tense process for the incarcerated individuals, the crime victims and society at large. During this process, the parties involved are often flooded with grief, sorrow and pain, and the fabric of their lives (and their families' lives) is ripped apart (Melnick and Roos 2007: 91). Even more, the penal process is often characterised by indeterminacy, uncertainty and doubt (Crewe 2011); processes of rehabilitation and desistance, when they occur, are also often viewed as lifelong journeys or chronic diseases that are hard to formally bring to an end (Peterson Armour and Umbreit 2006). Even after the formal completion of a sentence, incarcerated individuals are often stigmatised and excluded from employment, educational and social opportunities. Thus, it is likely that the mere legal termination of a sentence (eg serving the full prison term) in and of itself is not enough to allow closure (Albert 1984: 159–60). Parole, however, could in fact serve as a 'concluding experience', signalling the breaking of a cycle of censure, stigma and recidivism and the start of a new, post-prison life (Maruna 2011).

What makes the parole process an appropriate forum for investigating penal closure? First, parole is located in a liminal, spatio-temporal space between prison and community; as such, the parole phase may provide an opportunity to seek a symbolic 'ending' to the penal process, on both the individual and the social front. The parole board members, and the released individuals themselves, often include in their decisions or oral remarks well wishes of 'farewell', 'good luck' or similar such expressions, signalling the sense of an 'ending' (Doxat-Pratt et al 2022).

Second, during criminal trials, the sentenced individuals' voices are seldom meaningfully heard. At sentencing, the courts call the offenders to account for their wrongdoing, censure the sentenced individuals and seek from them an apologetic response, moral reform and reconciliation (Duff 2022). However, at sentencing, the sentenced individuals are usually not emotionally or morally open to receiving and/or responding to the courts' condemnatory messages (Dagan and Zimran 2023; Schinkel 2014). Instead, they often feel resentment, shame and humiliation at the 'degradation ceremony' that takes place at sentencing (Garfinkel 1956). However, the penal process should ideally take place in the context of a dialogue, not a monologue, as Duff (2022) noted: 'Punishment is a two-way process, which seeks an appropriate response from the offender, who has an active role in the process.' Parole can be viewed as a forum during which the punished individuals can offer their responses to the penal call of sentencing, based on their post-sentencing evolution. During parole, incarcerated individuals can show and communicate that they have heard and internalised the penal message. They can show that they are not passive objects of censure, but rather active and responsive moral agents (Duff 2001; Weaver 2009; Smith 2016; Dagan and Roberts 2019; Roberts 2019). They can demonstrate through remorse, apology and other reparative terms how they have internalised the law's authority and their moral wrongdoing; they can show how their 'core self' has not become irrevocably 'stained' despite their crime, and thus the penal dialogue could come to an end (Young and Chimowitz 2022).

To explore the meaning of parole as a kind of penal closure, in the following sections, I will analyse four closure-related elements of an ideal parole process. These closure-related functions are related to the construction of penal time, enabling recognition of prisoners' full status as citizens, allowing prisoners to come to terms with their penal past and reminding all stakeholders of the crime that was committed.

III. THE ELEMENTS OF PAROLE AS PENAL CLOSURE

A. Stopping the Prison Clock

Parole release can promote closure in the simplest sense by stopping the 'clock' of actual prison time served behind bars, marking the end of the person's life as a 'prisoner'. By doing so, parole marks a shift from quantitative to qualitative penal time (Dagan 2022). This temporal shift is inherent to the move from retributive sentencing to rehabilitative/risk parole. Modern retributive sentencing is a fundamentally *quantitative*-duration type of assessment, measured by temporal units of liberty deprivation (eg months, years) (Apt 2016; Kerr 2019; Hanan 2020). In this kind of retributive view, the time of punishment is often conceptualised as static and strict. The severity of the crime is crystallised in the past; no matter how remorseful the incarcerated individual, nothing can change the past (von Hirsch 2017; Roberts 2019). In accordance with this kind of temporal view, there is less need for penal closure, as everything is known at sentencing, and 'by waiting longer one learns nothing new' (von Hirsch and Hanrahan 1979: 29–30).

In contrast, the time of the parole process is more qualitative. This time is expansive, dynamic and fluid. It reflects the ongoing nature of human change, growth and transformation. There is thus an assumption, in accordance with this perspective, that during the punishment period, almost every aspect of an individual's life can be changed, and the punishment should therefore be reassessed according to these ongoing changes.

Moving from a quantitative to a qualitative 'clock' means that prison time can be stopped for several reasons even before the quantitative legal 'clock' of the sentence has officially stopped ticking. For example, early release should be allowed if the 'cup' of penal suffering was fulfilled as a result of an unexpected extra 'penal bite' in prison (eg a terminal medical condition).[2] The most common reason for parole, however, is related to the prisoners' reduced risk or rehabilitative progress. When the prisoner's self has qualitatively improved, the penal clock can be stopped.[3] In other words, serving a prison sentence should not merely be a matter of counting seconds, minutes, hours, days and years, looking passively at the penal hourglass, but more a matter of undergoing a change, transformation and improvement.

The shift of the clock from a quantitative to a qualitative one may also have meaning for the licence and supervision period. This period should reflect a different shift in time, to a qualitative process rather than an attempt to exhaust every moment of penal suffering possible, even though this time is spent in the community. Thus, the licence and supervision period should be used less as a punishment via various 'pains of parole' – such as extensive parole obligations; limitations on family and work; lack of a real possibility to find 'hooks' for developing new identities; and avoiding ongoing stigma and exclusion (Griffin and Healy 2019; McKendy and Ricciardelli 2021) – and more as a time to allow offenders to meaningfully re-enter the community.

In sum, the parole process can signify a stopping of the prison clock, which derives from a quantitative to a quantitative penal time change, and a shift from the crime to the punished individual.

[2] The Canadian Corrections and Conditional Release Act (SC 1992, c 20), s 121(1), for example, allows early release 'for whom continued confinement would constitute an excessive hardship that was not reasonably foreseeable at the time the offender was sentenced'. In drafting the Model Penal Code, the American Law Institute (2017: 544) proposed 'second-look' provisions that would include a judicial-based modification of prison sentences in circumstances of advanced age, physical or mental infirmity, exigent family circumstances or other compelling reasons as, in such cases, continuing imprisonment may be 'unnecessary, counterproductive, or inhumane'. Several systems allow *sentencing* mitigation for such extra harsh prison time. Indiana sentencing law, for example, permits mitigation if 'Imprisonment of the person will result in undue hardship to the person or the dependents of the person' (Ind Code Ann S 35-38-1-7.1(b)(10) (2011)). Some US courts allowed sentencing mitigation due to sexual violence in prison under solitary confinement conditions (*US v Blarek* 7 F Supp 2d 192 (EDNY 1998) or mental health deterioration in prison (*US v Ribot* 97 F Supp 2d 74, 84 (D Mass 1999).

[3] The complex normative relations between sentencing (particularly principles of proportionality, fairness and equality) and parole philosophies are beyond the scope of this chapter (for different normative and legal approaches to these issues, see American Law Institute 2017; Rhine et al 2017).

B. Enabling Recognition of Prisoners' Full Status as Citizens

Closure often involves validation, a renewed sense of belonging and membership, and the sense of a fresh start (Maruna 2011; Hamber and Wilson 2022). Parole can symbolise a formal recognition of the prisoners' reinstated citizenship and the community's trust in them as equal and valuable members of the community. It is an end, but also a beginning. Upon parole, the state signals that the released prisoners can renew the social-moral contract between them and the community and be included in the community's moral and social boundaries. Parole, from this perspective, indicates a fundamental symbolic recognition of the individuals' status change. This status change reflects a process; it is not a one-time act. Thus, parolees are under parole conditions, and are still considered legally to be under the state's custody until the formal end of their sentence (*Greenholtz v Inmates of the Nebraska Penal and Correctional Complex* 442 US 1 (1979)). Some degree of caution is reflected in this status, until the formal completion of their sentence (Dagan and Segev 2015). Viewed in this way, the parole hearing can be seen as a 'welcome home ceremony' that ritualises the 'rite of passage' of re-entry (Maruna 2011: 3). The parole board members reflect the 'conscience of the community', not only the judicial-censuring voice; they bring a wide range of perspectives and inputs – often including a judicial voice – that reflect the idea that the community is able to accept the incarcerated individual back into the community, and communicate a regaining of trust and the values of moral reform.[4]

The symbolic 'reminder' of parole as a reinstated societal status is especially important if prisoners served many years behind bars and possibly internalised their 'prisoner', 'other' or 'outcast' status, or if they were largely forgotten by the community. Looked at in this way, the parole process should act as a destigmatising forum, aiming to reverse the strong social-moral label of sentencing and seeking to nullify the condemnatory 'master status' of a 'permanent prisoner' (Becker 1963; Herbert 2024). Furthermore and relatedly, the parole process can signal to the community, the victims and the prisoners themselves the need to accept that the punishment has come to an end and the reasons the community thinks are relevant for having achieved such an end. Also, parole signals that good prison behaviour, making amends, showing remorse, expressing an apology and many other positive parole factors carry a moral value appreciated by the community, which should be recognised (Bibas 2003: 181). Even more, through parole, the community sends a message that the criminal justice system can work and that the judgement of prisoners is not deterministic: people *can* be rehabilitated, risk *can* be reduced and a return to the community *is* possible.

[4] For example, in Canada, the Corrections and Conditional Release Act 1992, s 105(1) states that 'members appointed to the board shall be sufficiently diverse in their background to be able to collectively represent community values and views in the work of the board'.

C. Allowing Prisoners to Come to Terms with their Past

Arriving at closure often involves identity-making and creating a sense of continuity between the present and the past (Maruna 2011). The parole process allows prisoners to construct their self-narratives of the past, present and future. During this process, often with the assistance of clinical officials, the prisoner can engage in emotional processing to work through the intense feelings of fear, sadness, anger and other emotions that the prisoner directs towards themself and/or towards the penal system.

The parole phase offers a temporally distant arena for incarcerated individuals to process and contextualise their 'penal story'. This process provides incarcerated individuals with the opportunity to look in retrospect at the penal process in a way that reconstructs a narrative ending with hope and optimism instead of despair and pessimism (see Maruna 2011). They can look back at their punishment period as not a complete failure. They can voice their successes in overcoming challenges, in their rehabilitation, education or their sheer survival of the penal experience, constructing and 'editing' their penal narrative and weaving it together with their future (Maruna and Liem 2021). During parole, ideally, prisoners no longer need to so forcefully involve themselves in defending their 'self' through denying their past crime and their moral guilt. Thus, they are possibly more open to reproaching themselves as moral agents, coming to terms with their past crime through remorse, apology and making amends (Crewe et al 2017).

Furthermore, parole narrative-making allows incarcerated individuals to communicate how they have learned to make a 'split' between their past-criminal and future-desisting 'self' and how they do not view themselves only through the lens of their crime. Through this process, they can take moral responsibility for the past, while also recognising the futility of trying to change said past. Such an acknowledgement allows them to express feelings of guilt and regret, but without being morally and psychologically swamped by what they once did, facing their future with self-acceptance (Crewe et al 2017).

The challenge of accomplishing the various elements of parole as closure can be found in the case of repeat offenders. Such offenders do not take their opportunities for penal closure, and thus sceptics may argue that for such prisoners the parole process is less a form of closure and more a stop on the way to the next recall to prison or new term of incarceration. Although no easy answers can be offered here, I would stress that the idea of parole as closure seems important, *especially* for repeat offenders. Such offenders may feel caught in an eternal spin of crime and punishment (eg recidivism motivated by drug addiction or mental health challenges; Matejkowski and Ostermann 2015). They move between the revolving door of prison and parole, feeling 'set up to fail', without really distinguishing between the different times of prison, parole and community that become just one penal experience in different forms (see Armstrong and Weaver 2013; Barry 2021). Marking the closure of one punishment period may send a message to repeat offenders and society that such prisoners are not deterministically locked in their past, and that their criminal lives are not routinised as bureaucratic risk management in prison and in the community (Garland 2001). Instead, every penal period represents an opportunity for stopping the prison clock; for a re-recognition of the offenders' full citizen status; and for offenders to come to terms with their past.

In sum, the parole process allows incarcerated individuals a forum for constructing their narratives and coming to terms with their 'criminal' past before starting their post-prison lives, even (or especially) for repeat offenders.

D. Remembering the Crime

Remembering is a key element of seeking closure and ending, especially in cases of loss and trauma (McEvoy and Conway 2004). The relation between crime, memory and closure is complex and controversial, as these aspects bring up the role that victims and public opinion play in the parole process.[5] Achieving closure can take time, and society, victims and prisoners themselves may need to give themselves time to process their emotions and thoughts in order to reach a sense of resolution (Roberts 2009; Bandes 2020: 112). During parole hearings, victims can give voice to the harm, suffering and loss they have had to endure, reclaiming a sense of recognition and emotional catharsis.[6] Victims, often with the assistance of prosecutors (or other state officials), can perform a 'moral memory' of the crime (Aviram 2020). Victims can engage during the parole process with 'grief work': dealing with loss and bereavement, focusing on memories, working towards a gradual detachment from the deceased and expressing their need to remember the victims (McEvoy and Conway 2004; Caplan 2010). The victims may also achieve a sense of closure in seeing the criminal justice system run its course, with lessons learned and future victims prevented (or at least with a feeling that there was a serious attempt to do so) (Padfield et al 2022: 130). In response, the incarcerated individuals, at a distance now from sentencing censure, can express remorse and apology, and offer reparations to assist victims in achieving such closure (Caplan 2010).

[5] NH Admin Code Rules (2024), para 302.01, for example, allows the parole board to consider 'the existence of adverse public concern or notoriety'. In contrast, several European systems (eg Scotland, Germany) do allow the parole board to consider punitive considerations, openly and less openly. The European Court of Human Rights criticised the use of 'public opinion' as an argument for punitive parole policies, viewed as failing to give weight to the prisoner's responsibility and being vague and inconsistent with the rule of law (*Stafford v UK* [2002] a35 EHRR 32 (28 May 2002)).

[6] For example, a victim impact statement often voices a sense of closure. See, eg *State v Rubio* Court of Appeals, 5th Circuit (2022), where the victim noted: 'I try my best every day not to let what you did get to me, and I remember how strong and brave I am for standing up and saying something after so long. Thank you for contacting me to write this. It's kind of a sense of closure. I really hope this helps in the decision-making process. I did the best I could.'

However, in reality, crime victims who participate in parole hearings have often been gravely harmed by the crime. Such victims may attempt to *counter* exactly such closure. For them, a sense of closure, well-being and solace is achieved through knowing that the prisoner received the maximum sentence allowed by the state (Peterson Armour and Umbreit 2006).

The very possibility of parole, as noted by one US court, may deny victims the sense of an ending, as it was the '*finality*' of the sentence that 'gave the victims' families a sense of closure' (*Commonwealth v Cunningham* 81 A.3d 1, 622 Pa 543 (2013)). For such victims, parole release may communicate a kind of disrespect for the memory of the deceased, a too easy sloughing off of the past and a premature ending to the process, before all the psychological-moral issues have been fully, or even partially, solved. However, the process of closure can work differently on different legal, societal and moral levels. Although attempting to reach closure of the *crime* indeed seems problematic, such problems should not negate the possibility of closure of the *penal process* and the *formal-legal* conflict between the *state and the prisoner*. This process requires the parole board to have sensitivity to the different layers of closure and the that take place in the parole process when communicating with the various stakeholders.

In sum, the parole process may allow crime victims and society at large a forum for remembering and processing the crime and the harm incurred by the crime. However, it may also come into direct conflict with victims' desire to prevent the ending of the penal process – an ending that, for them, signals a forgetting of the crime. These matters require a careful distinction by the parole board between what closure means for the different agents involved in the process, especially the victims, recognising that full synchronisation between closure for all parties is not always possible.

IV. PROMOTING CLOSURE: IMPLICATIONS FOR THE PAROLE PROCESS

So far, I have presented the conceptualisation of parole as a kind of closure for the penal process, as well as the ways in which such closure is manifested. The importance of this conceptualisation, however, is not merely theoretical: it can also serve as an analytical tool for shedding light on several key points in current parole policies. Without exhausting the issue here, I will point to several policy-related areas that would benefit from such an analysis.

Recognising the role of parole as offering a kind of penal closure carries implications for the parole hearing. The parole process should be recognised as a legitimate phase of the penal process that serves important penal and moral values, rather than as a hidden bureaucratic mechanism that focuses merely on prison overcrowding or prison discipline (Medwed 2008). Currently, the work of many parole boards, at least in some systems, is largely hidden, lacks formality, 'remains something of a mystery' and thus does not carry the symbolic meaning of closure. Taking seriously the role of parole as providing closure means the parole board should be public and symbolic, to reflect a 'reverse' process of the public censure of sentencing in the eyes of the community and various stakeholders (Taylor 2012; Bandes 2020).[7]

All of the above seems quite aspirational, given the reality that many parole boards work in accordance with the paradigm of risk-oriented, bureaucratic, actuarial risk management (Feeley and Simon 1992; Barry 2021). Taking seriously the idea of penal closure runs counter to these trends, as it requires an individualised, symbolic and inclusive event of closure rather than a narrow actuarial assessment of risk at parole hearings that often extends to other forms of risk in the community through parole conditions or supervision orders. Such a never-ending focus on risk in prison and in the community – which continues in one form of social governance and control or another – may curtail the very possibility of marking penal process closure.

Relatedly, sentencing courts should recognise the importance of achieving penal closure and the possibility of moving from quantitative to qualitative penal time; in addition, the communicative value of parole should be acknowledged by judges. Sentencing courts should not treat parole as an illegitimate or unjust phase, and they should not try to overcome parole release through artificially aggravating prisoners' sentences. Ideally, sentencing judges might even explain parole and its functions to the sentenced offender as part of the sentencing remarks, signalling to the incarcerated individual the possibility of moral improvement, a reinstated citizen status and a regaining of community trust. Parole decisions themselves, the reasons for these decisions and their effects – very much like the sentencing remarks – should be communicated in 'ordinary language' to the prisoner, along with the positive meaning of these decisions (eg recognition of trust, citizenship, or desistance success) (*cf* Sentencing Act 2020, section 52; Dagan and Zimran 2023). Viewing parole as a form of attaining penal closure requires thinking more carefully about the meaning of parole *denial*. Prisoners denied parole are released back into the community eventually, but without a meaningful opportunity for closure or symbolic recognition of their reinstated citizen status. As such, the closure experience of these incarcerated criminals needs to be taken into consideration by the criminal justice system as well. Possible thinking in this direction might be reframing release mechanisms based on prison conduct or overcrowding (eg 'good-time' credit, 'remission'), signalling at least some elements of closure.

[7] This point raises complex questions: will a public hearing not increase stigma and draw unwarranted attention and stigma to the parolees, preventing their effective return to the community? Should a public hearing also include local community representatives? Should the prisoner (or crime victims) demand a private hearing? These questions should be explored in future studies.

Further, in the event of parole denial, the parole board should explain to the prisoners the reasons for which their paroles were denied; in this way, they might avoid causing these incarcerated individuals further frustration, anger and hurt, having denied them not only release but also an opportunity to achive a meaningful ending (West-Smith et al 2000: 5; Yelderman et al 2022: 2091). However, even for these prisoners, it seems that the very possibility of parole may have, at least for some, a degree of significance in terms of *igniting* the internal process of closure. Although this claim is subject to future empirical assessment, it seems that a system with a meaningful parole phase could project this meaningfulness towards the whole prison experience, requiring incarcerated individuals to construct their narratives in a less pessimistic way and allowing them to more fully internalise the possibility of penal closure.

Finally, parole as penal closure also indicates that the role of the process is ideally to *end* the conflict between the community (and the crime victim/s) and the incarcerated individual. The parole process should not be viewed as a 'second sentencing' – an engagement in adversarial, 'legal combat' between the incarcerated individual and the state's counsel or the parole board members (see Dagan 2023; Aviram 2022). The parole process should not be focused on messaging re-censure for the past crime or for a lack of remorse, as an ongoing punitive relationship between the incarcerated individual and the state that deterministically associates the incarcerated individuals with their crime (Padfield et al 2000). Closure represents the sense of an end, or at least the attempt to achieve such. Thus, the parole board should not be viewed as a place for opening old wounds time and again or reinforcing incarcerated individuals' 'perpetual moral stain' (Herbert 2024). The message conveyed to them should not be that they are unworthy of collective trust or deserving of continued suspicion; rather, it should be one of encouraging their hope, integration, reform and desistance (Pogrebin et al 2015). As closure, the parole board should recognise that parole conditions are not just more punishment in a different guise, but a way to assist re-entry and reintegration until the incarcerated individuals fully regain the board's trust at the end of the formal sentence (Durnescu 2019). The parole release agencies should not treat the parolees as 'always precarious and as responsible for their own reformation', emphasising surveillance, sanctioning perceived misconduct, utilising or threatening to utilise their reimprisonment and messaging their never-ending punishment (Werth 2013).

V. CONCLUSION

In this chapter, I have suggested the importance of recognising the moral function of parole in one domain – that is, recognising its function as closing the dialogue between the community and the incarcerated individual, and possibly other actors (eg crime victims). Parole, *as it should be*, rather than as it is in many systems, can advance a sense of penal closure, given that parole can ideally provide a forum for: (i) stopping the prison 'clock'; (ii) enabling recognition of prisoners' full status as citizens; (iii) allowing prisoners to come to terms with their past; and (iv) reminding all stakeholders of the crime that was committed. Viewing parole as achieving closure means that parole should be more firmly acknowledged as a legitimate part of the penal process, as every beginning has an end and every end has a new beginning. Thus, parole policies should be viewed as achieving symbolic endings instead of reinforcing and extending punitive and condemnatory logic, in a process that is public and positive rather than secretive and punitive. Doing so would also require us to rethink more carefully the meaning of parole denial and the ways in which closure could be promoted, even in such cases, instead of reinforcing censure and exclusion.

Finally, one might argue that conceptualising parole as a kind of closure is over-idealising parole, considering the neo-liberal, under-resourced and punitive reality of parole in many systems. However, parole as it *is* should not prevent us from imagining parole as it *should be*. Future theoretical, legal and empirical research is much needed to explore under what conditions (if any), as well as when and for whom, parole can serve as closure.

REFERENCES

Albert, S (1984) 'The Sense of Closure' in K Gergen and M Gergen (eds), *Historical Social Psychology* (Hillsdale, NJ, Erlbaum) 159–72.

American Law Institute (2017) 'Model Penal Code: Sentencing', proposed final draft.

Annison, H and Guiney, T (2022) 'Populism, Conservatism and the Politics of Parole in England and Wales' 93(3) *The Political Quarterly* 416.

Apt, BL (2016) 'Do We Know How to Punish?' 19(3) *New Criminal Law Review* 43.

Armstrong, S and Weaver, B (2013) 'Persistent Punishment: User Views of Short Prison Sentences' 52(3) *Howard Journal of Criminal Justice* 285.

Aviram, H (2020) *Yesterday's Monsters: The Manson Family Cases and the Illusion of Parole* (Oakland, CA, University of California Press).

Barry, M (2021) 'Walking on Ice': The Future of Parole in a Risk-Obsessed Society' 25(2) *Theoretical Criminology* 325.

Bandes, SA (2020) 'Closure in the Criminal Courtroom: The Birth and Strange Career of an Emotion' in SA Bandes, JL Madeira, KD Temple and E Kidd White (eds), *Research Handbook on Law and Emotion* (Cheltenham, Edward Elgar Publishing) 102–18.

Becker, H (1963) *Outsiders: Studies in the Sociology of Deviance* (New York, Free Press).

Berns, N (2009) 'Contesting the Victim Card: Closure, Discourse and Emotion in Death Penalty Rhetoric' 50(3) *Sociological Quarterly* 383.

Bibas, S (2003) 'Using Plea Procedures to Combat Denial and Minimization' in B Winick and D Wexler (eds), *Judging in a Therapeutic Key: Therapeutic Jurisprudence and the Courts* (Durham, NC, Carolina Academic Press) 169–76.

Caplan, JM (2010) 'Parole Release Decisions: Impact of Victim Input on a Representative Sample of Inmates' 38(3) *Journal of Criminal Justice* 291.

Crewe, B (2011) 'Depth, Weight, Tightness: Revisiting the Pains of Imprisonment' 13(5) *Punishment & Society* 509.

Crewe, B, Hulley, S and Wright, S (2017) 'Swimming with the Tide: Adapting to Long-Term Imprisonment' 34(3) *Justice Quarterly* 517.

Dagan, N (2022) 'Overcoming Penal Boundaries: Exploring the Evolution of Retributive Time Through Parole Decision-Making' 62(1) *British Journal of Criminology* 37.

—— (2023) 'Parole as Resentencing: Exploring the Punitive Accounts of Parole Decision-Making Through the Comparative Case Study of Israel' 20(4) *European Journal of Criminology* 1231.

Dagan, N and Roberts, JV (2019) 'Retributivism, Penal Censure, and Life Imprisonment without Parole' 38(1) *Criminal Justice Ethics* 1.

Dagan, N and Segev, D (2015) 'Retributive Whisper: Communicative Elements in Parole' 40(3) *Law & Social Inquiry* 611.

Dagan, N and Zimran, A (2023) 'Punishment as Text' 25(5) *Punishment & Society* 1293.

Doxat-Pratt, S, Schliehe, A and Laursen, J (2022) '"Thank You for Having Me": The Experiences and Meanings of Release from Prison in Norway and England, and Wales' 3(2) *Incarceration* 1.

Duff, RA (2001) *Punishment, Communication, and Community* (Oxford, Oxford University Press).

—— (2022) 'Punishment as Communication' in J Ryberg (ed), *Oxford Handbook of Punishment Theory and Philosophy* (Oxford, Oxford University Press).

Durnescu, I (2019) 'Pains of Reentry Revisited' 63(8) *International Journal of Offender Therapy & Comparative Criminology* 1482.

Fitzgerald, R, Freiberg, A, Dodd, S and Bartels, L (2023) *Parole on Probation: Parole Decision-Making, Public Opinion and Public Confidence* (Palgrave Macmillan).

Feeley, M and Simon, J (1992) 'The New Penology: Notes on the Emerging Strategy of Corrections and Its Implications' 30 *Criminology* 449.

Garfinkel, H (1956) 'Conditions of Successful Degradation Ceremonies' 61(5) *American Journal of Sociology* 420.

Garland, D (2001) *The Culture of Control: Crime and Social Order in Contemporary Society* (Chicago, IL, University of Chicago Press).

Griffin, D and Healy, D (2019) 'The Pains of Parole for Life Sentence Prisoners in Ireland: Risk, Rehabilitation and Re-entry' 11(3) *European Journal of Probation* 124.

Habermas, T and Berger, N (2011) 'Retelling Everyday Emotional Events: Condensation, Distancing, and Closure' 25(2) *Cognition & Emotion* 206.

Hamber, B and Wilson, R A (2002) 'Symbolic Closure through Memory, Reparation and Revenge in Post-Conflict Societies' 1(1) *Journal of Human Rights* 35.

Hanan, ME (2020) 'Invisible Prisons'54(2) *UC Davis Law Review* 1185.

Herbert, S (2024) 'Degradation or Redemption? A Parole Board Polices a Moral Boundary' 49(1) *Law & Social Inquiry* 308.

Johnson, R and McGunigall-Smith, S (2008) 'Life Without Parole, America's Other Death Penalty: Notes on Life under Sentence of Death by Incarceration' 88(2) *The Prison Journal* 328.

Kanwar, V (2001) 'Capital Punishment as Closure: The Limits of a Victim-Centered Jurisprudence' 27 *New York University Review of Law & Social Change* 215.

Kerr, L (2019) 'How the Prison Is a Black Box in Punishment Theory' 69(1) *University of Toronto Law Journal* 85.

Liebling, A (2017) 'The Meaning of Ending Life in Prison' 23(1) *Journal of Correctional Health Care* 20.

Matejkowski, J and Ostermann, M (2015) 'Serious Mental Illness, Criminal Risk, Parole Supervision, and Recidivism: Testing of Conditional Effects' 39(1) *Law & Human Behavior* 75 https://doi.org/10.1037/lhb0000094.

Maruna, S (2011) 'Reentry as a Rite of Passage' 13(1) *Punishment & Society* 3.

Maruna, S and Liem, M (2021) 'Where Is this Story Going? A Critical Analysis of the Emerging Field of Narrative Criminology' 4(1) *Annual Review of Criminology* 125.

McKendy, L and Ricciardelli, R (2021) 'The Pains of Release: Federally-Sentenced Women's Experiences on Parole' 13(1) *European Journal of Probation* 1.

McEvoy, K and Conway, H (2004) 'The Dead, the Law, and the Politics of the Past' 31(4) *Journal of Law & Society* 539.

Medwed, DS (2008) 'The Innocent Prisoner's Dilemma: Consequences of Failing to Admit Guilt at Parole Hearings' 93 *Iowa Law Review* 491.

Melnick, J and Roos, S (2007) 'The Myth of Closure' 11(2) *Gestalt Review* 90.

Orlando, MS and Farrington, DP (2023) 'Desistance from Crime of Young Offenders in Argentina: A Qualitative Study' 3(2) *International Criminology* 116.

Padfield, N, Liebling, A and Arnold, H (2000) *An Exploration of Decision-Making at Discretionary Lifer Panels* (London, Home Office).

Padfield, N, Annison, HMJ, Calvert-Smith, D et al (2022) *A Parole System Fit for Purpose* (JUSTICE).

Penikett, J, Daly, C and Milton, E (2019) 'A Study of Mentors in Wales "Coming to Closure"' 45(3) *Professional Development in Education* 405.

Peterson Armour, M and Umbreit, MS (2006) 'Exploring "Closure" and the Ultimate Penal Sanction for Survivors of Homicide Victims' 19(2) *Federal Sentencing Reporter* 105.

Pogrebin, MR, Stretesky, PB, Walker, A and Opsal, T (2015) 'Rejection, Humiliation, and Parole: A Study of Parolees' Perspectives' 38(3) *Symbolic Interaction* 413.

Reitz, K (2012) 'The "Traditional" Indeterminate Sentencing Model' in J Petersilia and K Reitz (eds), *The Oxford Handbook of Sentencing and Corrections* (Oxford, Oxford University Press) 270–98.

Rhine, EE, Petersilia, J and Reitz, KR (2017) 'The Future of Parole Release' 46(1) *Crime and Justice* 279.

Roberts, JV (2009) 'Listening to the Crime Victim: Evaluating Victim Input at Sentencing and Parole' 38(1) *Crime & Justice* 347.

—— (2019) 'The Time of Punishment: Proportionality and the Sentencing of Historical Crimes' in M Tonry (ed), *Of One-Eyed and Toothless Miscreants: Making the Punishment Fit the Crime?* (Oxford, Oxford University Press) 149.

Schinkel, M (2014) 'Punishment as Moral Communication: The Experiences of Long-Term Prisoners' 16(5) *Punishment & Society* 578.

Singer, RG (1979) *Just Deserts: Sentencing based on Equality and Desert* (Cambridge, MA, Ballinger).

Smith, N (2016) 'Dialectical Retributivism: Why Apologetic Offenders Deserve Reductions in Punishment Even Under Retributive Theories' 44(2) *Philosophia* 343.

Strupp, H and Binder, JL (1984) *Psychotherapy in A New Key: A Guide to Time-Limited Dynamic Psychotherapy* (New York, Basic Books).

Taylor, CJ (2012) 'Balancing Act: The Adaptation of Traditional Judicial Roles in Reentry Court' 51(6) *Journal of Offender Rehabilitation* 351.

von Hirsch, A (2017) *Deserved Criminal Sanctions* (Oxford, Hart Publishing).

von Hirsch, A and Hanrahan, KJ (1979) *The Question of Parole – Retention, Reform and Abolition?* (Cambridge, MA, Ballinger).

Weaver, B (2009) 'Communicative Punishment as a Penal Approach to Supporting Desistance' 13(1) *Theoretical Criminology* 9.
Webster, DM and Kruglanski, AW (1994) 'Individual Differences in Need for Cognitive Closure' 67(6) *Journal of Personality & Social Psychology* 1049.
Werth, R (2013) 'The Construction and Stewardship of Responsible yet Precarious Subjects: Punitive Ideology, Rehabilitation, and "Tough Love" among Parole Personnel' 15(3) *Punishment & Society* 219.
West-Smith, M, Pogrebin, MR and Poole, ED (2000) 'Denial of Parole: An Inmate Perspective' 64 *Federal Probation*.
Yelderman, LA, Estrada-Reynolds, V and Lawrence, T I (2022) 'Release or Denial: Evaluating the Roles of Emotion and Risk in Parole Decisions' 125(4) *Psychological Reports* 2088.
Young, KM and Chimowitz, H (2022) 'How Parole Boards Judge Remorse: Relational Legal Consciousness and the Reproduction of Carceral Logic' 56(2) *Law & Society Review* 237.

Part II

Institutions

7

Parole for Life-Sentenced Prisoners in the New South Africa: Promise and Performance

DIRK VAN ZYL SMIT

I. INTRODUCTION

A. A Hard Case

ON 7 DECEMBER 2022, JANUSZ Walus, a 70-year-old Polish immigrant and right-wing extremist, was released on parole, having been in prison for 29 years on a life sentence.[1] The sentence flowed from Walus's conviction for murder in 1993 for assassinating Chris Hani, the leader of the South African Communist Party (SACP) and trusted lieutenant of Nelson Mandela, then leader of the African National Congress (ANC), the largest liberation movement in South Africa (Malala 2023). At his trial in October 1993, Walus had been sentenced to death, a sentence that was promptly upheld by the Appellate Division of the Supreme Court. Both trial and appellate courts stressed that this was a cold-blooded and premeditated murder undertaken to silence someone with whose political views Walus and his co-accused disagreed. They emphasised that the murder could have dramatic political consequences for the future of South Africa.[2]

In 2000, however, following the ruling in 1995 by the then newly established Constitutional Court that capital punishment was unconstitutional,[3] Walus's sentence was changed to one of life imprisonment.[4] At that time, the minimum term to be served before parole eligibility on a life sentence was unclear. By 2007 at the latest, however, it was clear that Walus had served the minimum period

[1] 'Janusz Walus: Killer of South African Anti-apartheid Hero Chris Hani Freed' www.bbc.co.uk/news/world-africa-63887332.

[2] *S v Walus* [1994] ZASCA 189.

[3] *S v Makwanyane and Another* 1995 (3) SA 391 (CC).

[4] *S v Walus and Another* 2000 JDR 0761 (SCA).

to qualify for consideration for release. Nevertheless, in subsequent years, his release, although recommended by parole boards and supported by the National Council on Correctional Services, was turned down four times for a range of inconsistent reasons by various Ministers of Justice.

Finally, on 21 November 2022, South Africa's apex court, the Constitutional Court, held unanimously, in a judgment written by Chief Justice Zondo, that the most recent decision by the Minister of Justice to refuse Walus's release was 'irrational'.[5] The Court did not refer the matter back to the Minister, but instructed him to release Walus on parole within 10 days. After a slight delay, caused by Walus being attacked by another prisoner, he was released on 7 December 2022.

Public opposition to the decision was loud. Given the high political profile of the victim, this was to be expected. Much of the opposition to Walus's release was led by Hani's revered widow, the ANC politician Limpho Hani, who had played an active role in ensuring that her husband's murderers remained in prison for as long as possible. Both Mrs Hani and the SACP had been parties in Walus's case before the Constitutional Court. They did not hold back in their public pronouncements. Both bitterly attacked the Court and denied its legitimacy. Mrs Hani saw the case as a vindication of critics of the Court, who had been arguing that it was 'anti-black'.[6] She was supported by SACP general secretary Solly Mapaila, who opined that 'Justice has given birth to injustice'.[7]

Other political parties took up the cause in a theatrical way that did not consider the complex questions raised by deciding whether, and if so when, to release life-sentenced prisoners on parole. The radical Economic Freedom Fighters decried the decision as 'callous, insensitive and regressive', and called for protests against the Court and Chief Justice Zondo.[8] It instigated public demonstrations that led to the blocking of the major highway outside the Court.[9] Even the governing ANC joined in the protest, with several of its Members of Parliament demonstrating outside Parliament in Cape Town, and demanding that the law be amended to prevent release on parole of people who had committed particularly heinous crimes.[10]

[5] *Walus v Minister of Justice and Correctional Services and Others* (CCT 221/21) [2022]), para 82.

[6] Eyewitness News video at https://www.youtube.com/watch?v=TcqMUSzFirw&t=3s.

[7] '"Karma will deal with them all" – Hani's widow furious with judges after Walus given parole' www.citizen.co.za/news/south-africa/hanis-widow-furious-with-judges/.

[8] '"Insensitive and Regressive" – EFF Rejects Chris Hani Killer's Parole, Calls for Rescission' *Times Live* www.timeslive.co.za/news/south-africa/2022-11-22-insensitive-and-regressive-eff-rejects-chris-hani-killers-parole-calls-for-rescission/.

[9] 'EFF Shuts Down N1 in Protest Against Walus' Release' *Newzroom Africa* www.youtube.com/watch?v=Hby-3Sqzu8A.

[10] 'ANC in Parly Calls for Justice System Review Following Walus Parole' ewn.co.za/2022/12/01/anc-in-parly-calls-for-justice-system-review-following-walus-parole. The ANC premier of Gauteng, South Africa's largest province where the Constitutional Court is situated, declared that the ANC was deeply betrayed by the decision: 'Panyaza Lesufi Unhappy with ConCourt's Decision on Janusz Walus' www.youtube.com/watch?v=Uhj8p3nrKcQ.

In some media, the attacks on the Constitutional Court decision on Walus's release were linked to the even more controversial matter of the Supreme Court of Appeal reversing the release from prison of ex-President Zuma on medical parole from a (relatively short, fixed-term) prison sentence for contempt of court imposed on him by the same Constitutional Court.[11] These linked attacks questioned the legitimacy of the Court and the Chief Justice. As the *Cape Times* put it:

> While Janusz Walus, the killer of one of the country's most prominent freedom fighters, was set free on parole by Chief Justice Zondo, Chris Hani's comrade [ex-President] Jacob Zuma was faced with the prospect of returning to finish his prison sentence in a case emanating from defying [Chief Justice] Zondo.[12]

On the other hand, the supporters of constitutional democracy rallied to defend the Constitutional Court. At times, however, they too did not address the difficult issues relating to the release on parole of life-sentenced prisoners. The General Council of the Bar, for example, called on South Africans to respect the rule of law amid the outcry over the ruling to free Walus, but it did not address the complexities of the case.[13] Two major online news outlets, the *Daily Maverick*[14] and *News 24*,[15] did carry opinion pieces offering support for the difficult decision that the Constitutional Court had made in ordering a release that they regarded as inherently just. Their more subtle responses were the exception, however.

B. Overview

The disputes around Walus's release are discussed below because they illustrate many factors that have contributed to South Africa having to face the most rapid growth in numbers of life-sentenced prisoners in the world (van Zyl Smit and

[11] 'South African Court Rules Former President Zuma's Medical Parole Unlawful' www.voanews.com/a/south-african-court-rules-former-president-zuma-s-medical-parole-unlawful-/6843455.html.

[12] 'Zondo Frees Chris Hani Killer Janusz Walus' www.iol.co.za/capetimes/news/zondo-frees-chris-hani-killer-janusz-walus-c6b45d61-f7a6-43e8-9a97-485500984a71.

[13] "General Council of The Bar Calls on South Africans to Respect the Rule of Law amid Outcry over Ruling to Free Hani killer Janusz Walus on Parole' www.iol.co.za/news/south-africa/gauteng/general-council-of-the-bar-calls-on-south-africans-to-respect-rule-of-law-amid-outcry-over-ruling-to-free-hani-killer-janusz-walus-on-parole-193110c9-976a-48e9-9c23-bca55ca031e0.

[14] 'Much as We May Hate It, the Decision to Release Janusz Walus Was Morally and Legally Correct' www.dailymaverick.co.za/opinionista/2022-12-11-much-as-we-may-hate-it-the-decision-to-release-janusz-walus-was-morally-and-legally-correct/; 'What Janisz Walus Did Was Heinous, but Vilifying the Chief Justice and the Constitutional Court Was Wrong' www.dailymaverick.co.za/opinionista/2022-11-28-janusz-walus-parole-vilifying-chief-justice-concourt-is-wrong/.

[15] 'Walus Parole – Politicians Agreed to Laws, so Why Attack the Judiciary?' www.news24.com/news24/opinions/columnists/guestcolumn/opinion-nkanyiso-ngqulunga-walus-parole-politicians-agreed-to-laws-so-why-attack-judiciary-20221201.

Appleton 2019). In these circumstances, if, when and how life-sentenced prisoners will be released has become the most intractable challenge facing parole in South Africa. This chapter argues that these challenges have arisen notwithstanding the idealism that accompanied the transition to majority rule, a new constitutional order designed to protect human rights and a judiciary dedicated to ensuring that justice is done in individual cases.

The chapter first highlights the almost casual way in which the release of life-sentenced prisoners was dealt with before 1990, when it was left to the almost unfettered discretion of the executive. It then considers the post-1990 transition to democratic rule. During this period, it became clear that life sentences would gradually replace the death penalty, and there were moves towards developing a more sophisticated parole system encompassing changed procedures for the release of life-sentenced prisoners.

The chapter then addresses the window of opportunity for prison reform that arose in the years immediately after 1994 with the advent of the new constitutional political order in South Africa. This period began with major riots by prisoners who rebelled against the existing release procedures. The response was fundamental prison law reform, which included overhauling the parole system, with some innovative ideas on when and how to release life-sentenced prisoners.

The chapter goes on to describe, and provide explanations for, the massive growth in the number of prisoners serving life sentences at around the same time as the new legislation dealing with their release became law. This leads to a description of the difficulties of implementing release procedures for life-sentenced prisoners during the long transitional period as the legal reforms were put into practice.

The focus then shifts back to the response of the courts to the inadequate release process, which was to interpret the transitional provisions in the new legislation in ways that fully recognised the liberty interests of life-sentenced prisoners and allowed their release to be considered positively at the first possible opportunity.

Finally, the chapter reflects on the wider shortcomings of the release system, which the courts have been unable to address. It concludes that a failure of ideas, compounded by administrative shortcomings, is largely responsible for the loss of legitimacy of the South African parole system for life-sentenced prisoners. These failures must be understood against the background of the wider challenges of dealing with serious crime in a period of massive political and social transition.

II. LIFE IMPRISONMENT BEFORE 1990

Historically, life imprisonment in South Africa was very rarely imposed directly. The sentence of death served as the ultimate penalty, and the majority of life terms were the result of the commutation of a death sentence. As in the UK, commutation happened almost routinely. Judges who imposed capital punishment in a particular case could write to the Governor General, and latterly to the Minister of Justice, suggesting commutation and sometimes also consideration of release after a specific number of years (Turrell 2004). The power of the Minister to order release of life-sentenced prisoners was largely unfettered. Little or no publicity was given to such releases, which were decided by the Minister of Justice (van Zyl Smit 1992).

Of course, there were exceptions. Directly imposed life sentences were recorded as early as 1907, and a small trickle of such sentences continued for the first nine decades of the twentieth century (Mujuzi 2008). A few of these life sentences did receive some publicity. Nelson Mandela famously was sentenced not to death but to life imprisonmen,t and served 27 years in prison before being released unconditionally.[16] It is noteworthy that the trajectory of political prisoners was different to that of 'ordinary' prisoners. Most were released as part of the amnesty process, which in many instances preceded the negotiated settlement that finally led to a new constitutional order in South Africa in 1994 or by further amnesties granted by the Truth and Reconciliation Commission (Bhargava 2002; du Bois-Pedain 2007). It is notable that Walus, as well as other life-sentenced prisoners whose release on parole was to become controversial, had their applications for amnesty denied by the Truth and Reconciliation Commission on the grounds that they did not meet the requirement of having been political offenders acting on superior orders.[17]

For the release of 'ordinary' life-sentenced prisoners, however, until 1990, the Prisons Act simply provided that the government minister responsible for prisons could order their release on parole following a report from a prison board.[18] Nothing was said of a minimum period in the primary or secondary legislation, but the Prison Standing Orders, internal instructions of the lowest legislative status, provided that such reports should be submitted to the minister after a minimum period of detention of 10 years. This minimum period could be increased administratively, however, after escapes or if the life-sentenced prisoner committed a disciplinary offence. It could also be reduced by amnesties or special remission (van Zyl Smit 1992). Informally, it appears that from 1991 to 1994 the minimum period was effectively 15 years, unless there were unusual circumstances, which brought it closer to 10 years.

[16] www.nelsonmandela.org/news/entry/nelson-mandela-sentenced-to-life-imprisonment-44-years-ago.

[17] https://sabctrc.saha.org.za/reports/volume6/section1/chapter4/subsection6.htm; Malala (2023: 223–26). du Bois-Pedain (2007: 58, 91) notes that the requirement of superior orders was not followed as strictly in several other cases. In Walus's case, the denial of amnesty was also based on doubts about whether he had made a full disclosure.

[18] See s 64 of the 1959 Prisons Act, which in 1991 was amended and renamed the 1959 Correctional Services Act.

III. LIFE IMPRISONMENT IN THE RUN UP TO DEMOCRATIC RULE

In President FW de Klerk's speech of 2 February 1990 (which foresaw the release of Nelson Mandela and the negotiations that would lead to South Africa becoming a constitutional democracy), the issue of capital punishment featured prominently, and a moratorium on its implementation was announced.[19] The speech was followed by the 1990 Criminal Law Amendment Act, which removed the presumption in favour of the death penalty for murder, thus increasing the direct imposition of life imprisonment (Mujuzi 2008). Walus was nevertheless sentenced to death during the period that this Act was in force as significant aggravating circumstances were found to apply in that case.

The 1990 Criminal Law Amendment Act also limited the power of the Minister of Justice to release life-sentenced prisoners and introduced a much more complicated release process. The initiative for releasing someone sentenced to life imprisonment had to come from the Minister who, in the first instance, had requested a new arm's-length body, the Advisory Release Board (subsequently renamed the National Advisory Council on Correctional Services and, after 1998, the National Council on Correctional Services) to advise him on a specific prisoner. Only if the Advisory Release Board, having considered a report from a parole board,[20] recommended the release could the Minister authorise the release of a life-sentenced prisoner, either unconditionally or on parole.

In 1993, credits that allowed earlier release for good behaviour were added to the mix by legislative amendment.[21] The assessment of good behaviour credits, however, gave wide discretion to prison officers. An additional policy change in 1994 made 20 years the minimum period before consideration of release from a life sentence, but this period could be reduced by granting credits and other forms of sentence reduction.[22]

IV. LIFE IMPRISONMENT LAW REFORM IN THE NEW SOUTH AFRICA

Shortly after the first democratically elected government came into power in April 1994, there were major prison riots, resulting in several deaths (Pete 1998). A subsequent judicial inquiry, the Kriegler Commission (1995), found that the root cause of the dissatisfaction was that prisoners believed that they would be granted amnesties when the first democratically elected president

[19] www.gov.za/address-state-president-mr-fw-de-klerk-dms-opening-second-session-ninth-parliament-republic-south-0. See also Phillips 1991.

[20] Called the Release Board, another new body in the Prisons Service added by the 1990 Act.

[21] By s 22A, which was added to 1959 Correctional Services by the 1993 Correctional Services Amendment Act.

[22] Moses (2012: 61) quotes the relevant Correctional Services B Order in this regard.

was inaugurated. Instead, they were faced with a complex and ill-understood system of credits, which they believed was designed to keep them in prison. The release system faced a fundamental crisis of legitimacy, and the Commission recommended that it be overhauled completely. At that stage, the Minister of Justice had already asked the National Advisory Council to begin work on comprehensive new prison legislation that would complement the constitutional principles of the new South Africa, and to give priority to legislation on release.

The prospect of developing a major new piece of legislation offered an opportunity for fundamental reform, and the drafting subcommittee of the National Advisory Council, which comprised the Chair of the Council, Judge MM Kumleben, Mr DJ Rossouw and me, paid much attention to considering what a release system would have to encompass to meet the standards of the new Constitution.

In an essay for a Festschrift for the retiring Chief Justice, MM Corbett, I had set out a comparative picture of what I considered best constitutional practice on life sentences worldwide at the time (van Zyl Smit 1995). I shared my ideas with the drafting committee, and argued that the system then current would fail to pass constitutional muster as it left too much power with the executive. Such power, a court in neighbouring Namibia had recently held, could render life imprisonment an unconstitutional form of punishment akin to the death penalty. I concluded that life imprisonment could be constitutional, but only if, following the German model as the Supreme Court of Namibia had done, there was a proper judicial process governing release after a minimum period that had been determined clearly in advance.

There was also an interesting South African precedent for some of these ideas. In 1993, the Criminal Procedure Act had been amended to enable courts to declare convicted persons to be 'dangerous criminals' if they represented a danger to the physical or mental well-being of other persons and the community should be protected against them.[23] With minor amendments, this provision for 'dangerous criminals' remains in force. Once a court has made such a declaration, it must sentence them to an indefinite term and set an individualised fixed period after which they must be returned to the same court to determine whether they are still 'dangerous' (Moses 2012; Hamman et al 2019).

In the new release legislation, which became the 1997 Parole and Correctional Supervision Amendment Act, the drafting committee and ultimately Parliament accepted the idea that, as a matter of constitutional principle, persons sentenced to life imprisonment who had served a minimum period should have their release on parole determined by the sentencing court. This was intended to be

[23] ss 286A and 286B of the 1977 Criminal Procedure Act, inserted by s 21 of the 1993 Criminal Matters Amendment Act. *S v Bashford* 2015 ZAGPPHC 146 (13 March 2015), paras 1–2.

a radical break with the past. Mrs Hani, who at that stage was the Chair of the Parliamentary Portfolio (select) Committee on Correctional Services, argued that having release decisions for life-sentenced prisoners determined by courts 'increases public accountability, as courts are more open and transparent than parole boards'.[24]

The minimum period that had to be served before life-sentenced prisoners could be considered for release proved to be highly controversial. While there was agreement that the uncertainty about the length of this period should be avoided and dealt with in primary legislation, there were disputes about how long it should be. The majority of the drafting committee did not support the idea that the minimum period should be flexible and, as with 'dangerous criminals', determined individually by the sentencing court. Instead, the majority preferred a single minimum period prescribed by primary legislation. Initially, the drafting committee favoured a 15-year minimum, based on the German model, both as a matter of principle and because it would allow for an easy transition for the system that until recently had routinely considered release after this period. However, the National Advisory Council supported a 20-year period – an early sign of a more punitive approach. When the matter reached the Portfolio Committee, Mrs Hani made it quite clear that she and the ANC, the majority party in Parliament, would be satisfied with no less than a minimum of 25 years. Only for prisoners who had reached the age of 65 were they prepared to reduce the minimum period to 15 years. At the second reading debate on the Parole and Correctional Supervision Amendment Bill in Parliament, the Minister of Justice emphasised proudly that 'with this 25 year minimum in primary legislation for the first time … we now know what we mean by life imprisonment'.[25] Mrs Hani added that, since the minimum period had been increased to 25 years, 'no prisoner serving a sentence of life imprisonment will be eligible for parole until a substantial portion of the sentence is completed'.[26]

The new legislation also did away with the credit system, which the Minister branded as discriminatory.[27] It did not spell out, however, how this would affect the minimum periods that existing life-sentenced prisoners would have to serve.

The composition and functions of parole boards were also changed. Instead of consisting exclusively of officials of the Department of Correctional Services, they were to have independent chairs, as well as some lay members and representatives from government departments other than Correctional Services. These new parole boards were to decide the release of prisoners serving fixed-term

[24] Second Reading of the Parole and Correctional Supervision Amendment Bill: *Hansard*, House of Assembly Debates 27 October 1997, col 5515.
[25] ibid col 5515.
[26] ibid col 5513.
[27] ibid.

sentences of more than two years, but in the case of life-sentenced prisoners they were only to feed information to the courts, which, according to the new Act, would decide on their release.

The 1997 Parole and Correctional Supervision Amendment Act 1997 was never put into effect. Instead, it was incorporated unchanged into the omnibus 1998 Correctional Services Act 1998, which, with some significant amendments, still governs parole for life-sentenced prisoners in South Africa today. The broader 1998 Act added further context to the new release provisions, spelling out clearly in section 36 that 'the implementation of a sentence of imprisonment has the objective of enabling the sentenced prisoner to lead a socially responsible and crime-free life in the future'.

V. THE GROWTH IN LIFE IMPRISONMENT NUMBERS

The bringing into effect of the 1998 Correctional Services Act proved to be highly challenging. Key provisions pertaining to parole boards and release from life imprisonment were delayed until 2004.[28] In the meantime, the number of life-sentenced prisoners grew apace, from 520, or 0.6 per cent of the sentenced prison population in 1994, to 17,173 or 18.5 per cent of the sentenced prison population in 2021.[29]

There are two primary reasons for this extraordinary increase. First, with the abolition of the death penalty, persons sentenced to death had their sentences converted to a life sentence (Mujuzi 2008).

Secondly, in 1997, mandatory life sentences were no longer limited to murder, but were also applied to other crimes such as rape.[30] The impact of the change was amplified by extending the jurisdiction of middle-level courts: regional magistrates could now impose life sentences, which hitherto could be done only by the High Court. Notwithstanding harsh criticism of the new mandatory sentencing regime (O'Donovan and Redpath 2006; Muntingh 2009), the 'temporary' measure was first prolonged and eventually became permanent.[31]

Mandatory life sentences became a subject of public debate, with successive Judicial Inspectors of Correctional Services pointing out the flaws and negative impact of the increased number of persons serving life sentences on both the overall prison population and the ability of the correctional system to consider their release adequately and in a timely manner.[32] This public debate led only

[28] s 138 provided that different sections of the Act could be brought into force at different times.

[29] Figures provided by Department of Correctional Services 25 April 2023. On file with the author.

[30] s 51 of the 1997 Criminal Law Amendment Act.

[31] 2007 Criminal Law (Sentencing) Amendment Act.

[32] Fagan (2004); Cameron (2017); '"Minimum Prison Sentences Must Go" Says Constitutional Court Judge' www.groundup.org.za/article/minimum-prison-sentences-must-go-says-constitutional-court-judge/#:~:text=Constitutional%20Court%20Judge%20Edwin%20Cameron,abbreviated%20version%20of%20his%20speech; Cameron 2020.

to some minor modifications in the scope of the application of the mandatory sentencing regime. The result has been that South Africa uses its ultimate penalty, life imprisonment, far more freely than it did when the sentence of death was the most severe punishment on offer. The pressures that these large and growing numbers of life-sentenced prisoners have put on the release system are severe.

VI. IMPLEMENTING THE NEW RELEASE PROCESS

A. Further Legislation

One response to implementation difficulties, perceived and real, was to amend the new 1998 Correctional Services Act even *before* it had been put into effect. Given the drastic changes that had been made, the first question was whether it would apply retroactively to persons sentenced to life admitted to prison prior to the 1998 Act coming into effect. Section 136 of the Act set out the initial transitional provisions. It provided simply that a person serving a sentence immediately before the commencement of the new Act would be subject to the provisions of the old 1959 Act relating to parole, empowering the Minister of Justice to make regulations to achieve a uniform policy in this regard. However, by 2001, before the new Act had come into force, a new section 136(3) was added, mandating that any prisoner serving a life sentence immediately before the commencement of the new release provisions would have to serve 20 years before being considered for release. This change was designed to reflect the release policy that had applied since 1994, and it remained in effect until the new 25-year minimum came into force.

A more drastic amendment came in 2008. It overturned a further piece of the new release procedure that has not yet come into force, namely that the release of life-sentenced prisoners was to be decided by the court that imposed them. The effect of this amendment has been to ensure that the National Council continues to consider recommendations of a parole board on the release of life-sentenced prisoners. The National Council may recommend that the Minister release such a person on parole, and the Minister then decides whether to do so and what parole conditions to set.[33]

B. The Crisis of Ideas

By the time the 2008 amendments were being debated, it should have been apparent to the government that the existing scheme for deciding the release

[33] s 78(1) of the 1998 Correctional Services Act, as substituted by s 54 of the 2008 Correctional Services Amendment Act.

of life-sentenced prisoners was problematic. The number of life-sentenced prisoners had already increased from the 520 inherited by the first democratic government in 1994 to approximately 7000 in 2007. However, in the debates of 2007 and 2008, on amending the release process, factors such as efficacy or the best form of release that would best reflect the new constitutional order were not considered.

The idealism expressed when the reforming legislation was adopted in 1998, through the idea that courts, with their additional legitimacy (and possibly also efficiency), would take these decisions, was largely forgotten. Instead, the Minister, who already had the final say on the release of life-sentenced prisoners in 'transitional' cases, chose to extend his powers to cover future cases. His dominant idea appears to have been to stress how tough the authorities would be with life-sentenced prisoners. This would be reflected in treating them harshly by placing those who refused to cooperate in what was effectively solitary confinement, and by ministers being parsimonious in using their powers of release.

When the 2008 amendments were first considered by the Parliamentary Portfolio Committee on Correctional Services, members of the Committee cautiously raised concerns about removing the power of judges to make final release decisions in the future.[34] However, these concerns were firmly brushed aside by the Department of Correctional Services, which provided a fig leaf of legal cover for the changes by referring repeatedly to a decision of the Supreme Court of Appeal, *S v Botha*.[35] In that case, the Court had held that on matters regarding the implementation of punishment, including release on parole, the executive was to decide. The decision had not been made in the context of life imprisonment, however. Instead, it had been designed to discourage courts, when imposing determinate sentences of imprisonment, from making additional orders that could distort parity in the sentencing structure by specifying what part of the sentence offenders would have to serve in prison and what part on parole.

Parliamentarians of all political parties, encouraged by the Department of Correctional Services, set aside their prior recognition that indeterminate sentences applied to both 'dangerous criminals' and life prisoners are different in that they do not guarantee release. In 1993, Parliament had mandated that *courts* decide whether or not to release 'dangerous criminals' serving indeterminate sentences. In 1998, the same protection had been written into the law prospectively governing the release of life-sentenced prisoners. Ten years later, in 2008, however, Parliament overlooked the need for the protection of a judicial process to ensure fairness in the decision-making process for release of life-sentenced prisoners.

[34] Parliamentary Research Unit 2007. Issues raised by the Portfolio Committee on Correctional Services on the Correctional Services Amendment Bill [B 32-2007] 31 August 2007.

[35] *S v Botha* 2006 (2) SACR 110 (SCA).

C. The Crisis of Administration

The complex bureaucracy established for the parole system from 1990 onwards proved to be problematic. Particular difficulties emerged at the level of parole boards, their reports being a key element in the decision to release life-sentenced prisoners. While Parliament was aware of these difficulties, it did not appear to have influenced the 2008 amendments to the release process. A meeting of the Portfolio Committee held with the chairpersons of these parole boards in 2009 gives a snapshot of the common difficulties of all parole boards. Notes from this meeting compiled by the Parliamentary Monitoring Group reveal that 'Almost all parole board chairpersons took issue with the lack of support, particularly by the South African Police Services (SAPS) and the Department of Justice'.[36] Most boards also complained that sentencing information was not made available to them. The issue of the composition of the board was a continuing concern: there was a particular problem in getting community members. One board described the resources at its disposal as 'pathetic', with the result that they had to outsource psychology or criminology work at great cost, while other boards also raised the issue of insufficient support.[37]

The problems faced by the parole boards persisted, in spite of several reports proposing reforms. In 2018, the Department of Correctional Services produced a detailed proposal for 'a Revised Parole System for South Africa'. This response to the Position Paper by the leading think tank, African Criminal Justice Reform, was largely dismissive, arguing convincingly that, in spite of its length, it did not provide sufficient concrete information and statistics to provide the basis for concrete reforms.[38]

Practical problems with the release of life-sentenced prisoners are compounded by the complexity of the layers of bureaucracy beyond the parole boards, namely the National Council on Correctional Services and the Minister of Justice, that are involved in all decisions to release such prisoners. The National Council is an unwieldy policy advisory body, not set up primarily to express opinions on the possible release of individual life-sentenced prisoners. An even greater bureaucratic hurdle is the Minister of Justice. By law, the Minister must personally make final decisions on the release of all life-sentenced prisoners, while having overall political responsibility for both the justice and correctional services portfolios. Given the large number of life-sentenced prisoners who must be considered, this task is probably beyond the capacity of even the most conscientious Minister. In 2021, the Judicial Inspector of Correctional

[36] Briefing by Selected Parole Board Chairpersons on Challenges in the Functioning of Parole Boards. Summary by the Parliamentary Monitoring Group of Correctional Services Portfolio Committee, 7 September 2009.

[37] ibid.

[38] 'ACJR Submission on "Position Paper: A Revised Parole System for South Africa"' dullahomarinstitute.org.za/acjr/resource-centre/acjr-submission-parole-2018.pdf.

Services, former Constitutional Court Judge Edwin Cameron, noted that there seemed to be a 'massive backlog on the Minister's desk'.[39] There were 4494 life-sentenced prisoners that were eligible for parole, but in that year only 36 had been granted parole. Cameron calculated that if the Minister 'considers each application for ten minutes, over seven hours, every day, for seven days a week, the backlog would take 409 days to eliminate'. An administrative crisis indeed![40]

VII. THE COURTS INTERVENE

Following the 2008 amendments, it was clear the executive was not only hampered by bureaucratic inertia, but was also not averse to using its control over the release from life imprisonment to bolster its tough-on-crime credentials. In four key cases, the South African courts, with the Constitutional Court taking the lead, had other priorities that focused on the human rights of individuals serving life sentences.

The thinking of the Constitutional Court on release from life imprisonment was revealed in 2011 in the case of *Minister of Correctional Services* v *Van Vuren*.[41] Van Vuren argued that, because at the time he was first sentenced the minimum period before life-sentenced prisoners were considered for release was effectively 15 years, he should also be considered for release at that stage. The difficulty was that section 136(3) of the 1978 Correctional Services Act as amended in 2001 appeared to specify that all life prisoners sentenced before the Act came into force should serve at least 20 years. A majority of the Constitutional Court disagreed and held that section 136(3) could be interpreted as applying only to life-sentenced prisoners who had initially been sentenced after 1994, when 20 years was in fact the minimum. If section 136 were considered as a whole, it could be understood as retaining the shorter minimum periods that were in force prior to 1994, when prisoners like Van Vuren were sentenced.

Critics argued that this interpretation was somewhat strained, but the principles underlying it were powerful (Ballard 2012). The Constitutional Court in *Van Vuren* emphasised the commitment of the new Constitution to all aspects of the rule of law, including the prohibition against retrospective punishments. The Court fully accepted that the minimum period was not a mere administrative matter. As Van Vuren had served more than the 15-year minimum that applied

[39] 'Our Faulty Approach to Life Sentences Is Catching Up with Us. Our Prisons Are Crowded with "Lifers", at Great Cost to Us All' www.groundup.org.za/article/our-faulty-approach-life-sentences-catching-us/.

[40] For an update, see www.dailymaverick.co.za/article/2024-09-17-sa-has-just-one-criminologist-to-deal-with-prison-parole-applications-mps-hear/.

[41] *Minister of Correctional Services v Van Vuren* 2011 JDR 0295 (CC).

when he was sentenced initially, the case was referred back to the Minister for immediate consideration of release.

A second key case, *Van Wyk v Minister of Correctional Services*,[42] concerned a different aspect of the life sentence, namely whether life-sentenced prisoners should have their minimum periods reduced by being granted credits for which correctional law had provided from 1993 onwards. (Like Walus, Van Wyk regarded his offences as 'political', but his application for amnesty had been turned down by the Truth and Reconciliation Commission.) Although the 1998 Correctional Services Act had prospectively abolished the credit system, Van Wyk argued that he should still benefit from it because the credit system applied at the time he was sentenced. The 1998 Act provided that, as a transitional arrangement, prisoners serving determinate sentences imposed before it came into effect should all be awarded maximum credits.[43] The Act was silent, however, on what should happen with credits for life-sentenced prisoners. Although in the past their minimum periods could be reduced for being awarded credits, the Department of Correctional Services decided as a matter of policy that post-1998 life-sentenced prisoners should not be awarded any credits at all. The High Court, which heard Van Wyk's application, held that this policy amounted to a retrospective increase in punishment and was therefore unconstitutional. Van Wyk was granted maximum credits. This effectively reduced the 20-year minimum term of Van Wyk and life-sentenced prisoners similarly situated to 13 years and four months. At the time of his application, van Wyk had already served 16 years, and the Court ordered that his release should be considered immediately.

In 2019, in a third case, the Constitutional Court returned to the fray in *Phaahla v Minister of Justice and Correctional Services*.[44] At issue was the rationality of section 136(1) of the amended 1998 Act, which provided that the minimum term of sentence should be the one applicable on the day of sentence. Phaahla had been sentenced to life imprisonment four days after the 1998 Correctional Services Act came into force on 1 October 2004 for an offence committed before that date. As the law stood, he had to serve 25 years before being considered for release. However, if the law had provided that his parole had to be considered according to the law that applied on the day he committed his offence, the minimum term would have been 20 years, reduced further to 13 years and four months by imputed credits.[45] The Constitutional Court responded that the legislative provision was unconstitutional because it irrationally denied Phaahla equal protection of the law and discriminated

[42] [2012] JOL 28491 (GNP).

[43] s 136(2) of the 1998 Correctional Services Act as amended in 2001.

[44] 2019 (7) BCLR 795 (CC).

[45] This could be reduced by a further 12 months by special remission of sentences from which life-sentenced prisoners were originally excluded: see Minister of Justice, Michael Masutha's media briefing of 29 June 2017, www.gov.za/speeches/minister-michael-masutha-media-briefing-status-political-offenders-and-parole-consideration.

unfairly against him, when compared to another offender who committed a similar offence prior to 1 October 2004 and who was sentenced before that date. Accordingly, it ruled that the impugned provision should be replaced by a provision that set the release policy applicable on the date of the commission of the offence for determining how long a life-sentenced prisoner should serve before being considered for release.

The fourth and most recent case was the Constitutional Court decision in *Walus v Minister of Justice* discussed in the introduction. Notwithstanding one unfortunate technical error,[46] it is a far-reaching and politically brave statement of the principles that should govern the release on parole of all life-sentenced prisoners.

What is particularly impressive about the *Walus* judgment is how it states and applies wider parole principles. Quoting an earlier judgment of the Constitutional Court, it begins by stating:

> Parole is an acknowledged part of our correctional system. It has proved to be a vital part of reformative treatment for the paroled person who is treated by moral suasion. This is consistent with the law: that everyone has the right not to be deprived of freedom arbitrarily or without just cause.[47]

The *Walus* judgment then makes much of the general principles on parole embodied in the 1998 Act, emphasising that section 36 of the Correctional Services Act establishes that the objective of the imprisonment phase of a sentence is to enable the prisoner to 'lead a socially responsible crime-free life in the future'.[48] From this principle, Chief Justice Zondo concludes that:

> Where, on all the evidence, the risk of a prisoner reoffending, if he or she were released on parole, is low, the relevant authorities should seriously consider releasing such prisoner on parole because the objective of the implementation of a sentence of imprisonment would have been achieved.[49]

This conclusion is then used to critique the reasons given by the Minister of Justice for his decision. In essence, the Minister reasoned that although Walus had not only been a model prisoner who had shown remorse and apologised for his crime and was highly unlikely to reoffend, he should nevertheless not

[46] The error is that Chief Justice Zondo assumed (*Walus*, para 55) that the original provision of the 1998 Act providing that the release of life-sentenced prisoners is to be decided by a court applies to life-sentenced prisoners sentenced after the Act came into force in 2004. The assumption overlooked the 2008 amendment of the Act, making the National Council and the Minister of Justice again the final decision-makers for new cases. Fortunately, the error is not material. Chief Justice Zondo is aware that Walus's release could not be determined in this way, as persons who committed offences before the 1998 Act came into force have to be dealt with according to the earlier procedures. He refers to the procedures, which he wrongly believes will apply in the future, only to bolster his conclusion that in Walus's specific case the Constitutional Court should make the final decision.

[47] *Jimmale v S* [2016] (2) SACR 691 (CC), para 1, quoted in *Walus*, para 3.

[48] *Walus*, para 36.

[49] ibid para 37.

be released. This was because the Minister gave great weight to the remarks of the original sentencing court, which had emphasised the heinousness of his crime, holding that it demanded the severest punishment permitted by law. The Minister concluded that these remarks would be 'negated', and the severity of the punishment wrongly diminished, if Walus were to be released on parole.

The Constitutional Court explained that the Minister cannot apply the remarks of the sentencing court in that way, since it would bar Walus from ever being granted parole. Given the importance of parole, the reasoning of the Minister was therefore 'irrational'.

The resultant Constitutional Court decision that the matter should not be referred back to the Minister but that Walus's release on parole should follow almost immediately was bold, but justified by precedent. Walus had been refused parole many times on varying and dubious grounds in the 16 years since he had first qualified for release. Under these circumstances, the Court was entitled to act directly to ensure that justice be done promptly.

The overall conclusion to be drawn from these four cases is that key South African courts have responded commendably to the cases before them and attempted to give life-sentenced prisoners every opportunity to be considered for release at the earliest permissible date. They have also not shied away from ordering the release on parole of life-sentenced prisoners by interpreting the rules governing this decision in a way that effectively removes the discretion of the decision-maker to keep the life-sentenced prisoner in prison when on the available evidence he qualifies for release.

VIII. FINAL REFLECTIONS

Given that the court decisions on the release of life-sentenced prisoners were clearly based on sound jurisprudence derived from legitimate constitutional principles, why were they so controversial? In particular, why did the *Walus* judgment lead to a direct attack on the legitimacy of the Constitutional Court, a key institution in the South African legal order? One explanation could be that the punitive emotions towards an assassin of someone such as Chris Hani are still so strong that any decision to release him could lead to attacks on those seen as responsible for the decision, even if it meant undermining the legitimacy of an important institution. These attacks could also have been facilitated by the legitimacy of the Constitutional Court and of Chief Justice Zondo already being questioned by some politicians because of the blocking of the release on medical parole of ex-President Zuma.

While the political context of the *Walus* decision is an important part of the story, there is an alternative explanation for the reaction to it. Attacks on the legitimacy of decisions of the courts on the release of life-sentenced prisoners in South Africa may also be explained by focusing on the structural shortcomings of the system that is now in place for the release of those prisoners.

The current system means that the Constitutional Court has had to take a politically unpopular decision by overruling on appeal a decision made by the Minister of Justice, a senior member of the elected government. If the 1998 Correctional Services Act had been implemented in the form it was initially enacted, release decisions would routinely have been taken by judges in the first instance. A body of precedent would have emerged, which would have clarified the law, thus avoiding the diverse justifications that different ministers have put forward for their decisions over the years. Routine decision-making on release by judges might still have resulted in controversial decisions, but, by avoiding a public stand-off between two branches of government, questions of legitimacy would have been less prominent.

In reflecting on the structural weaknesses of the South African system for considering the release of life-sentenced prisoners, one should not focus only on the role of courts that are limited to analysing, and in rare cases overturning, administrative decisions of officials. Appellate courts cannot repair all the shortcomings of the system, as they deal with individual cases on relatively narrow grounds. The South African Constitutional Court could directly challenge the mandatory life sentences, which since 2004 have been coupled to minimum periods of 25 years. Such periods are long but unexceptionable in international law, where they are regarded as harsh, but acceptable.[50] The much-praised new constitutional order that is a feature of the formally democratic post-1994 South Africa has not proved sufficient to guarantee a fair system of life imprisonment (Super 2024).

The problem was squarely a failure of ideas in the political development of the institutional structure for considering the release of life-sentenced prisoners. When mandatory life sentences were introduced (a problematic development in itself), it should have been recognised that less serious offences than in the past would become subject to life imprisonment, and that they would require shorter minimum periods before release could be considered if an enormous increase in the overall number of life-sentenced prisoners was to be avoided.

How this could have been achieved technically needs further evaluation of the different ways of determining when release of life-sentenced prisoners should be considered. Essentially, there is a choice between minimum periods set by the sentencing court and automatic consideration after a fixed period prescribed by legislation (van Zyl Smit and Appleton 2019). In the former case, the individualised minimum period is designed to reflect the heinousness of the offence and the blameworthiness of the individual offender before the court. Once that period has been served, offenders should be released if they pose no further danger to the public. However, there is the increased risk that sentencing

[50] This matters particularly in South Africa, where s 39 of the Constitution provides that, when interpreting the Bill of Rights, courts must consider international law.

courts will impose long minimum periods, as these periods are often seen by the public as the 'true' sentence of the court.

Legislatively fixed minimum periods remove that possibility, but their inflexibility means that they might not reflect the reality that offences carrying life sentences are not equally heinous. This objection could be met by setting a shorter minimum period before release can be considered, but at the same time allowing the releasing authority some flexibility in taking the offence into account. Particularly if the releasing authority were to be a court, it would be well placed to conduct a dispassionate retrospective review of the censure proportionate to the original offence (Dagan and Roberts 2019).

Moreover, contrary to what the Constitutional Court claimed in *Walus*, emphasising the seriousness of the original offence does not mean that release will never be granted. The doctrine of proportionality requires, however, that any weight given to the seriousness of the offence as a factor to be considered when contemplating release should be reduced in relation to the time that the prisoner has served beyond the minimum period. The reduced danger to society that a prisoner might still pose is a further factor that should also be given proportionate weight. While the *Walus* judgment rightly emphasises the importance of evidence of a prisoner's rehabilitation, the extent to which such rehabilitation has reduced the danger that life-sentenced prisoners pose to society is also a judgment call.

Finally, in South Africa, there have been failures of administration that are closely related to the failure of ideas on how to design a fair and effective release system. The reintroduction of a highly complex release structure, including a key role for the National Council, with the Minister of Justice again taking the final decision, paid no attention to the number of life-sentenced prisoners whose release would fall to be considered. More fundamentally, no matter at what stage and by whom release decisions are made, administrative failures of the kind that have been identified over the past 25 years leading to accurate information not being provided timeously, make release decisions harder. Such failures leave their outcomes wide open to harsh criticism that undermines the legitimacy not only of individual decision-making bodies, but of the legal system as a whole.

If, as is now widely recognised also in South Africa, the fundamental humanity of prisoners serving life sentences requires that at some stage they be considered fairly for release, the challenges posed by these failures, real and perceived, cannot be avoided. Creating a fair release system will require not only a return to the ideals of the 1990s, but also an acceptance that such a release system needs impartial decision-makers and carefully targeted resources to support them. The release process too must be reconsidered very carefully, for what the South African example shows is that failure to attend to detailed rules can lead to a system that, in spite of the best intentions of the courts and of human rights activists, produces unacceptable overall outcomes. Such outcomes are open to criticism from all positions on the political spectrum.

REFERENCES

Ballard, C (2012) 'Parole in South Africa: Understanding Recent Changes' *CSPRI Newsletter* Issue No 40.
Bhargava, A (2002) 'Defining Political Crimes: A Case Study of the South African Truth and Reconciliation Commission' 102 *Columbia Law Review* 1304.
Cameron, E (2020) 'The Crisis of Criminal Justice in South Africa' 137 *South African Law Journal* 32.
Dagan, N and Roberts, JV (2019) 'Retributivism, Penal Censure and Life Imprisonment Without Parole' 38 *Criminal Justice Ethics* 1.
Department of Correctional Services (2018) 'Position Paper: A Revised Parole System for South Africa'.
du Bois-Pedain, A (2007) *Transitional Amnesty in South Africa* (Cambridge, Cambridge University Press).
Fagan, H (2004) 'Curb the Vengeance: Laws on Minimum Sentencing and Parole Spell Worsening Prison Conditions' 10 *SA Crime Quarterly* 1.
Hamman, A, Albertus, C and Nortje, W (2019) 'Deciphering Dangerousness: A Critical Analysis of Section 286A and B of the Criminal Procedure Act 51 of 1977' 22 *Potchefstroom Electronic Law Journal* 1.
Kriegler Commission (1995) *Unrest in Prisons: Final Report of the Commission of Inquiry into Unrest in Prisons* (Pretoria, Government Printer).
Malala, J (2023) *The Plot to Save South Africa* ((New York, Simon & Schuster).
Moses, J (2012) *Parole in South Africa* (Cape Town, Juta).
Mujuzi, JD (2008) 'The Changing Face of Life Imprisonment in South Africa' CSPRI Research Paper No 15 (Bellville, University of the Western Cape).
Muntingh, L (2009) 'Sentencing' in ISS (ed), *Criminal (in)justice in South Africa: a civil society perspective* (Pretoria, Institute for Security Studies) 178–200.
O'Donovan, M and Redpath J (2006) *The Impact of Minimum Sentencing in South Africa* (Newlands, The Open Society Foundation for South Africa).
Pete, S (1998) 'The Politics of Imprisonment in the Aftermath of South Africa's First Democratic Election' 11 *South African Journal of Criminal Justice* 51.
Phillips, I (1991) 'Political Developments in 1990' 2 *South African Human Rights and Labour Law Yearbook* 176.
Super, G (2024) 'Porous Penality and the Myth of Liberal Punishment: Lessons from South Africa' 64 *British Journal of Criminology* 107.
Turrell, R (2004) *White Mercy. A Study of the Death Penalty in South Africa* (Westport, CT, Praeger).
van Zyl Smit, D (1992) *South Africa Prison Law and Practice* (Durban, Butterworths).
—— (1995) 'Taking Life Imprisonment Seriously' in E Kahn (ed), *The Quest for Justice: Essays in Honour of Michael McGregor Corbett, Chief Justice of the Supreme Court of South Africa* (Cape Town, Juta) 309–27.
van Zyl Smit, D and Appleton, C (2019) *Life Imprisonment: A Global Human Rights Analysis* (Cambridge, MA, Harvard University Press).

8

The Political and Legal Boundaries of Release, Recall and Risk: A UK Perspective

NICOLA PADFIELD

I. INTRODUCTION

THE INVITATION TO contribute to a book entitled *The Futures of Parole: The Rationalities, Institutions and Practices of Contemporary Prison Release* is both a privilege and a challenge. I have tried to take a specifically UK perspective to explore the possible futures of parole. I am a lawyer, better steeped in the law and practice of 'parole' in England and Wales than I am in the practice elsewhere in the UK. But, by looking beyond the boundaries of England and Wales, I provide some broader examples to illustrate my themes. I am writing at a time of political change in the UK – a Labour government has taken charge after a clear election win in June 2024. For the first time in years, the government may be committed to reducing the prison population. But it is impossible to know at the time of writing whether it will introduce dramatic changes – little was said about criminal justice and prisons in the election campaign. I argue here for significant change to the parole process in the UK, but I also reflect on the political and legal barriers, or boundaries, which make change so difficult.[1] My question is not simply what does a better parole system in England and Wales look like, but also what are the barriers to achieving that system.

The chapter is divided into a number of sections. I start with some definitional questions: introducing the nature of the UK constitution, and the meaning of 'parole' in this context. I then explore some key factors in relation to contemporary prison release, which inevitably shape any analysis of the future of parole: the state (and cost) of UK prisons today; the uncertain purposes of

[1] As I explain below, criminal justice matters are devolved to the Scottish government, so changes made by the UK Parliament may well have no wider impact than in England and Wales.

punishment; the burdens of 'risk' and 'offender management'; the complexity of political power. Only then do I consider possible futures.

II. CONTEXT AND DEFINITIONS

A. The UK Constitution

The UK is made up of four 'nations': England, Wales, Scotland and Northern Ireland. The UK has never really been a unitary state, since complex rules and conventions have governed the relationship between the different 'nations' for many centuries. The Acts of Union 1707 brought some sort of constitutional settlement, but calls for independence (or some degree of independence) have continued throughout recent centuries. A new chapter of devolved powers opened in 1998. The Scotland Act 1998 fixes the legislative competence of the Scottish Parliament by explicitly specifying powers that are 'reserved' to the UK Parliament; the Scottish Parliament may legislate in all areas which are not reserved. Criminal justice laws and practice are not reserved. The Welsh Assembly had no powers to initiate primary legislation until it was given limited law-making powers by the Government of Wales Act 2006. It can legislate in the 20 areas that are devolved, but this does not (yet) include criminal justice.

The political history of Northern Ireland is particularly complicated and contested, and a summary of how the UK government has devolved powers to the Northern Ireland Assembly is challenging (but see Dwyer and McAlinden 2015; Murray and Carr 2021). In brief, criminal justice policy was run directly from London during the 'Troubles'. After the Good Friday Agreement of 1998, policing and justice were not initially devolved, but the Hillsborough Agreement (2010) led to the devolution of policing and justice powers to the Northern Ireland Assembly.[2] The Assembly was suspended between 2017 and 2020, and again between 2022 and 2024, due to fundamental disagreements between the political parties. When the Assembly is suspended, the Department of Justice operates without a Minister. The Northern Ireland (Executive Formation etc) Act 2022 provides a framework for progressing decisions which enable some of the work of the Department to continue in the absence of a Minister.

Devolution has thus been complex, and continues to evolve. The powers of the state continue to be allocated to the legislature (Parliaments or Assemblies); the executive (the government); and the judiciary (the courts). As Elliott and Thomas (2024) put it, power is divided between these institutions according to their particular role. The executive governs the country. The legislature enacts legislation and should hold government to account (though how effective this is depends on electoral systems and power-sharing agreements). The courts are

[2] See the Northern Ireland Act 1998 (the Devolution of Policing and Justice Functions) Order 2010.

there to decide legal disputes and to uphold the rule of law. The purposes of the separation of powers are to avoid the overconcentration of power and to ensure checks and balances in the constitution. It is a matter of debate as to whether the UK constitution has got the balance of power right. A strong judiciary must stand up to an over-mighty executive (especially where Parliament is unable to be a significant check on the abuse of power). Yet, judges should not step into the political arena: their proper constitutional role is to apply fundamental rules of natural justice and fairness to the treatment of prisoners, for example, but not to second-guess executive decision-makers. It is hardly surprising that there is a degree of flexibility (instability?) in the relationships between the different organs of the state, reflecting a tension between 'legality' and 'democracy'. While remaining wary of 'judicial supremacism', the judiciary must speak out confidently about the abuse of power.

I may be criticised for an 'overriding Anglocentric focus, which sees the nations of the UK relegated to "the other" against an England/Wales marker' (McNaull 2016). For 25 years, I have been studying the parole system of England and Wales, and have made more comparisons to practice in France and elsewhere in Europe than I have to those nations to the north and west within the UK (see Dünkel et al 2010; Herzog Evans and Padfield 2015; Höffler and Padfield 2022). In this chapter, I reflect on law and practice throughout the UK, in order to identify the political and legal barriers to reform, but my Anglocentric focus remains.

B. Parole, Release and Recall

The meaning of 'parole' shifts over time, even within one jurisdiction. Parole has evolved completely in England and Wales in 50 years, from 'early' discretionary release to 'late' or 'delayed' release (Padfield 2020). Today, the UK jurisdictions have similar release rules, with similar understandings of such concepts as 'determinate' sentences (where the offender's longest possible period in prison is 'determined' on the day of the initial sentencing) and 'indeterminate' sentences (life sentences imposed with a minimum term fixed by the sentencing judge).[3] But as the sentencing regime in each jurisdiction becomes more complex, with extended sentences (a determinate sentence with an extended period of supervision after release), special sentences for 'offenders of special concern' etc, the legal frameworks may diverge.

Having explored the significant differences in the meaning of these sentencing terms in the USA and in Europe, van Zyl Smit and Corda (2017) speculate that the differences come from a key difference in approach 'to the restraints

[3] In England and Wales, the main sentencing provisions are found in the Sentencing Act 2020; in Scotland, it is the much-amended Prisoners and Criminal Proceedings (Scotland) Act 1993.

that ought to be placed on governmental power in the use of criminal penalties'. In Europe, they argue, the maximum prison term prescribed by law was meant to operate as a protection against excessive punitiveness. Their use of the words 'ought' and 'was meant to' reveals much, of course. Perhaps in the past the UK Parliament prescribed maximum penalties to limit the possibilities for punitive judges. But in recent decades, the many legislative changes, particularly in England and Wales, have revealed a deliberate attempt to make judges more punitive. It has been successful – sentence lengths have increased enormously. And yet, in Scotland, where the legislative language has been somewhat different, the prison population has also grown. This seems surprising at first blush and will be explored later in this chapter.

The loosest (and oldest?[4]) meaning of 'parole' today might be to use the term to describe any conditional release from custody. This release might be mandatory or discretionary, 'early' or 'late', after a minimum term. It might be decided by prison authorities or by a Parole Board. Prisoners in the UK are released on detailed conditions, which have significant bite. Whilst some media suggest that release at half time (or earlier) is a 'get out of jail free' card, the reality is very different. Lengthy licence conditions often include electronic monitoring. Prisoners who are alleged to have breached the terms of their licence are liable to be recalled to prison without any judicial oversight, and without necessarily any suggestion of further criminal behaviour.[5]

In England and Wales, most determinate sentence prisoners are released at half time, or earlier than that, with an electronic tag on HDC (home detention curfew) up to 135 days before half time. In recent months, many others have been released at 40 per cent in order to ease dramatically overcrowded prisons.[6] Those serving indeterminate sentences ('lifers') have to wait until they have served their minimum term, when the Parole Board decides on release. Those serving extended sentences and many others serving offences which deem them 'dangerous' may have to serve two-thirds before they are released, usually after consideration of their case by the Parole Board. The law has changed frequently in recent years.[7]

Most short-term prisoners in Scotland are released at the halfway point in their sentence, but those serving over four years have their cases considered, after they have served half time, by the Parole Board before they can be recommended for release. Currently, they must be released as soon as they have only six months

[4] The concept derives from the French word *parole*, which means word: prisoners are released on their word, trusted to behave, with sanctions attached when they fail.

[5] See Padfield (2020). Weaver et al (2012) explored the sharp rise in recall rates in Scotland.

[6] See the Criminal Justice Act 2003 (Requisite and Minimum Custodial Periods) Order 2024.

[7] See, eg the Legal Aid, Sentencing and Punishment of Offenders Act (LASPOA) 2012; the Offender Rehabilitation Act 2014; the Criminal Justice and Courts Act 2015; the Terrorist Offenders (Restriction of Early Release) Act 2020; the Prisoners (Disclosure of Information about Victims) Act 2020; the Counter-Terrorism and Sentencing Act 2021; the Police, Crime, Sentencing and Courts Act 2022; and the Victims and Prisoners Act 2024.

of their sentence left to serve.[8] In Northern Ireland, there is a similar framework of determinate, extended and indeterminate sentences, and the Parole Commissioners provide a similar function to the Parole Board in England and Wales. In all three jurisdictions, post-release supervision of offenders is compulsory, even where there is no evidence that the offender poses a significant risk of serious harm to the public (and in reality, the quality of this supervision is often poor, due to funding constraints).

So, in brief, the great majority of prisoners are released by the executive, not by the various Parole Boards.[9] Parole Boards are small cogs within the 'system'. Even in the small proportion of cases dealt with by Parole Boards, the prison authorities have a huge impact in shaping how prisoners progress through penal institutions, which in turn affects the likelihood of them being successful before a Parole Board. Thus, security classification or allocation to one prison rather than another can impinge greatly on 'progress'.

As well as HDC, there are other discretionary executive release mechanisms: the release of prisoners on compassionate grounds and release on temporary licence (ROTL), for example. Compassionate release is only granted after the personal agreement of the relevant Government Minister. In Scotland, the names of those released on compassionate release are published.[10] This reveals what is well known: that such release is rare and is only ever done on the grounds of terminal illness.[11] Secondly, ROTL is used to allow some prisoners to leave prison on day release, perhaps to work or for a family funeral. It can be invaluable in helping a prisoner prepare for release by securing accommodation, work, etc. The numbers fluctuate from year to year.[12] These forms of executive release, added to HDC, remind us that the executive continues to hold most of the keys to release.

Having explored some definitional issues and summarised release rules in the UK, I turn to the wider context surrounding decisions to release. I have chosen four key challenges facing anyone, or any body, seeking to reform or improve the 'system'.

[8] Under the Prisoners and Criminal Proceedings (Scotland) Act 1993. Those sentenced before 1 February 2016 are released on licence after serving two-thirds of their sentence, even if not granted parole. The Scottish government consulted in the summer of 2024 on a proposal to return to the position of automatic release at two-thirds.

[9] In 2023, 48,830 people were released from prison in England and Wales (see Offender Management Statistics 2023). In 2023–24, only 4370 were released by the Parole Board.

[10] www.gov.scot/publications/compassionate-release-cases-from-2016/.

[11] This underscores the weakness of the British government's argument that the power to release on compassionate grounds means that 'whole life' tariffs are acceptable under the European Convention on Human Rights. See *Hutchinson v UK UK* [2017] ECHR 65, after a succession of decisions such as *Vinter, Bamber, Moore v UK* (2013) 34 BHRC 605; *Vinter v UK* (2016) 63 EHRR 1; *McLoughlin and Newell* [2014] EWCA Crim 188. I am more convinced by *Vinter* and Judge Pinto's dissent in *Hutchinson*.

[12] In 2023, there were 416,621 incidences of ROTL in England and Wales: Annual Offender Management statistics.

III. BARRIERS TO CHANGE

A. The State of Prisons in the UK

The under-resourcing of prisons[13] is a huge issue. Prisons are currently both overcrowded and in a terrible state. If you actually wanted to rehabilitate a prisoner, you would not send them to the vast majority of our existing penal institutions.

The prison population in all UK jurisdictions has risen sharply in recent decades. In England and Wales, it more than doubled from 40,000 in 1991 to 88,521 in September 2024. In Scotland, the prison population has risen by around 13 per cent since the start of 2023, to 8348.[14] The imprisonment rate is similar in both jurisdictions, at 145 per 100,000 of the national population, whereas the rate in Northern Ireland is 98 per 100,000, with fewer than 2000 prisoners (Fair and Walmsley 2024). These are high rates by Western European standards, where the median rate is 73. Over the longer time frame, the main trend has been, in each jurisdiction, an increase in average sentence lengths. And yet, as the Scottish Prison Commission (2008: 2) put it, 'high prison populations do not reduce crime; they are more likely to create pressures that drive reoffending than to reduce it'.

Excellent sources of information are the reports of the Chief Inspectors of Prisons.[15] Prisons are currently described as being increasingly volatile, unsafe and failing to prepare prisoners for release. Reports are often shocking: 'The complacency with which such shocking standards seems to have been viewed by the prison service is extraordinary';[16] prisons 'had very poor regimes with too few prisoners taking part in interventions to reduce their risk, or education or employment to occupy their time meaningfully'.[17] The treatment of 15- to 18-year-old children at one young offenders institution was recently described as both 'scandalous' and 'appalling'.[18] Problems are not simply overcrowding (matched by understaffing), but include old, decaying, poorly maintained buildings, an ageing prison population, the difficulties of sustaining

[13] There are 117 prisons in England and five in Wales (17 of these 122 are run by private sector companies), 16 prisons in Scotland (now with only one run by the private sector since Kilmarnock was transferred to the Scottish Prison Service on 17 March 2024) and three in Northern Ireland.

[14] One of the main explanations for this recent change has been a reduction (by over one-third) in the backlog of court cases, with arrivals to prison exceeding departures: www.gov.scot/publications/prison-population-action/pages/country-comparisons/.

[15] https://hmiprisons.justiceinspectorates.gov.uk; https://prisonsinspectoratescotland.gov.uk. The Chief Inspector of Prisons in England and Wales also inspects the prisons in Northern Ireland; a separate inspectorate inspects Scottish prisons.

[16] https://hmiprisons.justiceinspectorates.gov.uk/news/hmp-exeter-vulnerable-men-receiving-shocking-standards-of-care-in-early-days-in-custody/.

[17] https://hmiprisons.justiceinspectorates.gov.uk/news/hmp-long-lartin-and-hmp-whitemoor-squalid-conditions-a-sign-of-wider-concerns/.

[18] https://hmiprisons.justiceinspectorates.gov.uk/hmipris_reports/hmyoi-cookham-wood-2/.

family contacts for those held far from home, limited access to rehabilitative (or any) purposeful activities, limited treatment for alcohol and drug abuse, and poor healthcare, often divorced from that available in the community.

Another long-standing problem is the failure to 'join up' the prison system, and especially the prison and probation systems. In England, an influential report in 2003 concluded that there needed to be more 'end to end offender management' (Carter 2003). An umbrella body, the National Offender Management Service (NOMS), was up and running within six months. It quickly became seen as a top-down 'bureaucratic behemoth emasculating prison governors under a deluge of dictates' (Podmore 2017). Recognising the problems, in 2017, NOMS was renamed Her/His Majesty's Prison and Probation Service (HMPPS).[19] The relationship between HMPPS and the Ministry of Justice remains complex, affected by the personalities involved in leadership at both (King and Wilmott 2022). In Scotland, interestingly, there is no probation service. Instead, criminal justice social workers, part of local authorities' social work departments, do the work done by probation officers elsewhere in the UK. This may suggest that the shift away from penal welfarism has been less sharp in Scotland (see McAra 2005; 2008), but, as McNeill (2019: 108) points out, 'despite an enduring commitment in policy and practice to supervision as a strategy for penal reduction … a dramatic growth in the use of supervision has enlarged rather than contracted the size of the penal system'.[20]

Part of the challenge is the status and role of probation. Established in England, Wales and Northern Ireland[21] in 1907, the role of probation officers in the first half of the twentieth century was ostensibly to 'advise, assist and befriend' offenders in the community.[22] Today, probation still 'feels' like a poor relation in criminal justice, and, whilst there is now a national probation service in England and Wales, after a failed attempt at privatisation, questions still hang over probation's local and national relationships with offenders and other criminal justice bodies (Padfield 2016).

The role of the third sector, voluntary and community organisations, is also contentious. Often highly dependent on key individuals, they rise and fall with the quality of their leaders. Funding is also often precarious. But they can be innovative and flexible, often recognising that ex-offenders, experts by

[19] HMPPS is an executive agency, 'sponsored' by the Ministry of Justice. In theory, HMPPS should be able to focus on 'service delivery', leaving the Ministry of Justice freer to focus on policy development.

[20] See also McNeill (2018).

[21] In Northern Ireland, the NI Prison Service, the agency charged with managing prisons (and prisoners) also manages prisoners on release through an aftercare scheme, Throughcare. But the Probation Board for Northern Ireland, another non-departmental public body sponsored by the Department of Justice, supervises those released on licence or parole if their sentence is longer than 12 months (for a critical analysis, see Northern Ireland Audit Office 2023). See also O'Mahony and Chapman (2007).

[22] There is a wealth of material on the history of probation: Raynor and Vanstone (2007); Burke and Collett (2014); Robinson and McNeill (2023).

experience, are more effective than 'technocratic' staff. In Northern Ireland, there is evidence that community-based networks of restorative justice projects can provide a useful way forward (see McEvoy and Mika 2002). But partnership working and inter-agency co-operation remains difficult and fragmented (see Hucklesby and Corcoran 2016; Tomczak 2018).

B. The Uncertain Purposes of Prison and the Penal System

A significant barrier to reform is the uncertainty surrounding the purposes of punishment. Conflicting purposes are enshrined in English law. Section 57(2) of the Sentencing Act 2020 (originally enacted in 2003) provides for the 'Purposes of sentencing: adults':

> (2) The court must have regard to the following purposes of sentencing –
>
> (a) the punishment of offenders,
> (b) the reduction of crime (including its reduction by deterrence),
> (c) the reform and rehabilitation of offenders,
> (d) the protection of the public, and
> (e) the making of reparation by offenders to persons affected by their offences.

When the Scottish Sentencing Council[23] published its first guideline in 2018, it took a more nuanced approach to these purposes, but perhaps introduced even more uncertainty:

> The sentence selected should best achieve the purposes of sentencing that are appropriate to the particular case but should always reflect the core principle of fairness and proportionality. In no particular order, the purposes may include:
>
> - Protection of the public. Sentencing may seek to protect the public from offending behaviour through preventative measures and by deterring offending behaviour.
> - Punishment. Sentencing may seek to punish the offender as a consequence of their criminal behaviour, normally resulting in some sort of loss depending on the sentence chosen.
> - Rehabilitation of offenders. Sentencing may seek to reduce the risk of reoffending through the effective rehabilitation of offenders, providing people with the opportunity to change and move away from past offending behaviour.
> - Giving the offender the opportunity to make amends. Sentencing acknowledges the harm caused to victims and communities. Sentencing may also aim to recognise and meet the needs of victims and communities by requiring the offender to repair at least some of the harm caused.
> - Expressing disapproval of offending behaviour. Sentencing may act as an expression of society's concern about and disapproval of the offending behaviour under consideration.

[23] A body set up in 2015 as an independent advisory body by the Criminal Justice and Licensing (Scotland) Act 2010.

In achieving the appropriate purpose(s) of a particular sentence, the efficient use of public resources may be considered.

Both these lists illustrate the confusion at the heart of the system. They allow, even encourage, sentencers to be eclectic in their choices. The purposes of sentencing children or young people are described somewhat differently. The 'principal' aim of the youth justice system in England and Wales is to prevent offending by children and young people (see section 37 of the Crime and Disorder Act 1998). A system which prioritises the reduction or prevention of reoffending would, I suggest, lead to more effective penal institutions.

It is not necessary in this chapter to consider in depth the age-old debates between penal philosophers. Suffice to say, in the 1970s/1980s in the UK (following a similar shift in the USA), retributive philosophers appeared to gain the upper hand in the debate with more consequentialist/utilitarian philosophers. The 'rehabilitative ideal' went out of fashion, replaced by a focus on desert, largely in the context of arguments for more consistent or proportionate sentences. The rise of the retributivist agenda allowed 'punitive' governments to force up punishment levels, without maintaining a keen eye on costs, fairness or effectiveness. 'The rehabilitative ethic, and perhaps still more the liberal-reformism which preceded it, was an ethic of coercive caring, but at least there was caring' (Bottoms 1980).

Sentencing is an ongoing process, not just a one-off event. An interesting philosophical question is whether the balance between the conflicting aims might change over the duration of a sentence. Dagan (2022) usefully challenges the division, or boundaries, between 'sentencing' and post-sentence implementation/parole. For him, the initial sentencing stage is seen as moral, retributive-oriented, proportionality-based, offence-focused, 'juridical' and public. In contrast, the stage of post-sentencing is largely seen as instrumental, risk-oriented, discretionary, offender-focused, 'carceral' and largely invisible. Building on the analysis in Roberts and Dagan (2019), Dagan suggests that 'retributive punishment' may evolve over time. This is a welcome argument, and fits with the idea that offenders are sent to prison as punishment, not for punishment. Once there, prisoners deserve not more punishment, but the opportunity for rehabilitation and reintegration.

C. Risk and 'Offender Management'

The fixation with 'risk' assessment has been identified as problematic for years (Harcourt 2007). In terms of prison and probation in England and Wales, the shift happened around the 1990s, as probation became more managerial and less social work-focused. Prior to this, probation tried to maintain a balance, as McCulloch and McNeill suggested, between the offenders' needs, rights and interests and those of the wider public. But as this changed, 'one corollary of this un-balancing has been the objectification of offenders as the "raw material" on which probation works, rather than one of the intended beneficiaries for whom and with whom it works' (McCulloch and McNeill 2007: 237). Barry (2021) explores how the aim of risk assessment and management in criminal justice is increasingly about minimising opportunities to create harm to the public rather than maximising opportunities to create change in offenders. As she argues, the 'balance' of public protection with rehabilitation has become increasingly unstable in prioritising the former. And yet the public are better protected if someone is properly 'rehabilitated'.

Risk assessment 'tools' are themselves risky. In a report for the Council of Europe, I argued that 'it cannot be emphasised too much that prediction tools can never be truly accurate' (Padfield 2010: para 31). Predicting harm in the future is highly unreliable. There are so many dynamic factors involved. The likelihood of reoffending increases if the prisoner is released without accommodation, money and a variety of support networks. It is easy to talk of 'risky' behaviour without adequately focusing on the precise risks involved. For example, it is vital to keep separate the risk of (serious?) harm and the likelihood of its occurrence.

Dwyer explores the 'politics' of risk assessments in the context of Northern Ireland. She shows how easily risk prediction can be used to sacrifice individual rights for 'political imperatives' (Dwyer 2015: 101). To many prisoners in England, the business of risk management feels deeply unfair and can provoke feelings of hopelessness. How can someone throw off the 'risky' label? I have met prisoners who will quote their OASys (Offender Assessment System) assessment ('I'm told I have a 65 per cent risk of reoffending within two years') and despair at their inability to shape these statistics. Unless a great deal more is done to support them when they leave prison, they may well be likely to reoffend and are understandably despondent.

D. The Political Complexity of 'Power'

The fourth barrier to change is manoeuvring the levers of change. Whilst the doctrine of the separation of powers suggests that power is divided between the three arms of government, the governance structures of the different players in the system are different in different parts of the UK, and these constitutional structures may disguise the reality of 'power'.

There have been extraordinary examples in England and Wales of the use and abuse of power by politicians. The most compelling examples may be drawn from the short tenure of Dominic Raab as Minister for Justice (September 2021–April 2023). First, he oversaw important legislative and quasi-legislative changes, which, whilst supposedly building 'public confidence' in parole,[24] in many

[24] On the complex issue of public opinion and public confidence, see Freiberg and Bartels (chapter two above).

respects weakened and undermined the process. The most obvious was the Police, Crime, Sentencing and Courts Act 2022. The Act increased the proportion of the sentence which many of those convicted of violent or sexual offences, and certain other 'offenders of particular concern', now have to serve. Particularly controversially, the Act gave to the Secretary of State the power to refer 'high-risk' offenders serving determinate, fixed-term sentences to the Parole Board, in place of automatic release.[25] The 2022 Act also introduced a new power to make provision for the *setting aside* of Parole Board decisions. As part of the Minister of Justice's determination to place further controls on the Board, this process can be used by either Minister or prisoner, but is predominantly being used by the Minister.[26]

Secondly, Raab's interventions into individual parole decisions was extraordinary. For example, in *R (Bailey and Morris) v Secretary of State for Justice* [2023] EWHC 555 (Admin), the High Court was damning of the Secretary of State's new Parole Board Rules 2022, which purported to prevent prison and probation staff from making any recommendations in their reports on prisoners. According to the Court, the Secretary of State's decision to make the rule

> was an impermissible interference with a judicial process … One of the Secretary of State's principal purposes in making [the rule] was to suppress or enable the suppression of relevant opinion evidence which differed from his own view in cases where he expressed one. That purpose was improper. (para 5(c))

The rule had also made the Parole Board's difficult job even more difficult: 'Any suggestion that the witness was tailoring their evidence so as to be consistent with their employer's view would substantially reduce the weight that could be given to it' (para 100). The rule 'may well have resulted in prisoners being released who would not otherwise have been released, and in prisoners not being released who would otherwise have been released' (para 5(f)).

The decision in *R (Simpson) v Secretary of State for Justice* [2022] EWHC 3181 (Admin) showed how far Raab was prepared to go in preventing the release of unpopular prisoners. Simpson and her partner were convicted in 2017 of causing or allowing her baby to sustain serious injury. The trial judge had decided that she was not 'dangerous' within the meaning of the law and imposed a 10-year determinate sentence. Even though no further evidence of 'dangerousness' emerged during the first five years of her sentence, Raab decided that she should not be released, and that the case should be referred to the Parole Board under the new provisions of the 2022 Act. Simpson was informed the day before she was due to be released that she was not to be released after all. Raab wanted the case referred to the Parole Board 'first of all for risk and second for public confidence' (see para 32). Unsurprisingly, the decision was struck down by the High Court, which held that the Secretary of State's arguments smacked

[25] See the discussion of the case of *Simpson* below.
[26] For reconsideration and set-aside decisions, see www.bailii.org/ew/cases/PBRA.

of resentencing and gave undue weight to the fact that the child's adoptive mother had been successful in keeping the case in the public eye. The judgment makes it clear that this was the Minister's personal decision, against the advice of civil servants. His decision also went against the spirit of the new legislation, which was designed to capture those cases where there is new or additional information which emerges during the sentence over and above that available to the court at the time of sentencing (Padfield 2024).

Another example is Raab's determination to stop life sentence prisoners being moved to open prisons even when this was recommended by the Parole Board: see *R (Wynne) v Secretary of State for Justice* [2023] EWHC 1111 (Admin). The Secretary of State had rejected the Parole Board's recommendation that Wynne should be transferred to an open prison, although this was supported by all six of the professionals who gave evidence. The High Court concluded that his decision was irrational:[27]

> [W]hether viewing the factors relied on by the Secretary of State individually, or stepping back and considering the decision as a whole, it is clear that the Secretary of State has provided no good reason for rejecting the Panel's recommendation. The lack of any good reason to depart from the Panel's recommendation is particularly striking given the Panel's depth of analysis, the clarity of their conclusion, and the consensus of opinion amongst the panoply of professional witnesses. For the reasons I have given, I conclude that the decision to reject the Panel's recommendation was outside the range of reasonable decisions open to the decision-maker' (para 86).

These are strong words! Courts in the UK do not easily leap in on behalf of prisoners. They are generally cautious, conservative and aware that they are unelected. The strength of the criticisms of the Secretary of State are therefore all the more surprising.[28]

The position in Scottish politics appears different, at least in law-making, as the following two examples show.[29] Scotland has had a presumption against short prison sentences since the Criminal Justice and Licensing (Scotland) Act 2010, and this was extended to a presumption against sentences of up to 12 months in 2019. The political message was focused on reducing reoffending:

> Such sentences often disrupt factors that can help prevent offending, including family relationships, housing, employment and access to healthcare and support.

[27] The courts in these cases are simply reviewing the legality of the Secretary of State's decision. They have the power to strike down a decision if it is outside the range of reasonable decisions open to the Minister, for which the word 'irrational' has become the legal shorthand.

[28] I am not arguing that the courts have somehow become more 'liberal' – simply that Raab's involvement in parole clearly exceeded what should have been the limits of his powers. For a critique of judicial decision-making, see Armstrong (2020), in particular her exploration of how the courts can use the language of rehabilitation and sentence management against prisoners.

[29] For an account of the contrasting approaches of the UK Parliament and the Scottish Parliament to mandatory life sentences in the early 2000s, see Bild (2014). Here, too, we see that despite contrasting legislative approaches (the one punitive, the other more liberal or flexible), the substantive outcomes in practice have been similar: longer minimum terms. See also Brangan (2019).

> Around 90% of women sent to prison are given a custodial sentence of a year or less, many of whom have experienced abuse, mental health and addiction problems'.[30]

Secondly, the Bail and Release from Custody (Scotland) Act 2023 was designed to be 'a first step in a wider discussion about how custody should be used in a modern, progressive Scotland'.[31] The government's summary of the consultation which preceded the Act suggests that the debate was largely focused on the reduction in reoffending:

> The majority of respondents agreed with the proposal that enabling a prisoner to serve part of their sentence in the community could help their reintegration. There was considerable agreement with the proposal that releases on a Friday (or the day before a public holiday) should be restricted … Whilst the majority of respondents agreed that a 'specific duty to engage' in release planning was required, it was seen as important that this duty involved collaboration between all community justice partners. Across all of the proposals it was generally felt that key to the success of the proposed changes would be collaborative working (including between statutory and third sector organisations). Overall, subject to refinement and suitable safeguards many of the proposals were seen as potentially contributing to the underlying aim of reducing crime, reducing reoffending and having fewer people experience crime.

So, the 2023 Act was enacted to improve the support available to prisoners on release. It also requires certain public bodies to engage in sentencing planning, and requires Scottish ministers to produce minimum standards for through-care support. At the time of writing, there is another public consultation on the long-term prisoner release process.[32] This rehabilitative message from the Government of Scotland may be merely 'performance' (see Buchan and McNeill 2023), but, for me, it raises questions of political will, and maybe of political dynamics.[33]

Nothing is straightforward. The prison population has surged in Scotland, as it has in England and Wales. In chapter one in this volume, Annison et al (at page x) are critical of 'political elites' seeking to drive public policy reform from the top down. My examples from Scotland seem to me to show genuine consultation with 'the public', and those from England and Wales show a much more punitive government, being restrained only slightly by the courts. Is the 'political elite' in Scotland driving a different agenda?

The power of public opinion is complex. Parole is no longer invisible, and indeed Parole Boards themselves have attempted to diminish the secrecy often associated with their decision-making. Whilst more public engagement

[30] www.gov.scot/news/presumption-against-short-sentences-extended/.

[31] https://consult.gov.scot/justice/bailandreleasefromcustody/.

[32] www.gov.scot/publications/long-term-prisoner-release-process-consultation/pages/7/.

[33] Another issue is jurisdictional size. Scotland and Northern Ireland are tiny jurisdictions compared with England and Wales. Does size make a difference to political leadership? Should the penal system in England and Wales be regionalised?

is welcome, greater scrutiny may drive Parole Boards to focus more on public protection than on reintegration (Fitzgerald et al 2022). Bartels et al (2018) conclude that two key themes emerge from the literature on public opinion and parole: first, that although respondents typically express dissatisfaction with sentencing, they tend to impose sentences that are on a par with or more lenient than the sentence imposed by the judge when provided with relevant information about sentencing. The second theme was support for alternatives to prison, especially for non-violent offenders, young offenders and those with substance abuse issues and/or mental illness.[34]

Is the involvement of the 'public' or 'communities' in criminal justice more sophisticated in Scotland than in England and Wales? McAra (2008), exploring the shifting modalities of power and identity in Scotland, suggested that communities are increasingly regarded as 'stakeholders' in criminal justice. I am sailing beyond my expertise as a lawyer into political science, but the 'power' to change the process clearly does not lie only with politicians, or courts, or policy-makers or communities. Goodman et al (2017) usefully remind us that punishment expands, contracts and morphs because of contestation and struggles between real people in real contexts, not simply because of a mechanical 'swing' of the pendulum. Academics should engage more in the public debate.

IV. A POSSIBLE FUTURE?

Having identified some of the significant barriers to change, I now turn to those changes which may be crucial. The first issue is to identify some basic values and principles. We need a fair system, fit for purpose. But what is that purpose? Contrary to the current eclectic mix of purposes, a primary aim of reducing the likelihood of reoffending would be invaluable. Fairness, humanity and respect[35] come near the top of my values.

There are those who would argue for 'honesty in sentencing': a system of fixed release, when the release date is known at the start of a sentence. It is more 'honest' – everyone serves one-third, half or two-thirds of their sentence, before being conditionally released. Lifers could be released the moment they have served their 'tariff'. This would bring a lot more certainty into the system. But it is also rigid. I am not going to argue for an inflexible system.

The current system already involves a lot of flexibility, with both early and delayed release. The executive decides when the majority of prisoners are released, with the Parole Board deciding only on release for the most serious cases. I have no strong views on whether people should routinely

[34] See also Freiberg and Bartels (chapter two above).
[35] See Watson (2020).

serve 30, 40 or 50 per cent of their sentence in custody before the rest is in effect suspended, subject to good behaviour. But we must explore carefully by whom, and how, decisions should be taken, and on what criteria and on what evidence.

Currently, the Parole Board of England and Wales is an executive, non-departmental, public body, not a court. In some ways, this might not matter. If parole decisions were simply 'early' release decisions, an executive body making the decision is acceptable, subject always to judicial review to ensure fairness and legality. But Parole Boards currently delay release: people on life sentences sit in prison long after their tariff or minimum term, and all those people who have been recalled during the period of supervision in the community on licence, if they are not executively re-released, await a decision of the Parole Board. Administrative delay also remains a huge problem. Prisoners wait for courses and health treatments, wait for the preparation of reports, face postponements and adjournments of hearings: these problems are mentioned in the most recent Annual Reports of all three parole boards in the UK.[36] They should surely be a 'court'. First, because the law requires it. Article 5(4) of the European Convention on Human Rights provides:

> Everyone who is deprived of his liberty by arrest or detention shall be entitled to take proceedings by which the lawfulness of his detention shall be decided speedily by a court and his release ordered if the detention is not lawful.

The executive is not permitted to detain people arbitrarily against their wishes. The law on habeas corpus evolved hundreds of years ago to prevent unlawful imprisonment. Secondly, a court or tribunal may well have greater 'power' to improve practice.

In 2018, I was encouraged to explore a better parole system by the Howard League for Penal Reform (Padfield 2018). There too, as in this chapter, I explored many of the problems facing the 'system', as well as the difficulties prisoners face in trying to negotiate their unclear pathways through the minefield of the prison system, powerless in the face of an apparently uncaring and unpredictable system. Legal advice is often not available to prisoners, and even practical advice may be hard to access. Luck plays a significant part in a prisoner's progress, eg in whether they find staff who have the time and commitment to champion their progress. Widespread variations in treatment undermine perceptions of legitimacy and leave prisoners feeling both frustrated and angry. I imagined a system where the sentencing process could be seen as dynamic and integrative, and where a Sentence Monitoring Court might oversee all release and recall processes (see also Herzog-Evans and Padfield 2015; Herzog-Evans 2019).

[36] See the annual reports of all three Boards, which identify the number of postponed or adjourned hearings. On the pains of indeterminacy and parole, see Padfield (2002, 2013); Annison and Condry (2022).

I remain convinced that a release scheme fit for purpose involves a more judicialised process. The non-governmental organisation JUSTICE produced a report in January 2022, entitled 'A Parole System Fit for Purpose'.[37] Despite a group of 17 very different members (judges, prisoners, lawyers, academics and a member of the Parole Board), we came up with unanimous recommendations. We suggested that the Parole Board should be replaced by a more obviously court-like body, a Parole Tribunal (the name already used in Scotland when the Board sits in oral hearings). We argued for a clear burden of proof, resting on the state rather than on the prisoner, to justify any continued detention beyond the minimum term. Perhaps most importantly, we argued that rehabilitation should be at the heart of the parole process.

A. The Case against

Nevertheless, the voices against such reforms have seemed to dominate. To the recently removed Conservative government, the Parole Board of England and Wales needed 'greater ministerial oversight'.[38] Their *Root and Branch Review of the Parole System* (2022) promised to make the statutory release test 'clearer', ie more restrictive (as was enacted in the Victims and Prisoners Act 2024). Annison and Guiney (2022)[39] suggest that the *Review* represented a continuation of a well-researched political strategy based upon

> the symbolic power of parole to demonstrate 'toughness' with respect to violent and sexual offending, to express solidarity with the victims of crime and reaffirm a populist credo that purportedly stands in opposition to an unaccountable and out of touch penal elite.

My argument is that this political strategy is misplaced, and perhaps the recent election may mark a shift.

B. Signs of Hope?

In this chapter, I have explored some of the reasons why challenging this populist credo is so difficult. Perhaps we are now at a 'critical juncture' which might sow the seeds of long-term change (see Karstedt et al 2019). The first signs are that the new government has recognised that they must reduce the prison population. But even where early release is seen as a way of reducing the prison

[37] Which I chaired. See https://justice.org.uk/our-work/criminal-justice-system/current-work-criminal-justice/post-conviction-decision-making-a-parole-system-fit-for-purpose/.

[38] https://assets.publishing.service.gov.uk/media/6424028e2fa848001 3ec0e3d/victims-and-prisoners-bill-impact-assessment-victims-of-criminal-conduct-impact-assessment.pdf.

[39] See also Guiney (2023).

population, it can be a self-defeating strategy. Weaver et al (2012) argued that early release can feed public cynicism, especially about community supervision. Releasing people 'early' with little supervision and support may well result in new offences. Hard-pressed probation officers are likely to recall many of those released. Resourcing the 'system' is a prerequisite to reform.

Today's government is rightly confronting the prison crisis (overcrowding, if not yet understaffing and dreadful prison conditions). But simply tinkering with executive early-release schemes is hardly a solution. Throughout the UK, the prison population must be reduced, by reducing the flow into prison as much as the routes out, by building the credibility of punishments in the community, challenging the frequency of life sentences and reducing the length of individual prison sentences, for example.

In this chapter, I have focused on the barriers to achieving any of these ambitions: the state of prisons; uncertainties about the purposes of sentencing and of prisons; the fixation with risk and offender management; and the politics of power. These are clearly largely 'political' challenges. Ismail (2020), pointing out that imprisonment and austerity policies have been political choices in the UK, suggests that governments should find more cost-effective alternatives to incarceration. Indeed, these challenges could be dealt with: prisons and probation could be improved (especially if there was a real attempt to cut the number of people sent to prisons); and an honest ambition to reduce reoffending might turn more attention to fairness and rehabilitation.

My main conclusion is not new. A Parole Board is one small cog in a complicated system. It sits amidst a chain of processes, each link of which has to be effective for the Board to function well. The 'parole' system will not improve without a vast improvement to the prison and probation system. Without dealing with the four barriers to reform outlined in this chapter, improvements are unlikely.

REFERENCES

Annison, H (2022) 'The Role of Storylines in Penal Policy Change' 24 *Punishment & Society* 387.

Annison, H and Condry R (2022) 'The Pains of Hope: Families of Indeterminate Sentenced Prisoners and Political Campaigning by Lay Citizens' 62 *British Journal of Criminology* 1252.

Annison, H and Guiney, T (2022) 'Populism, Conservatism and the Politics of Parole in England and Wales' 93(3) *The Political Quarterly* 416.

Armstrong, S (2020) 'At Risk of Rights: Rehabilitation, Sentence Management and the Structural Violence of Prison' 28 *Critical Criminology* 85.

Barry, M (2021) 'Walking on Ice': The Future of Parole in a Risk-Obsessed Society' 25(2) *Theoretical Criminology* 325.

Bartels, L, Fitzgerald, R and Freiberg, A (2018) 'Public Opinion on Sentencing and Parole' 65(3) *Probation Journal* 269.

Bild, J (2014) 'The Mandatory Life Sentence for Murder: Lessons from Two Neighbours' (unpublished PhD diss, University of Cambridge).
Bottoms, A (1980) 'An Introduction to "The Coming Crisis"' in AE Bottoms and RH Preston (eds), *The Coming Penal Crisis. A Criminological and Theological Exploration* (Edinburgh, Scottish Academic Press).
Brangan, L (2019) Civilising Imprisonment: The Limits of Scottish Penal Exceptionalism 59 *British Journal of Criminology* 780.
Buchan, J and McNeill, F (2023) 'Progressive Penality as Performance' 62 *The Howard Journal of Crime and Justice* 325.
Burke, L and Collett, S (2014) *Delivering Rehabilitation: The politics, governance and control of probation* (London, Routledge).
Carr, N and Blay, E (2019) 'Parole and Prisoner Release: Exploring Rationalities Across Time and Place' 11(3) *European Journal of Probation* 119.
Carter, P (2003) 'Managing Offenders, Reducing Crime: A New Approach' (Strategy Unit).
Cracknell, M (2020) 'Post-Sentence Supervision: A Case Study of the Extension of Community Resettlement Support for Short Sentence Prisoners' 67 *Probation Journal* 340.
Dagan, N (2022) 'Overcoming Penal Boundaries: Exploring the Evolution of Retributive Time Through Parole Decision-Making' 62(1) *British Journal of Criminology* 37.
Dünkel, F, Padfield, N and van Zyl Smit, D (eds) (2010) *Release from Prison – European Policy and Practice* (Cullumpton, Willan Publishing).
Dwyer, C (2015) 'Governing Justice Through Risk: The Development of Penal and Social Policies in a Transitional Context' in A-M McAlinden and C Dwyer (eds), *Criminal Justice in Transition: The Northern Ireland Context* (Oxford, Hart Publishing).
Dwyer, C and McAlinden, A-M (2015) 'Crime and Criminal Justice in Northern Ireland: Conflict, Transition and the Legacy of the Past' in A-M McAlinden and C Dwyer (eds), *Criminal Justice in Transition: The Northern Ireland Context* (Oxford, Hart Publishing).
Elliot, M and Thomas, R (2024) *Public Law*, 5th edn (Oxford, Oxford University Press).
Fair, H and Walmsley, R (2024) *World Prison Population List*, 14th edn (Institute for Crime and Justice Policy Research, Birkbeck University of London).
Fitzgerald, R, Freiberg, A, Dodd, S and Bartels, L (2023) *Parole on Probation: Public Opinion, Public Confidence and Parole Decision-Making* (Basingstoke, Palgrave Macmillan).
Goodman, P, Page, J and Phelps, M (2017) *Breaking the Pendulum: The Long Struggle over Criminal Justice* (Oxford, Oxford University Press).
Guiney, T (2023) 'Parole, Parole Boards and the Institutional Dilemmas of Contemporary Prison Release' 25(3) *Punishment & Society* 621.
Harcourt, B E (2007). *Against prediction: Profiling, policing, and punishing in an actuarial age*. University of Chicago Press.
Herzog-Evans, M (2019) 'French Early Release: McProcedures and McRe-entry' 11(3) *European Journal of Probation* 188.
Herzog-Evans, M and Padfield, N (2015) 'The JAP: Lessons for England and Wales?' (Criminal Justice Alliance).
Höffler, K and Padfield, N (2022) 'The Implementation of Sentences' in K Ambos, A Duff, A Heinze, J Roberts and T Weigend (eds), *Core Concepts in Criminal Law and Criminal Justice*, vol II (Cambridge, Cambridge University Press).

Hucklesby, A and Corcoran, M (eds) (2016) *The Voluntary Sector and Criminal Justice* (Basingstoke, Palgrave Macmillan).

Ismail, N (2020) 'The Politics of Austerity, Imprisonment and Ignorance: A Case Study of English Prisons' 60(2) *Medicine, Science and the Law* 89 https://doi.org/10.1177%2F0025802419899744.

JUSTICE (2022) 'A Parole System Fit for Purpose' https://justice.org.uk/our-work/criminal-justice-system/current-work-criminal-justice/post-conviction-decision-making-a-parole-system-fit-for-purpose/.

Karstedt, S, Bergin, T and Koch, M (2019) 'Critical Junctures and Conditions of Change: Exploring the Fall of Prison Populations in US States' 28(1) *Social & Legal Studies* 58 https://doi.org/10.1177/0964663917747342.

King, R and Wilmott, L (2022) *The Honest Politician's Guide to Prisons and Probation* (Abingdon, Routledge).

Maruna, S, Immarigeon, R and LeBel, TP (2004) 'Ex-offender Reintegration: Theory and Practice' in S Maruna and R Immarigeon (eds), *After Crime and Punishment* (Cullumpton, Willan Publishing).

McAra, L (2005) 'Modelling Penal Transformation' 7 *Punishment and Society* 277.

—— (2008) 'Crime, Criminology and Criminal Justice in Scotland' 5 *European Journal of Criminology* 481.

McNaull, G (2016) 'Review of Criminal Justice in Transition: The Northern Ireland Context, A-M McAlinden and C Dwyer (eds)' 55 *Howard Journal of Criminal Justice* 537.

O'Mahony, D and Chapman, T (2007) 'Probation, the State and Community – Delivering Probation Services in Northern Ireland' in L Gelsthorpe and R Morgan (eds), *The Handbook of Probation* (Cullumpton, Willan Publishing).

McEvoy, K and Mika, H (2002) 'Restorative Justice and the Critique of Informalism in Northern Ireland' 42 *British Journal of Criminology* 534 https://doi.org/10.1093/bjc/42.3.534.

McNeill, F (2019) 'Contesting Probation in Scotland: How an Agonistic Perspective Travels' 44(3) *Law & Social Inquiry* 814.

—— (2018) *Pervasive Punishment: Making Sense of Mass Supervision* (Bingley, Emerald).

Northern Ireland Audit Office (2023) 'Reducing Adult Re-offending in Northern Ireland' www.niauditoffice.gov.uk/files/niauditoffice/documents/2023-06/NI%20Audit%20Office%20Report%20-%20Reducing%20Adult%20Reoffending%20in%20NI_0.pdf

Padfield, N (2002) *Beyond the Tariff: Human Rights and the Release of Life Sentence Prisoners* (Cullompton, Willan).

(2010) 'The Sentencing, Management and Treatment of "Dangerous" Offenders' (Council of Europe) https://rm.coe.int/168070f091.

—— (2013) 'Understanding Recall 2011' University of Cambridge Faculty of Law Research Paper No 2/2013 https://ssrn.com/abstract=2201039, http://dx.doi.org/10.2139/ssrn.2201039.

—— (2016) 'The Magnitude of the Offender Rehabilitation and "Through the Gate" Resettlement Revolution' *Crim LR* 99.

—— (2018) 'Parole: Reflections and Possibilities: A Discussion Paper (Howard League for Penal Reform) https://howardleague.org/wp-content/uploads/2018/05/Parole-reflections-and-possibilites.pdf.

—— (2020) 'The Function of the Parole Board – Avoiding Failure or Promoting Success?' (July) *Public Law* 468.
—— (2024) 'Victims at Parole' in M Manikis and G Watson (eds), *Sentencing, Public Opinion, and Criminal Justice* (Oxford, Oxford University Press).
Podmore, J (2017) 'A Farewell to NOMS: We Need More Than a Name Change' (The Justice Gap) www.thejusticegap.com/farewell-noms-need-name-change/.
Raynor, P and Vanstone, M (2007) 'Towards a Correctional Service' in L Gelsthorpe and R Morgan (eds), *The Handbook of Probation* (Cullumpton, Willan Publishing).
Roberts, J and Dagan, N (2019) 'Just Deserts, Penal Censure, and Parole' in A du Bois-Pedain and A Bottoms (eds), *Penal Censure: Engagements Within and Beyond Desert Theory* (Oxford, Hart Publishing).
Robinson, G and McNeill, F (2023) 'Punishment in the Community: Evolution, Expansion, and Moderation' in A Liebling, S Maruna and L McAra (eds), *The Oxford Handbook of Criminology*, 7th edn (Oxford, Oxford University Press).
Scottish Prisons Commission (2008) *Scotland's Choice: The Report of the Scottish Prisons Commission.*
Tomczak, P (2018) *The Penal Voluntary Sector* (Abingdon, Routledge).
van Zyl Smit, D and Corda, A (2018) 'American Exceptionalism in Parole Release and Supervision: A European Perspective' in KR Reitz (ed), American Exceptionalism in Crime and Punishment (New York, Oxford University Press) 410–86.
Weaver, B, Tata, C, Munro, M and Barry, M (2012) 'The Failure of Recall to Prison: Early Release, Front-Door and Back-Door Sentencing and the Revolving Prison Door in Scotland' 4 *European Journal of Probation* 85.

9

Between Ideal and Practice: What's Wrong with Discretionary Early Release?

KRISTEL BEYENS AND LARS BREULS

I. INTRODUCTION

THIS CHAPTER FOCUSES on the discretionary early release system for long-term prisoners in Belgium, which was legally introduced in 2006.[1] Since then, persons with a prison sentence totalling more than three years usually pass different stages of semi-liberty, such as short leaves, prison furloughs, semi-detention, electronic monitoring and conditional release (parole), before being finally released. This is frequently referred to in practice as 'the progressive system of release'.

At each stage, decisions are taken by the Penitentiary Administration and/or a Sentence Implementation Court, which introduces consecutive moments (or phases) of uncertainty surrounding the result of each decision. Reparation of the harm caused to victims and reintegration of the (formerly) incarcerated persons are important official leading principles for release decision-making in Belgium. This approach starts from the expectation that incarcerated individuals must actively engage with their re-entry into society and life after prison whilst being in prison.

This chapter questions the feasibility of the reintegration requirements in the progressive system of release. These expectations are particularly problematic given the limited (temporal) agency and the ongoing institutional impediments, lack of support and access to services within and outside prison during detention (Scheirs and Beyens 2019). The observation that in Belgium a growing number of convicted persons get stuck in the progressive release system and a

[1] The Act of 17 May 2006 on the External Legal Position of sentenced prisoners and the right of the victims in the framework of modalities of implementation of sentences, *Belgian Gazette*, 15 June 2006, 30.455.

growing number even 'max out' their full sentence (Robert 2018; Beyens 2019) suggests the existence of 'pains of discretionary gradual release'. These pains also result from the substantial difficulties prisoners face preparing their reintegration whilst in prison, which is of paramount importance to obtain a modality of (semi-)release during the detention trajectory. We argue that this situation creates a 'reintegration paradox' for imprisoned people, who must work towards the future while physically and mentally being stuck in prison.

The gradual discretionary release system is considered from a political, normative, legal-systemic and experiential perspective. How and under which political circumstances is the current Belgian release system legally constructed and what is the normative rationale behind it? How does this system 'work' in practice and how is it experienced by those who are subjected to it? What are the tensions between the ideal, abstract principles and grounded dynamics? And what are the unintended consequences of this progressive system for the use of parole?[2]

The requirements of the discretionary progressive early release are linked to temporal detention experiences. We show how the release system imposes additional constraints on an imprisoned person's temporal agency, by creating consecutive temporal uncertainties. We end this chapter with reflections on the desirability of the discretionary progressive early release system, as implemented in Belgium, and discuss a proposal for reform. We also question the ideal of reintegration as a guiding principle for parole in a context of risk averseness and demand for retribution and public protection.

II. POLITICAL CONTEXT OF THE ESTABLISHMENT OF THE CURRENT DISCRETIONARY PROGRESSIVE RELEASE SYSTEM IN BELGIUM[3]

A. Juridification of Parole and the Establishment of Sentence Implementation Courts

With the introduction of the Act Lejeune in 1888, Belgium became one of the first countries in Europe to introduce conditional release. An administrative discretionary system was installed and for more than 100 years, parole was granted following an administrative but non-transparent procedure, where the Minister of Justice or the members of the Cabinet could reject or accept requests for release, without any motivation or judicial guarantees. This gave ministers

[2] Although we are aware that parole has a specific meaning, depending on the jurisdiction where it is applied, for the sake of easy readability, we use the concepts of parole and conditional release interchangeably.

[3] This section builds on Scheirs (2014; 2016) and Beyens (2019).

a lot of penal power and raised substantial criticism, not least from the parole candidates. This ministerial decision-making power could, however, also lead to political backlashes, particularly when a parolee committed new, mediatised crimes.

The infamous *Dutroux* case of 1996, which involved the abduction, rape and murder of several young girls while Dutroux was on parole, and whose conditional release was decided by the then Minister of Justice Melchior Wathelet, raised questions regarding his decision and credibility. This context was therefore a catalyst to hand over the release decision-making responsibility to multidisciplinary Parole Commissions in 1998 and finally to independent multidisciplinary Sentence Implementation Courts in 2006. The Act on the External Legal Position of 2006 transferred the decision-making authority from the executive power to the judiciary to reinforce procedural and substantive statutory rights of prisoners (eg due process, fairness, legitimacy) and to meet the criticism of the lack of judicial guarantees of the release procedure in Belgium. Since then, Sentence Implementation Courts have decided on cases of people convicted to prison sentences of more than three years. The multidisciplinary composition of these courts was regarded as a necessary condition to improve the quality of the release decision-making, which required a combination of legal reasoning and expertise in social reintegration and the effects of the deprivation of liberty (Snacken et al 2010; Scheirs et al 2015).

The juridification and strengthening of the legal position of the parole candidates and the professionalisation of the members of the Sentence Implementation Court were particularly welcomed, as was the multidisciplinary composition of the court, which was seen as a guarantee for expert and deliberate decision-making through which the quality of the decision-making could be improved. Politicians were relieved of the burden of deciding on sensitive cases, but at the same time, they lost their control over the release process for prisoners serving longer sentences. For persons sentenced to a prison term of no more than three years, a ministerial–administrative system of quasi-automatic early release remained in place until the decision-making power for this group was also recently (2022/2023) transferred to the judiciary – something that was already stipulated in the aforementioned 2006 law. In this chapter, however, we focus only on the parole system for prison sentences exceeding three years.

B. A Discretionary Progressive Release System

In these cases, multidisciplinary Sentence Implementation Courts decide on early release after a judicial procedure and an adversarial court hearing where the Public Prosecutor, the prison governor and the convicted person and/or their lawyer is heard. Conditional release is often the end of a longer trajectory of inside-outside prison, which is constructed around different and consecutive 'sentence implementation modalities', such as short leaves, penitentiary furloughs, semi-detention and/or electronic monitoring, which should be applied for and granted on an individual basis.

Persons sentenced to more than three years of imprisonment can be conditionally released after serving one-third of their sentence. However, those sentenced to 30 years or life imprisonment must serve longer periods. The legally defined parole date is the anchor point for eligibility for all sentence implementation modalities, and is thus an important moment in the sentence trajectory. Imprisoned persons can ask for short leaves or prison furloughs, for periods of 16 and 36 hours respectively, one or two years prior to the eligibility date of their conditional release. According to the law, these furloughs are framed in a rehabilitative logic and must be used to look for a job, housing or education in society. Although these leaves and furloughs are part of the 'standard regime', they are granted – and thus can be refused – by the Prison Administration on an individual basis, which, for many prisoners, is the first hurdle to overcome.

Six months before the eligibility date for conditional release, imprisoned persons can apply for electronic monitoring or semi-detention (leaving prison to work daily for a maximum of 12 hours). The Sentence Implementation Courts decide whether to grant this. And although the time conditions are fixed, the discretionary aspect of the process is introduced with the evaluation of five 'counter-indications': (i) the absence of prospects for the social reintegration of the imprisoned person; (ii) the risk of committing further serious offences; (iii) the risk that the imprisoned person would harass victims; (iv) the attitude of the imprisoned person towards the victim(s) of the offence they were convicted of; and (v) the efforts undertaken to pay the civil parties. These counter-indications reflect the importance of social reintegration, but also the concern to avoid the risk of recidivism and to safeguard the interests of victims. Parole candidates must provide a 'reintegration plan' showing their prospects for post-prison reintegration and the efforts that they have already made in this regard. As the counter-indications are very wide-ranging, they offer considerable discretion to the decision-makers of the Sentence Implementation Courts (Scheirs 2014).

Although a system of progression is not explicitly stipulated in the 2006 Act on the External Legal Position, in practice, Sentence Implementation Courts mainly do not grant conditional release, electronic monitoring or semi-detention if the prisoner has not been previously granted a penitentiary furlough or short prison leave. This has instigated a practice that has been called 'the path of progressive release' (Scheirs 2014; 2016; Beyens 2019; Vander Beken 2021). This progressive system also gives the Prison Administration, which takes decisions about short leaves and furloughs, considerable power in opening, delaying or cutting off the possibility for conditional release. And although the logic of this system is formally framed as rehabilitative, Beyens et al (2022) showed that these stages through which imprisoned persons are required to pass to move towards release are experienced as recurring obstacles to be overcome, which hinder, rather than support, the pathway out of prison.

III. A REINTEGRATION-ORIENTED PAROLE SYSTEM VERSUS PAROLE POPULISM

The Belgian Prison Act of 2005,[4] which enacts the imprisoned person's rights (the so-called internal legal position), and the Act on the External Legal Position of 2006, which regulates the release of imprisoned persons, are both based on the principle of the autonomy of the aims of the implementation of sentences and of the aims of sentencing. This principle reflects and justifies the different priorities in decision-making at the different stages of the punishment process. It states that, whatever the aims may have been at the time of sentencing, which are inherently backward-looking and focused on the committed offences, such as retribution, these should not be considered as mandatory goals to be pursued during the actual implementation of the sentence (Dupont 1998: 134–36; Snacken 2004; van Zyl Smit and Snacken 2009; Snacken et al 2010).

The execution of the sentence is instead primarily future-oriented, prioritising the mitigation of the harmful effects of the punishment, the reparation of the harm caused to the victims and the reintegration of the offender. So, the principle of relative autonomy recognises the competing aims of punishment at each stage of the criminal justice process and emphasises that their importance may vary between the imposition of a sentence and its implementation. While there is (or should be) a logical coherence between the legal framework for sentencing and that for the implementation of the sentence, this coherence is considered to be 'relative'. Both legal frameworks recognise, for example, that retribution at the level of sentence implementation is confined exclusively to the deprivation of the 'freedom of movement' and the establishment of a minimum custodial period that must be served before eligibility for (early) release can be considered (for an in-depth analysis, see Maes 2009: 176–80, 1129–31).[5]

It should immediately be recognised, however, that the theory of relative autonomy may not be persuasive to all. Both politicians and the public may regard 'relative autonomy' as a weakening of the retributive, deterrent or incapacitatory effects of punishment, and may therefore call for a 'truth in sentencing policy', where all sentences are served in prison until the last day.

[4] The Prison Act of 12 January 2005 on the prison system and the legal position of prisoners, *Belgian Gazette*, 1 February 2005, 2.815.

[5] This paragraph is based on Beyens et al (2013) and Beyens (2019).

Indeed, through legislation, politicians have sought to limit the decision-making power of the Sentence Implementation Court, aiming to reclaim the control they relinquished when transferring parole decision-making authority to the judiciary. For example, in 2013, the time conditions for persons serving very long sentences, such as 30 years or life imprisonment, were tightened.[6] As a result, at least 15 years must now be served before becoming eligible for parole, instead of the previous 10 years. Long-term-sentenced recidivists must serve at least 19 or 23 years, depending on the nature of their earlier convictions. The eligibility dates for short leaves, prison furloughs, semi-detention and electronic monitoring are adapted accordingly, implying that the period of 'deep imprisonment' (Crewe 2011) is extended. Moreover, these eligibility dates are only theoretical dates, as in most cases, they are exceeded by a considerable margin (Maes and Tange 2014; unpublished data of the Prison Service 2022).

This 2013 reform was a direct political reaction to the highly mediatised conditional release of Michelle Martin, the ex-wife of Marc Dutroux, who was convicted as a co-offender in his crimes. Public outrage followed her release, with widespread protests demanding stricter release policies. The media also played a crucial role in shaping public sentiment by closely documenting every aspect of Martin's post-release life, often focusing on even the most mundane details. For example, the press reported on her visit to a hairdresser in Knokke, her completion of a first-aid course with the Red Cross and her efforts to find a job. This relentless media attention not only intensified public outrage, but also posed significant barriers to Martin's rehabilitation, turning her every move into a public spectacle rather than allowing for a more discreet reintegration process (Daems 2014; Breuls et al 2015).

In this context, politicians tend to quickly compete with one another to address the public's emotional needs and demands (Karstedt 2002: 303). After Martin was granted conditional release in 2011, politicians from across the political spectrum swiftly called for stricter legislation on conditional release. Following her actual release in 2012, the then Prime Minister Elio Di Rupo further fuelled the debate by strongly advocating for 'incompressible prison sentences', implying that certain offenders should never be released early (Breuls et al 2015).

Another clear example of such political reaction emerged in the aftermath of the 2016 Brussels bombings. Two of the attackers had been released early from prison, violated their parole conditions, and subsequently disappeared from the authorities' radar. This fuelled the introduction of the 2017 provision allowing the imposition of a 'security period' for 'extremely serious offences', such as terrorism, rape or the murder of police officers, during the sentencing phase. This provision permits the sentencing judge or the Court of Assizes to set a

[6] The Act of 17 March 2013, which amends the Act of 17 May 2006 on the external legal position of sentenced prisoners and the right of the victims in the framework of modalities of implementation of sentences, *Belgian Gazette*, 19 March 2013, 16.363.

period – typically two-thirds of the sentence instead of one-third – during which conditional release is not possible. For sentences exceeding 30 years, the security period can range from 15 to 25 years.[7] The introduction of such a security period was clearly a response to criticisms that the release policy for long-term prisoners was too flexible or lenient. At the same time, it appears to be a flagrant violation of the relative autonomy principle, and it effectively sidelines the Sentence Implementation Courts for an extended period before eligibility.

These two examples clearly illustrate the influence of public opinion, political pressure and media scrutiny on parole policies in Belgium, undermining expert judgement in the phase of sentence execution and rehabilitation-focused justice. In response to public outrage, particularly in high-profile cases involving serious crimes, governments frequently impose more restrictive parole measures or reduce the discretion traditionally held by parole authorities – examples of what is coined 'parole populism' (Moffa et al 2019; Fitzgerald et al 2023). Indeed, in Belgium, highly mediatised cases have made parole 'a focus of political debate in the name of prioritising victims, community safety and appearing tough on crime, which has resulted in divergence from the original purpose of parole' (Moffa et al 2019: 75).

IV. UNREALISTIC REINTEGRATION EXPECTATIONS WITH LITTLE SUPPORT? DELAYED RELEASE AND MAXING OUT

Despite these tightening measures, the decision-making practices of the Sentence Implementation Courts have remained strongly focused on reintegration. Reintegration is still a guiding principle of the Belgian conditional release system. However, it is not something that happens effortlessly. Candidate parolees face numerous legal and practical demands, including the responsibility to provide a reintegration plan to demonstrate their readiness for parole. The reintegration plan typically must meet minimum requirements, including securing housing, employment or education, and treatment for issues underlying the criminal conduct (Scheirs 2016).

A. Delayed Release

The support incarcerated persons receive to prepare their reintegration plan, however, differs between prisons, depending on, inter alia: the efforts of the psychosocial service, which is increasingly overloaded with writing risk assessments instead of providing support to the detained persons; the availability of

[7] The Act of 21 December 2017 changing several provisions to introduce the implementation of a security period and to change the Act of 20 July 1990 regarding remand imprisonment and immediate arrest, *Belgian Gazette*, 11 January 2018, 1.185.

local services in the community; and the available infrastructure for education and work in prison. In general, the support is very modest and the availability of services for treatment of sexual offenders, for example, is clearly insufficient, leading to long waiting lists, resulting in extension of the detention periods of these individuals and thus exceeding their eligibility dates (Scheirs and Beyens 2019). We argue that this situation creates a 'reintegration paradox' (Beyens et al 2022) for imprisoned persons, who are expected to plan for their future while remaining physically and mentally trapped in often overcrowded prisons with minimal support.

Ideally, and according to the Belgian Prison Act of 2005, the (preparation of the) social reintegration of imprisoned individuals should start at the very beginning of the detention period. From this perspective, the requirement of a 'detention plan' is outlined in Article 75 of the Belgian Prison Act:

> The Prison Service shall ensure that the prisoner is given the widest possible access to the full range of training activities made available with regard to his personal development, to the meaningful spending of his detention time, and to maintaining or improving prospects of successful reintegration into society. (own translation).

In this plan, the different steps and activities to be carried out during detention in the preparation for progressive release should be identified. In particular, the specific obstacles to successful reintegration of the detained persons must be identified and solutions must be proposed in the detention plan (Dupont 1998). The detention plan is thus a condition for the elaboration of a sound reintegration plan. However, the stipulations about the detention plan were only implemented in 2019[8] and the investment in practice is very limited. So, to date, the necessary support for preparing a reintegration plan is still very minimal, and in the context of continuing prison overcrowding in Belgium, it does not look like it will change any time soon. All these factors add up to the reality that preparations for release only begin when the possible release date is approaching, resulting in serious delays in the actual release date. We should therefore speak of *delayed release* instead of early release.[9]

To illustrate the delays, recent non-published internal data from the Prison Service show that in 2016, 93 per cent of all released persons with a sentence of three years or more were released later than after one-third of their sentence. In 2021, this percentage had slightly decreased to 86 per cent, indicating that only 14 per cent of all parolees were released having served just one-third of their sentence, as is stipulated in the law. Of all parolees, 69 per cent stayed in prison for more than half of their sentence.[10] Although very general, these data put the legal eligibility date of release after one-third in perspective.

[8] The Royal Decree of 5 April 2019 determining the date of effect of Title IV of the Belgian Prison Act of 12 January 2005, *Belgian Gazette*, 26 April 2019, 40 557.

[9] We thank Nicky Padfield for this comment on our chapter.

[10] These data refer to all releases, including after electronic monitoring, semi-detention or parole, and they do not differentiate between first offenders and recidivists.

The delay in granting parole is also demonstrated by the mean number of days of delay per year compared to the legal eligibility date. In 2016, the mean delay was 408 days; in 2021, this had increased to 742 days.[11] This not only indicates that the exceedance period for granting parole is quite long, but also that it has increased by 75 per cent in six years, which is quite remarkable. However, these data do not provide any insight into the reasons for the delay, which can be systemic, caused by the complex procedure, lack of support and treatment facilities or risk-averse decision-making, or caused by individual characteristics of the parole candidates, such as lack of motivation, lack of initiative, estimated dangerousness, lack of personal resources in society, lack of residence permit, earlier recalls to prison, etc. For example, Aydin's (2024) recent research of one Sentence Implementation Court shows that a considerable number of cases of maxing out is linked to persons without a residence permit who are awaiting expulsion to their country of origin after their sentence, which points to the link between release policies and immigration control policies (*cf* 'crimmigration').

B. Maxing Out

A final legal aspect worth mentioning is that if parole is granted, the Sentence Implementation Court also imposes a period on licence, which lasts at least for the remaining term of the prison sentence. This ranges from a minimum period of one year for those with a sentence of up to five years, to between five and 10 years if the person is serving a prison sentence of more than five years, and up to 10 years for those with life sentences. Consequently, the licence period can exceed the remaining prison sentence, which demonstrates how control in the form of extended supervision after early release was already on the legislator's mind when developing the Act of 2006. This can lead to the unintended side effect of imprisoned persons maxing out their sentences instead of asking for parole.

The more denials parole candidates face for prison leaves, furloughs or electronic monitoring, the longer their path to obtaining parole becomes (*cf* the progressive path of early release). As they approach the end date of their sentence, the risk increases that, if granted parole, the period of supervision will exceed the time remaining on their sentence. Consequently, they may adjust their aspirations and reduce or stop their efforts to meet the requirements of the Sentence Implementation Courts. Therefore, when a critical point is passed,

[11] It remains unclear to what extent this increase is linked to a policy change, specifically the alignment of parole eligibility dates for first-time offenders and recidivists. Previously, recidivists were required to serve at least two-thirds of their sentence in prison. Although this has not been the case since 2021, in practice, their risk of recidivism may still be assessed as high for an extended period by the Sentence Implementation Courts, delaying their release for a longer period of time than is legally defined.

parole candidates become discouraged, lose hope and 'prefer' to max out their sentence in prison, thereby leaving prison without supervisory conditions or support, which contrasts markedly with the aim of reintegration.

In 2013, the number of persons maxing out their sentence surpassed the number of those who got parole (Beyens and Maes 2017: 281). According to unpublished internal data of the Prison Service, in 2016, 735 persons with a sentence of more than three years served their full sentence in prison, which is 56 per cent of all released convicted persons with such a sentence (for comparison, only 585 individuals were released on parole). This was an alarming number, and in 2021 the number of prisoners maxing out their sentence had decreased to 508 (43 per cent of all releases), compared to 668 prisoners who got parole. This is, however, still a high percentage for a system that officially proclaims that all imprisoned persons are eligible for parole after a certain period of detention. This high number of 'maxing outs', which is clearly linked to the discretionary gradual release system, is thus not in line with the spirit of the law and the ideal of reintegration.

V. LIVED EXPERIENCES OF THE DISCRETIONARY GRADUAL SYSTEM OF RELEASE[12]

What is the impact of these release practices on the to-be-released subjects themselves? How do they cope with this reality? Based on interviews with persons with experience of detention in Belgium, Beyens et al (2022) analysed their experiences from a temporal perspective. They found that the way prison life is organised and how detention time is experienced are completely at odds with the stringent requirements that the system attaches to early release. Throughout the interviews, strong emphasis was placed on the absence of support in prison. The expectations to work towards the future were experienced as unrealistic.

Imprisoned individuals, however, do not passively endure their incarceration, release policies or the expectations placed upon them. To some extent, they are able to exercise agency and resist the system's demands (Rubin 2015). This agency applies not only to their experience of prison life, but also to how they adjust their temporal expectations concerning release. As Flaherty (2020: 13) notes, prisoners attempt 'to control, manipulate, and customize their own temporal experience', adapting their expectations to the uncertainty and frequent delays of the release process.

[12] This section is based upon Beyens et al (2022).

A. Lack of Assistance

Imprisonment leads, amongst other things, to the weakening of ties with family and friends, the loss of residence and the loss of work, all of which created a feeling of 'having to start from scratch again' (eg Tom, a person whose conditional release has been recounted in Beyens et al 2022). Complaints about the lack of support from the psychosocial services – or even about the way in which, for some, these services obstructed the reintegration process – were omnipresent throughout the interviews.

Offers of assistance (eg treatment for addiction and psychological problems) in prison are limited. Only 35 per cent of the prisoners have access to jobs in prison and only 5 per cent have access to education and training for qualifications (FOD Justitie 2019: 18). So, just to get a job or to participate in classes inside prison, incarcerated individuals often must spend several months on a waiting list, even though these are important activities in preparing for their return to society.

Without working or studying, imprisoned people spend most of their days and nights in their cell, watching TV, playing games, cleaning, drawing or writing as the main boredom management strategies to kill time. Time in prison is generally experienced as slow and 'sticky' (Griffiths 2014: 1994). While in prison, time is experienced as standing still, whilst life outside, of course, continues. The implication here is that imprisoned people often have the feeling of 'losing' time as they miss out on transitional events, such as children's birthday parties, family reunions and funerals, which makes them feel alienated from their friends, who all continued with their lives. Whilst people outside evolve, the life of the prisoners is put on hold.

The ways in which temporal agency is exercised by imprisoned individuals generally varies throughout the different stages of a prison sentence, reflecting a renewed or heightened focus on life outside in preparation for release (Wheeler 1961; Irwin 1970; O'Donnell 2014; Crewe et al 2020). But in a discretionary release system, convicted persons are expected to prepare for a release date that might not come, or is postponed several times. The waiting for decisions by administrative decision-makers and/or courts, which follow a bureaucratic framework of procedural time, therefore generates frustrations, which we call 'pains of discretionary gradual release'.

B. Early Release, Anticipatory Waiting, Despair and Dropping Out

The 'path of progressive release', to which most judicial actors adhere so enthusiastically, is thus a daily concern for many parole candidates. Although not required by law, short prison leaves and furloughs are considered by the majority of decision-makers as the first steps in this gradual path to liberty. They can be used for job interviews or for an intake meeting for a training course, and are thus important and necessary steps towards the reintegration plan. Once imprisoned individuals are eligible for sentence implementation modalities, a process of anticipatory waiting starts. This is a period of waiting for something meaningful and/or of hoping for good news. However, if the applications for short leaves, furloughs or other sentence modalities are rejected several times, the risk of becoming cynical and desperate is real. This was confirmed by several interviewees, who felt that the modalities in the progressive pathway of release were used as a privilege to be handed out rather than steps towards their release. One interviewee, for instance, called the uncertainty associated with the discretionary gradual early release system 'the worst punitive experience', or an additional psychological punishment. The interviewees had the feeling that working out a reintegration plan was their sole responsibility, and their frustrations were compounded by lengthy administrative procedures.

The discretionary early release system, with its uncertain release dates, imposes contextual constraints that limit imprisoned persons' ability to exercise temporal agency, such as planning ahead and making arrangements with family, friends and employers. Despite being in a highly controlled environment, imprisoned individuals still attempt to exercise some degree of temporal agency, finding ways to control and adapt their experience of time (*cf* Sayer 2012; Flaherty 2020). As a coping strategy, many prisoners abandon any expectations of early release. The 'pains of discretionary gradual release' have led a significant number of convicted persons to intentionally forgo applying for early release, opting instead to serve their full sentence, which has contributed to the phenomenon of maxing out. While the choice to 'max out' might appear desperate, it can also be understood as a rational response to the constraints of the current system – an intentional exercise of temporal agency. Maxing out then becomes a calculated decision to avoid the uncertainty of the parole process and its psychological burdens.

However, the 'choice' to stay in prison until the end of the sentence comes at a significant cost: not only does the length of the sentence increase, but so too does its perceived depth, with incarcerated persons finding themselves 'being buried far from liberty, deep below the surface of freedom' (Crewe 2011: 521), away from associated life plans, social ties and attachments. Paradoxically, those leaving prison at the end of their sentence are the least prepared for reintegration into society, which opens the doors to recidivism. Besides being an act of despair, maxing out can also be regarded as an act of resistance or subversion against the discretionary gradual parole system. 'Voluntarily refusing' parole means that supervision and judicial control after the detention period are avoided, undermining the goal of reintegration and the claims that current systems strive for reintegration. Maxing out can also be a rational choice to escape certain conditions, such as compensating victims, which is one of the conditions to be met before being conditionally released. Robert (2018), who studied maxing out with a small group of imprisoned persons in one Walloon prison, refers to the existence of a certain critical 'tipping point', which he describes as a 'threshold beyond which the prisoner sees more benefits in maxing out than he does in obtaining early release' (Robert 2018: 262). He found that the timing of the tipping point differs, and depends on many issues, including the time that has already been served, the exact time that is left to serve and the minimum duration of the supervisory period after detention. The tipping point can also be linked to elements of the release system, such as the number of negative decisions, or negative release experiences, such as recall.

VI. DISCUSSION: WHICH FUTURE FOR PAROLE?

Research shows how persons with a prison sentence of more than three years face numerous unrealistic expectations while preparing for release in a discretionary system. Within Belgian prisons and beyond, incarcerated individuals are expected to actively work towards change during their detention, with limited, if any, structural and emotional support to do so. This can be considered a 'reintegration paradox' (Beyens et al 2022). This paradox is compounded by the uncertainties of the discretionary release system, which impose psychological burdens on prisoners.

The combination of expected progression and uncertainty, due to a discretionary release system that seeks to reduce recidivism and risk (Scheirs 2016; Vander Beken 2021) and which is susceptible to parole populism, is at the heart of the pains described in this chapter. The combination of the aim of reintegration, which supposes a positive and future-oriented approach of the parole candidate by the decision-makers, with risk awareness and even risk aversion is noxious. The ideas of dangerousness, public protection and retribution are hard to leave behind, particularly at moments when high-profile cases are widely covered in the media and politicians publicly question the legitimacy of parole, which has led to stricter legislation, particularly for certain serious and highly mediatised offences. The discretionary decision-making, even with the best intentions, introduces a lot of uncertainties, leading to disengagement towards the preparation of parole.

It could be argued that temporal pains and uncertainties could be eased if imprisoned people knew what to expect in terms of release dates – an argument that is supported by the observation that an increasing number of convicted people 'choose' to stay in prison until the only date they are certain of, ie the end of their sentence. From this perspective, a system with fixed dates of release after a certain period in prison, of one-third, half or two-thirds of the imposed sentence, may be preferable. In any case, this idea is alive and well, since Van De Voorde, the then Director-General of the Belgian Prison Service, outlined such a proposal in 2020: 'Let us define the sentence of deprivation of liberty as the sequential composition of an intramural part of deprivation of liberty and an extramural part of restriction of liberty. Let both be fixed in time at the sentencing process' (Van De Voorde 2020: 346; own translation).

This would provide 'the most solid basis for a real detention planning. A planning that from the start has a perspective in time and space' (Van De Voorde 2020: 349; own translation), and would lead to a greater continuity between the intramural and extramural periods of the sentence.

This proposal avoids the uncertainties of a discretionary release system and proposes to make release less conditional and discretionary. It also ensures that incarcerated individuals will make the transition to society in a supervised (and controlled!) way, as all imprisoned persons would get the opportunity for, or would be directed to, an extramural part of their sentence with restrictions or conditions. It also avoids the situation where the licence period exceeds the imposed sentence, which at present is a reason to stay in prison until the last day.

Belgian criminologists/criminal law scholars, such as Vander Beken (2021), also endorse such a reform, albeit with the important caveat that such a transition should be part of a broader policy of penal moderation (*cf* Snacken 2015), limiting the use and length of prison sentences in general. Indeed, the primary concern with such a system is the risk of 'compensatory sentencing' – a tendency to increase the length of the imposed sentence in order to ensure a long enough detention period, thereby undermining the goal of penal moderation. This dilemma reflects a deeper tension between the desire for certainty in release decisions and the persistent demand for retribution and incapacitation of ('dangerous') offenders, which remains strong in both public opinion and political discourse. Without accompanying reforms to reduce sentence lengths and reliance on incarceration, the risk is that the fixed release system could unintentionally lead to an increase in the number of people in prison.

In any case, based on the testimonies presented in this chapter, reforms that limit the temporal uncertainties seem more than warranted. Moreover, efforts must be made to reduce the 'reintegration paradox'. An important driver of this paradox is the limited offer of meaningful activities in prison to prepare for re-entry. This offer should, however, be part of a 'normalised' prison regime designed to prepare for reintegration. Article 5 of the European Prison Rules defines normalisation by stating that 'life in prison shall approximate as closely as possible the positive aspects of life in the community'. Snacken (2005) distinguishes between two levels of normalisation. On an individual level, normalisation refers to the idea that prison regimes should be organised in such a way that they allow imprisoned people to keep, or fulfil, their social roles, such as being a father, a friend, a student or employee, as far as possible. This should be guaranteed by normalisation on a collective level, which recognises imprisoned people's right to access the same (quality of) services and activities as is provided in society. The distinct lack of many aspects of a normalised regime contributes to the reintegration paradox, revealing that this issue is a result not only of the complex discretionary release system, but also of a deficient, overcrowded prison environment.

This raises the question of whether it is sustainable, or even desirable, to put reintegration forward as a legitimate aim of imprisonment within the context of a deficient system. In this regard, our analysis advocates for a realistic understanding of what can be accomplished in the current prison environment. It demonstrates that parole reforms, despite being well-intentioned, can only succeed if they are accompanied by broader reforms within the penitentiary system.

VII. CONCLUSION

This chapter has highlighted the complexities and challenges of Belgium's discretionary release system for convicted persons serving over three years of imprisonment. We traced the political rationale behind the 2006 reforms, aimed at depoliticising release decisions, and explored how parole remains vulnerable to political populism. Indeed, this chapter has demonstrated that parole remains a contentious practice, often scrutinised during incidents, and is therefore a particularly sensitive political issue. Moreover, the principle of relative autonomy between sentencing aims and sentence implementation aims forms the foundation of the system, but there is a significant gap between the ideal of reintegration and the reality of its implementation. Delayed releases, rather than early releases, are common, driven by systemic constraints both within and outside the prison, as well as by risk-averse decision-making. We argue that the current system's reliance on discretion imposes considerable uncertainty on imprisoned people, creating additional 'pains of discretionary release'. We suggest that a semi-automatic release system could mitigate some of these issues by reducing uncertainty and offering a clearer path towards reintegration.

REFERENCES

Aydin, H (2024) 'Achter slot en grendel tot strafeinde? Een onderzoek naar langgestraften in de Belgische gevangenissen' ['Behind Bars Until the End? A Research to Long-Term Prisoners in the Belgian Prisons'] (Masters thesis, Vrije Universiteit Brussel).

Beyens, K, Snacken, S and van Zyl Smit, D (2013) 'Truth in (the Implementation of) Sentencing: Belgium and Elsewhere' in T Daems, D van Zyl Smit and S Snacken (eds), *European Penology?* (Oxford, Hart Publishing) 271–92.

Beyens, K (2019) 'Belgian Release Policies, Rationales and Practices' 11(3) *European Journal of Probation* 169.

Beyens, K and Maes, E (2017) 'Gevangeniscapaciteit, gevangenisbevolking en gevangenispersoneel: kwantitatieve evoluties' ['Prison Capacity, Prison Population and Prison Staff: Quantitative Evolutions'] in K Beyens and S Snacken (eds), *Straffen. Een penologisch perspectief* (Antwerp, Maklu) 253–93.

Beyens, K, Breuls, L and Gilbert, E (2022) 'The "Reintegration Paradox": Working Towards the Future While Standing Still' in N Carr and G Robinson (eds), *Time and Punishment. New Contexts and Perspectives* (Basingstoke, Palgrave Macmillan) 143–69.

Breuls, L, De Leener, F and Redmond, I (2015) '"They Came Back": Media Coverage after the Release of Maxine Carr and Michelle Martin from Prison' (Masters paper, Vrije Universiteit Brussel).

Crewe, B (2011) 'Depth, Weight, Tightness: Revisiting the Pains of Imprisonment' 13(5) *Punishment & Society* 509.

Crewe, B, Hulley, S and Wright, S (2020) *Life Imprisonment from Young Adulthood: Adaptation, Identity and Time* (London, Palgrave Macmillan).

Daems, T (2014) 'Naschokken van de zaak-Dutroux: Zoeklicht op de strafuitvoering' ['Aftershocks of the Dutroux Case: Spotlight on Sentence Implementation'] in K Beyens, T Daems and E Maes (eds), *Exit gevangenis? De werking van de strafuitvoeringsrechtbanken en de wet op de externe rechtspositie van veroordeelden tot een vrijheidsstraf* (Antwerp, Maklu) 13–30.

Dupont, L (1998) 'Proeve van een Voorontwerp van Beginselenwet gevangeniswezen en tenuitvoerlegging van vrijheidsstraffen' ['Draft Proposal for a Preliminary Draft of a Basic Law on the Prison System and the Execution of Custodial Sentences'] in L Dupont (ed), *Op weg naar een beginselenwet gevangeniswezen* (Leuven, Universitaire Pers Leuven) 15–250.

Fitzgerald, R, Freiberg, A, Dodd, S and Bartels, L (2023) *Parole on Probation: Public Opinion, Public Confidence and Parole Decision-Making* (Basingstoke, Palgrave Macmillan).

Flaherty, MG (2020) 'The Lathe of Time: Some Principles of Temporal Agency' in MG Flaherty, L Meinert and AL Dalsgård (eds), *Time Work: Studies of Temporal Agency* (New York, Berghahn Books) 13–28.

FOD Justitie (2019) *Jaarverslag 2017. Directoraat-generaal Penitentiaire Inrichtingen* [*Annual Report 2017. Belgian Prison Service*] (Brussels, FOD Justitie).

Griffiths, MBE (2014) 'Out of Time: The Temporal Uncertainties of Refused Asylum Seekers and Immigration Detainees' 40(12) *Journal of Ethnic and Migration Studies* 1991.

Irwin, J (1970) *The Felon* (Englewood Cliffs, NJ, Prentice Hall).

Karstedt, S (2002) 'Emotions and Criminal Justice' 6(3) *Theoretical Criminology* 47.

Maes, E (2009) *Van gevangenisstraf naar vrijheidsstraf, 200 jaar Belgisch gevangeniswezen* [*From Prison Sentence to Deprivation of Liberty, 200 Years of Belgian Prisons*] (Antwerp, Maklu).

Maes, E and Tange, C (2014) 'Langgestrafte veroordeelden in de SURB-wachtkamer voor voorwaardelijke invrijheidstelling: "En attendant Godot?"' ['Long-Term Prisoners in the Waiting Room for Conditional Release: "Waiting on Godot?"'] in K Beyens, T Daems and E Maes (eds), *Exit gevangenis? De werking van de strafuitvoeringsrechtbanken en de wet op de externe rechtspositie van veroordeelden tot een vrijheidsstraf* (Antwerp, Maklu) 97–131.

Moffa, M, Stratton, G and Ruyters, M (2019) 'Parole Populism: The Politicisation of Parole in Victoria' 31(1) *Current Issues in Criminal Justice* 75.

O'Donnell, I (2014) *Prisoners, Solitude, and Time* (Oxford, Oxford University Press).

Robert, L (2018) 'Maxing Out in Prison. A Study of Pre-release Long-Term Prisoners' (PhD thesis, KU Leuven).

Rubin, AT (2015) 'Resistance or Friction: Understanding the Significance of Prisoners' Secondary Adjustments' 19(1) *Theoretical Criminology* 23.

Sayer, A (2012) 'Power, Causality and Normativity: A Critical Realist Critique of Foucault' 5(2) *Journal of Political Power* 179.

Scheirs, V (2014) *De strafuitvoeringsrechtbank aan het werk* [*The Sentence Implementation Court at Work*] (Antwerp, Maklu).

Scheirs, V (2016) 'Doing Reintegration? The Quest for Reintegration in Belgian Sentence Implementation' 8(2) *European Journal of Probation* 82.

Scheirs, V and Beyens, K (2019) 'Prisoners' Resettlement in Belgium: Also a Responsibility of Civil Society' in F Dünkel, I Pruin, A Storgaard and J Weber (eds), *Prisoner Resettlement in Europe* (London, Routledge) 37–50.

Scheirs, V, Beyens, K and Snacken, S (2015) 'Mixed System: Belgium. Who Is in Charge? Conditional Release in Belgium as a Complex Bifurcation Practice' in M Herzog-Evans (ed), *Offender Release and Supervision: The Role of Courts and the Use of Discretion* (Oisterwijk, Wolf Legal Publishers) 151–66.

Snacken, S (2004) 'De voorstellen van de commissie externe rechtspositie' ['The Proposals of the Commission on External Legal Status'] in Aertsen, I, Beyens, K, De Valck, S and Pieters, F (eds), *De Commissie Holsters buitenspel?* (Brussels, Politeia) 34–70.

—— (2005) 'Forms of Violence and Regimes in Prison: Report of Research in Belgian Prisons' in A Liebling and S Maruna (eds), *The Effects of Imprisonment* (Cullumpton, Willan Publishing) 306–39.

—— (2014) 'De commissie Holsters dan toch buitenspel?' ['The Holsters Commission Sidelined After All?'] in K Beyens, T Daems and E Maes (eds), *Exit gevangenis? De werking van de strafuitvoeringsrechtbanken en de wet op de externe rechtspositie van veroordeelden tot een vrijheidsstraf* (Antwerp, Maklu) 155–76.

—— (2015) 'Punishment, Legitimate Policies and Values: Penal moderation, Dignity and Human Rights' 17(3) *Punishment & Society* 397.

Snacken, S, Beyens, K and Beernaert, M-A (2010) 'Belgium' in N Padfield, D van Zyl Smit and F Dünkel (eds), *Release from Prison: European Policies and Practice*. (Cullumpton, Willan Publishing) 70–103.

Vander Beken, T (2021) *Als je klaar bent, mag je naar huis. Reflecties over doel en inhoud van vrijheidsberovende straffen en maatregelen* [*When You're Done, You Can Go Home: Reflections on the Aims and Content of liberty-Depriving Sentences and Measures*] (Brussels, VUBPress).

Van De Voorde, R (2020) 'Het einde van de voorwaardelijke invrijheidstelling' ['The End of Conditional Release'] 41(3) *Panopticon* 345.

van Zyl Smit, D and Snacken, S (2009) *Principles of European Prison Law and Policy: Penology and Human Rights* (Oxford, Oxford University Press).

Wheeler, S (1961) 'Socialization in Correctional Communities' 26(5) *American Sociological Review* 697.

10

Reconsidering Parole: The Interplay of Purpose, Expertise and Institutional Structure

JASMINA ARNEŽ AND MOJCA M PLESNIČAR

I. INTRODUCTION

THE PROCESS OF leaving prison and the mechanisms governing reintegration are as crucial as those that determine incarceration (Padfield 2014). How a person transitions out of prison can have profound implications for their future and for the broader community to which they return. The impact of a successful or unsuccessful reintegration can influence recidivism rates, community safety and the overall effectiveness of the criminal justice system.

Consider an offender who has served a significant portion of their prison sentence and is now anticipating a decision on early release. Who should determine if they are ready to re-enter society? The judge who originally sentenced them? A prosecutor whose role is to secure punishment for crimes? Or perhaps a psychologist who can assess their capacity for change? The answer is complex, lying at the intersection of law, institutional roles and varying interpretations of what parole should accomplish. The purpose and institutional setup of parole decision-making bodies have a significant impact on their outcomes.

The purpose of parole is often seen through various lenses – rehabilitation, behavioural management, risk assessment, or even as a practical tool to reduce prison overcrowding. Each of these perspectives suggests a different basis for decision-making, which can lead to inconsistencies when the purpose is not clearly defined. In Slovenia, which will be the focus of our discussion, as in many other jurisdictions, parole decisions are made by a board composed of members from different institutional backgrounds, each carrying distinct professional biases. This chapter aims to explore how the lack of a unified purpose for parole and the institutional setup of the parole board affect parole decisions.

In the chapter, we examine the Slovenian parole system, focusing on how the institutional composition of the parole board influences its functioning and alignment with the intended purposes of parole. The analysis begins with a literature review of the varied purposes of parole and the types of institutions involved in parole decision-making. This is followed by an empirical examination of the Slovenian system, drawing on interviews with parole board members. The findings emphasise the importance of clearly defining the purpose of parole and ensuring that the board's composition aligns with these objectives. We conclude by discussing broader implications for parole systems globally and the importance of institutional coherence in achieving fair and effective parole outcomes.

II. THE PURPOSES OF PAROLE AND THE COMPOSITION OF PAROLE BOARDS

Parole, as a component of criminal justice systems worldwide, exhibits substantial diversity in its implementation and the philosophies that underpin it (van Zyl Smit and Corda 2016). Criminal justice systems across the globe widely utilise parole to facilitate the conditional release of prisoners back into society, yet the nature of parole varies significantly between jurisdictions. This leads to diverse practices and procedures that govern its implementation. In many systems, parole is characterised by rigorous supervision and monitoring, aimed at ensuring public safety and aiding rehabilitation (Petersilia 1999; Kleiman and Hawken 2008; Werth 2013). Conversely, other systems may adopt a more lenient approach, allowing for early release with minimal oversight (Šugman Stubbs and Ambrož 2012). This also results in different understandings of the term 'parole' – for American readers, it might be a much more wholesome notion than for European ones, who are more likely to understand it as simply the 'release from incarceration with conditions' (van Zyl Smit and Corda 2016: 416). The terminology used for parole across Europe also reflects this distinct approach. In many European languages, 'parole' is translated as 'conditional release' (eg *liberazione condizionale* in Spanish, *libération conditionnelle* in French, *pogojni odpust* in Slovenian, *villkorlig frigivning* in Swedish), aligning the term closely with discretionary early release rather than post-release supervision. The Council of Europe's Recommendation on Conditional Release (Parole) (2003) reinforces this perspective, framing parole as 'the early release of sentenced prisoners under individualised post-release conditions'.

This understanding and variation deeply impact our understanding of what parole aims to achieve: whether it functions as a system of supervision and monitoring and is seen as an extension of sentencing (Dagan 2021; Vîlcică 2018) or, in some cases, simply facilitates an early release from prison with minimal subsequent oversight. For example, in Slovenia, parole might mean releasing individuals from prison early, with few follow-up measures (Ambrož and Šugman Stubbs 2011) – a practice we will explore in more detail.

Moreover, a variety of different stakeholders are involved in parole decisions in different systems (Guiney 2022). These differences in parole systems raise critical questions about the underlying purposes of parole, as the objectives can differ markedly depending on whether parole is viewed primarily as a tool for supervision or as a reward for rehabilitation. Understanding these distinctions is essential, as they directly influence the expectations and outcomes associated with parole (Paparozzi and Demichele 2008).

A. The Nature of Parole

In the European context, the ongoing debate regarding the nature of parole – whether it should be viewed as prisoners' right (mandatory or automatic release) or as a benefit that must be earned through good behaviour (discretionary release) – reflects significant philosophical differences across jurisdictions about the objectives of penal systems (Tournier 2004; Rhine 2012; van Zyl Smit and Corda 2016). In some countries, for instance, such as Sweden, Finland, Greece and Turkey (van Zyl Smit and Corda 2016), parole is conceptualised more as a rehabilitative right. There, it is often considered an integral part of the prisoner's rehabilitation process, aimed at supporting a successful reintegration into society (Carr and Blay 2019; Healy and Griffin 2023). This view fosters an environment where parole is expected and planned, focusing on preparing the inmate for eventual release (Dagan 2021). In contrast, many other jurisdictions, such as Austria, the Netherlands, France and Italy, adopt a more traditional view, treating parole strictly as a privilege contingent upon the prisoner's conduct and participation in rehabilitation programmes (Ambrož and Šugman Stubbs 2011; van Zyl Smit and Corda 2016; Guiney 2022). There, it is granted selectively to those who meet specific criteria demonstrating their readiness and potential for reintegration. This conditional approach frames parole as a privilege rather than an inherent right, emphasising compliance and the prisoner's behaviour as central to earning early release.

The debate surrounding the nature of parole significantly shapes how different systems define its primary purposes. While parole always serves multiple objectives, the complexity of these purposes varies based on its conceptualisation (Mackey and Rudes 2021). Whether viewed as a right or a privilege, each interpretation leads to a distinct set of priorities and practices within the parole system.

B. The Purposes of Parole

The purposes and aims of parole are multifaceted and reflect the evolving philosophies of the criminal justice system. Traditionally, parole has been envisioned as a rehabilitative measure designed to smooth the transition from incarceration to freedom, aiming to reduce the likelihood of reoffending (Hibbert 1965; Jones et al 2012). This perspective posits that parole should be granted as a right or benefit, contingent upon demonstrated rehabilitation and readiness to reintegrate into society (Reitz and Rhine 2020). This rehabilitative focus is supported by research indicating that parole can facilitate reintegration into society, thereby promoting desistance from criminal behaviour (Doekhie et al 2018). The concept of rehabilitation is central to many penal systems, which view parole as an opportunity for individuals to demonstrate their readiness to return to the community (Mackey and Rudes 2021).

Another significant purpose of parole is the management of behaviour within prison settings. It serves as a strategic tool within prison settings, employed as an incentive for inmates to comply with regulations and engage in rehabilitative activities. This approach encourages prisoners to engage positively with the correctional system, thereby fostering an environment conducive to rehabilitation. However, this incentive-based approach might conflict with the overarching rehabilitative objectives. The awareness that adherence to rules can accelerate release may lead to superficial behavioural changes among prisoners, effectively a 'performance' of good conduct maintained only until release. This raises concerns about the authenticity of rehabilitation, as the observed behaviour may not truly reflect an inmate's reformation (Brinc 2003; Dünkel et al 2010).

In addition to rehabilitation and management, discussions surrounding parole have increasingly focused on risk management, prioritising public safety and scrutinising the conditions under which prisoners are released. This perspective aligns with the punitive elements often associated with parole decision-making, where the severity of the original offence and the perceived risk of recidivism play significant roles in determining eligibility for release (Dagan 2021; Harding 2006; Mackey and Rudes 2021). While this approach underscores the importance of public safety, it also necessitates continuous support and monitoring in the community, particularly for individuals deemed at higher risk of reoffending (Kuziemko 2013; Yesberg and Polaschek 2019; Alfandari et al 2022). The integration of risk management into parole discussions reflects a broader trend within criminal justice to prioritise community safety (Monahan 2006; Doekhie et al 2018; Goel et al 2021).

Moreover, the pragmatic use of parole to address prison overcrowding has gained prominence, especially in contexts of economic strain and limited resources. Parole may serve as a mechanism to alleviate immediate logistical challenges associated with overcrowded prisons (Ambrož and Šugman Stubbs 2011; Meško et al 2011). While this approach can provide short-term relief, using parole predominantly as a tool to manage prison populations might erode the foundational goals of rehabilitation and reintegration.

As we delve deeper into the institutional frameworks that govern parole, it becomes essential to consider how these philosophical underpinnings manifest in practice. The institutions responsible for parole decisions operate within these varying conceptual frameworks, which can significantly influence their decision-making processes and the criteria they prioritise when evaluating parole applications (Guiney 2022).

C. The Institutions of Parole

The decision-making bodies involved in parole decisions vary significantly across different jurisdictions, reflecting each system's unique legal frameworks, cultural contexts and penal philosophies. Typically, the bodies responsible for parole decisions include a panel composed of legal, correctional and sometimes psychological experts. Depending on the size of the system, the parole board may be a larger, independent institution or part of a judicial or administrative entity.

In England and Wales, for example, the parole board consists of judicial members (mostly retired judges), psychologists, psychiatrists and independent members, in an attempt to bring diverse expertise to parole decisions (Padfield 2019; Beard 2023). While this parole decision-making structure aims to incorporate diverse expertise through its mixed panel, the approach in France, for example, takes a more judicial turn, with the process being managed by the judge of the application of sentences (*Juge de l'application des peines*, JAP) or the Tribunal of Sentence Application (*Tribunal de l'application des peines*), emphasising legal oversight. Judges are supported by social workers and psychologists, who contribute assessments regarding the social and rehabilitative aspects of the parolee's readiness for release (Baratta et al 2011). Another option is presented by Belgium's parole system, characterised by a more complex, bifurcated structure. For shorter sentences (up to three years), parole is almost automatic and handled administratively by prison authorities. For longer sentences, Sentence Implementation Courts, composed of a judge and assessors with backgrounds in law, criminology and psychology, make the decisions (Beyens 2019). Finally, in Scandinavian systems, parole decisions are handled administratively by the correctional services rather than by traditional parole boards. Parole is generally granted after a predetermined portion of the sentence is served, while the process also focuses on ensuring that inmates meet predefined conditions, such as participation in rehabilitation programmes (Kriminalvården nd).

Research shows that individual parole board members differ significantly in how they weigh various factors when deciding whether to grant early release (Metchik 1988; Hancock et al 2018; Ruhland 2020). Personal factors, such as values, risk tolerance and perspectives on rehabilitation versus public safety, shape these differences. However, we think these differences are also influenced by the institutional structures and authority of the organisations that board members belong to and their educational backgrounds.

The role of institutions in shaping outcomes is undisputable in numerous contexts (Dixon 1995; Scott 2013), including parole (Guiney 2022). We are particularly interested in how the institutional affiliations and qualifications of board members may shape their perceptions of parole's role and purpose within criminal justice, influencing both individual decisions and how board members conceptualise parole's broader systemic goals.

Moreover, the dynamics within parole board decision-making may reflect institutional influences, where the authority and respect given to board members often vary based on their professional backgrounds. Members from legal, psychological or corrections fields may have differing levels of influence during discussions, with some voices – often those from legal backgrounds – being louder or perceived as more authoritative (*cf* Barry 2021; Sunstein and Hastie 2014). This imbalance can lead to prioritising certain purposes, such as public safety, over others, like rehabilitation, depending on whose expertise is more valued within the board.

This suggests that the purpose of parole may be inherently linked to the composition of the parole board and the broader institutional context in which these members operate, making it critical to explore whether board composition directly affects how parole is conceptualised or whether broader systemic factors play a more defining role.

III. PAROLE IN SLOVENIA

To further explore the influence of institutional factors on parole decision-making, the empirical part of this chapter focuses on the Slovenian parole system. Slovenia's criminal justice system is distinctive for its low imprisonment rates, often drawing parallels with the more lenient Nordic countries and described as 'Slovenian exceptionalism' (Dünkel 2013; Flander and Meško 2016). The execution of criminal sentences in Slovenia involves a collaboration between judicial and administrative sectors: courts impose sentences, and administrative bodies, particularly the Prisons Administration or the Probation Service, administer their execution (Plesničar 2013). The parole board, a crucial administrative entity, underscores this approach by facilitating conditional releases, which align with the national focus on rehabilitation and reintegration of offenders (*cf* Ambrož and Šugman Stubbs 2011).

In Slovenia, the parole board is officially known as the Committee for Conditional Release. The Committee, in individual cases, consists of three key members. The chairperson is a civil servant from the Ministry of Justice (MoJ). The first member is drawn from the judiciary, specifically either from the judges of the Supreme Court or of one of the four Higher Courts, while the second member is appointed from among the supreme or senior state prosecutors. This composition, defined by the Enforcement of Penal Sanctions Act (ECSA-1), ensures that the Committee includes key stakeholders from the criminal justice system. Sessions of the Committee are held three times a year in all prisons, with the composition of the panel varying based on geographic and availability considerations, while still maintaining the mandated structure of a judge, a prosecutor and a MoJ representative. Importantly, the Slovenian parole board is merely a committee that decides on parole, not a specialised department or service within the MoJ that would be responsible for implementing conditional release or supervising parolees.

The Committee relies on detailed assessments provided by prison staff, who evaluate each parolee's potential risk of reoffending and recommend or advise against granting parole. This structured approach is meant to ensure a balance between informed risk management and the principles of rehabilitation and reintegration in the parole decision-making process.

Two types of conditional release exist in Slovenian law. 'Conditional release' means that a convicted person may be released from serving a prison sentence that they have not yet served in full if they do not commit a new offence during the period for which the prison sentence was imposed. In the case of 'conditional release with protective supervision', the convicted person must also comply with the Probation Service's supervision demands and fulfil other tasks potentially set for them by the Committee. Notably, simple conditional release – which is by far the most frequently used – does not involve any form of monitoring or conditions beyond the requirement to avoid reoffending. The absence of ongoing oversight after release signals confidence in the offender's readiness for reintegration and the rehabilitative processes experienced within the prison system (*cf* Plesnicar and Tripkovic 2024).

In theory, the legal aspects of conditional release in Slovenia are well regulated by the Criminal Code and ECSA-1. Conditional release can be granted if a convicted person has served a specified part of their sentence and if there is a reasonable expectation that they will not reoffend while at liberty.

IV. METHODOLOGY

This chapter is part of broader research into parole in Slovenia, in which we have examined existing legislation, collected statistical data on parole, conducted a survey with prison and Probation Service staff, and held in-depth interviews with members of the Committee for conditional release. Our aim was to critically assess the legal framework and practices of parole in Slovenia. In this chapter, we draw from all these findings but focus specifically on interviews and focus groups with Committee members to explore how differences in understanding the aims of conditional release correlate with the Committee's composition and influence its decisions.

The participants in this study included 12 judges, prosecutors and civil servants from the MoJ, who were at the time part of the Committee. The semi-structured nature of the interviews allowed us to delve deeply into both the procedural and substantive aspects of the Slovenian parole system. Informed consent was obtained prior to the interviews and, to safeguard the anonymity of our participants, we only use broad identifiers such as 'judge', 'prosecutor' or 'civil servant' when presenting their perspectives.

We transcribed the interviews verbatim and analysed them using thematic analysis (Braun and Clarke 2019). This approach helped us identify and interpret key themes that emerged from the discussions, such as the perceived purposes of parole and how these are influenced by institutional roles.

V. THE INTERPLAY BETWEEN PURPOSE AND INSTITUTION

A. The Nature of Parole

Similar to other European systems mentioned earlier (eg the Austrian, Dutch, French and Italian systems), the Slovenian legal framework implies that parole is not a right but a benefit the convicted person has to deserve (Bavcon et al 2013). The perspectives of our participants reflect a similar consensus on the nature of conditional release in the Slovenian legal framework: it is not a right but a privilege. Most Committee members view parole as a benefit that must be earned by the convicted person rather than an automatic entitlement. As a prosecutor explained, parole is 'a right … for which [the convicted person] has to fulfil certain conditions' or '[it] is a right, it is just not [always] granted'.

Similarly, a judge described conditional release as 'an option, not a right', emphasising that even if the formal and material conditions are met, the Committee still deliberates on whether the individual should be granted release. This viewpoint highlights the discretionary nature of parole decisions, where meeting criteria does not guarantee release but only makes it possible.

The notion that parole is a privilege was further articulated by a civil servant from the MoJ, who stated:

> Parole … is not a right, of course, it is … a privilege. If someone is granted conditional release, they should … be given some treatment by the state, by the community, to make sure … that such a person … is capable of participating fully in society. (Civil servant)

The members of the Committee unanimously agreed that conditional release is a benefit, not a right. It can be granted if specific criteria are met after serving the required portion of the sentence, but it is not automatic and requires Committee approval (Ambrož and Šugman Stubbs 2011). The Committee's assessment considers both the individual's conduct in prison and their potential future behaviour, incorporating a retrospective and forward-looking evaluation of their likelihood to reintegrate successfully.

B. The Undefined Purpose of Parole

In discussing the purpose of parole, Committee members expressed diverse views, reflecting both the operational realities and ideological aspirations of the system. These differing perspectives illustrate the complexity of defining conditional release, as stakeholders see it as a rehabilitative opportunity, a behavioural incentive or a pragmatic response to institutional challenges.

(i) Rehabilitation as a Primary Purpose

Several Committee members emphasised that rehabilitation and humanity are the core justifications for conditional release. The focus here is on giving prisoners a genuine opportunity to demonstrate personal change and reintegrate into society. As one judge put it:

> [The purpose of conditional release] is to re-socialise the prisoner and to give them a chance to prove themselves during that time. (Judge)

This sentiment was echoed by others, who highlighted that conditional release should not be about remitting the sentence but rather about changing how it is served, reflecting a belief in the individual's capacity for change and the idea of humanity:

> [If we grant conditional release, we] are not remitting the sentence; we are only changing the way the prisoner is serving a sentence … because … we believe they have changed. (Civil servant);

> [The point of conditional release is adhering to] the principle of humanity in criminal proceedings (Judge).

These perspectives suggest that some Committee members view conditional release as an essential element of rehabilitative justice – focused on supporting personal growth and reintegration.

(ii) Parole as a Behavioural Incentive

At the same time, many Committee members viewed conditional release as a tool to incentivise good behaviour during incarceration. This perspective positions conditional release as a means of maintaining order within the prison and encouraging compliance with institutional rules.

> [Conditional release] can be a reward for the convicted person for many things [and] a good instrument of the prison. The ['performance'] can go both ways. (Prosecutor)

> As a prisoner, you have the right to conditional release. If you behave nicely, you might be released early. Otherwise not. This way … the convicted person is forced … to behave as correctly as possible … (Judge)

> [In decision-making on conditional release,] we should emphasise what the convicted person is doing [while serving their sentence]. Are they involved in education and attending courses because there are a million workshops in the institutions? (Prosecutor)

The perspectives of our participants reflect familiar dilemmas in the academic debate on the purposes of conditional release, particularly the balance between promoting good behaviour during incarceration and fostering genuine resocialisation. As explained above, these objectives can sometimes be at odds. For instance, prisoners may perform good behaviour solely to accelerate release, without genuine rehabilitation – what is referred to as the 'treatment performance' (Brinc 2003; Dünkel et al 2010; Plesničar 2012). This issue was articulated well in an exchange between two prosecutors, highlighting the backward-looking nature of the current system and its focus on past behaviour rather than future reintegration potential:

> Prosecutor 1: [At the moment, conditional release] is more of a reward for [prisoners] behaving well in prison rather than a way to rehabilitate [prisoners] or to ease their path to life in the community. It is more … a measure of the prison … their tool to keep [the prisoner] in line with the prison rules.
>
> Prosecutor 2: I agree with that, but I would add that the fundamental problem with the current … administration of conditional release is precisely that it is backward-looking; it looks back at the time the prisoner has already served instead of being forward-looking and assessing whether the person who is going to get out has all the conditions – job prospects, housing, etc. – to be in a position not to reoffend. This is completely misguided and must be fundamentally changed if conditional release is to achieve its true purpose. But this also depends on the conditions that society is prepared to provide for [people who are conditionally released from prison]. In the old days, conditional release was only possible if it was established exactly how [the conditionally released prisoner] would be integrated into the community. Nowadays … this question is usually solved by some generalised statement that they have a job, by some letter that someone will employ them without a contract, without anything. So, the task [of resocialisation and facilitating the transition of the convicted person from prison to the community] is not fulfilled by responsible institutions, but [conditional release is about] rewarding behaviour in prison. … The court imposes the prison sentence. Conditional release is … then a primary tool in the hands of the prison administration to be able to run the institution successfully and to influence the convicted person appropriately, thereby stimulating them to (1.) behave appropriately in the institution and (2.) to be able to expect an earlier release … if they behave the way that the internal rules dictate.

This perspective reveals the dual role of conditional release: both as an opportunity for personal growth and as a tool for ensuring compliance. The second prosecutor highlighted that conditional release initially focused on reintegration, requiring clear community re-entry plans like job prospects and housing. Over time, this focus has shifted to managing inmate behaviour and institutional pressures. This shift from a forward-looking, rehabilitative approach to a more compliance-focused mechanism creates conflicts between rehabilitative goals and pragmatic needs like maintaining order and reducing overcrowding.

(iii) The Pragmatic Use of Parole

Additionally, some participants articulated an even more contentious purpose of conditional release, reflecting concerns within the broader criminal justice community. They felt that conditional release is increasingly used as a tool to manage prison populations, particularly in the face of overcrowding. They expressed concerns that prison authorities might primarily promote conditional release to alleviate the pressures of overcrowded facilities, a trend supported by academic findings (Dünkel et al 2010, 435). While acknowledging prison overcrowding is a significant issue, they felt that it should not have any bearing on their decisions on conditional release.

> [In Slovenia], the problem arose because the prisons became overcrowded, and they wanted to get rid of [prisoners]. We can understand that, but it must not be to the detriment of conditional release. (Judge)

Another judge explained how this has become an unintended consequence of recent amendments:

> One of the motivations of the Committee [to grant conditional release] is prison overcrowding. Especially with foreign prisoners, where [prison staff] can't communicate with them when they have a problem, so they try to get rid of them. [In reality, the purpose of conditional release] is to resocialise the prisoner and to give them a chance to prove themselves during that time. (Judge)

The pragmatic use of conditional release raises significant ethical and operational concerns. The shift towards using parole as a response to overcrowding may undermine its rehabilitative intent and shift the focus from individual readiness to broader systemic needs. This practice represents a significant deviation from the rehabilitative aspirations of conditional release, leading to what some participants termed a 'short-term solution' mentality.

(iv) The Need for a Clearer Purpose

The diverse perspectives on the purpose of conditional release reflect a lack of consensus and a broader challenge in the Slovenian system – there is no clear statutory definition of what conditional release is meant to achieve. Several Committee members argued for a formal definition that would clarify whether the goals of conditional release should focus on encouraging better behaviour, facilitating rehabilitation or easing the transition from prison to community life.

Some members suggested that defining the purpose would prevent the misuse of conditional release as a mere tool to alleviate prison overcrowding.

A prosecutor emphasised that a clear definition could stop conditional release from being instrumentalised as 'a means for the prison to get rid of overcrowding or manage troublesome convicts'. This clarity would ensure that conditional release remains a mechanism for principled rehabilitation rather than a pragmatic solution to systemic issues. A civil servant further elaborated on the importance of having an explicit purpose:

> I miss … an explicitly determined purpose of conditional release on a statutory level. For me, that is where it all begins and ends. [Conditional release] should help integrate the prisoner into life in the community if we can reasonably expect that they will not reoffend, that the sentence has achieved its purpose, and the conditionally released person does not pose a risk to society … I believe conditional release … should be the crown of resocialisation. I do not know whether I am right or wrong, but if that is the case, then the current composition of the Commission is wrong. (Civil servant)

This lack of clarity also raises questions about the structure and operation of the Committee itself. As noted by a prosecutor, reform is needed

> [Conditional release] needs to be reformed and [its] purpose, means, decision-making, the composition of the Committee, and the nature of the procedure need to be comprehensively reconsidered and regulated. (Prosecutor)

The calls for a more clearly defined purpose underline the importance of ensuring that conditional release serves its intended rehabilitative function, rather than being swayed by short-term institutional pressures. Establishing a clear statutory purpose would provide a consistent framework for decision-making, helping to ensure that the system prioritises rehabilitation and reintegration over purely pragmatic concerns.

The findings in this section reflect the diverse and, at times, conflicting perspectives on the purpose of conditional release among Committee members. Civil servants were more likely to emphasise the rehabilitative purpose of conditional release, highlighting its role in helping individuals reintegrate into society and demonstrating a clear belief in the value of resocialisation. Judges, while also supporting the rehabilitative function, often viewed conditional release through a dual lens – balancing rehabilitation with the need to maintain institutional order and promote good behaviour. Prosecutors were more critical of the current system, pointing out how conditional release has shifted from being a forward-looking reintegration tool to a more backwards-looking mechanism focused on managing behaviour and alleviating prison overcrowding.

The differing views between civil servants, judges and prosecutors indicate the complexity of defining the purpose of conditional release and the need for a more unified understanding of its role within the Slovenian criminal justice system. The absence of a clear statutory purpose has allowed conditional release to be understood and perhaps used inconsistently, sometimes as a rehabilitative tool and other times as a pragmatic response to institutional pressures.

In the next section, we will explore how the structure and composition of the Committee for Conditional Release influence the implementation of these varied purposes.

C. The Committee's Composition

If conditional release is indeed the 'crown of resocialization', as described by an interviewed civil servant from the MoJ, then the composition of the Committee for conditional release in Slovenia is fundamentally flawed. A recurring theme in our discussions was the belief among Committee members that either they themselves, their colleagues or the entire institution lacked the appropriate qualifications to serve on the parole board. This perceived inadequacy was attributed to both institutional limitations and a lack of individual expertise, suggesting deeper issues within the system's ability to effectively fulfil the goals of parole.

(i) Self-Criticism and Recognition of Inadequacies

Throughout our interviews, Committee members expressed significant self-criticism, highlighting their limitations and those of their colleagues in effectively fulfilling their role. They felt that their backgrounds, primarily in law and the civil service, did not equip them sufficiently to assess an individual's readiness for reintegration into society – particularly if the goal of parole is rehabilitative.

The interviewed judges, for example, felt that civil servants at the MoJ were not competent to assess whether a prisoner had been rehabilitated. As one judge explained:

> We have a certain knowledge that the President of the Committee (representative of the MoJ) does not have. We know perpetrators of fraud when we see them, for example. We know what it means for a perpetrator of fraud to behave in a certain way; we know when they are sweet-talking, etc … In other words, we know more about whether someone is being honest. When I started working as a young trainee at the State Prosecutor's Office, my mentor told me I would come to recognise a drug addict immediately. I didn't at the time, but now I can spot them from a hundred kilometres away. That's just the way it is, that's experience, and we have experience with perpetrators of fraud behaving in a certain way. This is the experience that the Committee member from the MoJ does not have. (Judge)

Judges believed that civil servants, by the very nature of their work, lack exposure to the wide variety of offenders and cannot adequately assess their prospects for positive prognosis and resocialisation. This sentiment reflects a broader concern that those without direct experience with criminal behaviour may not be suited to make nuanced parole decisions.

However, judges and prosecutors also questioned their own suitability to serve on the Committee. They pointed out that assessing the material conditions for parole – such as whether a convicted person presents a low risk of reoffending – is inherently complex. Some members argued that while they are qualified due to their legal experience, their predictions are often subjective and based on a 'legal sense' that may not always be reliable:

> If all the conditions are met, [the applicant for conditional release] will get out at 50% [of the sentence served]. But the assessment is really whether all the conditions are met so that the expectation [that they will not commit any more crimes] is justified. I can honestly say that these conditions cannot be weighed … When I look at [the prison's report on the prisoner's progress], and I go through everything they write, my feeling can be that [the prisoner] has not done enough time yet. [This feeling] comes – it's hard to capture – from everything you've experienced as a prosecutor … You assess the situation based on your experience. This assessment can be different; one Committee member assesses it this way, and another assesses it another way. It's like assessing non-pecuniary damages; how much is fear worth, for example? (Prosecutor)

> [The assessment of the condition of] a positive prognosis … is not a matter of rational judgment but primarily of experience. (Judge)

Despite their legal training, some members acknowledged that assessing a prisoner's readiness to reintegrate requires expertise beyond what the legal profession provides. This concern was compounded by the recognition that parole decision-making operates 'in a field that is not so exact', where 'no expert … can reliably guarantee that what they predict will be true' (Prosecutor). Interestingly, while many Committee members admitted they were not adequately equipped to perform these assessments, there was also a sense of relief in this acknowledgement. They believed that since no one could reliably predict outcomes, their shortcomings were not unique. Among some legal professionals, there was even a sense of superiority – an attitude that if anyone could handle these decisions, it would be them, but ultimately, they felt it did not matter much because accurate assessment was inherently impossible. This sentiment was reflected in the idea that their legal experience, or 'legal sense', gave them an advantage, even if the task itself was impossible from the outset.

(ii) Challenges of Balancing Roles

The sense of inadequacy among Committee members was also tied to the demanding nature of their primary roles. Judges and prosecutors often expressed that their participation in the Committee was merely a secondary duty, not their main focus. Many felt overwhelmed by their other tasks, and parole decision-making became an afterthought – a responsibility they did not have the time or energy to prioritise effectively. For example, judges noted the work overload faced by Supreme and Higher Court judges, leading some to believe that appointing first-instance judges would be more appropriate as they are more grounded in day-to-day judicial activities.

Moreover, prosecutors highlighted concerns about their systemic role as members of the Committee. Several pointed out that their primary function is to secure convictions, which conflicts with the rehabilitative purpose of parole. This conflict was described as undermining the impartiality of their participation in parole decisions:

> What specialist knowledge do I have to decide whether or not someone should get out? Secondly, have I not, as a prosecutor, fulfilled my task, which the Constitution gives me in the context of prosecution, to secure a conviction? Finally, is this in line with the Constitution? I have been saying all along: I am waiting for a lawyer to bring the case before the Constitutional Court and put forward that – and I will put this crudely – conditional release [as it currently exists in the Slovenian system] is a Stalinist tool from the days when the State Prosecutor interfered with everything, including civil disputes … This needs to be reformed so that conditional release is put in the hands of the court. The court should decide on the sentence and whether it must change as part of conditional release, but of course, with the participation of professionals with the skills to assess this. (Prosecutor)

Judges, too, questioned whether they should be involved in parole decisions, arguing that their role had already been fulfilled when they imposed the original sentence. These concerns were echoed by civil servants from the MoJ, who also felt that judges and prosecutors are not appropriate Committee members. More specifically, the judiciary 'has already had its say when it imposed a sanction', while the prosecutors 'have exhausted their powers to prosecute' (Civil servant).

Such reflections indicate a fundamental discomfort with the current composition of the Committee and point to a broader institutional misalignment between the Committee's goals and the professional expertise of its members.

(iii) Proposals for a Different System

Given these challenges, Committee members proposed several alternatives to the current structure. Many suggested that senior staff from the Probation Service would be better suited to participate in parole decisions. These individuals would have more direct experience with rehabilitation processes and better understand the social factors contributing to a prisoner's successful reintegration.

In addition to replacing judges and prosecutors, some interviewees advocated for expanding the Committee to include professionals from fields such as psychology, social work, criminology and penology. A civil servant expressed the need for expertise beyond the legal sphere:

> It would be ideal to have a psychologist [as a Committee member] who would interview [the convicted person applying for conditional release] and give a professional

> psychological assessment. Unlike now, when it's us [lawyers] assessing whether the applicant is stable enough that they will be able to behave acceptably [when released back into the community] … I would like a psychologist there to look under the convict's hood … Better than [having only] … the prosecutor, the judge, and the civil servant making decisions. (Civil servant)

> Suppose the purpose of conditional release is to assess the convict's resocialisation and the prognosis for their integration into the community. In that case, we cannot bypass assessing the social factors. We need a Committee member from social work, pedagogy, and perhaps psychology. Someone with softer skills … As a lawyer, I do not feel … competent to … assess adequately the prognosis of that person's integration back into society. For these purposes, we have social services and experts who went to school and have practical experience in this field … (Civil servant)

Some interviewees also proposed that the judge who imposed the sentence should be responsible for decisions about conditional release. This suggestion was based on the idea that the sentencing judge knows the case best and could better determine whether the individual has been rehabilitated:

> I think it would be best if the judge specified what part of the sentence the convicted person should serve in prison and what part at liberty as part of conditional release. The judge knows the case well because they have been dealing with it for several months. The sentencing judge also knows why they imposed such a sentence, and I would expect them to know how that sentence should be enforced. (Prosecutor)

While this idea seemed promising to some, others argued that it was impractical given the workload of Slovenian courts. Instead, they suggested the appointment of an executive judge – one specialising in the execution of custodial sentences, similar to the French JAP. However, there was also scepticism about whether such judges could adequately handle the complexities of assessing rehabilitation without additional expertise in social sciences.

> It seems flawed that the executive judge would determine the prison regime – whether it is open or closed – because determining the regime is a typical means of the prison administration. If the judge determined the execution of the sanction in advance, this would not stimulate the convicted person. You always have to give a person hope. (Prosecutor)

> An executive judge cannot make the Committee's decisions, that's for sure. (Judge)

These reflections illustrate the diverse viewpoints and debates around the current structure of the Committee. The idea of involving an executive judge is not without merit; however, it faces practical and conceptual challenges, as expressed by several Committee members.

The scepticism about whether any single professional group – whether executive judges, prosecutors or civil servants – could adequately fulfil the requirements for making effective parole decisions is apparent. Ultimately, the views expressed by Committee members about their inadequacies and the shortcomings of the current structure were significantly influenced by their professional roles and institutional affiliations. Prosecutors, whose primary function is to secure convictions, expressed discomfort with a rehabilitative process that seemed at odds with their punitive responsibilities. Judges, too, found it difficult to reconcile their role as decision-makers in the original sentencing with the task of evaluating rehabilitation. Civil servants, on the other hand, were more inclined to view parole through a rehabilitative lens. They emphasised the importance of social support and community integration, and their critiques of the Committee's composition often focused on the absence of professionals with experience in rehabilitation and social services.

VI. DISCUSSION AND CONCLUSION

The findings of our study align with and add nuance to the broader debates on the purposes of parole and the institutional structures that oversee its implementation. By examining the Slovenian parole system, we wanted to highlight how institutional setup, professional roles and a lack of unified purpose impact the functioning of parole boards.

A. A Defined Purpose

One of the critical insights derived from our analysis is the need to establish a clear statutory purpose for parole. Literature has consistently pointed out that the purpose of parole varies significantly across jurisdictions, ranging from a rehabilitative right to a privilege linked to compliance with prison rules (van Zyl Smit and Corda 2016; Dagan 2021). In Slovenia, this ambiguity manifests in the differing perspectives of Committee members, who view parole through lenses of rehabilitation, behavioural management, or even as a pragmatic tool for alleviating prison overcrowding. The diversity of these perspectives complicates decision-making and risks undermining the rehabilitative potential of parole.

The necessity for a clear definition of purpose has become evident through the critiques voiced by Committee members. For parole to function effectively, especially within discretionary parole systems, its purpose must be outlined more explicitly. A defined purpose would create a consistent framework that informs decision-making, helps to avoid instrumentalising parole purely for logistical reasons and aligns parole decisions more closely with the rehabilitative aims of the criminal justice system. As highlighted in our results, without a shared understanding of its objectives, parole remains subject to differing interpretations, which can not only dilute its effectiveness as a tool for rehabilitation and reintegration, but also lead to unequal treatment and injustice (*cf* Hogarth 1971).

B. Expertise and Multidisciplinary Perspectives

Our analysis also emphasises the importance of the institutional setup and the composition of parole boards. The current composition of the Slovenian Committee – comprising a judge, a prosecutor and a civil servant – reveals a misalignment between the expertise of its members and the rehabilitative goals parole is supposed to achieve. Prosecutors and judges often felt that their legal backgrounds did not equip them to assess an individual's readiness for reintegration accurately. The existing structure leans heavily towards a legalistic approach, which is at odds with the rehabilitative ideals that parole is meant to promote.

This misalignment was evident in the critiques offered by Committee members, who were not only critical of the backgrounds of their colleagues, but also doubted their own ability to fulfil the rehabilitative mandate of parole effectively. As our findings show, judges and prosecutors were often overwhelmed by their primary responsibilities and treated parole decisions as an afterthought. They acknowledged that assessing rehabilitation required expertise they did not possess, such as insights into psychological and social factors. This challenge is echoed in the literature, which advocates for multidisciplinary parole boards that incorporate experts in criminology, psychology and social work to provide a holistic evaluation of parole candidates (Guiney 2022; Beard 2023).

To align parole decisions more closely with rehabilitative goals, our findings suggest the necessity of rethinking the parole board's composition. This aligns with comparative practices where parole boards include professionals from diverse fields to enhance their decision-making capacity and ensure that parole serves its intended purpose (Baratta et al 2011; Padfield 2019). The involvement of probation officers, psychologists or social workers could provide a more balanced perspective that considers the parolees' social reintegration needs. To improve parole decision-making, reform must address both the clarity of its purpose and the qualifications of those who make the decisions. Parole, as a means to support reintegration into society, cannot function effectively if its gatekeepers lack the appropriate expertise or if the overarching goals are ambiguous.

C. The Power of the Institution

However, the issue extends beyond lack of expertise. It also concerns the fundamental roles and institutional perspectives of the individuals serving on the parole board. Prosecutors, whose primary function is to secure convictions, often find it difficult to assess an offender's readiness for release. Their institutional role is inherently punitive, focusing on proving guilt and ensuring that offenders are punished. Their institutional focus on proving guilt and ensuring punishment makes it challenging for them to transition to evaluating rehabilitative progress and reintegration despite their personal beliefs, which might be rehabilitative.

Similarly, judges face a parallel conflict of interest. They are responsible for sentencing based on the severity of the offence and what they consider fair punishment. This judicial perspective can carry over into the parole process, where decisions may focus more on whether the sentence has been adequately served rather than on the individual's rehabilitative progress. This mindset may not always align with the rehabilitative goals of parole.

On the contrary, civil servants were, perhaps unexpectedly, more inclined to view parole through a rehabilitative lens. They emphasised the importance of social support and community integration, and their critiques of the Committee's composition often focused on the absence of professionals with experience in rehabilitation and social services.

The differing perspectives among Committee members highlight how professional identity and institutional culture may shape their views on parole. Those accustomed to punitive and legalistic approaches to justice were more likely to question the rehabilitative ideal of parole and their ability to contribute to it effectively. This suggests that to align parole practices more closely with rehabilitative goals, reforms must consider not only the professional qualifications of Committee members, but also the institutional biases that influence how they understand the purpose of conditional release.

The coherence of the parole board is further undermined by its lack of formal independence. The Slovenian parole board operates under the MoJ, with no independent employees and members drawn from various institutions. This structure limits the board's ability to function as a unified, cohesive entity, complicating efforts to establish a consistent approach to parole decisions. Even if a clear purpose for parole were defined, the fragmented nature of the board's composition would remain a significant barrier. The lack of an independent body dedicated solely to parole means that members bring perspectives and priorities from their respective institutions, making it difficult to achieve a shared vision.

D. Broader Implications

The findings of this study, though focused on Slovenia, have broader implications for parole systems generally. Similar challenges – such as a lack of unified purpose, the composition of parole boards and the influence of institutional roles – are observed in other jurisdictions. Van Zyl Smit and Corda (2016) discuss how distinct penal philosophies, from rehabilitative to punitive, shape parole systems. Our study adds depth by illustrating how institutional structures and professional roles within parole boards can either align with or contradict these philosophies.

In many jurisdictions, parole boards are still predominantly composed of individuals with legal or correctional backgrounds (Hancock et al 2018; Padfield 2019). The emphasis on legal expertise often results in a focus on risk management and public safety, rather than on rehabilitation and reintegration (Guiney 2022). Our findings suggest that a multidisciplinary approach, involving professionals in social work, psychology and criminology, could help parole boards better fulfil rehabilitative goals, aligning with calls for a more holistic perspective in parole systems (Dagan 2021; Beard 2023).

Moreover, the issue of institutional independence is not unique to Slovenia. In several jurisdictions, parole boards operate within the administrative framework of justice ministries or corrections departments, which can compromise their ability to function independently and focus on rehabilitation (Baratta et al 2011). Our study illustrates how the lack of an independent identity can undermine coherence and effectiveness. Addressing both the expertise of board members and the structural frameworks in which they operate is crucial to reform.

Ultimately, the effectiveness of parole as a tool for rehabilitation depends on both the clarity of its purpose and the composition of those who administer it. With this study, we wish to contribute to the broader discourse by emphasising the importance of both institutional independence and multidisciplinary expertise in realising the rehabilitative potential of parole.

REFERENCES

Alfandari, R, Taylor, BJ, Baginsky, M et al (2022. 'Making Sense of Risk: Social Work at the Boundary between Care and Control' *Health, Risk & Society* https://doi.org/10.1080/13698575.2022.2147904.

Ambrož, M and Šugman Stubbs, K (2011) 'Conditional Release (Parole) in Slovenia: Problems and Possible Solutions' 91(4) *The Prison Journal* 467 https://doi.org/10.1177/0032885511424394.

Baratta, A, Schwartz, P and Milosescu, G-A (2011) 'Place et Méthodes de l'expertise Post-Sentencielle Dans Le Dispositif de Libération Conditionnelle. Comparaison Des Procédures En Belgique et En France' 109 *Médecine & Droit* 177 https://doi.org/10.1016/j.meddro.2011.05.001.

Barry, BM (2021) *How Judges Judge: Empirical Insights into Judicial Decision-Making* (London, Routledge).

Bavcon, L, Šelih, A. Korošec, D, Ambrož, M and Filipčič, K (2013) *Kazensko Pravo: Splošni Del*, 6. Izdaja (Ljubljana, Uradni list Republike Slovenije).

Beard, J (2023) 'The Parole System of England and Wales' (London, House of Commons Library).

Beyens, K (2019) 'Belgian Release Policies, Rationales and Practices' 11(3) *European Journal of Probation* 169 https://doi.org/10.1177/2066220319895776.

Braun, V and Clarke, V (2019) 'Reflecting on Reflexive Thematic Analysis' *Qualitative Research in Sport, Exercise and Health* 1 https://doi.org/10.1080/2159676X2019.1628806.

Brinc, F (2003) 'Kriminalna Prognoza – Iluzija Ali Resničnost' 54(4) *Revija Za Kriminalistiko in Kriminologijo* 341.

Carr, N and Blay, E (2019) 'Parole and Prisoner Release: Exploring Rationalities Across Time and Place' 11(3) *European Journal of Probation* 119.

Dagan, N (2023) 'Parole as Resentencing: Exploring the Punitive Accounts of Parole Decision-Making Through the Comparative Case Study of Israel' 20(4) *European Journal of Criminology* 1231 https://doi.org/10.1177/14773708211039635.

Dixon, J (1995) 'The Organizational Context of Criminal Sentencing' 100(5) *American Journal of Sociology* 1157 https://doi.org/10.1086/230635.

Doekhie, J, van Ginneken, E, Dirkzwager, A and Nieuwbeerta, P (2018) 'Managing Risk or Supporting Desistance? A Longitudinal Study on the Nature and Perceptions of Parole Supervision in the Netherlands' 4(4) *Journal of Developmental and Life-Course Criminology* 491 https://doi.org/10.1007/s40865-018-0097-6.

Dünkel, F (2013) 'Slovenian Exceptionalism?: Die Entwicklung von Gefangenenraten in Internationalen Vergleich' in M Ambrož, K Filipčič and A Završnik (eds), *Zbornik Za Alenko Šelih: Kazensko Pravo, Kriminologija, Človekove Pravice* (Ljubljana, Inštitut za kriminologijo pri Pravni fakulteti; Pravna fakulteta; Slovenska akademija znanosti in umetnosti) 61–93.

Dünkel, F, van Zyl Smit, D and Padfield, N (2010) 'Concluding Thoughts' in N Padfield, D van Zyl Smit and F Dünkel (eds), *Release from Prison: European Policy and Practice* (Cullumpton, Willan Publishing) 395–444.

Flander, B and Meško, G (2016) 'Penal and Prison Policy on the "Sunny Side of the Alps": The Swan Song of Slovenian Exceptionalism?' (January) *European Journal on Criminal Policy and Research* 1 https://doi.org/10.1007/s10610-015-9299-1.

Goel, S, Shroff, R, Skeem, J and Slobogin, C (2021) 'The Accuracy, Equity, and Jurisprudence of Criminal Risk Assessment' in R Vogl (ed), *Research Handbook on Big Data Law* (Cheltenham, Edward Elgar) ch 1 https://china.elgaronline.com/edcollchap/edcoll/9781788972819/9781788972819.00007.xml.

Guiney, TC (2023) 'Parole, Parole Boards and the Institutional Dilemmas of Contemporary Prison Release' 25(3) *Punishment & Society* 621 https://doi.org/10.1177/14624745221097371.

Hancock, K, Brown, P, Hadgis, A, Hollander, M and Shrider, M (2018) 'Parole Board Personality and Decision Making Using Bias-Based Reasoning' in DD Schmorrow and CM Fidopiastis (eds), *Augmented Cognition: Users and Contexts* (Cham, Springer) 255–72 https://doi.org/10.1007/978-3-319-91467-1_21.

Harding, J (2006) 'Some Reflections on Risk Assessment, Parole and Recall' 53(4) *Probation Journal* 389 https://doi.org/10.1177/0264550506069363.

Healy, D and Griffin, D (2023) 'Unnesting the Matryoshka Doll: An Ecological Model of Probation and Parole Decision-Making in Ireland' 39(1) *Journal of Contemporary Criminal Justice* 75 https://doi.org/10.1177/10439862221138678.

Hibbert, C (1965) *Zgodovina Zločinstva in Kazni* (Ljubljana, Cankarjeva založba).

Hogarth, J (1971) *Sentencing as a Human Process* (Toronto, University of Toronto Press).

Jones, M, Wolfe, NT and Johnstone, P (2012) *History of Criminal Justice*, 5th edn (Waltham, Elsevier).

Kleiman, M and Hawken, A (2008) 'Fixing the Parole System' (June) *Issues in Science and Technology*.

Kriminalvården (nd) 'Villkorlig Frigivning' www.kriminalvarden.se/fangelse-frivard-och-hakte/fangelse/villkorlig-frigivning/.

Kuziemko, I (2013) 'How Should Inmates Be Released from Prison? An Assessment of Parole versus Fixed-Sentence Regimes' 128 *Quarterly Journal of Economics* 371 https://doi.org/10.1093/QJE/QJS052.

Mackey, BJ and Rudes, DS (2021) 'Discretion in the US Parole System' in *Oxford Research Encyclopedia of Criminology and Criminal Justice* https://doi.org/10.1093/acrefore/9780190264079.013.227.

Meško, G, Fields, C and Smole, T (2011) 'A Concise Overview of Penology and Penal Practice in Slovenia: The Unchanged Capacity, New Standards, and Prison Overcrowding' 91(4) *The Prison Journal* 398.

Metchik, E (1988) 'Parole Decisionmaking: A Comparative Analysis' 32(3) *International Journal of Offender Therapy and Comparative Criminology* 233 https://doi.org/10.1177/0306624X8803200307.

Monahan, J (2006) 'A Jurisprudence of Risk Assessment: Forecasting Harm Among Prisoners, Predators, and Patients' 92(3) *Virginia Law Review* 391.

Padfield, N (2014) 'Front Door and Backdoor Sentencing' in G Bruinsma and D Weisburd (eds), *Encyclopedia of Criminology and Criminal Justice* (New York, Springer) 1846–55 https://doi.org/10.1007/978-1-4614-5690-2_492.

—— (2019) 'Giving and Getting Parole: The Changing Characteristics of Parole in England and Wales' 11(3) *European Journal of Probation* 153 https://doi.org/10.1177/2066220319895798.

Paparozzi, M and Demichele, M (2008) 'Probation and Parole: Overworked, Misunderstood, and Under-Appreciated: But Why?' 47(3) *Howard Journal of Criminal Justice* 275 https://doi.org/10.1111/j.1468-2311.2008.00522.x.

Petersilia, J (1999) 'Parole and Prisoner Reentry in the United States' 26 *Crime and Justice* 479 https://doi.org/10.1086/449302.

Plesničar, MM (2012) 'Slovenska Ureditev Pogojnega Odpusta v Luči Sodobnih Razvojnih Trendov' 63(2) *Revija Za Kriminalistiko in Kriminologijo* 136.

—— (2013) 'The Individualization of Punishment: Sentencing in Slovenia' 10(4) *European Journal of Criminology* 462.

Plesnicar, MM and Tripkovic, M (2024) 'Communicating Confidence: Suspended Sentences as Communicative Punishment' 2024(1) *Pravni Zapisi* 239 https://doi.org/10.5937/pravzap0-50554.

Rhine, EE (2012) 'The Present Status and Future Prospects of Parole Boards and Parole Supervision' in J Petersilia and KR Reitz (eds), *The Oxford Handbook of Sentencing and Corrections* (Oxford, Oxford University Press) https://doi.org/10.1093/oxfordhb/9780199730148.013.0026.

Ruhland, EL (2020) 'Philosophies and Decision Making in Parole Board Members' 100(5) *The Prison Journal* 640 https://doi.org/10.1177/0032885520956566.

Scott, WR (2013) *Institutions and Organizations: Ideas, Interests, and Identities*, 4th edn (Los Angeles, CA, SAGE).

Šugman Stubbs, K and Ambrož, M (2012) 'Recalling Conditionally Released Prisoners in Slovenia' 4(1) *European Journal of Probation* 98.

Sunstein, CR and Hastie, R (2014) *Wiser: Getting Beyond Groupthink to Make Groups Smarter*, 1st edn (Boston, MA, Harvard Business Review Press).

Tournier, PV (2004) 'Systems of Conditional Release (Parole) in the Member States of the Council of Europe' I *Champ pénal/Penal field* https://doi.org/10.4000/champpenal.378.

van Zyl Smit, D and Corda, A (2016) 'American Exceptionalism in Parole Release and Supervision: A European Perspective' (July) *Law & Society: Public Law – Crime*.

Vîlcică, ER (2018) 'Revisiting Parole Decision Making: Testing for the Punitive Hypothesis in a Large US Jurisdiction' 62(5) *International Journal of Offender Therapy and Comparative Criminology* 1357 https://doi.org/10.1177/0306624X16668512.

Werth, R (2013) 'The Construction and Stewardship of Responsible yet Precarious Subjects: Punitive Ideology, Rehabilitation, and "Tough Love" among Parole Personnel' 15(3) *Punishment & Society* 219 https://doi.org/10.1177/1462474513481720.

Yesberg, JA and Polaschek, DLL (2019) 'How Does Offender Rehabilitation Actually Work? Exploring Mechanisms of Change in High-Risk Treated Parolees' 63(15–16) *International Journal of Offender Ther apy and Comparative Criminology* 2672 https://doi.org/10.1177/0306624X19856221.

11

Conditional Release in Spain: More Incapacitation and Less Reintegration? A Balance of Two Decades of Legal Reforms

MIKEL ANDEREZ BELATEGI

I. INTRODUCTION

THE 1979 GENERAL Prison Law established the so-called model of 'scientific individualisation', which, in line with the constitutional principle of reintegration, establishes a flexible system of execution of prison sentences, which should be adapted to the individual characteristics and treatment needs of the detained person.[1] This model of individualisation constitutes an evolution from purely progressive systems, which generally require all prisoners to spend fixed periods of time in different phases in order to move from closed to less restrictive conditions (Fernández Bermejo 2019). The express recognition of the aim of reintegration in Article 25.2 of the Constitution provided a strong foundation for the penitentiary model of scientific individualisation, in line with the principle of relative autonomy of prison law, which distinguishes the aims of punishment at the moment of sentencing and at the later stage of implementation of the sentence (van Zyl Smit and Snacken 2009: 76–80). Conditional release (parole) can therefore be seen as a key instrument of a prison system which should primarily serve the constitutional aim of reintegration.[2] It should

[1] As a result, Art 72.4 of the General Prison Law provides that 'In no case shall an inmate be kept in a lower grade when the evolution of his treatment merits progression'.

[2] In this vein, see, eg the Judgment of the Constitutional Court No 120/2000, of 10 May, FJ 4, affirming that the constitutional clause of reintegration established by Art 25.2 'operates as a parameter for weighing up the entire system for the execution of [prison] sentences and the institutions that comprise it. Therefore, it is not so much a question of evaluating a specific custodial sentence but of weighing it up within the framework of a system in which institutions such as the suspended sentence, the alternatives to prison, or, finally, the different regimes for serving a sentence, are key elements.' Along the same lines, see Judgment No 160/2012, of 20 September, FJ 3.

be noted that there is no exact equivalent in Spanish of the English legal term 'parole'. I therefore use the term 'conditional release' (*libertad condicional*) throughout this chapter in reference to the early release from imprisonment under post-release conditions (Van Zyl and Corda 2018).

As in other European countries, conditional release in the Spanish criminal justice system has undergone profound structural reforms during the last two decades. Different legislative reforms have progressively narrowed the scope of this institution, particularly concerning specific groups of offenders (eg sexual offenders or those convicted of terrorism) and the execution of long-term imprisonment. Since its inception, conditional release had been conceived as the last phase in the execution of imprisonment, but the 2015 reform of the Spanish Criminal Code (SCC) converted this institution into an alternative to imprisonment, thus becoming a form of suspending the execution of the sentence. On the other hand, parole decision-making in Spain is based on a purely discretionary release model, which has led to a relatively limited application of conditional release when compared to other European countries (Cid Moliné 2021: 280; Gómez Martín 2022: 1480).

The aim of this chapter is twofold: first, to describe how the recent legal reforms have led to a considerable limitation of the application of the critical rehabilitative instruments of the model of individualisation, with a strong legislative emphasis on retributive and incapacitative aims of punishment. Although the focus here is on conditional release, the overview will show that legislative reforms have impacted the key instruments of rehabilitation, including prison leave and open prison (semi-liberty). Second, I will argue that the legal status of prisoners is further weakened by a restrictive constitutional interpretation of the clause of reintegration, which has filtered down to the judicial review of decisions made by the prison administrations. It is argued that, in relation to conditional release, there needs to be more consistency in applying the relevant legal criteria for release. I conclude by arguing that the Constitutional Court's recognition of a fundamental right to reintegration would provide valuable guidance to legal operators when reaching fair and transparent decisions on conditional release, and enhance the legal status of prisoners.

II. THE LEGAL OBSTACLES TO PRISON PROGRESSION AND INDIVIDUALISATION: TWO DECADES OF LEGAL REFORMS

As set out in the General Prison Law, which crystallised in the 1995 Criminal Code and the 1996 Prison Rules, the rehabilitative path of the prisoner is comprised of three fundamental 'milestones' designed to both reduce the harms of imprisonment and to adapt the execution of the sentence to the individual characteristics of prisoners: ordinary prison leave (*permisos ordinarios*); open prison (*tercer grado*); and conditional release (*libertad condicional*). While there are considerable differences in nature and scope, these three institutions constitute the essential instruments of an individual sentence path, which should allow the prisoner to move progressively from a closed prison to more open conditions. In this sense, the prison regime is to be determined through a process of classification through the individual study (observation) of each prisoner's criminogenic needs for treatment.[3]

The flexible nature of the individualisation system allows the classification in open prison or semi-liberty (third degree) at any stage of the execution of the sentence, even initially, according to the individual needs and evolution of the prisoner. In contrast to the requirement in progressive systems, the stay in previous phases or 'degrees' of classification is not generally required to classify a prisoner in an open prison.[4] Nevertheless, the flexibility in the classification system is not at odds with an 'upward' sense in the manner of serving the sentence (Solar Calvo 2019: 312), conditional release being the last phase (fourth degree) and requiring the previous classification in open prison (third degree). One should not lose sight of the fact that an open prison is a form of imprisonment, meaning that the prisoner continues to serve his or her sentence for all purposes, even though it can be served in different establishments which entail varying levels of supervision and control.[5]

In any event, it should be noted that under the model of individualisation, the discretion of the prison administration remains limited by the duration of the sentence, which has been determined judicially according to the culpability of the offender and the seriousness of the offence. In this sense, at least for determinate prison sentences, the maximum duration of the sentence marks a fundamental limit of state intervention and a clear distinction from the authoritarian conception of rehabilitation which powered, for instance, the growth of North American indeterminate imprisonment and conditional release in the late nineteenth century (Rotman 1990).

[3] Art 65.1 of the General Prison Law states that 'The evolution in the treatment will determine a new classification of the inmate, with the consequent proposal of transfer to the establishment of the corresponding regime, or from one section to another of a different regime'. Art 72 further provides that 'Whenever it appears from the corresponding observation and classification of an inmate that he is fit for it, he may initially be placed in a higher degree of treatment, except that of conditional release, without necessarily having to pass through those that precede it' and that 'In no case will an inmate be kept in a lower grade when the evolution of his treatment makes him worthy of progression'.

[4] See Art 72.3 of the General Prison Law: 'Whenever it appears from the observation and classification of an inmate that he or she is fit, he or she may be initially placed in a higher degree, other than parole, without necessarily having to pass through the grades preceding it.' In this vein, although it is possible to classify a detainee in open prison (third degree) at the initial phase of imprisonment after a minimum period of observation, the Prison Rules demand special care before placing in open prison a detainee who has not served at least one-quarter of his sentence (Art 104.3 of the Prison Rules). However, a Prison Service Instruction has recently regulated the possibility of initial allocation in open prison for short-term prisoners who have been imprisoned for the first time (see Instruction 6/2020, of 17 December, establishing a protocol for direct admission to open prison).

[5] In practice, the most frequent form of open prison is implemented in the Social Insertion Centres *(Centros de Inserción Social)*, where the regime is much more relaxed. Offenders are generally allowed to leave the centre during the day and on the weekends. In its least stringent form, open prison can be served from home, and the offender remains subject to certain measures of supervision and control (electronic monitoring).

Contrary to open prison, conditional release is circumscribed to the final phase of imprisonment (Rodríguez Yagüe 2013: 61–62), with a temporary minimum requirement of having served at least three-quarters of the sentence (ordinary conditional release), with the exceptional possibility of earlier release in some cases.[6] In this sense, Article 72.1 of the General Prison Law establishes conditional release as the last stage of imprisonment, which follows open prison: 'Prison sentences shall be executed according to the system of scientific individualisation, separated into grades, the last of which shall be that of conditional release, as determined by the Criminal Code'.[7] Therefore, prison legislation conceives conditional release as the last part of the sentence, as a fourth degree of treatment which must be considered once the objective requirements set out in the Criminal Code have been met.

Taking the aforementioned general constitutional design of the prison system into account, the Organic Law 7/2003, on reform measures 'to ensure the full and effective execution of prison sentences', made profound legislative changes to the Criminal Code and the General Prison Law, establishing a less rehabilitative and a more punitive system of execution (Faraldo Cabana 2004: 299–340; Landa Gorostiza 2006: 165–202; Cervelló Donderis 2019a: 45–54). The subsequent reforms in the penal system have exacerbated the internal shortcomings in executing custodial sentences and limited the use of its primary tool for rehabilitation, the flexibility and individualisation principles proclaimed by the General Prison Law.

The erosion of this individualisation model has taken place through different legal avenues. Firstly, criminal law provisions have been introduced, establishing fixed time parameters as prerequisites for obtaining higher levels of freedom. For instance, Article 36.2 SCC establishes the so-called security period (*periodo de seguridad*) blocking the access to open prison until at least half of the sentence period has been served in closed conditions. The need to introduce this security period and, more generally, the truth in sentencing measures set out by the reform were justified by the need to increase the 'legal certainty' in the execution of imprisonment and to give citizens more certainty on the implementation of sentences.[8]

[6] Early conditional release (Art 90.2 SCC) may be granted once two-thirds of the relevant sentence has been served, provided that the prisoner has participated in prison work or other vocational training. Exceptionally, conditional release can be moved forward to half of the sentence for those prisoners who are serving their first prison sentence and qualify for early conditional release (Art 90.3 SCC).

[7] This provision is complemented by Art 192 of the Prison Rules, which states that 'Prisoners classified in the third degree [open prison] who meet the other requirements established for this purpose in the Criminal Code shall serve the remainder of their sentence on parole, in accordance with the provisions of the Criminal Code'.

[8] The memorandum of the Organic Law referred to the need to establish a security period as a bridge between the Criminal Code and the penitentiary system: 'When determining the proportionality of sentences, their specific length and their suitability for the purposes of general and special prevention, proposals cannot be made outside the scope of penitentiary legislation. In fact,

For all sentences exceeding five years, the sentencing judge retains, in general, the discretion to apply this security period. However, for certain offences – terrorism offences, crimes committed within a criminal group, human trafficking and certain sexual offences against minors – the application of the security period is mandatory *ex legem* and can only be overruled by the prison supervision court based on a favourable prognosis of reintegration. Nevertheless, in its most stringent original form, this reversion was not possible for prisoners convicted of terrorist offences.[9] For prisoners convicted of crimes of terrorism, a specific (additional) requisite of abandonment and collaboration with authorities was added, which raises serious problems of legitimacy from the perspective of the right not to incriminate oneself and the right to freedom of conscience (Garro Carrera 2017). This exceptional treatment of terrorist offending paved the way for a more restrictive regime, which has progressively expanded to long-term imprisonment.

Also in relation to open prison, the 2003 reform introduced the payment of civil liabilities derived from the offence (reparation) as an objective requisite of the progression to the third degree. In the same vein, certain offenders are being increasingly excluded from the possibility of accessing specific rehabilitative measures (prison leave, open prison, conditional release) through more complex criminal law provisions. A significant example is found in Article 78 SCC (*cumplimiento íntegro y efectivo*), blocking the possibility of applying rehabilitative measures where the sentences to be served notably exceed the maximum legal limits of effective imprisonment (20, 25, 30, 40 years).[10]

When particularly long sentences are accumulated, the offender may be hindered from getting any rehabilitative measure for the whole sentence period, so the totality of the sentence will be served in closed conditions, without any measure of regime relaxation. If this limitation is applied at the sentencing stage, there remains a get-out clause that will allow the prison supervision court to reverse its application if a 'favourable individual prognosis of social reintegration' is made. This get-out clause does not apply to prisoners convicted of terrorist offences or crimes committed within a criminal group as, in their case, the access to open prison and conditional release is locked until serving four-fifths and seven-eighths of the sentence, respectively. As a result, for the first

the system of progression through degrees of treatment, prison leave, open prison and conditional release can mean that the sentence provided for in the Criminal Code and by the sentence is very far removed from the sentence actually served.'

[9] See Art 36.2 SCC (as redacted by Organic Law 7/2003, of 30 June): 'The Prison Supervision Court, after an individualised and favourable prognosis of social reintegration and assessing, where appropriate, the personal circumstances of the offender and the evolution of the rehabilitative treatment, *when the offence is not a terrorist offence* under section two of Chapter V of Title XXII of Book II of this Code *or committed within criminal organisations*, may agree, after hearing the Public Prosecutor, the Prison Service and the other parties, the application of the general regime of execution' (emphasis added).

[10] This was coupled with the increase to 40 years of the maximum effective time of imprisonment fixed at 30 years by the 1995 Criminal Code.

time, the 'phantom' of de facto life imprisonment appeared for prisoners who began to serve their sentence at an advanced age (Rodríguez Yagüe 2013: 74).

Lastly, and in relation to conditional release, the 2003 reform expressly provided that, in case of revocation, the time spent on conditional release would be lost and that the sentence would resume from the point at which conditional release was given.[11]

In 2015, a second relevant reform of the Spanish Criminal Code made substantial changes, further eroding the autonomy of prison law and scientific individualisation. The statement of purpose of the law justified the reform because of the sense of impunity in certain segments of the population.[12] On the one hand, the indeterminate sentence of life imprisonment (*prisión permanente revisable*) was established for the first time in democratic times, introducing mandatory (reviewable) life imprisonment for certain aggravated types of murder. It should be noted that life imprisonment had been abolished in 1928 for humanitarian reasons in Spain. For almost a century, under different political regimes – democratic or dictatorial – Spain has been an abolitionist country in terms of life imprisonment or indeterminate sentences for criminally liable offenders. This was so even in the periods when the death penalty was in force, its commutation carrying a determinate sentence, which ordinarily took place after 30 years of imprisonment (Acale Sánchez 2016: 47). As pointed out by legal scholars, in the case of life imprisonment, conditional release departs even further from its original conception as the last stage of imprisonment, becoming the only instrument which permits the prisoner's release (Cervelló Donderis 2022). The introduction of life imprisonment, despite being justified on the grounds of retribution or general prevention (deterrence), can be rightly seen as the triumph of a new penology which rejects reintegration as the aim of imprisonment and focuses on the incapacitation and control of the 'dangerous' offender (Daunis Rodríguez 2013).

In this context, the 2015 penal reform profoundly altered the institution of conditional release for life prison sentences (as well as determinate or fixed-period prison sentences), by turning it into a form of suspension of the execution of the sentence and regulating it within the framework of the 'alternative forms to the execution' (probation). With this modification, conditional release is currently conceived as an alternative measure to enforcement, which brings it closer to the conception of conditional release in common law countries

[11] Art 93.3 (as redacted by Organic Law 7/2003, of 30 June reads: 'In the case provided for in the previous paragraph [prisoners convicted of terrorist offences], the convicted person shall serve the remaining time of the sentence with the loss of the time spent on probation.'

[12] See the statement of purpose of Organic Law 1/2015, of 30 March, reforming the Criminal Code: 'The need to strengthen confidence in the Administration of Justice makes it necessary to provide it with a legal system that guarantees predictable judicial decisions that are also perceived by society as fair. To this end, following the model of other European countries, permanent revisable prison was introduced for extremely serious crimes, in which the public demanded a sentence proportional to the crime committed.'

(Solar Calvo 2019: 291). Surprisingly, this decisive change in the nature of conditional release was not preceded by any scholarly debate (Mir Puig 2022: 184) and was taken despite the opposition expressed by the Prosecution Council during the legislative process.[13]

The main practical consequence of this change in nature has been that, in case of revocation, the period of time spent in conditional release does not count towards the sentence, as the prisoner resumes the sentence from the moment the suspension was accorded, losing the time spent on conditional release.[14] As a result, even though conditional release still constitutes the last stage of imprisonment, from the prisoner's perspective, it can be seen as a worse alternative compared to open prison (Ortega Calderón 2015; Cervelló Donderis 2022), which pushes many prisoners to 'max out' their sentences in ordinary or open prison conditions (Guisasola Lerma 2017: 69).

Table 11.1 Classification of prisoners and corresponding prison regime (excluding remand prisoners)

Degree of treatment	**1st degree**	**2nd degree**	**3rd degree (open prison)**	**4th degree (before 2015)**
Prison regime	Closed regime (segregation/ solitary confinement)	Ordinary regime	Semi-freedom	Conditional release
Minimum time served (legally required)	n/a	n/a	No • In practice: at least ¼ of the sentence • Security period for long sentences (exceeding 5 years): ½ of the sentence	¾ (ordinary) ⅔ (extraordinary) ½ (first-time serving prison sentence)

(continued)

[13] In its Report to the Draft Bill to Reform de Criminal Code, dated 20 December 2012, the Prosecution Council (Consejo Fiscal) criticised the reform of parole as constituting 'a radical transmutation of the penal and penitentiary theory and praxis in force in our country to date' and declared that its timeliness was 'more than dubious'.

[14] Art 90.6 SCC expressly imposes the loss of time spent on parole in case of revocation: 'The revocation of the suspension of the rest of the sentence and probation shall result in the enforcement of the part of the sentence still to be served. The time spent on probation shall not be counted as part of the time spent serving the sentence.'

Table 11.1 *(Continued)*

Degree of treatment	1st degree	2nd degree	3rd degree (open prison)	4th degree (before 2015)
Legal criteria or requisites	'Extreme dangerousness or clear and serious inadaptation to other regimes'	'Prisoners in personal and penitentiary circumstances of normal cohabitation, but without the capacity to live, for the time being, in semi-liberty'	'Prisoners who, due to their personal and prison circumstances, are capable of living a regime of semi-liberty'	• Being classified in the 3rd degree • Having satisfied: – civil liability – personality – previous records – circumstances of the criminal offence – the significance of the legally protected rights that may be affected by a repeat offence – behaviour while serving the sentence – family and social circumstances – the expected consequences of the actual suspension on the serving and fulfilment of the measures imposed
Decision-making	Prison Administration	Prison Administration	Prison Administration	Prison Supervision Court

Another related effect of the 2015 reform is the decoupling between the duration of the sentence and the period of suspension, as the parole period can extend far beyond the remainder of the sentence. Article 90.5 SCC establishes a variable period of suspension for a minimum of two and a maximum of five years. The lower limit of two years is applicable even if the imprisonment term left to be served is under that threshold. And, in reality, the upper limit of five years is frequently exceeded in cases where the prisoner has significant time remaining on their sentence, because the period of conditional release will never be shorter than the time remaining as part of the sentence. As Cervelló Donderis has pointed out, this two-to-five-year period of conditional release carries numerous interpretive problems

> because its starting point is that parole is a trial period similar to suspension [probation], but it forgets that it constitutes the final phase of the execution of the prison sentence, not the alternative to its initiation; and therefore, the duration of the sentence has already been fixed in the judgment. (Cervelló Donderis 2022: 325)

In this regard, a significant problem is that the legal provision does not provide any guidance that will aid the Prison Supervision Court in individualising the period of conditional release during which the sentence will be suspended. Finally, many scholars have criticised the conversion of conditional release into a modality of a suspended sentence on the grounds that this interrupts the prison treatment inherent to the execution of the sentence. Because treatment ceases with the suspension of the sentence, this can have generally negative consequences for the individualisation of the prison intervention and the prospects of social reintegration (Cervelló Donderis 2019a:130–31).

III. A RIGHT TO CONDITIONAL RELEASE? ADMINISTRATIVE AND JUDICIAL DECISION-MAKING CONCERNING REHABILITATIVE FIGURES

Rights-based approaches to parole have emphasised the fundamental importance of the decision to release (van Zyl Smit and Snacken 2009: 316). The fairness of the process by which the decision on conditional release is made is therefore an essential aspect of the legitimacy of conditional release as an institution. In Spain, the decision on conditional release is discretionary and is vested in the judiciary, in contrast to the decisions to grant prison leave or open prison, which are generally a competence of the executive through the Prison Administration. The three basic legal requirements for ordinary conditional release are set out in the Criminal Code: (i) having attained open prison treatment (the so-called third degree); (ii) having served three-quarters of the sentence handed down; and (iii) having a record of good conduct (understood as the absence of disciplinary sanctions in prison).[15] In addition, where civil liability has been imposed, the granting of conditional release is subject to the fulfilment of this prerequisite. For those prisoners who have been convicted for terrorist offences or those related to criminal organisation, additional specific requirements of abandonment and collaboration apply,[16] as for the progression to open prison.

Surprisingly, the reference to the 'individualised prognosis of social reintegration' in the previous wording of Article 90.1 SCC has been repealed. This assessment of reintegration, together with the classification in open prison/third degree, constituted the central criterion for the decision of conditional release.[17]

[15] Art 90.1 SCC.

[16] Art 90.8 SCC.

[17] The prognosis of social reintegration was understood in the sense of Art 67 of the General Prison Law, which reads: 'Once the treatment has been completed or the release of the inmate is imminent, a final prognosis report shall be issued, stating the results achieved by the treatment and a judgement on the probability of the inmate's future behaviour on release, which, where appropriate, shall be taken into account in the file for the granting of conditional release.' Surprisingly, the 2015 reform of the Criminal Code did not adjust the General Prison Law, and consequently the final prognosis report by prison authorities is still required.

However, the 2015 reform replaced the explicit reference to the prognosis of social reintegration with a set of criteria that should inform the judicial decision on conditional release, namely:

> [T]he personality of the convict, his criminal record, the circumstances of the criminal offence committed, the significance of the legally protected rights that may be affected by reoffending, his or her behaviour while serving the sentence, his or her family and social circumstances and the expected consequences of the suspension and the compliance with the measures imposed.[18]

In this way, reintegration has ceased to be the overarching criterion for the decision on conditional release and is dissolved into a plethora of criteria which the prison supervision court must consider, with the prevalence of static risk factors linked to the offence and unrelated to any rehabilitative consideration (Cervelló Donderis 2019a: 148). As Cervelló Donderis has rightly pointed out, since the 2015 legal reform, the criteria that inform the decision to release are mainly grounded on considerations of retribution and/or general prevention, whereas only two of them are linked to special prevention (rehabilitation), namely the conduct of the offender during the execution of the sentence and the conduct expected upon release. These criteria are identical to the ones foreseen for the conditional release review of life imprisonment.[19] Surprisingly, in the case of the newly introduced sentence of life imprisonment, the legislator maintains the express reference to the 'positive prognosis of social reintegration' after repeating the legal criteria for deciding on conditional release. In any event, it should be noted that, whereas the decision on conditional release for determinate prison sentences is vested in the competent Prison Supervision Court, the sentencing court retains the power to release for indeterminate sentences of life imprisonment.

Apart from the legal obstacles to conditional release, the access to this figure is further complicated by the restrictive approach taken by the Constitutional Court when interpreting the constitutional clause of reintegration. It must be noted that a right to conditional release has not yet been recognised by

[18] In addition, express reference is made to the (continued) payment of civil liability as a requisite that must be maintained when deciding on conditional release. In this sense, Art 90.1 SCC remits to the general requisites established in Art 72 of the General Prison Law for the progression to open prison.

[19] For life imprisonment, Art 92.1 SCC provides that: 'The Court of Law shall order the suspension of permanent, revisable imprisonment with the possibility of parole when the following circumstances are fulfilled: a) The convict has served twenty-five years of his sentence … b) That he has attained open prison treatment; c) That the Court of Law, taking into account the personality of the convict, his record, the circumstances of the criminal offence committed, the significance of the legally protected rights that may be affected by a repeat offence, his behaviour while serving the sentence, his family and social circumstances and the expected consequences of the actual suspension on the enforcement and fulfilment of the measures imposed, can establish the existence of a favourable assessment of social integration, upon evaluating the progress reports submitted by the prison and by those specialists determined by the Court of Law itself.'

constitutional jurisprudence, despite the unequivocal wording of the prison rules that conditional release 'shall' be granted to those prisoners who fulfil the relevant legal requirements.[20] The Court has firmly established that the Constitution does not impose that social reintegration should be the basis of punishment, nor even that it should constitute the sole guiding criterion for the execution of custodial sentences. However, the mere fact that sentences can serve multiple legitimate preventive purposes (both general and specific) does not exempt the prison administration and the judiciary from their responsibility to protect the constitutional rights at stake, delimiting the legitimate content of the deprivation of liberty.

Both the principle of legality and the principle of legal certainty make it necessary to develop constitutional criteria to resolve conflicts between the different legitimate purposes of punishment which arise during the execution of prison sentences and which, in the absence of clear constitutional guidance, end up being resolved by the ordinary courts in a disparate manner. Thus, the current constitutional interpretation by the Spanish Constitutional Court of the constitutional reintegration principle (Article 25.2) significantly devalues the weight of this constitutional mandate, showing complete deference to the Prison Administration even where there is a total disregard for the principle of reintegration. The case law shows that the weak constitutional commitment to the reintegration clause – its degradation to a mere guiding principle and its understanding as 'just one more' of the legitimate aims of punishment – has filtered down to the level of the judicial application of punishment and tends to give way, without any need for balancing, to other considerations of general prevention or retribution.

The refusal to recognise a fundamental right to reintegration, far from being a theoretical question, has practical implications for the protection of prisoners' fundamental rights, as this restrictive interpretation devalues reintegration to a mere symbolic mandate. In this sense, the prisoners' interest in reintegrating into society is not balanced against other legitimate aims of imprisonment when conducting the judicial review on the decisions which restrict prisoners' rights. This also affects the decisions to deny conditional release once the objective legal criteria are met, or when controlling other restrictions of fundamental rights by prison authorities. Thus, even when the prisoner fulfils the legal requirements to access the key rehabilitative instruments, the Constitutional Court has rejected the idea that the prisoner has any subjective right to their concession, which usually results in rubber-stamping the reasons put forward by the Administration, whether of a penological nature (general prevention, retribution) or an administrative one (eg prison organisation needs).

[20] According to Art 90.1 SCC, 'The Parole Board Judge shall order the suspension of the rest of the prison sentence and *shall grant* parole to convicts who fulfil the following circumstances' (emphasis added).

The recognition of a constitutional right to reintegration as an integral part of the prisoner's legal status would allow the system of scientific individualisation proclaimed in the General Prison Act to operate with enhanced guarantees for prisoners, counteracting the supremacy of the prison administration in the penitentiary relationship and modulating the limitations of fundamental rights in prison. The consequences of such a recognition would be both qualitative and quantitative: on the one hand, the principle of reintegration would be surrounded by the guarantees inherent to fundamental rights, among which the access to the appeal for protection before the Constitutional Court stands out; on the other hand, and even more relevantly, the reintegration clause would be given specific weight in the balancing exercise against other interests that lack constitutional recognition.

The recognition of such a right would not imply the denial of the existence of the frequent tensions between the different purposes of punishment during the implementation of prison sentences, nor would it mean proclaiming that reintegration constitutes the only criterion that should guide the adoption of decisions affecting fundamental rights in prison, since the conflict between the prisoner's individual interest for reintegration and other legitimate constitutional interests or goods is inherent in the execution of prison sentences. Among these is the need to consider and control the risks to intra-penitentiary security (the safety and good order of the prison) and extra-penitentiary security (the risk of further offending) when deciding on any rehabilitative measure that involves a certain relaxation of the control measures inherent to closed conditions.

It is relevant that the Constitutional Court itself came to apply a standard close to the one proposed here, although it did so without recognising a constitutional right to reintegration. In its Judgment No 112/1996, of 24 June, the Court granted protection to a prisoner who, despite meeting the objective conditions for access to ordinary prison leave at the time – completion of a quarter of his sentence, classification in the second or third grade and absence of misconduct – had been denied ordinary prison leave, with the prison administration citing the 'remoteness' of the date of completion as the reason for denial.

In constitutional protection proceedings, the standard of control applied by the Court on that occasion was very different from the one that would end up being consolidated: the starting point was the connection between the constitutional principle of reintegration and the figure of prison leave, which meant that the decision on release must take this purpose into account. The Constitutional Court did not derive from the principle of reintegration – an unconditional right to being granted prison leave once the objective requirements had been met. Instead, it established a prima facie right to leave, subject to the non-existence of other interests or constitutional values that conflict with the interest of reintegration. In other words, once the legal requirements for prison leave have been met, the denial of leave requires the existence of other constitutional interests at stake that are 'connected with the meaning of the sentence and with the aims pursued by its enforcement', thus requiring the prison administration to carry out a balancing exercise of the various interests at stake and giving individualised reasons for the decision to deny leave. The Administration could not legitimately invoke generic reasons of general prevention or retribution to deny prison leave.

IV. CONCLUSIONS

The last two decades of reforms of the conditional release system can be seen against the background of wider truth in sentencing measures that have restricted the application of key rehabilitative institutions such as prison leave (*permisos ordinarios*) and open prison (*tercer grado*), eroding the constitutional principle of reintegration (Article 25.2 of the Constitution). In Spain, the criminal policy changes have blurred the model of scientific individualisation proclaimed by the 1979 General Prison Law, which was crystallised in the 1995 Criminal Code and the 1996 Prison Rules. As shown, the last two decades of prison law reforms have substantially increased the minimum periods of incarceration required for conditional release and have further restricted access to rehabilitative instruments for certain categories of offenders. In this sense, there is an increasing legislative emphasis on the retributive and incapacitative aims of punishment, which prevail over reintegration and challenge the principle of relative autonomy of imprisonment (Landa Gorostiza 2006: 168–69; Cervelló Donderis 2019b: 236; Solar Calvo 2019: 479).

At the same time, the change in the nature of conditional release – from a form of enforcement to a form of suspension – implies the interruption of prison treatment at the last phase of the prison sentence, thereby 'emptying' the system of scientific individualisation by making its last phase (the fourth degree) disappear. It is, then, perhaps surprising that the described toughening of the prison system coincides with a notable decrease in the overall prison population in Spain, from its peak in 2010 (73,929 prisoners) down to 56,698 prisoners in 2023, which represents a 23 per cent reduction in absolute numbers. However, the average length of imprisonment has increased significantly and steadily in the last two decades (from 13 months in 2000, up to 18 months in 2010 and 22 months in 2021), together with the proportion of prisoners serving long prison sentences (Rodríguez Yagüe 2023).

The relatively low use of conditional release in Spain can also be explained by the pure discretionary model of conditional release decision-making and the low standard of reintegration set by the constitutional case law when controlling administrative and judicial decisions on rehabilitative institutions. However, despite its historic hands-off approach in the field of imprisonment, recent constitutional case law in Spain has opened the door to a more demanding interpretation of reintegration, which is manifested in several judgments that correct the decisions of prison authorities (and the judiciary) limiting the fundamental rights of prisoners (Anderez Belategi 2024; Solar Calvo and Lacal Cuenca 2024: 168). These decisions deal not with conditional release but with the restriction of rights, such as freedom of information (access to the media in prisons), freedom of expression in relation to disciplinary proceedings and the right to due process concerning prison leave. In all of them, the Court controls the administrative decisions requiring that any restriction of fundamental rights is provided by law, based on specific legitimate aims and subject to the test of proportionality.

In this way, the Court has laid the ground to develop a more demanding standard of review of the prison figures connected to reintegration, which would go beyond the minimum scrutiny exercised by the Strasbourg Court in the field of conditional release, at least as far as determinate sentences are concerned (van Zyl Smit and Corda 2018: 435).[21] As seen, the recognition of a fundamental right to reintegration harbours an enormous potential for more demanding judicial control of decisions affecting the rehabilitative path of prisoners (leave, open prison, conditional release) and, more broadly, of restrictions on the exercise of fundamental rights in prison (allocation of prisoners, disciplinary regime, freedom of expression, etc).

As indicated, this alternative line of jurisprudence, despite having been abandoned by the Court in subsequent decisions, shows the possibilities of an interpretation which gives practical consequences in the penitentiary sphere to the reintegration clause and raises the standard of protection applicable to persons deprived of their liberty. As Rotman (2023) points out, this understanding of reintegration as an individual right departs from other paternalistic and authoritarian conceptions of rehabilitation, strengthening the state's power by increasing judicial or administrative discretion. In his words, under the rights-based model,

> rehabilitation is no longer a matter of the state's largess, subject to the vicissitudes of policy change. Instead, rehabilitation is the culmination of a continuum of the perpetrator's rights, as it guarantees the dignity of human beings confronted with criminal prosecution and conviction. (Rotman 2023: 25)

However, the formal recognition of a right to reintegration may not suffice to improve the position of prisoners or to reverse the steep decline in the use of conditional release in Spain. As Cid Moliné has pointed out, even if judicial discretion were correctly delimited and the legal provisions interpreted in the light of the principle of reintegration, the requisite of a positive prognosis

[21] van Zyl Smit and Corda cite as an example of the 'hands-off' approach in relation to parole the case of *Dybeku v Albania* ECLI:CE:ECHR:2007:1218JUD004115306, where the court held that 'the Convention does not guarantee, as such, a right to conditional release or to serve a prison sentence in accordance with a particular sentencing regime'.

of reintegration and the previous access to open prison constitute structural limits which determine a comparatively low use of conditional release. It is noteworthy that, according to the data compiled by that author, the proportion of prisoners in Spain who ended their sentences in conditional release halved from a maximum of nearly 40 per cent for the 2010–14 period to around 20 per cent after the 2015 legal reform, and this decrease has not been compensated by a comparable increase in the progressions to open prison (Cid Moliné 2021: 291).

In the Spanish case, whilst the introduction of a privileged form of conditional release for first-time prisoners serving sentences below three years (Article 90.3 SCC) constitutes a positive step, the maintenance of a completely discretionary model of conditional release for all sentences of imprisonment is a key limit to the use of conditional release. As comparative research has shown and international human rights instruments recommend,[22] a progressive transition from closed to open conditions is a crucial aspect of reducing reoffending and improving reintegration prospects. Therefore, adopting automatic conditional release with adequate supervision for certain offenders would improve their reintegration prospects by reducing the rate of unsupervised release from closed conditions. In the case of short sentences, a model of automatic release would find express normative support in the materials of the Council of Europe.[23] In this sense, even though prisoners who pose a higher risk of reoffending also have a higher likelihood of failing the conditional release period, the key is whether progressive and supervised release is more beneficial than release from closed conditions.[24]

REFERENCES

Acale Sánchez, M (2016) *La prisión permanente revisable: ¿pena o cadalso?* (Madrid, Iustel).

Anderez Belategi, M (2024) *La reinserción como garantía individual en la ejecución penitenciaria* (Valencia, Tirant lo Blanch).

Cervelló Donderis, V (2019a) *Libertad condicional y sistema penitenciario* (Valencia, Tirant lo Blanch).

[22] Recommendation Rec(2003)22 of the Committee of Ministers to member states on conditional release (parole), adopted by the Committee of Ministers on 24 September 2003 at the 853rd meeting of the Ministers' Deputies: 'In order to reduce the harmful effects of imprisonment and to promote the resettlement of prisoners under conditions that seek to guarantee safety of the outside community, the law should make conditional release available to all sentenced prisoners, including life-sentence prisoners' (No 4.a).

[23] ibid general principle No 7: 'Consideration should be given to the savings of resources that can be made by applying the mandatory release system in respect of sentences where a negative individualised assessment would only make a small difference to the date of release.'

[24] See Cid Moliné (2021) 296.

—— (2019b) 'Individualización garantista en el ejercicio de la discrecionalidad penitenciaria' 72 *Anuario de Derecho Penal y Ciencias Penales* 217.

—— (2022) *Derecho penitenciario* (Tirant lo Blanch, Valencia).

Cid Moliné, J (2021) 'La libertad condicional. ¿Está en Europa la solución?' 4 *Indret* 280.

—— (2022) 'La libertad condicional y su orientación preventiva' in V Gómez Martín et al (eds), *Un Modelo Integral de Derecho Penal. Libro Homenaje a la Profesora Mirentxu Corcoy Bidasolo* (Madrid, Agencia Estatal Boletín Oficial del Estado) 1479–93.

Daunis Rodríguez, A (2013) 'La prisión permanente revisable. Principales argumentos en contra de su incorporación al acervo punitivo español' 10 *Revista de Derecho Penal y Criminología* 65.

Faraldo Cabana, P (2004) 'Un derecho penal de enemigos para los integrantes de organizaciones criminales. La Ley Orgánica 7/2003, de 30 de junio, de medidas de reforma para el cumplimiento íntegro y efectivo de las penas' in P Faraldo Cabana, LM Puente Aba and JA Brandariz García (eds) *Nuevos retos del derecho penal en la era de la globalización* (Valencia, Tirant lo Blanch) 299–340.

Fernández Bermejo, D (2019) 'Del sistema progresivo a la individualización científica. La elaboración de la Ley General Penitenciaria y la relevancia del bienio 1978–1979 en el derecho penitenciario' 72 *Anuario de Derecho Penal y Ciencias Penales* 483.

Fiscalía General del Estado (2012) Informe del Consejo Fiscal al Anteproyecto de Ley Orgánica por la que se modifica la Ley Orgánica 10/1995, de 24 de noviembre, del Código Penal.

Garro Carrera, E (2017) 'Tercer grado y libertad condicional de condenados por delitos de terrorismo: una mirada desde la libertad ideológica y el derecho a no incriminarse. La gestión penitenciaria del final de ETA' 28 *Revista General de Derecho Penal*.

Guisasola Lerma, C (2017) *La libertad condicional. Nuevo régimen jurídico conforme a la LO 1/2015, CP* (Valencia, Tirant lo Blanch).

Landa Gorostiza, JM (2006) 'Delitos de terrorismo y reformas penitenciarias (1996–2004). Un golpe de timón y correcciones de rumbo ¿hacia dónde?' in M Cancio Meliá and C Gómez-Jara Díez (eds), *Derecho penal del enemigo: el discurso penal de la exclusión* (Madrid, Edisofer) 165–202.

Mir Puig, C (2022) *Derecho penitenciario. El cumplimiento de la pena privativa de libertad* (Barcelona, Atelier).

Ortega Calderón, JL (2015) 'El nuevo régimen temporal de la libertad condicional en el Código Penal tras la reforma operada por la LO 1/2015 de 30 de marzo' 8652 *Diario La Ley*.

Rodríguez Yagüe, C (2013) *El sistema penitenciario español ante el siglo XXI* (Madrid, Iustel).

Rodríguez Yagüe, C (2023) 'La evolución legislativa de las penas de prisión de muy larga duración' in C Rodríguez Yagüe (ed), *Penas perpetuas* (Valencia, Tirant lo Blanch) 335–414.

Rotman, E (1990) *Beyond Punishment: A New View of the Rehabilitation of Criminal Offenders* (Westport, CT, Greenwood Publishing).

—— (2023) 'The History of Rehabilitation as a Penological Principle' in F Coppolla and A Martufi (eds), *Social Rehabilitation and Criminal Justice* (Routledge, London) 13–26.

Solar Calvo, P (2019) *El sistema penitenciario español en la encrucijada: una lectura penitenciaria de las últimas reformas penales* (Madrid, Agencia Estatal Boletín Oficial del Estado).

Solar Calvo, P and Lacal Cuenca, P (2024) 'En defensa del tercer grado. Su importancia como tiempo efectivo de cumplimiento' 168 *La ley penal: revista de derecho penal, procesal y penitenciario*.

van Zyl Smit, D and Corda, A (2018) 'American Exceptionalism in Parole Release and Supervision: A European Perspective' in KR Reitz (ed), *American Exceptionalism in Crime and Punishment* (New York, Oxford University Press) 410–86.

van Zyl Smit, D and Snacken, S (2009) *Principles of European Prison Law and Policy: Penology and Human Rights* (Oxford, Oxford University Press).

Part III

Practices

12

Prison Release in Cases of Old Age and Chronic or Life-Limiting Illness

CHRISTOPHER SEEDS AND DELANEY MOSCA

I. INTRODUCTION

DISCUSSING THE FUTURE of parole, as an exercise in normative theorising, is a project done best with attention to context and awareness of the variety of circumstances in which one encounters parole. This chapter examines and analyses parole release decision-making, in contrast to parole supervision, in the United States of America. Historically, as a general matter, in late nineteenth-century and early twentieth-century USA, the theory and practice of parole emerged alongside a penal philosophy attuned to rehabilitation; partnered with indeterminate sentencing, parole entered as an alternative to fixed sentencing regimes, then predominant in US jurisdictions, under which expiration of time or executive clemency were the bases for release from prison. In present-day USA, parole decision-making has become risk averse to the point of frustrating its original purpose – prison release; so broken, in this sense, as to lead some scholars to call for the reform of parole, if not its abolition. Simultaneously, the USA faces a contemporary reality in which, over the past half a century, prison populations have grown as never before and sentencing has hardened, so that many of the people imprisoned, having spent decades incarcerated, are growing old and approaching the ends of their lives – that is, dying – inside. The bloated US prison system poses financial, organisational and ethical challenges – challenges that in the case of older and terminally ill incarcerated people demand urgent, expedient solutions.

There is, then, a tension between, on the one hand, the tendency to risk-averse decision-making that characterises American parole boards of late and, on the other hand, the singular combination of pressures that mass incarceration and the excessive incarceration of older adults present, as limited resources and human decency urge release from prison for people approaching the end of life.

That tension is apparent in the recent interest and slow but steady expansion of approaches to prison release that are based on health, the use of which accelerated during COVID-19 but continues in its wake. That tension is also apparent in jurisdictions' experimentation with approaches to prison release that vest decisions not with parole boards, but elsewhere – for example, with courts. Both developments should be recognised as something of a shift. Indeed, following the millennium, some scholars called for abolition of parole in the USA and some recommended that the judiciary rather than the parole board make release decisions (see, eg Travis 2002; American Law Institute 2011); yet scholars just as often dismissed the idea that parole boards be replaced by specialised courts as something beyond the realm of realistic possibility (based on an assessment that in the USA this would require an arduous amount of institution building). At present, however, in what one might call 'late mass incarceration', the intersecting crises of *over-incarceration* and *older-incarceration* have produced circumstances in which jurisdictions are exploring multiple review and release pathways for older and/or dying incarcerated adults. These are circumstances, this chapter suggests, in which calls for the reform, if not the abolition, of parole deserve another look.

This chapter revisits parole in the context of medical-based release for the ageing and terminally ill and, therein, judicial officials as prison release decision-makers for US penal systems. In doing so, the chapter gives attention, beyond the position of the decision-maker (eg parole board versus court), to the different types of evaluations in which prison release decision-makers engage and the different justifications upon which decision-makers base their conclusions. If contemporary developments in penal thought and practice – in penality – have stimulated the production of a variety of forms of prison release (Guiney 2023), that splintering involves both an array of decision-makers and a variety of underlying logics. In California today, a jurisdiction we examine in what follows, as the state makes some effort to undo the excesses of mass incarceration and address the challenges posed by the escalating number of older, dying prisoners, there exist multiple pathways by which older and/or dying incarcerated adults might obtain review and release: *elderly parole*, a parole-board hearing and determination rooted in traditional parole considerations of safety available to people over 50 who have served more than 20 years inside; *medical parole*, a conditional parole grant available to incarcerated people diagnosed with less than a year to live who can obtain outside housing, but revocable upon regaining health; *compassionate release*, a judicial determination initiated by a prison Chief Medical Examiner finding that a person has less than a year to live; and *clemency*, a grant of mercy from the governor or another executive body, such as a board of pardons.

As this variety suggests, it is not only the institutional position of the decision-maker at issue, but also how decision-makers approach and ground their decisions. On the latter count, compassionate release deserves special note, because of its renewed vitality (a surge in use that began during the

COVID-19 pandemic and has continued, if to a lesser extent), and also because of the rather ambiguous or multifaceted bases of decision for such grants. As practised in most US jurisdictions (including California), compassionate release involves, by statute, a recall of sentence or a resentencing by a court. Yet, as the name suggests, the determination is often approached from the perspective of charitability, rather than as something the law demands.

Further, as the chapter examines parole boards and courts as alternative sites for prison release decisions, as well as the varying logics underlying those decisions, the chapter emphasises that the historical trajectories by which these splintering forms take shape may not be a simple matter of choosing one decision-maker or one logic over another. In day-to-day decisions on the ground, in the practicalities that separate laws from their implementation, the matter of who decides on release and on what basis they justify their decision may be driven by local circumstances and by expediency (Simon 1993; see generally Garland and Duff 1995). Put another way, the avenue more travelled for release of older incarcerated people may not result from a selection made after debate and deliberation over who decides or on what basis they should decide, but rather as a matter of interactions between people and institutions, events and structures in society – that is, as a matter of social construction and, often, as a response to crisis. As this chapter will discuss, in California, compassionate release and medical parole have a complicated and interwoven recent history. Compassionate release, initiated in the 1970s, and medical parole, initiated in the 2010s, provide alternative pathways for release of people suffering from serious illness. Interestingly, these different forms have been turned to by lawmakers less for reasons of who decides, and less for reasons concerning what justifies prison release, than for practical efficacy and what an approach offers in response to immediate needs. Individual case decisions under these different release mechanisms reflect this fractured history, rather than finding anchoring in a particular logic. This chapter concludes, however, that for a release form to work optimally, a grounding logic is important. Considering the judiciary as an alternative to parole boards, as such, not only demands exploring the distinct underlying logics of courts and parole boards, it also demands an examination of the different bases for judicial resentencing, and therein a close and critical look at the concept and practice of compassionate release.

In sum, this chapter considers the 'future of parole' by using the present problem of ageing and dying in prison as a frame to examine the pros, cons and challenges of doing prison release in a different way. As a foundation, we begin with a historical look at parole in the USA. We then turn to contemporary USA, in which the size of prison populations as well as the number of older adults approaching the end of life in prison pose significant challenges. For empirical depth and for generating ideas and questions about what matters in the policy and practice of prison release based on medical and health concerns, we use recent developments in California as a case study. The chapter closes with a reconsideration of judicial recall of sentence (or resentencing) based on age, illness and dying as a basis for determining release from prison.

II. PAROLE AND ITS ALTERNATIVES

In the USA, the history of parole is, as a general matter, intricately tied to indeterminate sentencing. This began during the mid- to late-nineteenth century, when persistent criticisms confronted the then-common approach to sentencing: fixed sentences meted out by courts with any back-end adjustments to release dates made through executive clemency. In general, the critique had two parts. One part concerned the principle of fixed sentencing: identifying the prison term and an automatic release date at the outset, it was argued, was impossible to do in a reliable and meaningful way. As criminal justice system reformer Frederick Wines (1904: 11–12) put it:

> Justice is an abstraction, elusive as a sunbeam … A criminal court is a trap to catch sunbeams. Neither the legislature nor the court can make use of a non-existing pair of scales with imaginary weights … How long a time is uncertain and cannot ever be foretold in advance.

The 'life' sentence – a sentence without a minimum or maximum term, in which the release date is determined later, after a period of incarceration has passed – was presented as an alternative, paradigmatic of the indeterminate sentencing model.

A second part of the critique concerned who served as the decision-maker on prison release. If courts were poorly positioned to make decisions at the outset, executive clemency, it was argued, was given to arbitrariness and ripe for favouritism. Concerns were also raised about the qualifications of certain other decision-makers to assess release from prison. Timing of the decision aside, it was proposed that a judge, an expert in law, was less fit to determine readiness for release than a panel of individuals who were ostensibly experts in incarceration, human behaviour, and risk and safety – in effect, in assessing dangerousness. Wines (1904: 11) wrote of this body of reviewers, commonly referred to today as a parole board, in the following way:

> Has not the governor of the state the power to grant pardons and commutations of sentences? Yes, but the grant is an act of arbitrary sovereign power. What is needed is something quite different, to wit, the establishment of a system under which the authorities who have the custody of the prisoner and who, being appointed by the governor, as his representatives and agents, and are empowered to establish rules … governing the date and the conditions of the prisoner's release … They are in a position to gain, by observation and inquiry, a full knowledge of the life history of the convict, and of his character and intentions, such as no court ever can. They are, or should be, experts in criminal chicanery, who cannot easily be deceived by hypocritical professions or by simulated and self-interested obedience to rules, who are capable of forming a tolerably accurate judgment as to his actual genuine change in

> his attitude to the law and to the commonwealth. If any analogy is needed, in order to justify the confidence reposed in them, it may be found in the grant of precisely similar powers to the medical superintendent of every American hospital for the insane.

Wines's perspectives are representative of reform thought at the time, the currents of which were reflected in new state laws authorising, and practices implementing, indeterminate sentencing and parole.[1] States varied as to when each adopted the parole model, as to the crimes and sentences they authorised parole boards to review and in local operations. But common at root was an idea about a certain sort of expertise: parole purported to rely on a speciality in assessing readiness for release from prison and, on the flip side, identifying dangerousness and malingering. As Wines specified (1904: 13), the basis for the indeterminate sentencing model, in which the ultimate length of a sentence would not be determined at the outset, was not retribution, but rather 'social self-defence'; and that needed to be determined by a body invested, in theory, not with a proficiency in law, but rather with an expertise in ascertaining rehabilitation and risk. As we will see in looking at California's recent history, the difference between specialities in law or in 'dangerousness' has been absent in conversations about forms of prison release. The thought of Progressive Era reformers, such as Wines, however, offers a reminder that the training of prison release decision-makers and the knowledge and measures to which they turn ought not be disregarded; in fact, it is arguably the crux of the matter.

Over the course of the twentieth century, parole was widely adopted, and indeterminate sentencing and rehabilitation represented the guiding philosophy of carceral systems (see generally Garland 2001). In practice, the influence of the rehabilitation paradigm differed across jurisdictions, and even jurisdictions that utilised an indeterminate model did not do so exclusively (Rhine et al 2017: 280–81). Recognising the variation in authority given to the parole board across jurisdictions, one might choose to identify systems as parole-oriented, and, as Reitz and Rhine note, 'for purposes of policy analysis, it is useful to think in terms of degrees of indeterminacy' (2020: 284). The weakening of rehabilitation as a penal paradigm in the USA in the late twentieth century brought with it a departure from parole in some states. In the last quarter of the twentieth century, 16 US states abolished parole. Today, there are 33 states with parole-oriented systems.[2]

Yet, despite the fall of the rehabilitative ideal and partial retrenchment of parole, and even given the variation that exists in parole-oriented systems across states, the influence of parole decisions on time served in prison has been significant at a national level. Reitz and Rhine estimate that approximately two-thirds of prison release decisions in the USA in recent decades have

[1] Wines was also influenced by 'scientific' advances of the times, including disciplinary practices and eugenics (see, eg Wines 1904: 14).

[2] As of 1 August 2024, Louisiana fully discontinued the practice, leaving 33 states with discretionary parole.

been determined or 'heavily influenced' by parole board decisions (2020: 283). Hence, it is important to recognise that parole decision-making, if often unheralded, has been a significant, even primary, site of the growth of the US prison population during the mass incarceration era (Reitz 2012).

In addition to acknowledging the powerful influence of parole decisions, even in the wake of the so-called 'fall of the rehabilitative ideal', it is important to recognise that parole practices changed in resonance with broader transformations in the penal field. The shifts that affected sentencing policy and clemency in late-twentieth-century USA – including risk aversion and law and order politics (see generally Garland 2001; Simon 2007), managerialism (Feeley and Simon 1992) and increased roles of victims in policy and legal proceedings (Gottschalk 2006) – also affected parole. This ought not be surprising: parole boards, if vested with high discretion over prison release, nevertheless possess low institutional clout (far lower than a governor, legislature or court). Parole decision-makers, as such, are particularly susceptible to penal trends and institutional pressures.[3] Parole boards, moreover, are situated in the executive branch, and in some states, such as California, the governor has review power over parole decisions (Ghandnoosh 2017). Accordingly, the length of a prison sentence that depends on parole review for determining its end point is likely to shift, not only according to the particularities of decision-makers, but with the times, not to mention the many recognised problems or 'procedural shortfalls' (Reitz and Rhine 2020) of local parole processes. If one wants to refer to parole decision-making as an expertise or science, as Progressive Era reformers did, it has proven to be one especially susceptible to political, cultural or even organisational influence.

Given the foregoing, it is understandable that some scholars called for an end to parole in the USA at the turn of the millennium. Yet, beset with the exorbitant costs of state prison administration and in the midst of a national financial recession in the late 2000s, policy took a different course. Rather than facing abolition, parole became a key site of intervention in a national wave of state-level policy reform. Bipartisan reforms with a general aim of downsizing prison populations and saving money often worked through parole, and in the process also diversified the routes that states relied on for prison release (see, eg LaVigne et al 2014: 26–27). Since that era of reform subsided in the late 2010s, scholarly calls that courts take over release decisions from parole boards have resurfaced. For example, van Zyl Smit and Corda (2018: 466) recommended

[3] van Zyl Smit and Corda (2018: 454) put it well: 'Indeed, parole board members are vulnerable to the loss of their livelihoods on every day of their tenure of service, whereas elected prosecutors and judges face ouster only at intervals of several years, depending on the length of their election cycles. Arguably, parole board members live with a degree of political insecurity more acute than other responsible officials in American criminal justice systems'. Or, per Reitz and Rhine (2020: 286): 'American parole boards are supremely powerful institutions in their influence on prison policy, but they are exceedingly weak agencies in terms of professional status, political insulation, and member job security'.

that specialised courts handle parole, perhaps modelled after re-entry courts, which had become prevalent in the USA:

> While … reforms [to parole] could certainly improve current US parole systems substantially, we think that in the long run a transition to a 'judicial model' for parole boards would be advisable in order to achieve full independence from the executive branch of government. In other words, parole boards should be removed from the correctional environment and conceived anew as specialist sentence implementation courts squarely within the judicial branch.

Rhine et al (2017: 287) also preferred 'judicially led parole decision making'; but they noted (citing other scholars who concurred) that there was little likelihood of judicially led parole decision-making catching on in the USA, and therefore recommended 'concentrat[ing] on evolutionary changes to existing institutions rather than a "ground-up" building of new infrastructures'.

Why so unlikely? In part, because, as those authors suggested, parole agencies already exist in many jurisdictions, whereas specialised resentencing courts dedicated to determining prison release do not. But it also may be because historically in the USA, as discussed above, parole decisions and judicial sentencing decisions have been cast as fundamentally different operations, governed by different logics and requiring different forms of expertise. A court knows the law; a parole board knows rehabilitation, risk and safety. This perspective, which undergirded the inception of parole in the USA, to the extent it continues in recent policy, buttresses scepticism about courts taking over the discretionary area that parole has occupied.

The remainder of this chapter takes a second look at the possibility of judicially led prison release decision-making in the context of an added crisis – the growing number of incarcerated people approaching or facing the end of life.

III. MEDICAL RELEASE FROM PRISON: THE CALIFORNIA EXAMPLE

There is another crisis facing incarceration in the USA that comes with its own costs and its own ideological challenges. The increase in the prison population and those serving long sentences has brought with it a swell of men and women who are ageing into senior-citizen status and dying in prison. Growing old and experiencing the death process generates unique 'pains' for those incarcerated, who must contend with the challenging material and social conditions of the prison (see also chapter five in this volume). The swell of older and dying individuals also poses challenges for the day-to-day administration of prisons. In financial terms, operating a prison that is also in effect a nursing home is extremely expensive. The situation introduces new demands in terms of what incarcerated people who are older and chronically ill require, and, with respect to prison release, introduces added cost- and resource-related reasons that releasing people is desirable from the perspective of prison administration.

As one of the largest and most influential carceral systems in the USA, and one that has made some attempts to ameliorate the excesses of mass incarceration, California is a compelling case in which to examine developments in prison release processes and their logics. This is particularly true with regard to prison release as it relates to California's ageing incarcerated population. To understand the current context of medical release in California, we need to take a step back to the 1970s, a time when the currents leading to the circumstances noted above first become noticeable, and in doing so highlight the introduction of medical-based reasons in prison release decision-making.

California's history with parole began at the end of the nineteenth century, earlier than in most US states, when parole served in effect as a substitute for executive clemency (Messinger et al 1985; Simon 1993). At the turn of the century and in the early twentieth century in California, as in other US jurisdictions, concerns over sentence lengths coincided with Progressive Era reform arguments that prison release decisions were best made on the basis of expert knowledge and indeterminate sentences rather than predetermined lengths or mercy. This resulted in the California Adult Authority, entrusted with broad discretion to decide prison release (in effect, to determine ultimate sentence lengths), revoke parole and set new parole dates (Cassou and Taugher 1978). From 1913 to 1976, parole was California's primary release mechanism (Weisberg 2019).

In the 1970s, as indeterminate sentencing and rehabilitation fell into disfavour as a guiding logic for the prison, California shifted to determinate sentencing and curtailed parole in the process (Messinger et al 1985). Two lines of legal precedent fuelled the changes. The first afforded due process rights in the parole process, and thereby curtailed the Adult Authority's broad discretionary power to grant and revoke parole without review and strict procedure (*Morrissey v Brewer* 408 US 471 (1972)). The second challenged the broad sentencing power of the parole authority as cruel and unusual (see *In re Lynch* 8 Cal 3d 410 (1974); *In re Foss* 10 Cal 3d 910 (1976)). These judicial attacks on parole authority created administrative disorder, as the Adult Authority was required to amend its procedures in accordance with the parolees' newly accorded rights, leading to legislative pressures on the indeterminate sentencing system (Cassou and Taugher 1978). Combined with a growing disillusionment with rehabilitation, these circumstances undergirded California legislators' turn to determinate sentencing. In the process, the legislature eliminated the Adult Authority and in effect eliminated parole, abolishing it for most felony crimes.

Importantly, as the determinate sentencing bill discontinued parole, it also introduced a provision for recall of sentence and resentencing by courts. The sentence-recall provision authorised judges to modify sentences years afterwards for 'for any reason rationally related to lawful sentencing' (*Dix v Superior Court* 53 Cal 3d 442, 456 (1991); see the California Penal Code, § 1170(d)(1)). The sentence-recall provision, initially used principally to reward informants, was turned to by the California Department of Corrections (CDC) as a route for releasing from prison people who were close to death, a form of compassionate release (Demyan 2013). The process, however, was a slow one. Initiated by a recommendation from the CDC (in determinate sentence cases), it then required approval by the Board of Prison Terms (BPT) before going to a judge for a resentencing proceeding.[4] In the early 1990s, legislative attempts were made to accelerate the review process by allowing incarcerated people who were terminally ill to apply directly to the courts. The CDC and BPT opposed the bills, expressing concerns about 'abuse' of release 'power' (Demyan 2013: 36), and the bills, after passing in the legislature, were vetoed by successive governors who upheld the gatekeeping role of the CDC. In the mid-1990s, however, as the AIDS crisis worsened in prisons and public support for more efficient release processes grew, Governor Pete Wilson eventually signed into law a bill supported by the CDC, the BPT and the California Peace Officers Association, all agreeing in that conjuncture that the cost of incarcerating people dying of AIDS outweighed the risk to public safety. The bill allowed the Chief Medical Examiner of a prison or the CDC director to initiate the process, and gave the CDC or BPT only a month to review and recommend the case to a court, which then had 10 days to issue a decision.[5]

Public discontent with release rates, along with support for the release of people who were terminally ill, however, continued into the millennium. The number of people who died while awaiting compassionate release decisions – as well as the increasing number of people in custody who required extensive medical care but did not meet the requirements for sentence recall, as they were not actively dying or medically incapacitated – led legislators to consider a new mechanism: medical parole. Introduced in 2011, medical parole was heralded as an opportunity for the state to save millions of dollars annually on the care of exceptionally sick individuals with little public safety risk (Dolan 2011; Lagos 2011). Medical parole reduced the fiscal burden of ailing prisoners by offloading the expense of their care to the Center for Medicare and Medicaid Services (CMS), and did so without sacrificing public safety by providing they could be returned to prison if their condition improved. In 2014, after the US Supreme Court decision in *Brown v Plata* 563 US 493 (2011) held that living conditions and health care in California prisons violated the Eighth Amendment, medical parole was expanded by court order. Even so, between January 2011 and September 2020, only 183 people achieved prison release by medical parole (CDCR nd) – approximately 19 per year.

The three-judge court ordered as a result of *Brown v Plata* and related litigation also required that the CDCR establish a mechanism to review people

[4] The California Department of Corrections was renamed the California Department of Corrections and Rehabilitation (CDCR) in 2004. The California Board of Prison Terms was abolished and replaced by the Board of Prison Hearings in 2005 (California Penal Code, ch 3, § 5075(a)).

[5] For a detailed account of this policy history, supported by archival legislative materials, see Demyan (2013: 20–36).

over the age of 60 who had been incarcerated for more than 25 years (but not sentenced to death, life without parole (LWOP), or for a second or third strike) (CDCR 2021). This led to the creation of 'elderly parole', which requires that the parole board give special consideration to age, diminished physical condition and long-term confinement. In 2021, the California legislature modified elderly parole by reducing the eligible age to 50 years and the time-served requirement to 20 years. While, in an elderly parole hearing, the board considers age and associated physical condition, it still weighs this against psychological and risk evaluations, the nature of the crime, criminal record and behaviour while incarcerated.[6] In 2023, 34 per cent of elderly parole hearings resulted in a decision to grant parole – a total of 627 people, which pales in comparison to the 26,970 individuals in state custody aged 50 or over at the end of that year (CDCR 'Offender Data Points').

The parole board's status as a key decision-maker in the release of chronically ill and older prisoners came into question, however, after a dispute between the CDCR and the CMS and an investigation into the quality of care that was being provided to medical parolees. When an individual was released on medical parole, they were placed into skilled nursing facilities, licensed by the CMS. An investigation by the *LAist* magazine, however, uncovered that the CDCR moved and released most medical parolees to a single, unlicensed, skilled nursing facility, in which patients were living in unclean conditions and experienced inhumane treatment (some patients, for example, had been handcuffed, leading to pressure ulcers) (Mendelson and Yu 2022). The medical parole process was scandalised. Contemporaneously, a bill had been introduced in the state legislature to expand medical parole access to patients experiencing chronic pain or eligible for hospice treatment. After the investigation was publicised, and as a result of tension between CDCR practice and the CMS protocol, however, the bill's author shifted focus (Yu 2022). What began as legislation to expand eligibility for medical parole was modified to instead revise the compassionate release process rooted in California's recall-of-sentence statute. Passed in 2022, AB960 instituted a presumption of release and specified that the compassionate release process would begin with a recommendation from a primary care physician and the Chief Medical Examiner of a prison, and then move – without other CDCR decision points – directly to the courts. The new law also requires that court hearings must take place within 10 days of the referral to court and release, if granted, must occur within 48 hours. In the 12 months after the new law went into effect in January 2023, 67 individuals were released under the procedure, 15 were denied and five died awaiting a decision (Judicial Council of California 2024).

[6] Note, too, that local and national news often cite the concerns of victims, prosecutors and police as elderly parole hearings approach (Metz 2019; Bakersfield Californian 2024).

IV. CONSIDERATIONS FOR THE FUTURE OF MEDICAL RELEASE

A. Splintering of Forms: Deep-Rooted Philosophies and Exigent Circumstances

As this volume emphasises (see chapter one in this volume), one way to theorise the impact of contemporary changes in penal landscapes on parole is to see those changes – put very generally, the punitive turn – as generating a trio of crises that challenged the institution of parole, leading to a diversification of prison release decision-makers and decision-making logics: a crisis of legitimacy, concerning a lack of public trust in government; a crisis of administration, concerning how to actually carry out prison release decision-making in a context of mass incarceration; and a crisis of ideas, in which 'the decision to release has become imbued with all the anxieties and contradictions of late-modern penality' (Guiney 2023: 629). As a consequence, the landscape of parole is now peppered with a variety of decision-makers and decision-making styles: 'administrative-bureaucratic, non-executive committee, legislative pre-commitment and judicial body' (Guiney 2023: 623).

The California case set out above, which illustrates movement between parole boards and the courts as release decision-makers, offers an example of the complex ways in which such mosaics take shape, a process in which claims of authority and expertise work alongside social and political circumstances. On the one hand, the role of the decision-maker is a matter with roots in penal philosophy and US penal history, and one influenced by competing institutional positions and structures of the penal state (Garland 2013). Parole became entwined a century ago in the USA with the *indeterminate* sentencing paradigm; and in the mid-1970s, California's recall-of-sentence statute, from which the contemporary practice of judicial-based compassionate release stems, was introduced as part of the *determinate* sentencing statute that eschewed indeterminate sentencing. Yet the shift away from parole was not entirely clean. Recall of sentence, if ultimately a judicial determination, still depended on the department of corrections (the CDC/R) to initiate a recommendation, and on the parole board (the Board of Prison Terms) to approve the recommendation, before a court could consider it. What followed was a dispute – animated most clearly in the BPT's concerns about an 'abuse' of power – rooted in how release decisions should be made. At the crux of the BPT's complaint, alongside some concern over institutional survival, was a belief in which one sees Progressive Era justifications for parole boards still in play: that the parole board possesses an expertise – in determining risk and dangerousness – that is most relevant for the decision at hand, that the courts do not.

On the other hand, the shifts back and forth between parole-based and court-based release decisions in California have depended significantly on expediency and local social and political circumstances. The reform bill that succeeded, after multiple failed attempts, in the 1990s was the one that received the support of the department of corrections and the parole board, support it received due to the overwhelming demands of the AIDS crisis. Those were unique circumstances in which an urgent need existed to release large numbers of terminally ill incarcerated people, as well as an urgent need for a process that could do so rapidly, before applicants died onsite awaiting release decisions. At that moment, matters of health could override safety. Less than a decade into the twenty-first century, law-and-order opposition to expanding release decisions was again mitigated, this time by a budget crisis in the late 2000s and, several years later, by the US Supreme Court holding that conditions in California prisons violated the US Constitution. In that context, the legislature turned back to the parole board, expanding medical parole and introducing elderly parole. Certainly, the parole board's concern with abuse of power was satisfied by this move, but that was not its impetus.

Immediate needs and unique social and political circumstances also underlie the most recent shift back to prison release as a judicial determination. Again, the bill that brought about the change was set against a background dispute between the Department of Corrections and the state medical services, coupled with the crisis that COVID-19 brought to the California prison system (see generally Aviram and Goerzen 2024), alongside the increase in the number of older incarcerated adults. The bill originally sought to reform medical parole, but, after the nursing home scandal, veered back to judicial resentencing as the site for reform, reintroducing a streamlined process running directly from a Chief Medical Examiner to the courts, with no CDCR or Board of Prison Hearings decision points along the way. Significantly, the basis for the move was not the shortcomings of a parole board to make release decisions about older and terminally ill people; rather, it was the inability of the Department of Corrections to provide for people, upon release to community nursing homes, in a humane way. Urgent needs to release for material reasons, efficacy of process and aversion to political scandal drove the oscillation between parole board and court more than arguments about expertise or logic of decision.[7]

B. The Role of Dangerousness in Deciding Applications Grounded in Illness and Age

If one should not assume that arguments over penal philosophy drive shifts in prison release decisions, one also should not assume that the decision-maker's

[7] Researching parole in California in earlier eras led Messinger et al (1985) and Simon (1992) to similar conclusions. As Simon (1992: 103) wrote, 'Parole supervision should not be treated as a generic type of state control, the unchanging significance of which can be read off from its founders' declarations. It is most usefully seen as a discontinuous series of power configurations involving both public and private actors'. Or per Messinger et al (1985: 103), 'inquiries into the development of penal reforms must be alert to changes over time in the problems of the organizations they serve'.

position necessarily determines a decision's guiding logic. While compassionate release hearings are held in the courtroom, not before a parole board, the prevailing logic will nevertheless be that of the presiding judge; and given the discretion accorded to individual judges, and diversity of viewpoints across jurisdictions and local offices, judicial decisions on prison release can be and have been anchored in varying rationales. See, for example, the California case of Adnan Nijmeddin (*Nijmeddin v Superior Court* 90 Cal App 5th 77 (2023)). Nijmeddin suffered from advanced pancreatic cancer and had a prognosis of less than a year to live. At the sentence recall hearing, the Monterey County judge expressed concern about Nijmeddin's 'ability to pick up the phone and obtain things that he might need to go somewhere or do something to be a risk of dangerousness to others', and denied the compassionate release application. Reviewing the case, the California Court of Appeals ruled the lower court relied on insufficient evidence of a risk of public danger and found the sentencing court abused its discretion. Nijmeddin was released shortly thereafter and died two months later in the care of his family. The case shows how individual judges can take dangerousness into account, not unlike a parole board (see *In re Martinez* 210 Cal App 4th 800 (2012), finding the BPH decision was not supported and ordering release on medical parole).

One finds a similar variety in the grounding of judicial decisions elsewhere in the USA as compassionate release has waxed with the second look movement. The second look movement, spurred by the US Supreme Court's decisions limiting the use of LWOP for juveniles, has been accelerated by increasing recognition of the greying incarcerated population (Feldman 2024; see FAMM 2022). Age and illness, like youth, race and trauma contexts such as domestic violence and military service, have become the subject matter of second-look reforms. The federal First Step Act, which authorises direct petitions for resentencing to US federal courts based on 'extraordinary and compelling reasons' (18 USC § 3582(c)(1)), provides a notable example. What constitutes 'extraordinary and compelling reasons' under the federal law was not initially well defined, leading to a variety of bases for decisions (see Esser 2024: 29–31). The US Sentencing Commission later provided a Guideline Amendment that expanded and clarified the 'extraordinary and compelling' circumstances under which federal judges are authorised to grant release for medical reasons (US Sentencing Guidelines Manual, 1B1.13 (2023)). The development of the First Step Act underscores a takeaway from the *Nijmeddin* case in California: compassionate release often lacks clear guidelines, and in such circumstances, courts may turn to 'dangerousness' to guide decisions much as a parole board would (albeit, if one follows the Progressive Era reformers, without expertise in making such assessments).

More generally, the California example is a reminder that laws are not simply prepackaged and put to work, they are created and implemented in historical and social contexts, which include existing structures and ideologies, existing ways of doing and thinking. One consequence relevant to prison release decisions is that in practice opportunistic or expedient choices involving the allocation of discretion over release decisions may gloss over significant differences between the decision-making bodies and their respective forms of expertise. Caught up in this as well is that the logic or basis of the release decision – for instance, traditional bases for parole decisions such as rehabilitation, risk, safety and dangerousness versus traditional bases for decisions of law such as justice, fairness, equality and consistency – may also become obscured. Who holds power over prison release decisions may be less a matter of which position, parole or court is deemed best situated to make a determination on the relevant facts than a matter of which route is actually functioning.

C. Approaching Compassionate Release as a Change in the Original Circumstance

The lack of a clear grounding for compassionate release decisions has led some scholars to suggest that a more clearly defined logic for resentencing decisions is needed. Legal scholar Meredith Esser, for example, argues that the Eighth Amendment prohibition of cruel and unusual punishments should be a basis for releasing people from prison for physical health reasons, particularly physical maladies stemming from medical neglect (Esser 2023; Esser 2024: 45–46). In this closing section of the chapter, we return to the California example to explore yet another grounding logic for judicial decisions on prison release – one, in fact, already present in the statute.

In recent years, the California legislature has created multiple paths along which individuals may have prison sentences reconsidered based on changed circumstances in the interest of justice. The legislature, for example, has authorised resentencing for people convicted under mass incarceration policies now deemed unduly harsh – including two- and three-strikes resentencing, resentencing on gang- and gun-related enhancements, as well as resentencing for people convicted of crimes in which trauma related to intimate partner violence or military service affected the crime. The justification for resentencing and prison release in these cases is not mercy or equity. Rather, it is *recognition of a change of legal landscape* and, based on that change, the necessity under law for change of sentence 'in the interest of justice'. Claims by eligible parties for resentencing on these grounds have worked their way through state courts, not without hurdles, but resulting in release for many.

A release decision based on medical and health reasons *could also* be conceived as a resentencing required by changed circumstances. In fact, judicially based compassionate release in California is rooted in the same statute as the aforementioned examples of resentencing. While terms of the California law have changed significantly with the amendments noted above, the statute's foundation remains: 'the resentencing court may, in the interest of justice … reduce a defendant's term of imprisonment by modifying the sentence' (California Penal

Code, § 1172.1(a)(3)). It is important to recognise two distinct types of analysis contained within this statutory authorisation (see § 1172.1(a)(5)).[8] The first is an assessment that looks back to the original sentence and recognises that the sentence itself warrants reconsideration in light of changed circumstances. This is a primarily legal determination – for example, as to whether trauma was involved in the crime or the original sentence was based on a gang or gun enhancement. The second is an assessment that regards post-conviction factors, including rehabilitation and diminished physical condition, which may also be balanced with 'defendant's risk of future violence'. This latter determination focuses on changes in the person rather than the circumstances of the crime of commitment. As such, it is harder to distinguish from parole board determinations. The *Nijmeddin* case exemplifies how some courts approach compassionate release applications prioritising the latter type of analysis, and in doing so step outside the bounds of squarely legal expertise, which may loosen the grounding of the decision. But what if, instead, courts considering compassionate release took the former track? It is worth asking whether old age, terminal illness and impending death can be considered as more than matters of change in a person over time.

V. CONCLUSION

In conclusion, building on the prior discussion, we sketch the following argument: (i) that *old age*, *terminal illness* and *death* can also be viewed as circumstances that affect the original sentence; (ii) that approaching compassionate release petitions from this analysis, placing courts more squarely within their sphere of expertise (the law), could provide stronger decisions; and (iii) that approaching compassionate release petitions as evidence reflecting changed circumstances demanding reconsideration of the original sentence could, in turn, result in more grants of release on more consistent grounds. The argument may be clearest with respect to dying. If the original sentence is not formally a death sentence, then the process of dying incarcerated, based on illness at any age, arguably constitutes a changed condition that conflicts with the original sentencing logic. One may think of old age and terminal illness in

[8] The text of California Penal Code, § 1172.1(a)(5), reads: 'In recalling and resentencing pursuant to this provision, the court may consider postconviction factors, including, but not limited to, the disciplinary record and record of rehabilitation of the defendant while incarcerated, evidence that reflects whether age, time served, and diminished physical condition, if any, have reduced the defendant's risk for future violence, and evidence that reflects that circumstances have changed since the original sentence so that continued incarceration is no longer in the interest of justice … The court shall consider if the defendant has experienced psychological, physical, or childhood trauma, including, but not limited to, abuse, neglect, exploitation, or sexual violence, if the defendant was a victim of intimate partner violence or human trafficking prior to or at the time of the commission of the offense, or if the defendant is a youth …, and whether those circumstances were a contributing factor in the commission of the offense'.

similar ways: rather than factors to be added to a risk calculus, they may be encountered as physical conditions that did not exist at the time of the original sentencing, conditions that do not simply matter to an assessment of the dangerousness of the person but that matter as well to the proportionality of the sentence to the crime. If courts are authorised to judge retrospectively that certain punishments are overly harsh for certain criminal conduct (as multiple forms of recent resentencing legislation in California do), courts might also be authorised to judge that a punishment imposed upon a younger, healthier person was not imposed with the experience of an aged, terminally ill person in mind.

The case of California and older and chronically ill incarcerated adults illustrates the complexity of processes (fuelled by competing positions of authority, decision-making logics, forms of expertise, and immediate social and political circumstances) that generate laws and practices governing parole and prison release. In doing so, it points to a possible future of 'parole' – one in which the condition of ending life in prison is recognised not merely as a fate calling for compassion, but as a circumstance changing the nature of a prison sentence by law.

REFERENCES

American Law Institute (2011) 'Model Penal Code: Sentencing, Tentative Draft No 2'.

Aviram, H and C Goerzen (2024) *Fester: Carceral Permeability and California's COVID-19 Correctional Disaster* (University of California Press).

Bakersfield Californian (2024) 'DA: Drive-by Shooter Denied Elderly Parole' (12 January).

California Department of Corrections and Rehabilitation (CDCR) (nd) 'Medical Parole' www.cdcr.ca.gov/bph/medical-parole/#:~:text=Referrals%20and%20Approvals, medical%20parole%20and%20denied%2088.

—— (nd) 'Offender Data Points' https://public.tableau.com/app/profile/cdcr.or/viz/OffenderDataPoints/SummaryInCustodyandParole.

—— (2021) 'Initial Statement of Reasons … Parole Consideration Hearings for Elderly Inmates' www.cdcr.ca.gov/bph/wp-content/uploads/sites/161/2021/09/BPH-RN-21-04-elderly-parole-ISOR-filed-with-OALdocx.pdf.

Cassau, AK and Taugher, B (1978) 'Determinate Sentencing in California: The New Numbers Game' 9(1) *Pacific Law Journal* 5.

Demyan, A (2013) 'What's Compassion Got to Do with It?' (PhD diss, University of California, Irvine).

Dolan, J (2011) 'Inmate May Be First To Be Set Free Under "Medical Parole"' *LA Times* (6 June).

Esser, MB (2023) 'Extraordinary Punishment: Conditions of Confinement and Compassionate Release' 92(4) *Fordham Law Review* 1369.

—— (2024) 'Unpunishment Purposes' *Minnesota Law Review* forthcoming.

Feeley, M and Simon, J (1992) 'The New Penology: Notes on the Emerging Strategy of Corrections and Its Implications' 30 *Criminology* 449.

Feldman, B (1994) 'The Second Look Movement: A Review of the Nation's Sentence Review Laws' (Washington, DC, The Sentencing Project).
Garland, D (2001) *The Culture of Control: Crime and Social Order in Contemporary Society* (Chicago, IL, University of Chicago Press).
—— (2013) 'Penality and the Penal State' 51(3) *Criminology* 475.
Garland, D and RA Duff (1995) 'Thinking about Punishment' in D Garland and RA Duff (eds), *A Reader on Punishment* (Oxford, Oxford University Press).
Ghandnoosh, N (2017) 'Delaying a Second Chance' (Washington, DC, The Sentencing Project).
Gottschalk, M (2006) *The Prison and the Gallows* (Princeton, NJ, Princeton University Press).
Guiney, TC (2023) 'Parole, Parole Boards and the Institutional Dilemmas of Contemporary Prison Release' 25(3) *Punishment & Society* 621.
Judicial Council of California (2024) 'Report on the Compassionate Release Program'.
Lagos, M (2011) 'Calif. Convict Wins States' First Medical Parole' *SF Gate* (15 June).
Lavigne, N et al (2014) *Justice Reinvestment Initiative State Assessment Report* (The Urban Institute).
Mendelson, A and Yu, E (2022) 'Medical Parole Got Them Out of State Prison. Now They're in a Decertified Nursing Home' *LAist* (3 May).
Messinger, S et al (1985) 'The Foundations of Parole in California' 19(1) *Law & Society Review* 69.
Metz, S (2019) 'Parole Reform Gives Older Californians, including David and Louise Turpin, Hope for Early Release' *Desert Sun* (19 April).
Reitz, KR (2012) 'The "Traditional" Indeterminate Sentencing Model' in *The Oxford Handbook of Sentencing and Corrections* (Oxford, Oxford University Press) 270–98.
Reitz, KR and Rhine, EE (2020) 'Parole Release and Supervision: Critical Drivers of American Prison Policy' 3 *Annual Review of Criminology* 281.
Rhine, EE, Petersilia, J and Reitz, KR (2017) 'The Future of Parole Release' 46(1) *Crime and Justice* 279.
Simon, J (1993) *Poor Discipline: Parole and the Social Control of the Underclass 1890–1990* (Chicago, University of Chicago Press).
Simon, J (2007) *Governing through Crime* (Oxford, Oxford University Press).
Travis, J (2002) 'Thoughts on the Future of Parole', remarks delivered at The Vera Institute, 22 May 2002.
van Zyl Smit, D and Corda, A (2018) 'American Exceptionalism in Parole Release and Supervision: A European Perspective' in KR Reitz (ed), *American Exceptionalism in Crime and Punishment* (New York, Oxford University Press) 410–86.
Weisberg, R (2019) 'The Wild West of Sentencing Reform: Lessons from California' 48(1) *Crime and Justice* 35.
Wines, FH (1904) *The New Criminology* (Kempster Print Company).
Yu, E (2022) 'CA Bill Aims to Release Severely Ill Patients from Prisons vs Parole in Nursing Homes' *LAist* (4 August).

13

Paradox of Parole Practices in Japan: Progress, Challenges and a Possible Way Forward

SAORI TODA

I. INTRODUCTION: THE PARADOX OF PAROLE PRACTICES

JAPAN IS OFTEN regarded as an 'exception' in comparative penal studies. For instance, Cavadino and Dignan (2005: 171) describe Japan as 'the most paradoxical' and 'highly distinctive' country in their study. They identify key contradictions: Japan has maintained a uniquely low and stable crime rate despite rapid urbanisation, industrial growth, and significant economic and social disruptions. Further, while its criminal justice and penal institutions resemble those of Western countries, their practices are deeply influenced by traditional Japanese attitudes and values. Third, its penal policy initially appears lenient but, upon closer inspection, is repressive and totalitarian in some respects. Fourth, while informal social control generally promotes social inclusion, the state also employs exclusionary punishments like the death penalty. While their study did not delve deeply into parole, they might also find recent parole practices paradoxical given the recent contradictory trends in current practices: an increasing proportion of prisoners are being released on parole, yet the timing of their release is being delayed. In other words, although the scope of prisoners released on parole has expanded to facilitate reintegration and rehabilitation, parolees typically undergo only a brief period of community supervision, as they are released near the end of their term.

In Japan, discretionary release is the only form of parole available for all prisoners serving a custodial sentence. Parole practices in Japan have remained stable over the last half-century. Following the turmoil of the immediate post-war era, the proportion of prisoners released on parole among the total number of released prisoners each year ('the parole rate') has been consistently between 50 and 60 per cent (Japan, Ministry of Justice Research and Training

Institute 2023a: 77–78; 2023b: 32).[1] The other 40 per cent serve their entire sentence in prison and are released unconditionally upon the expiration of their term. However, recent trends indicate a shift towards broader use of parole. The parole rate has been on upward trajectory since reaching a post-war low of 49.1 per cent in 2010, surpassing 60 per cent in 2021 for the first time since 1972 (Japan, Ministry of Justice Research and Training Institute 2023a: 77–78; 2023b: 32). Furthermore, the current government has advocated for the expanded use of parole in a recent policy statement (Japan, Ministry of Justice 2023c: 220). On the other hand, the timing of parole has gradually been deferred towards almost the end of sentences. In most cases, parole release occurs typically after 80 per cent of the term has been served (Table 13.1).

Table 13.1 Proportion of the original sentence served by Japanese determinate sentence prisoners before release, 1992–2022

Year	Total	X*>70%	70%≦X<80%	80%≦X<90%	90%≦X
1992	100% (12,511)	9.8% (1230)	26.4% (3299)	34.7% (4342)	29.1% (3640)
2002	100% (15,854)	11.7% (1860)	33.1% (5253)	35.1% (5560)	20.1% (3181)
2012	100% (15,033)	1.5% (231)	21.4% (3223)	47.0% (7071)	30.0% (4508)
2022	100% (10,692)	1.2% (132)	18.9% (2018)	46.1% (4927)	33.8% (3615)

*X means a proportion of the original sentence served before parole release.

Source: Japan, Ministry of Justice Research and Training Institute (2023a: 79; 2023b: 33).

Contradictory directions in parole practices have often been explained through the lens of the 'penal bifurcation' theory in other jurisdictions (Padfield 2010; Beyens 2019; Guiney 2019; Herzog-Evans 2019). This theory, coined by Anthony Bottoms (1977; 1980), explains the distinction between the treatment of dangerous, violent and sexual offenders and 'ordinary' offenders in sentencing. In the context of parole, this distinction often centres around the boundary between discretionary release and automatic release (Guiney 2018; 2019: 141). Some might think that the recent contradictory trends in Japan could also be explained by this theory. However, Japanese trends do not align with this theory, not just because Japan only has a discretionary release system. For instance, the parole

[1] The English language version of the 'White Paper on Crime', released by the Ministry of Justice in Japan, offers only a summary of the original publication and lacks detailed information. The comprehensive statistics cited in this chapter can be downloaded in Excel format (in Japanese) from www.moj.go.jp/EN/housouken/houso_hakusho2.html.

rate for sex offenders increased between 2010 and 2014, surpassing the average increase (from 62.6 per cent to 66.5 per cent for forcible sexual intercourse and from 55.0 per cent to 62.7 per cent for indecency through compulsion, compared to an average increase from 49.1 per cent to 56.5 per cent) (Japan, Ministry of Justice Research and Training Institute 2015).[2]

Moreover, the parole rate for long-term prisoners (those who have served more than 10 years) rose from 34.1 per cent in 2007 to 47.2 per cent in 2022, while the rate for short-term prisoners (sentences less than six months) (18.3 per cent, 734 cases in 2022) remains much lower than average (Japan, Ministry of Justice 2023a). Certainly, long-term prisoners and sex offenders are being released later than others (Japan, Ministry of Justice Research and Training Institute 2015; 2023a: 79; 2023b: 33). However, the timing of release has generally been deferred, not just for these offenders. These statistics indicate that the contradictory trends are not based on a clear distinction between dangerous and 'ordinary' offenders. To understand these paradoxical practices, it is necessary to explore the functions of parole in Japan, considering the contexts in which parole policies and practices have developed.

Given the importance of local analysis (Nelken 2010; Brangan 2022), this chapter examines parole practices in Japan, presenting the benefits and limitations of its unique approach as an effort to engage in normative discussions of the future of parole. First, the chapter outlines the basic legal provisions of the Japanese parole system and identifies the main functions of parole along with the key characteristics of Japanese parole practices. Second, it examines recent developments in Japanese criminal justice policy that influence current parole practices and policies, contextualising the contradictory directions in parole. Third, the chapter critically analyses the present approach, revealing its benefits and limitations in light of the normative functions of parole. The chapter concludes by highlighting a crucial first step towards fundamental parole reform in Japan, emphasising the importance of procedural justice in parole decision-making. The focus of this chapter is determinate-sentenced prisoners, as they constitute the majority of the cases for parole decision-makers[3] and the contradictory directions are primarily observed in these cases.[4]

[2] Statistics on sex offenders from 1996 to 2014 are available in the 'White Paper on Crime' featuring sex offences. Data from 2015 onwards is not currently available.

[3] While 10,692 determinate sentence prisoners were released on licence in 2022, only five life-sentenced prisoners were released (Japan, Ministry of Justice, Research and Training Institute 2023a: 78–79; 2023b: 32).

[4] Even considering the rarity of life-sentenced prisoner releases in recent years, the overall picture of Japanese parole practices does not squarely fit penal bifurcation theory. These practices are not primarily driven by the belief that life-sentenced prisoners are inherently 'dangerous'. Instead, the main reason for the recent rigorous release practices is that release practices of life-sentenced prisoners are more vulnerable to public concerns and shifts in penal philosophies due to the indeterminate and ambiguous nature of the life sentence (Toda 2024).

II. UNDERSTANDING THE JAPANESE PAROLE SYSTEM

A. Overview of Japanese Parole

The current release requirements are specified in section 28 of the 1908 Penal Code (Keiho, Act No 45 of 1908) as follows:

> When a person sentenced to imprisonment evinces signs of substantial reformation, the person may be paroled by a disposition of a government agency after that person has served one-third of the term sentenced or ten years in the case of a life imprisonment.

The release requirements have not undergone any changes for over 100 years and remain in effect to this day.

Since the release requirement, 'signs of substantial reformation', is too vague to provide guidance for parole decision-makers, the Ministry of Justice developed specific parole criteria. Section 28 of the Rules on Community Treatment for Persons Who Have Committed Crimes and Juvenile Delinquents (Hanzai wo shita Mono oyobi Hiko no aru Shonen ni taisuru Shakainai ni okeru Shogu ni kansuru Kisoku, Ministerial Order No 28 of 2008) lays down the current parole criteria as follows:[5]

The release decision may be approved if:

(i) the prisoner feels remorse and is willing to reform and rehabilitate;
(ii) there is no risk of reoffending;
(iii) parole supervision is suitable for the prisoner's reformation and rehabilitation; and
(iv) unless it is found that public sentiments are against the release.

The Ministry of Justice circular (2008) states that the prisoner needs to satisfy all these criteria, which are assessed in the order listed above, emphasising that the first criterion is 'the central criterion' among the four. The first criterion (referred to as 'remorse and willingness to rehabilitate' hereinafter) is judged mainly based on behaviour in prison and remarks in interviews with parole board members, compensation to victims, adherence to prison rules and the candidate's rehabilitation plan. Additional weight is given if prisoners demonstrate particularly strong remorse and repentance, suggesting that inner reformation is highly valued in Japan. The second criterion, 'no risk of reoffending', requires that an individual poses no reasonable risk of reoffending during the licence period and no substantial, realistic risk thereafter. This indicates a higher threshold of risk assessment is applied during the licence period than the post-licence period. The third criterion is the overarching criterion. The fourth criterion (referred to as 'public acceptability' hereinafter) is assessed 'from the

[5] The original text does not include Roman numerals. They were added by the author of this chapter.

perspective of whether a prisoner's release would undermine the penological principle and function', which is understood in practice as 'the retributive principle and general preventive function' (Udo 2021: 155).

A prison governor regularly assesses these criteria and will refer a case to the Regional Parole Board, one of the local branch offices of the Ministry of Justice, if they believe all criteria are satisfied. While the parole board can initiate parole reviews on its own initiative, most cases (99 per cent, 13,656 cases) are handled through the two-tier review process involving prison governors and parole boards (Japan, Ministry of Justice 2023b). The parole review is then conducted by a panel of three board members. The whole panel discusses a case based on the results of a paper review and an interview usually conducted by one of the panel members. Data shows that, for determinate sentenced prisoners, there is a very high probability of receiving a favourable decision – 93.0 per cent (12,651 cases) on average between 2013 and 2022 (Japan, Ministry of Justice Research and Training Institute 2023a: 77) – indicating that governors act as gatekeepers.[6]

B. Key Characteristics of Japanese Parole Practices

This section of the chapter identifies three characteristics of Japanese parole practices. These characteristics, which gradually evolved over the years within a legal framework granting wide discretion to decision-makers, underpin the paradoxical practices in Japan.

1. **A strong risk aversion to reoffending during the licence period**: this aversion is exemplified by one of the parole criteria, 'no risk of reoffending', focusing on a reoffending risk during the licence period, rather than on long-term risk. It contributes to practices where prisoners are released near the end of their sentence, with most serving more than 80 per cent of their term before release (Table 13.1). Since sentence lengths in Japan are typically short[7] and the licence period corresponds to the remainder of the original sentence, delayed release timing means that parolees spend only a brief period on licence: approximately 80 per cent (7606 cases) are on licence for six months or less (Japan, Ministry of Justice Research and Training Institute 2023a: 84). The short licence period also correlates with the low recall rate, which was 3.4 per cent in 2022 (Japan, Ministry of Justice Research

[6] In life sentence cases, the majority of reviews are initiated by the parole board after a prisoner has served 30 years in prison. The average positive decision rate between 2013 and 2022 was only 24.0% (84 cases), a stark contrast to determinate sentence cases (Japan, Ministry of Justice 2023d: 16).

[7] 80.4% of newly incarcerated prisoners in 2022 (11,584 prisoners) were serving sentences of three years or less (Japan, Ministry of Justice Research and Training Institute 2023a: 61).

and Training Institute 2023a: 92; 2023b: 112).[8] In essence, the focus of the current practices is avoiding reoffending during the licence period.

2. **Weak surveillance in parole supervision**: Japan does not prioritise long-term risk reduction through rigorous parole supervision. While parole decision-making is risk averse, parolees are usually not subject to strict surveillance in the community. This is reflected in Japan's recall practices, where minor technical breaches of licence conditions typically do not result in a recall decision, which are more commonly triggered by reoffending (Ota 2018: 112). The weak surveillance structure is also evident in the absence of an electronic monitoring system in community supervision and the heavy reliance on *hogoshi* (volunteer probation officers) who support public probation officers. These volunteers are unpaid part-time national public officials, but remain private citizens (Watson 2018). Many of them retired individuals, they serve more as 'supporting neighbours' or 'significant others' (Japan, Ministry of Justice Rehabilitation Bureau 2020: 2) rather than rigorous risk managers. They assist offenders by utilising their strong connections with the local community and access to social resources. While public probation officers play supervisory and coordinating roles, such as crisis intervention, rehabilitation planning and offender assessment, volunteer probation officers engage more directly with offenders: these volunteers occasionally invite offenders into their homes, offer them meals and listen to their daily concerns (Japan, Ministry of Justice Rehabilitation Bureau 2020: 2).[9] The central role assigned to volunteer probation officers, who vastly outnumber public probation officers,[10] is a distinctive feature of the Japanese community supervision system (Ellis et al 2011; Minoura 2018; Watson 2018).
3. **Emphasis on retributive justice and regard for the original sentence**: although the 1908 Penal Code significantly relaxed the minimum term for determinate sentence prisoners from three-quarters to one-third and for life-sentenced prisoners from 15 years to 10 years, under the concept of individualised punishment (Uematsu 1964), retributive rationalities in the implementation stage of punishment have increasingly gained prominence over time. This shift reflects the growing dominance of retributive justice

[8] The term 'recall rate' here refers to the 'revocation rate' as defined in the statistics provided by the Ministry of Justice. This rate indicates 'the percentage of probationers/parolees whose full suspension of the execution of their sentence or parole was revoked due to either a violation of their conditions for probation/parole supervision or reoffending, among the total number of probationers/parolees whose probation/parole supervision terminated in the respective years' (Japan, Ministry of Justice Research and Training Institute 2023b: 112).

[9] The future of the volunteer probation officer system has been under discussion at the Ministry of Justice since May 2023 with a view to making the system sustainable. Securing an interview location other than home has been a long-standing issue, which became urgent after a volunteer probation officer was murdered by a supervisee at his home in May 2024.

[10] While Japan currently employs approximately 1000 public probation officers (Japan, Ministry of Justice 2011), there were 46,956 volunteer probation officers in Japan in 2022 (Japan, Ministry of Justice Research and Training Institute 2023a: 94; 2023b: 40).

> as the prevailing penological philosophy in sentencing (Otsuka 2008). The criterion of public acceptability in parole decision-making represents this retributive focus and a respect for the original sentence. However, it is important to recognise that this shift has been a gradual, long-term process. The significant disparity between the statutory minimum terms and the actual time served before release was evident as early as 1959 (Japan, Ministry of Justice Research and Training Institute 1961).

With these characteristics in mind, the functions of parole are analysed in the following section.

C. Functions of Parole in Japan

The conceptions of parole outlined in a United Nations document (United Nations 1954: 1–2) serve as a valuable framework for analysing the functions of parole in Japan. The four types of conceptions of parole can be summarised as follows.

1. **Parole as an act of clemency**: this perspective views parole as a means of exercising leniency, often linked to its ulterior function as a tool for controlling prison behaviour.
2. **Parole as a penological measure in harmony with the original sentence**: this approach emphasises rehabilitation and individualisation, focusing on prisoners who demonstrate good behaviour and the potential to reintegrate into the community.
3. **Parole as a social defence measure**: this conception targets dangerous offenders, ensuring the possibility of intervention when there is a perceived imminent risk of further criminal activity.
4. **Parole as a transitional measure**: this view considers parole as a necessary step in the transition from prison to community life, applicable to all prisoners regardless of their behaviour or perceived risk, acknowledging the challenges of reintegration due to the inherent gap between prison and the community.

In Japan, the purposes of parole are generally understood to be 'promoting offenders' rehabilitation by providing the hope of early release and offering community supervision with guidance and support after release' (Hayashi 2015: 713). This aligns with the broader objectives of the Offenders Rehabilitation Act (Koseihogo ho, Act No 88 of 2007), a basic law pertaining to the rehabilitation system, including parole. It aims 'to prevent reoffending, rehabilitate offenders, ensure proper operations of pardons and promote crime prevention activities, thereby protecting society and enhancing the welfare of individuals' (Article 1). Given the generally understood purposes of parole, its main function seems to be promoting rehabilitation, aligning with the second conception in the UN document.

However, parole often serves multiple, sometimes contradictory, functions. As Padfield (2019: 164) notes, there need not be a single overriding rationale for parole. In Japanese parole practices, there are also elements resonating with the first and fourth conceptions. For instance, considering the filtering role of prison governors and the practical importance of prison behaviour in assessing the first parole criterion, parole release can be seen as a reward for good behaviour in practice. Additionally, there is the perspective of parole as a transitional measure from prison to the community, although this applies only to 'safe' prisoners due to risk aversion during the licence period. While it is difficult to deny the element of the third conception in Japan, this perspective appears to be of only limited influence due to the generally weak surveillance in parole supervision. It should also be noted that while the main function of parole in Japan – promoting rehabilitation – is more commonly associated with indeterminate sentences in other jurisdictions, this objective is stifled by a notable emphasis on retributive justice in Japan. This highlights a gap between the main functions of parole as outlined in law and its practical application. As a result, parole is typically granted only near the end of a determinate sentence.

While the three characteristics and the balance of parole functions in Japan identified above might explain why prisoners are released near the end of the sentence, they fall short of fully addressing the contradictory trends in parole practices. Specifically, they do not explain why the parole rate is currently rising or why the timing of release is being deferred further. To make sense of these paradoxical trends, it is necessary to explore the repercussions of recent developments in broader penal policies in Japan.

III. CONTEXTUALISING PARADOXICAL TRENDS IN PAROLE PRACTICES

A. Recent Developments in Recidivism Prevention Policies

Recent government policies aimed at reducing recidivism have garnered academic attention due to their broad impact extending over offenders' rehabilitation, social welfare services, diversion and sentencing (Keiji Rippo Kenkyukai 2018). These initiatives began with a 2003 action plan published in recognition of rising reported crime since 1996 and growing security concerns among the public (Japan, Cabinet Secretariat 2003). It marked the first time crime issues gained political significance in Japan (Honjo 2021: 6). Reported crime began declining from 2002, hitting a record low in 2015 and remaining low since (Japan, Ministry of Justice Research and Training Institute 2023a: 2–3; 2023b: 3). However, this decline has brought recidivism to the forefront as a significant political concern. While crimes committed by first-time offenders has significantly decreased, crimes committed by repeat offenders have not decreased as much, and indeed reached a peak in 2020, at a 49.1 repeat offender percentage[11] in 2020 (Japan, Ministry of Justice 2023c: 20).

Another strand of policy development has been a growing awareness of the difficulties elderly and disabled prisoners face in reintegration. Public attention was captured by the prison autobiography of a former Member of Parliament (Yamamoto 2003) and a high-profile 2006 arson case committed by a 74-year-old man with a minor intellectual disability who set fire to a train station because he had nowhere else to go and wanted to return to prison (Blaze destroys JR 2006). These incidents highlighted gaps in social welfare services for individuals involved in the criminal justice system, prompting enhanced collaboration between criminal justice and social welfare services.

Reflecting increased concern about recidivism and the importance of aftercare, the government published a series of policy statements. The 2012 policy statement emphasised the importance of providing *ibasho* (a place to belong) and *deban* (a role to play in a society) for recidivism prevention, leading to expanded housing options and job opportunities for offenders (Japan, Cabinet Secretariat 2012). These developments culminated in the 2016 Act for the Prevention of Recidivism (Saihan no boshi to no suishin ni kansuru horitsu, Act No 104 of 2016), passed with bipartisan cooperation. The fundamental principle of the Act is to enable offenders to reintegrate into society by supporting them, with public understanding and cooperation, so they are not isolated from society (Article 3, paragraph (1)).

The 2016 Act led to the 'Recidivism Prevention Plan' in 2017, a five-year project running from 2018 to 2022, aiming to reduce the reimprisonment rate within two years to less than 16 per cent (Japan, Ministry of Justice 2023c: 190). Parole is encouraged as a part of this plan (Japan, Ministry of Justice 2023c: 220). As the government met its target, with the reimprisonment rate dropping to 15.1 per cent in 2021 (Japan, Ministry of Justice 2023c: 44), the new 'Recidivism Prevention Plan' was created for 2023–27, aiming for further reductions (Japan, Ministry of Justice 2023c: 224–54).

Given the public appeal of a goal of recidivism prevention for securing budgets, combined with the success of the previous plan in meeting its numerical targets, recidivism prevention remains a priority in the Japanese criminal justice policy. Recent policies promoting parole have gained political legitimacy by emphasising recidivism prevention, particularly in a context where the crucial role of parole in reducing prison populations has diminished in significance due to declining prison occupancy rates (48.5 per cent in 2022) (Japan, Ministry of Justice Research and Training Institute 2023a: 58–59; 2023b: 23–24). Given these

[11] The term 'percentage of repeat offenders' refers to 'the percentage of repeat offenders among the total number of cleared persons for Penal Code offenses' (Japan, Ministry of Justice Research and Training Institute 2023b: 101).

factors, the current direction of parole policy as a part of comprehensive recidivism prevention strategies is likely to continue.

B. Impact of Recidivism Prevention Policies on Parole Practices

Recent years have seen an unprecedented emphasis on aftercare in Japanese criminal justice policy. Although recidivism prevention policies primarily target prisoners released at the end of their sentences without parole, these policies have also indirectly facilitated an increase in parole releases. By expanding housing options and job opportunities, and strengthening cooperation between criminal justice officials and social workers, these policies enhance the chances for prisoners to develop robust rehabilitation plans that support their successful reintegration into society. A government survey of prison governors revealed that issues related to securing a place to return were the most common reasons (62.5 per cent, 4400 cases) for not referring a case to the parole board (Japan, Ministry of Justice 2021: 7). Prisoners without a stable place to return are often perceived by parole decision-makers as failing to meet the 'no risk of reoffending' criterion. If housing options continue to improve due to recent policies, the parole rate is likely to rise further.

However, it is important to recognise concerns among scholars that recidivism prevention policies might turn social services into a new form of social control (Ikehara 2017; Kakegawa 2020). Doi (2018) cautions that the concept of recidivism prevention encompasses both support and public protection, which could lead to an overemphasis on the latter. Honjo (2021) argues that whether these policies become tools of social control or genuine support for desistance depends on how they are implemented. While vigilance in policy implementation is crucial, the rising parole rate and increased focus in aftercare suggest that the function of parole in providing transitional support has gained greater significance under recent policies.

C. Interpreting the Contradictory Trends in Parole

The recent conflicting trends can be fully understood only by considering Japan's unique concept of risk. Parole decision-makers in Japan place significant importance on a prisoner's behaviour during interviews and in prison, instead of actuarial risk assessment. In Japan, if a prisoner meets the first parole criterion (remorse and willingness to rehabilitate), it is generally assumed they meet the second criterion (no risk of reoffending) (Japan, Ministry of Justice 2008). This assumption is based on the belief that a remorseful prisoner who is committed to reform is unlikely to reoffend. However, this subjective approach can make it challenging for parole board members to maintain accountability when high-profile reoffending occurs, as their risk assessment is not primarily grounded in structured assessments.

Such subjective risk assessments, combined with broad discretion, can lead to overly cautious decision-making. This is particularly true given that strict legal obligations can sometimes prevent parole decision-makers from overemphasising public opinion (Fitzgerald et al 2022: 1402). The public acceptability criterion further constrains positive decisions, as parole board members are keenly aware of the potential for public backlash if their release decisions result in reoffending during the parole period. Consequently, the requirement to examine public sentiments, intended as an abstract measure of retribution and general deterrence, often blurs the boundary between these rationalities and risk perspective.

On the other hand, parole release appears to be seen as a tool for recidivism prevention among parole decision-makers. The reimprisonment rate within two years of release for parolees is significantly lower (9.3 per cent, 1011 cases) compared to those released unconditionally (21.6 per cent, 1504 cases). Interestingly, the recent improvement in the parole rate has led to a reduction, rather than an increase, in the reimprisonment rate of parolees (Japan, Ministry of Justice 2023c: 23). Even acknowledging that parolees generally pose a lower risk of reoffending than those released without parole, these statistics suggest that aftercare provided through parole supervision potentially reduces recidivism, at least within the first two years after release. As a result, decision-makers prioritise releasing 'safe' prisoners to ensure a smooth transition and minimise recidivism. However, this strategy remains cautious and is limited by short parole periods to reduce the risk of reoffending during the licence period. Although recent policies have expanded the scope of 'safe' prisoners by offering welfare support, housing and job opportunities, the traditional cautious approach to parole decision-making remains unchanged. The ongoing focus on recidivism prevention might further delay release timing. In this way, the intricate interplay of factors surrounding recidivism prevention drives the recent paradoxical trends in parole practices. Bearing these complex dynamics in mind, this chapter critically analyses the current practice, highlighting the challenges that need to be addressed.

IV. FUTURE DIRECTIONS FOR PAROLE REFORM

A. Assessing the Benefits and Limitations of the Current Approach

Before engaging in a critical analysis of current practices, it is crucial to first explore the normative debate regarding which function of parole should be prioritised. Emphasising its latent function as a tool for controlling prison behaviour, often linked to the first UN conception of parole (parole as an act of clemency), is problematic, as parole could be deprioritised as long as order within prison is maintained (Takeuchi and Honjo 2019: 254). While the rehabilitative function of parole, aligned with the second conception (parole as a penological measure in harmony with the original sentence) focusing on 'good' prisoners, remain significant, it has been argued that support and guidance under parole supervision might be even more important for dangerous offenders (Ota 2017: 17–18). Focusing on public protection, associated with the third conception (parole as a social defence measure), risks overreliance on recall decisions, potentially hindering reintegration, given experiences in England and Wales (Barry 2021). Meanwhile, prioritising transitional support and aftercare, consistent with the fourth conception (parole as a transitional measure), has garnered widespread support since the UN document was published (UN 1954: 2). Recent developments in Japan's recidivism prevention policies underscore the importance of aftercare. Given the significant gap between life in prison and the community, parole is essential for a gradual transition, suggesting the need for broader access to parole release. However, recent policies have yet to fundamentally shift the traditional approach.

On the bright side, the current approach has contributed to a low recall rate and fostered community-based, support-oriented parole supervision. Given that the recidivism rate for parolees is less than half that of individuals who serve their sentence in full (Japan, Ministry of Justice 2023c: 23), it potentially facilitates the rehabilitation and reintegration of parolees by ensuring that they can restart their community lives in environments conducive to these goals, with the assistance of public probation officers and volunteer probation officers who have strong local ties. Moreover, given the recent reduction in the recidivism rate, the welfare-oriented direction of recent policies seems to enhance the reintegration process, although care must be taken to prevent this support from becoming a form of indirect coercive social control. Additionally, the current approach has somewhat helped to avoid parole populism and maintain public confidence in the system, preserving the current discretionary parole release system even in the face of public scrutiny following high-profile reoffending cases (Toda 2024).

On the other hand, the current approach has notable limitations. First, it restricts the scope of prisoners eligible for parole. Since only 4.3 per cent of cases (499 cases) are denied parole by the board (the second stage of review), most who serve their full sentence in prison are filtered out by prison governors (the first stage) (Japan, Ministry of Justice Research and Training Institute 2023a: 77–78; 2023b: 32). The reasons for non-referral extend beyond the lack of place to return, an issue the government has indicated a willingness to address. Membership in *yakuza* (gangs) or other criminal organisations, as well as poor behaviour in prison or rule violations, accounted for 7 per cent (544 cases) and 33.2 per cent (2342 cases), respectively, of the reasons for non-referral by prison governors (Japan, Ministry of Justice 2021: 7). Such prisoners are often perceived as lacking remorse and willingness to rehabilitate, with a high likelihood of reoffending and violating licence conditions, rendering them unsuitable for parole supervision.

While expressing remorse during the interview with board members appears crucial at the second stage, prison behaviour seems to carry weight at the first stage. Prison behaviour is regarded as an indicator of remorse and willingness to rehabilitate, reoffending risk and suitability for community supervision (Japan, Ministry of Justice 2008). However, this linkage can be problematic. Non-compliance with prison rules does not necessarily reflect a lack of remorse or lead to a breach of licence conditions in the community, much less reoffending, as various factors contribute to violations of 'a highly detailed and restrictive set of prison rules' in Japan (Cavadino and Dignan 2005: 184). For instance, some prisoners may refuse to work in an assigned prison factory due to conflicts with colleagues, potentially resulting in rule violations.[12] This connection reflects the latent function of parole as a tool for controlling prison behaviour, which, as discussed earlier, is normatively problematic.

Second, current practices significantly constrain the possibility of earlier release. Despite the statutory minimum eligibility for parole being set at one-third of the sentence, in practice, parole is typically granted only after prisoners have served 80 per cent of their term (Table 13.1). This delay is primarily driven by a combination of a pronounced aversion to reoffending during the licence period and an emphasis on retributive justice. This aversion to reoffending is particularly evident in cases involving long-term prisoners whose term is more than 10 years, where the timing of release has been further delayed. Notably, most long-term prisoners (97.8 per cent, 136 cases) serve more than 90 per cent of their sentence before being considered for parole (Japan, Ministry of Justice 2023a: 79; 2023b: 33).

These limitations highlight the need for a fundamental rebalancing of the main parole functions in Japan. While the transitional function of parole has gained more emphasis recently, it has not become the primary focus, as current practices still prioritise releasing only those deemed 'safe'. To address these limitations, a combination of discretionary and automatic parole release is proposed, based on the idea that parole should be extended to all prisoners to mitigate the harmful effects of custody (Takeuchi 2003: 2017).[13] While this proposal is ambitious, especially in the absence of practical drivers like prison overcrowding or mass incarceration, it is normatively ideal given the importance of the transitional function of parole. In the interim, a provisional approach could involve revisiting parole criteria such as 'no risk of reoffending' and 'public acceptability', incorporating more evidence-based risk assessments and

[12] Japanese prisons have been undergoing reform, prompted by the upcoming amendment of the Penal Code, effective 1 June 2025, which eliminates the distinction between imprisonment with and without work, and by scandalous incidents of assault by prison staffs in Nagoya Prison between 2021 and 2022. As a result of these reforms, it is currently unclear whether refusal to work will result in penalties.

[13] Under the proposed system, prisoners would remain eligible for discretionary release after serving one-third of their original sentence, consistent with the current legal framework. However, if discretionary release is not granted, automatic release would occur after the prisoner has served five-sixths of their original sentence (Takeuchi 2003; 2017).

further expanding community support options for released prisoners, thereby broadening the scope of parole to include a wider range of prisoners.

B. Procedural Development as Leverage for Further Parole Reforms

Challenging the conventional approach in Japan is difficult due to the country's long-standing commitment to its current parole practices.[14] However, procedural improvements are not only crucial for upholding the rule of law and protecting prisoners' rights, but also hold the potential to drive further reforms in the parole system. The existing approach to parole decision-making has persisted largely due to the lack of procedural guarantees: while prisoners have the right to appeal a parole revocation decision to the National Offenders Rehabilitation Commission, the upper administrative agency of the Regional Parole Board,[15] they cannot challenge a negative release decision made by the parole board. Judicial review of negative parole decisions and non-referrals by prison governors is exceedingly rare.[16] Moreover, prisoners are not granted the right to apply for a review, the right to legal representation or the right to access their dossiers. Without these procedural safeguards, the current approach remains insulated from meaningful scrutiny or reform.

Establishing the right to apply for a review and providing a mechanism to challenge parole decisions could illuminate the criteria that prevent release in individual cases, thereby stimulating broader discussions about parole criteria. For example, in cases involving sex offenders, the time served before release is notably longer than the average (Japan, Ministry of Justice 2015: part 6, chapter 2, section 5). This appears to be driven by concerns about the risk of reoffending during the licence period and considerations of public acceptability. However, it remains unclear which specific factors cause this delay in sex offender cases. While some sex offenders might be persistent, the reimprisonment rate within two years for sex offenders is 8.2 per cent, lower than the average (14.1 per cent) (Japan, Ministry of Justice 2023c: 24–25). This discrepancy suggests that the general deferral of release based on a perceived risk of reoffending amongst this group is not fully justified by the available evidence. While considerations of retributive justice and the original sentence are valid to some extent, if these

[14] The parole criterion of 'no risk of reoffending' was first introduced in 1931 as a part of the guidance provided to prison governors for referring decisions. This focus on preventing reoffending during the licence period was further emphasised in 1952, when the parole criteria for parole boards explicitly articulated 'no risk of reoffending during the licence period' (Azuma 1934; Japan, Ministry of Justice 1952).

[15] Offenders Rehabilitation Act, Art 4, para (2).

[16] A case in which an applicant sought compensation from the state, arguing that a prison governor has caused mental distress by treating the applicant unequally by not referring the case to the parole board, was dismissed by the court. The Tokyo District Court recognised the broad discretion granted to prison governors and ruled against the applicant (Tokyo District Court judgment, 31 October 2019, No 2575, LEX/DB 25582149).

considerations vary based on public reaction to specific offences, they risk leading to biased practices influenced by public moral judgements (Toda 2024). By making the reasons for negative decisions and deferrals transparent and subject to challenge, the issues within the current parole decision-making process could be exposed, creating momentum for reform.

Current parole practices in Japan focus on releasing a select group of 'safe' prisoners for short periods, with decisions shaped by considerations of 'public acceptability' and made through a closed, secretive process to avoid triggering public concern and resulting in wholesale changes (Toda 2024). While increased transparency in parole decision-making can be a double-edged sword – potentially leading to 'parole populism', as seen in some anglophone jurisdictions (Annison and Guiney 2022; Fitzgerald et al 2023) – such a risk appears less pronounced in Japan. The centralised and relatively insular nature of Japan's criminal justice policy-making, which allows criminal justice elites to remain largely insulated from external pressures (Fenwick 2013), makes it unlikely that greater transparency would result in radical populist reforms.

V. CONCLUSION

This chapter has explored the recent paradox in Japanese parole practices, where an increasing proportion of prisoners are granted parole, yet the timing of their release is delayed. By examining Japanese parole practices, the chapter has illuminated the distinctive features of the Japanese practices: a strong aversion to the risk of reoffending during the licence period, a relatively weak surveillance in parole supervision and an emphasis on retributive justice. Over time, Japan has developed nationally standardised practices that prioritise the release of selected 'safe' prisoners on parole for short durations, while preserving lenient and abstract release requirements that afford parole decision-makers considerable discretion.

While recent criminal justice policies aimed at preventing recidivism through welfare services and community-based care have indeed expanded the scope of prisoners deemed 'safe' for release, these developments have not fundamentally altered the traditional practices of parole. The growing acknowledgement that robust support for parolees could contribute to reducing recidivism is somewhat stifled by the persistent concern for reoffending during the licence period. This complex interplay of factors surrounding the concept of recidivism prevention has resulted in paradoxical parole practices. The analysis has further revealed that the broad discretion afforded to parole decision-makers and the subjective nature of risk assessments tied to remorse and prison behaviour has perpetuated this cautious approach.

Recognising the critical function of parole in bridging the gap between prison and community (see, eg chapter eleven in this volume), this chapter advocates for a fundamental rebalancing of parole functions, with greater emphasis on its function as a transitional support mechanism. In the meantime, revisiting parole criteria, especially those related to 'no risk of reoffending' and 'public acceptability', along with incorporating evidence-based risk assessments and expanding housing and employment opportunities, may be important in broadening the scope of parole. Although challenging the deeply entrenched traditional approach is difficult, opportunities for change may lie in procedural improvements, an area where the Japanese parole system currently falls markedly short.

REFERENCES

Annison, H and Guiney, T (2022) 'Populism, Conservatism and the Politics of Parole in England and Wales' 93(3) *The Political Quarterly* 416.

Azuma, K (1934) 'Karishakuho Shinsa Kitei Shakugi' ['The Exegesis of the Regulations for Review of Conditional Release'] in A Masaki, G Oka and K Azuma (eds), *Saishin Gyoukeirei Shakugi* [*The Exegesis of the Latest Prison Orders*] (Tokyo, Gansuido) 137–202.

Barry, M (2021) 'Walking on Ice': The Future of Parole in a Risk-Obsessed Society' 25(2) *Theoretical Criminology* 325.

Beyens, K (2019) 'Belgian Release Policies, Rationales and Practices' 11(3) *European Journal of Probation* 169.

'Blaze Destroys JR Shimonoseki Station' (2006) *Japan Times* (8 January) 1–2.

Bottoms, AE (1977) 'Reflections on the Renaissance of Dangerousness' 16(2) *Howard Journal of Criminal Justice* 70.

—— (1980) 'An Introduction to "The Coming Crisis"' in AE Bottoms and RH Preston (eds), *The Coming Penal Crisis. A Criminological and Theological Exploration* (Edinburgh, Scottish Academic Press).

Brangan, L (2022) *The Politics of Punishment: A Comparative Study of Imprisonment and Political Culture* (Abingdon, Routledge).

Cavadino, M and Dignan, J (2005) *Penal Systems: A Comparative Approach* (London, SAGE).

Doi, M (2018) '"Keijishiho to Fukushi no Renkei" no Kenrironteki kosei: Saihan boshi Suishin keikaku no Hihanteki Kento wo toshite' ['Rights-based Construction of "Cooperations between Criminal Justice and Social Welfare": Through Critical Analysis of the Recidivism Prevention Plan'] in Keiji Rippo Kenkyukai (ed), *'Shiho to Fukushi no Renkei' no Tenkai to Kadai* [*Developments and Challenges of 'Cooperations between Criminal Justice and Social Welfare'*] (Tokyo, Gendai jinbun sha) 3–23.

Ellis, T, Lewis, C and Sato, M (2011) 'The Japanese Probation Service: A Third Sector Template?' 58 *Probation Journal* 333.

Fenwick, M (2013) '"Penal Populism" and Penological Change in Contemporary Japan' 17 *Theoretical Criminology* 215.

Fitzgerald, R, Freiberg, A, Dodd, S and Bartels, L (2022) 'Building Public Confidence in Parole Boards: Findings from a Four-Country Study' 66 *British Journal of Criminology* 1395.

—— (2023) *Parole on Probation: Public Opinion, Public Confidence and Parole Decision-Making* (Basingstoke, Palgrave Macmillan).

Guiney, T (2018) *Getting Out: Early Release in England and Wales, 1960–1995* (Oxford, Oxford University Press).

—— (2019) 'Marginal Gains or Diminishing Returns? Penal Bifurcation, Policy Change and the Administration of Prisoner Release in England and Wales' 11(3) *European Journal of Probation* 139.

Hayashi, M (2015) 'Karishakuho' ['Parole'] in H Otsuka, K Kawakami, Y Nakayama and Y Furuta (eds), *Dai Kommentar Keiho* [*The Great Commentary of Criminal Law*] vol 1, 3rd edn (Tokyo, Seirin shoin).

Herzog-Evans, M (2019) 'French Early Release: McProcedures and McRe-entry' 11(3) *European Journal of Probation* 188.

Honjo, T (2021) 'Naze Saihan boushi ka: Kikaku syushi wo kanete' ['Why Do We Discuss and Try to Achieve Recidivism Prevention?'] 46 *Hanzai Shakaigaku Kenkyu* [*Japanese Journal of Sociological Criminology*] 5.

Ikehara, Y (2017) 'Saihan boshi to Bengonin no Yakuwari' ['Recidivism Prevention and the Role of Defence Lawyer'] 89(4) *Horitsu jiho* [*Law Review*] 40.

Japan, Cabinet Secretariat (2003) 'Hanzai ni tsuyoi Shakai no Jitsugen no tameno Kodo keikaku: "Sekaiichi anzen na Kuni, Nihon" no Fukkatsu wo mezashite' ['The Action Plan for the Realisation of a Society Resistant to Crime 2003: Towards Making "Japan as the Safest Country in the World" Again] December, www.kantei.go.jp/jp/singi/hanzai/kettei/031218keikaku.html.

—— (2012) 'Saihan boushi ni muketa Sogo taisaku' ['Comprehensive Measures to Prevent Recidivism'] 20 July, www.moj.go.jp/hisho/saihanboushi/html/ns170000.html.

Japan, Ministry of Justice (1952) 'Karishakuho narabini Zaikan mataha Zaiin chu no Mono ni taisuru Futeikikei Sikko Shuryo mataha Taiin no Shinri Kettei to ni kansuru Tetsuzuki ni tuite' ['Procedures Regarding Review and Decision Making of Parole, the Termination of Indeterminate Sentence and Release from a Juvenile Training School'] 25 December.

—— (2008) 'Hanzai wo shita Mono oyobi Hiko no aru Shonen ni taisuru Shakainai ni okeru Shogu ni kansuru Jimu no Unyo ni tuite' ['Administrative Operations of the Rules on Community Treatment for Persons Who Have Committed Crimes and Juvenile Delinquents'] 9 May.

—— (2011) 'Hogokansatsusho' ['Probation Offices'] www.moj.go.jp/hisho/seisakuhyouka/hisho04_00040.html.

—— (2021) 'Saihan boshi suishin Hakusho 2021' ['White Paper on Recidivism Prevention 2021'] December, www.moj.go.jp/hisho/saihanboushi/hisho04_00104.html.

—— (2023a) 'Kyosei Tokei Chosa' ['Statistical Survey of Correction'] 31 July, www.e-stat.go.jp/index.php/stat-search/database?statdisp_id=0003278320.

—— (2023b) 'Hogo Tokei Chosa' ['Statistical Survey of Rehabilitation'] 31 July, www.e-stat.go.jp/stat-search/files?stat_infid=000040079981.

—— (2023c) 'Saihan boshi suishin Hakusho 2023' ['White Paper on Recidivism Prevention 2023'] December, www.moj.go.jp/hisho/saihanboushi/hisho04_00009.html.

—— (2023d) 'Mukikei no Shikkou Jokyo oyobi Mukikei Jukeisha ni kakaru Karishakuho no Unyo Jokyo ni tuite' ['Monitoring of Execution of Life Sentence and Operation of Parole for Life-Sentenced Prisoners'] December, www.moj.go.jp/content/001408824.pdf.

Japan, Ministry of Justice Rehabilitation Bureau (2020) 'Hogoshi: Volunteer Probation Officers', March, www.cep-probation.org/wp-content/uploads/2020/04/Hogoshi-Volunteer-Probation-Officers-in-Japan.pdf.

Japan, Ministry of Justice Research and Training Institute (1961) 'Hanzai Hakusho 1961' ['White Paper, Japanese Version 1961'] March, https://hakusyo1.moj.go.jp/jp/2/nfm/mokuji.html.

—— (2015) 'Hanzai Hakusho 2015' ['White Paper, Japanese Version 2015'] November, https://hakusyo1.moj.go.jp/jp/62/nfm/n62_2_6_2_5_1.html.

—— (2023a) 'Hanzai Hakusho 2023' ['White Paper, Japanese Version 2023'] December, www.moj.go.jp/housouken/housouken03_00127.html.

—— (2023b) 'White Paper on Crime 2023' (English Version) December, www.moj.go.jp/EN/housouken/houso_hakusho2.html.

Kakegawa, N (2020) *Hanzai karano Shakaifukki wo Toinaosu: Chiiki kyosei shakai ni okeru social work no katachi* [*Reconsidering Reintegration from Crime: Social Work in Community-Based Inclusive Society*] (Tokyo, Junposha).

Keiji Rippo Kenkyukai (ed) (2018) *'Shiho to Fukushi no Renkei' no Tenkai to Kadai* [*Developments and Challenges of 'Cooperations between Criminal Justice and Social Welfare'*] (Tokyo, Gendai jinbun sha).

Minoura, S (2018) 'Offender Rehabilitation Reform in Japan: Effective Cooperation between Professional and Volunteer Probation Officers' 54 *International Journal of Law, Crime and Justice* 111.

Nelken, D (2010) *Comparative Criminal Justice: Making Sense of Difference* (London, SAGE).

Ota, T (2017) *Karishakuho no Riron: Kyosei, Hogo no Renkei to Saihan boshi* [*Theory of Parole: Prevention of Reoffending through Co-operation between Institutional and Community Treatment*] (Tokyo, Keio University Press).

—— (2018) *Kei no Ichibu shikko yuyo: Hanzaisha no Kaizen kosei to Saihan boshi* [*Partial Suspended Execution of Sentence: Offenders Rehabilitation and Prevention of Reoffending*], revised and enlarged edn (Tokyo, Keio University Press).

Otsuka, H (2008) *Keiho Gaisetsu (Soron)* [*Overview of Criminal Law (General Principles)*], 4th edn (Tokyo, Yuhikaku).

Padfield, N (2010) 'England and Wales' in N Padfield, D van Zyl Smit and F Dünkel (eds), *Release from Prison: European Policy and Practice*, 2nd edn (Abingdon, Routledge) 104–34.

—— (2019) 'Giving and Getting Parole: The Changing Characteristics of Parole in England and Wales' 11(3) *European Journal of Probation* 153.

Takeuchi, K (2003) 'Karishakuho seido no horitsuka to shakaika: Hitsuyoteki karishakuho seido to Niniteki karishakuho seido no teisho (Legalisation and Socialisation of Parole System: A Case for Mandatory Release System and Discretionary Release System)' in Keiji Rippo Kenkyukai (ed), *21 Seiki no keiji shisetsu: Global Standards to Shimin sanka (Prison in the 21st century: Global standards and civil participation)* (Tokyo, Nippon Hyoron Sha) 228–34.

—— (2017) 'Karishakuho: Hitsuyoteki karishakuho wo meguru giron wo chushin ni (Parole Release: Focusing Discussions on Mandatory Release)' in T Honjo and K Takeuchi (eds), *Keibatsu seido kaikaku no mae ni kangaeteoku beki koto (What Needed to Consider Before Penal Reform)* (Tokyo, Nippon Hyoron Sha) 103–19.

Takeuchi, K and Honjo, T (2019) *Keiji seisaku gaku* [*Criminal Policy Jurisprudence*] (Tokyo, Nippon Hyoron sha).

Toda, S (2024) 'A Place for Public Concerns in Parole Decision Making in Japan' 63 *The Howard Journal of Crime and Justice* 98.

Udo, G (2021) '*Kaishun no jo (Jisshitsuteki yoken)*' ['Signs of Substantial Reformation (the Substantive Requirement)'] in Nihon Koseihogo Gakkai (ed), *Koseihogo gaku jiten* [*Encyclopaedia of Offenders Rehabilitation Jurisprudence*] (Tokyo, Seibudo) 154–55.

Uematsu, T (1964) 'Trends of the Revision of the Penal Code in Japan' 3 *Hitotsubashi Journal of Law and Politics* 1.

United Nations (1954) *Parole and After-care* (New York, United Nations Department of Social Affairs).

Watson, A (2018) 'Probation in Japan: Strengths and Challenges and Likely New Tasks' 10(2) *European Journal of Probation* 160.

Yamamoto, J (2003) *Gokusoki* [*Prison Life*] (Tokyo, Popolar Publishing).

14

The Future of Parole in Chile: Reconciling Social Reintegration and Public Safety[1]

CAROLINA VILLAGRA, CATALINA DROPPELMANN AND SERGIO FAÚNDEZ

I. INTRODUCTION

THE PAROLE SYSTEM in Chile has undergone significant transformations over time, influenced by evolving crime control policies and shifting public sentiment regarding safety and punishment. As societal perceptions of security change, so does the political response, often steering the discourse towards punitive measures at the expense of rehabilitative objectives. This dynamic mirrors global trends, where high-profile criminal cases and public outcry frequently result in more restrictive parole policies, driven by a desire for control rather than reintegration.

The Chilean experience with parole reflects a broader phenomenon observed in many parts of the world, where the interplay of political pressures, media portrayals and societal attitudes towards crime has redefined the purpose and function of conditional release. Once envisioned as a mechanism for fostering social reintegration, parole in Chile has increasingly adopted a managerial approach focused on risk mitigation, with stricter eligibility criteria and discretionary decision-making processes.

This chapter explores the socio-political forces that have shaped Chile's parole system, analysing the implications of these reforms within a comparative and critical framework. Drawing from Southern criminology, it highlights the need for a balanced parole policy that integrates public safety with social reintegration, while also considering the structural challenges and inequalities that prisoners face after release.

[1] This chapter is derived from and utilises data presented in the prior study conducted by Droppelmann et al (2023), thereby building upon the foundational work established in that research.

The analysis presented in this chapter is based on a review of legal regulations and literature, along with empirical data from two studies, conducted in 2015 (Villagra and Droppelmann 2017) and 2022 (Droppelmann et al). These studies examined the application of legal modifications and the effectiveness of parole as a mechanism for social reintegration.

The first section offers an overview of the historical development and regulatory evolution of parole within the Chilean legal system. Following this, we examine two significant normative reforms and analyse their influence on decision-making processes and practices, placing parole discussions within a broader sociological and political context. The subsequent section delves into the effects of these reforms and media pressures on the current state of parole. Next, we explore empirical findings from recent studies that reveal the practical challenges faced by parole boards, including discrepancies in decision-making and the impact of public sentiment on legal processes. The final section reflects on the implications of Chile's parole experience for the future, drawing from Southern criminology to propose a more balanced approach that prioritises both public safety and social reintegration.

II. THE PAST: TRACING THE ORIGINS AND DEVELOPMENT OF PAROLE IN CHILE

In Latin America, most countries introduced parole in their Penal Codes within the first decades of the twentieth century,[2] over a century later than Europe (Tebar 2004). Parole was incorporated into Chile's legal system in 1925 as part of a broader modernist effort to facilitate prisoner reintegration, following nineteenth-century debates critiquing poor prison conditions and ineffective punitive measures (Sepúlveda and Sepúlveda 2008; León 2019).

The original regulation described parole as

> a means of proof that the offender sentenced to a custodial sentence and to whom it is granted is corrected and rehabilitated for social life … It does not extinguish or modify the duration of the sentence but is a particular way of enforcing it in freedom. (Decree Law No 321, Article 1)

Any individual sentenced to a custodial term exceeding one year had the right to apply for parole, provided they met several stipulated criteria, including serving half of their imposed sentence, maintaining impeccable behaviour and acquiring a trade or attending school (Ministerio de Justicia 1925, Decree Law No 321, Article 2). Once parole was granted, individuals had to meet a

[2] Argentina, 1922; Perú, 1924; Chile, 1925; México, 1931; Uruguay, 1934; Colombia, 1936, Ecuador, 1938; Brasil, 1940.

number of conditions: (i) establish a fixed residence; (ii) attend school or work; (iii) report weekly to a designated institution for administrative control; and (iv) follow instructions from the Prison Conduct Tribunal. Parole could be revoked if any condition was breached or if a new sentence was imposed, leading to the person's return to prison to serve the remaining sentence. The Prison Service (Gendarmería, as it is known in Spanish)[3] had been the institution responsible for the monitoring of parolees and maintaining statistical records.[4]

Parole was a fundamental stone for setting the progressive principle that guides the prison regime, which implies that individuals in custody should be granted increasing levels of freedom to ensure a gradual and safe reintegration into the community (Eurosocial 2015). In 1983, temporary release permits were introduced in the Prison Regulations, allowing inmates who meet certain requirements – such as time served, good behaviour and having a social support network in the community – to apply for these permits, with Gendarmería responsible for assessing applications and granting permissions.

A century later, an analysis of the statistics of the granting of temporary release permits and parole calls into question the adherence to and effective respect for the principle of progressivity within the Chilean penal system. Over the past two decades, early release mechanisms, particularly parole, have been increasingly restricted. Sixteen legal modifications to parole, 10 in the last 20 years, have made it one of the most contentious instruments in Chile's penal landscape. Two of these reforms are considered structural, fundamentally altering the rationale, institutions and practices surrounding parole. They have shifted its nature from a means of demonstrating an inmate's readiness to reintegrate into society to a privilege that must be earned. Through these reforms, more rigorous eligibility criteria have been established, necessitating that inmates meet higher standards in terms of minimum time served, demonstrate good behaviour over extended periods and actively participate in reintegration programmes (Decree Law No 321, Articles 1 and 2).

Collectively, these reforms have led to a marked decline in the number of applicants granted parole, even as the prison population continues to grow, as illustrated in Figure 14.1.

[3] The prison system, known as Gendarmería in Spanish, is a public service established in 1921 and operates under the Ministry of Justice and Human Rights. It is composed of trained prison staff and a professional civic team responsible for managing the control and rehabilitation of individuals in custody, as well as those serving community penalties (Gendarmería 2024).

[4] It is worth noting that, from 1925 to 2020, Chile's parole system lacked individualised supervision or structured assistance to assist parolees with community reintegration, health issues, housing or employment. The prison service only managed administrative tasks. This lack of post-release support, given the burdensome nature of the application process, drew criticism from experts who highlighted the system's failure to adequately facilitate reintegration into the community (Villagra and Droppelmann 2016; Figueroa 2018).

Figure 14.1 Parole trends 2013–23: prison population, applications and granted parole

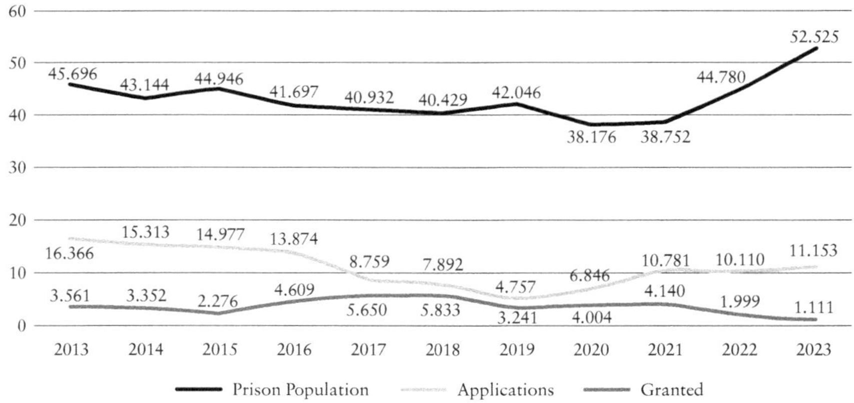

Source: Own elaboration, based on data from Gendarmería de Chile (2024).

The reforms of the last decade have emerged in response to political crises and high-profile media cases, underscoring, as posited by Fitzgerald et al (2022), the tensions governments face in reconciling the contradictions between penal politics and penal policies. Moreover, as Annison and Guiney (2022) assert, crises and scandals currently serve as significant drivers of penal policy.

In the following section, we will examine two significant reforms to the parole system. To set the context, we will first situate the discussion within a broader social framework and historical perspective, reviewing the most significant change in the history of the Chilean justice system and how this has created a scenario that adversely impacted parole.

III. CRIMINAL PROCEDURE REFORM AND ITS IMPACT ON PAROLE: A SHIFT FROM INQUISITORIAL TO ACCUSATORY JUSTICE

From 1906 until the early twenty-first century, Chile operated under an inquisitorial justice system, a legacy from Spanish colonisation. This predominantly written system vested a single judge with responsibility for investigation, prosecution and judgment. As a result, cases often took years to resolve, with further delays caused by the frequent appeal of decisions and the lack of transparency of the decision-making processes (Villagra 2022). This was a justice system aligned with the rationales of the military dictatorships that governed much of the region between the 1960s and 1980s. However, in the 1990s, as most Latin American countries recovered democracy, they began reforms to modernise their criminal legislations to align with international treaty standards and to reflect the principles of the rule of law (Riego and Duce 2008).

In 2000, the Criminal Procedure Reform (CPR) implemented the accusatory justice system in Chile, a profound shift in the rationale and procedures in criminal justice. It established oral and public hearings; created guarantee courts and oral trial courts, which replaced the single judges in criminal courts; set a clear separation of the functions of investigation, prosecution and judgment; and introduced new institutions, such as the Public Prosecution Office and the Public Defender's Office (Biblioteca del Congreso Nacional (BCN) 2018).

Several studies show how the CPR had a profound impact on the prison system (Alvarez et al 2007; Salinero 2012; Wilenmann 2020; Arriagada et al 2021). The prison population increased from 32,000 in 2000 to 54,000 in 2010, reflecting a growth of approximately 68.75 percent over this 10-year period. This large rise in custodial sentences was inversely proportional to the granting of parole, which saw a sharp decline in the grant rate (percentage of the prison population granted parole), dropping from 11.5 percent to 1.4 percent during the first decade of the twenty-first century, as illustrated in Figure 14.2.

Figure 14.2 Trends in parole granting and grant rate, 2000–10

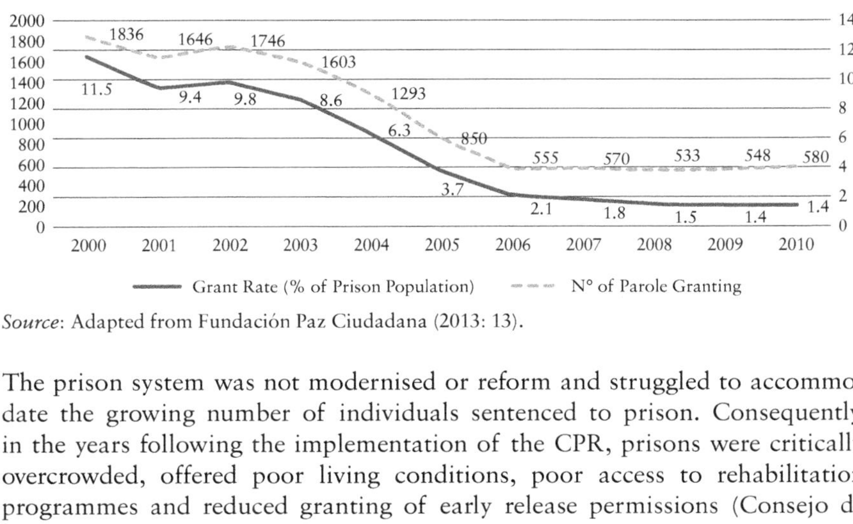

Source: Adapted from Fundación Paz Ciudadana (2013: 13).

The prison system was not modernised or reform and struggled to accommodate the growing number of individuals sentenced to prison. Consequently, in the years following the implementation of the CPR, prisons were critically overcrowded, offered poor living conditions, poor access to rehabilitation programmes and reduced granting of early release permissions (Consejo de Reforma Penitenciaria 2009).

The government prompted several initiatives to decompress the prison system, including a motion to modify parole, presented by the President to the Senate in March 2011 (BCN 2012). This led to the approval of Law No 20,587 in 2012, aimed at reducing overcrowding and improving prison conditions to promote reintegration and lower crime. The reform also changed the institution responsible for granting parole decisions (BCN 2012; Ministerio de Justicia 2012).

This represents a significant juncture where a crisis within the Chilean criminal justice system catalysed a substantive reform in the parole framework. In this case, however, the application of parole appears to demonstrate public trust in its potential, as the highest executive authority in the nation endorsed its utility both as a strategic mechanism for prison population management and as a tool for the broader governance of criminal behaviour.

IV. THE 2012 REFORM: ESTABLISHMENT OF PAROLE BOARDS AND RISE IN GRANTING RATES

In June 2012, Law No 20,587 came into effect (BCN 2012). Until then, the process of applying for and granting parole had involved three institutions. The Conduct Tribunal, which operates in prisons and is composed of staff from the prison service, was responsible for approving or rejecting inmate applications and subsequently submitting the lists of candidates to a second institution, the Parole Commission. This Commission was made up of judges who reviewed the lists and conducted a second assessment in accordance with the legal criteria. The Commission then presented this second list to the third institution, the Regional Ministerial Secretariat of Justice, a political–administrative body responsible for making the final decision (Droppelmann et al 2023).

This institutional framework underwent a complete reform with Law No 20,587, with the Commission being replaced by parole boards that operate within the Courts of Appeal. They are directly responsible for reviewing applications and granting parole, a process carried out biannually in April and October (Article 4).

The first results of the reform showed an increase in parole-granting figures, from 13 per cent[5] in 2012 to 22 per cent in 2013. However, despite the quantitative improvement, the historical qualitative problems in administrative and decision-making processes became more apparent. An empirical study conducted in 2015 (Villagra and Droppelmann 2017) revealed that the parole process imposed a significant bureaucratic burden on prison staff, and practitioners felt that their work was undervalued as their recommendations had little influence on the decisions made by judges. From the perspective of parolees, the experience was marked by a sense of helplessness as, despite years of effort to meet the legal requirements and undergoing a rigorous evaluation process, they were released on parole with no post-release support, leaving them in a state of 'no man's land' (Villagra and Droppelmann 2017: 191). One of the study's key

[5] These figures represent the percentage of inmates who were granted parole out of the total number of applicants.

recommendations was to establish a post-release supervision system staffed by specialised professionals, such as parole officers.

Empirical evidence supported the view that parole was an effective mechanism for both social reintegration and public safety. Studies of the time indicate that parole had the lowest recidivism rate among all forms of prison release (Gendarmería de Chile 2013; 2019). This aligns with comparative data, which demonstrates that parole can serve as a penal tool for supervising offenders, as well as fostering prosocial behaviour and facilitating reintegration into society (Armstrong and Durnescu 2017; Vîlcică 2018).

Despite the seemingly positive outcomes, 2016 proved to be a contentious year for parole. Following the first review process in April, the granting rate had surged from 16 per cent in 2015 to 44 per cent. A notable example was the Valparaíso Parole Board, where the granting rate soared to 87 per cent. This situation was characterised by the Senate's institutional website as a 'mass release of inmates', which drew considerable criticism towards the judiciary. The Parole Board maintained that the grants were made strictly in accordance with established legal procedures.

The case of the Valparaíso Parole Board received extensive media coverage and was employed to support arguments advocating for more stringent criminal prosecution and harsher sentencing in various bills under consideration at the time. These legislative efforts occurred amid penal policy decisions influenced by prevailing perceptions of insecurity (BCN 2016) and a crisis of legitimacy of parole. From a populist perspective, parole might be linked to a sense of impunity. Individuals with populist attitudes may argue that granting offenders conditional release, rather than requiring them to serve their full sentence, undermines the justice system. They contend that this practice allows offenders to evade the full extent of their punishment, thereby fostering a perception that they are not being held fully accountable for their crimes. This view often reflects broader concerns about the leniency of the penal system and its perceived failure to ensure appropriate retribution (Garland 2002; Pratt 2007).

Two legal initiatives underscore the prevailing punitive spirit of the era. On May 2016, a parliamentary motion – which would reform parole in 2019 – was proposed to introduce amendments to the existing parole legislation, which would impose stricter eligibility criteria for applications and establish a framework for post-release supervision system (BCN 2016). In July 2016, Law No 20,931 was enacted, after just six months of legislative processing (Ministerio de Justicia y Derechos Humanos 2016). This law intensified the prosecution of robbery, theft and handling of stolen goods, facilitated the effective enforcement of penalties for such offences and established a minimum requirement of two-thirds of the sentence served before applying for parole. This legislation, informally referred to as the 'Short-Term Anti-Crime Agenda', garnered widespread bipartisan support in Congress and initiated a series of legislative reforms aimed at increasing penalties and enhancing oversight of property-related crimes.

This legislative change and the public questioning of parole granting had a substantial impact on the number of individuals eligible to apply for parole, resulting in a dramatic decline from 37 per cent in 2016 to just 13 per cent in 2017. Concerns have been raised regarding the discriminatory nature of the 'Short-Agenda' legislation, particularly in relation to the demographic characteristics of the incarcerated population in Chile (Figueroa 2018). A significant proportion of these individuals possess inadequate educational backgrounds, experience socioeconomic deprivation, lack access to vocational training and have been convicted predominantly for property-related offences. As a result, this law has exacerbated the punitive measures directed at already vulnerable groups, facilitating the intensification of criminal prosecution and incarceration rates while prolonging the duration of confinement that individuals must endure prior to becoming eligible to apply for parole.

This is an example of how legal reforms can, in fact, exacerbate and reproduce structural inequalities. In Chile, as in other countries of the Global South, inequalities and social exclusion are central to the question of access to justice. Carrington et al (2016: 4) argue that 'Southern criminology' refers not only to the geographical division between the Global North and South, but also serves as a metaphor for 'the other, the invisible, the subaltern, the marginal, and the excluded'. This disparity is evident in the fact that inmates from low-income backgrounds and marginalised social groups are overrepresented in prisons while simultaneously being underrepresented in reintegration programmes and early-release schemes, such as parole.

V. HIGHLIGHTS AND CHALLENGES OF THE 2019 PAROLE REFORM

In 2017 and 2018, both parole applications and granting significantly declined amidst heightened political debates on public security. The 2019 parole reform, enacted through Law No 21,124 (Ministerio de Justicia y Derechos Humanos 2019), introduced substantial changes to the rationale, institutions and practices surrounding parole in Chile. The changes sought to address concerns about public safety while also modernising the parole system to enhance supervision and support for parolees.

One of the main changes in the rationale introduced by this reform was the modification of the legal status of parole, reclassifying it as a benefit rather than a right. This alteration granted parole authorities discretionary power, meaning that while meeting legal requirements remained necessary, it was no longer sufficient to guarantee parole. This change aimed to curb concerns about 'mass grants' of parole, which had sparked controversy in 2016. The law introduced the mandatory submission of a psychosocial report to provide the parole board with crucial information on the applicant's potential risk to public safety. This was an early sign of how the managerial approach gradually replaced a psychosocial model with a management-based model in parole. Despite the importance placed on this report, it does not bind the parole board's decision, paradoxically increasing the workload of prison professionals without necessarily influencing the outcome.

With regard to institutional changes, parole boards were reorganised to include a judge from the Court of Appeals, four criminal or oral trial judges and a secretary appointed by the Court of Appeals. This restructuring was intended to improve the decision-making process by bringing more judicial expertise into the evaluation of parole cases. Moreover, the law established a specialised post-release supervision system, overseen by newly created parole officers under the authority of Gendarmería. These officers are tasked with monitoring parolees' compliance with legal conditions and providing psychosocial support through an intervention plan. This element of the reform represents a key strength, as research has shown that individuals with greater social support tend to have better reintegration outcomes (Hochstetler et al 2010; Cochran 2014). The introduction of such a system aligns with international best practices, as comparative studies underscore the importance of supervision and support in reducing recidivism (Schaefer and Williamson 2018).

Procedurally, the reform introduced a range of new requirements. In addition to the submission of a psychosocial report elaborated by prison staff, the law increased the number of bimonthly good-conduct periods required for parole eligibility from three to four. Parole officers were tasked with ensuring compliance with the individual intervention plan. Non-compliance with this plan could result in the revocation of the parole benefit.

The reform introduced valuable changes, such as the much-needed supervision and support system, facilitating the gradual departure from perceiving parole as a state of 'no-man's land' and envisioning a future in which parole would be reinforced as a specialised mechanism for social reintegration. Simultaneously, the reform restricted access to parole by tightening the legal requirements even more. The reform ultimately reflected the contradiction between punitive and rehabilitative aims in the Chilean criminal justice system.

The specialised post-release supervision system was expected to start in September 2020. However, in August 2020, a high-profile case involving a murder committed by an individual on parole garnered widespread attention. As anticipated, the public is particularly sensitive to such incidents (Tversky and Kahneman 1973, as referenced in Fitzgerald et al 2022), and this case provoked substantial public outcry. Known as *The Ambar Case*, it involved the murder of a 16-year-old girl, daughter of the parolee's partner. The accused, who had been serving a sentence for double homicide, had been granted parole during a highly publicised process in the Valparaíso region.

The crime incited a political debate aimed at identifying those accountable for the release of the murderer, and public discussions were frequently framed as expressions of empathy for the victims of violent crime (Annison and Guiney 2022). In September 2020, the Chamber of Deputies filed a constitutional accusation against the President of the Valparaíso Parole Board, an initiative that was critiqued as a threat to judicial independence (Judicial Observatory 2020; National Association of Chilean Judges 2020). Although ultimately rejected, it set a precedent for public scrutiny and highlighted the vulnerability of judges to political pressure.

In response to this scandal, several legislative initiatives were introduced aiming to further restrict access to parole by tightening eligibility requirements. In 2020, four out of five parliamentary motions proposed the incorporation of a favourable prognosis as a condition for granting parole. Although none of these initiatives succeeded, from 2021 onwards, a marked reduction in both parole applications and approvals was observed. This decline reflects the punitive shift in penal policy, wherein legislative discourse around parole increasingly emphasised risk management and control over rehabilitation and reintegration.

VI. THE PRESENT

The ramifications of this reform prompted an empirical study conducted in 2022, which aimed to assess the state of parole in Chile following the structural changes implemented in 2019 (Droppelmann et al 2023). Twenty-eight interviews were carried out with a range of stakeholders involved in the parole selection, evaluation and granting processes, including key informants, public defenders, practitioners from Gendarmería, parole board judges, parole officers and inmates applying for parole. The findings of the study underscored the effects of the 2019 reform and the 2020 media case on the practices of prison practitioners and Parole Board judges. The most significant findings are presented below.

A. Controversies and High-Profile Criminal Cases that Changed Parole Practices

High-profile cases that attracted extensive media coverage and eroded public confidence in the parole system were a recurrent topic among interviewees. Most identified *The Ambar Case* and the subsequent constitutional accusation as pivotal events that significantly shaped parole board practices. Since then, parole boards have adopted a more cautious approach, often deferring complex cases to the Court of Appeals. From 2020 to 2023, there was a sharp increase in parole approvals via appeals, with over 60 per cent of paroles being approved by the Court. Judges, public defenders, parole officers and practitioners collectively view this trend as indicative of a structural shift, signalling a profound transformation in the administration of parole in Chile.

The growing reliance on appeals reignites the previously settled legislative debate over whether parole is a right or a privilege. Some stakeholders argue that the Court of Appeals tends to base parole decisions solely on compliance with legal criteria – such as time served, good behaviour and participation in school or work – while overlooking the assessment of psychosocial and criminological reports.

Despite the various factors contributing to the increase in parole approvals by the Court of Appeals, this trend has significant systemic implications. Professionals in the field have raised concern that numerous cases, initially rejected by parole boards due to unfavourable psychosocial reports, are later granted parole on appeal. This dynamic effectively turns the parole boards into preliminary review bodies, where legal arguments overshadow the technical evaluation of psychosocial backgrounds. As a result, the process of granting parole is increasingly viewed as a legal matter, rather than a decision grounded in a comprehensive assessment of an individual's rehabilitation and potential for social reintegration.

B. The Application Report: A Tool for Better Decision-Making?

These developments have sparked important debates about the actual role and impact of the psychosocial reports introduced by the 2019 reform. Parole evaluations are now seen more as legal determinations rather than being rooted in criminological and psychosocial evidence. Nevertheless, some professionals within the Prison Service argue that the 2019 reform has improved the scientific rigour of these reports, particularly through the establishment of higher standards. Additionally, some claim that the use of standardised risk assessment tools has helped to standardise the information presented, providing a more uniform basis for decision-making. From the judiciary's perspective, the incorporation of these instruments has contributed to the professionalisation of the selection and evaluation process, providing technical criteria to guide the Parole Board's decision-making.

Conversely, some practitioners have raised concerns about practices that may undermine the integrity of these reports. They argue that excessive standardisation, coupled with a lack of cultural adaptation of the risk assessment tools to the Chilean context,[6] results in evaluations that inadequately capture the social realities of applicants. Consequently, these assessments tend to overemphasise risk factors while downplaying elements that foster change and desistance from crime. Furthermore, professionals report that the significant administrative burden and workload involved in producing these reports adversely affect their quality. Many evaluators lack direct contact with the applicants they assess, relying instead on limited application information. Additionally, insufficient training in the use of the required instruments further compromises the quality of the reports.

[6] Chile adapted the Canadian instrument LSI Level of Service Inventory to measure the recidivism risk of offenders and identify the areas in which re-entry programmes should be focused on.

From the perspective of parole applicants, the reports are perceived as deficient, which they identify as a critical factor in the rejection of their applications. Applicants cite the superficial nature of the evaluation process, noting that brief interviews often fail to capture their life trajectories or their progress in rehabilitation and reintegration during incarceration. Notably, the concerns expressed by applicants resonate with those articulated by professionals regarding the constraints they face in generating high-quality reports.

Two key issues emerge concerning prisoners' understanding of the parole process. First, there exists a widespread lack of knowledge regarding the eligibility criteria and procedural requirements for parole. Second, confusion persists about the legal nature of parole – whether it is a right or a privilege. This ambiguity creates uncertainty among prisoners regarding whether meeting the established criteria suffices for obtaining parole or whether additional, discretionary factors may influence the Parole Board's decision. Consequently, parole is not broadly regarded by prisoners as a legitimate mechanism for early release. Finally, the reports are expected to identify and detail the progress applicants have made towards reintegration. A fundamental issue within the Chilean prison system, however, is the lack of substantial opportunities for prisoners to engage in rehabilitation and reintegration programmes. The limited availability of such programmes was further exacerbated by the COVID-19 pandemic, which led to many applicants between 2020 and 2022 receiving negative evaluations due to the absence of documented progress. This presents a significant challenge for parole practices, as applicants are required to meet reintegration standards that the state itself is unable to provide.

C. The Diversity of Practices within Parole Boards

As mentioned, once the Prison Conduct Tribunal have selected the applicants, the cases are forwarded to the parole boards operating within each Court of Appeals, which convenes biannually. As the regulations do not specify internal procedural rules, a diversity of practices has emerged in the operation of these boards across the country. Such practices largely depend on the criteria and guidelines established by the chairperson of the parole board.

This variability in practices is evident in quantitative data, revealing different functions across the country's regions. For instance, during the study period, 87 per cent of parole applications were granted in the Antofagasta region, compared to only 34 per cent in the Atacama region.

Regarding evaluation criteria, representatives of parole boards have indicated that some judges prioritise the formal compliance with the law, whereas others adopt a more interpretative approach. Consequently, there is an express need for more clearly defined criteria outlining the aspects to be considered in each application. Nevertheless, there is a consensus among parole board members that the most pertinent variables for decision-making include the applicant's progress in social reintegration while incarcerated and the strength of their support network for reintegration in the community. Both variables are incorporated into the application report prepared by Gendarmería.

Given the multidisciplinary nature of the decision-making process, various participants in the study recognised the importance of integrating clearly defined criteria to aid judges in their decisions regarding psychosocial interventions. They also emphasised the necessity for enhanced training in psychosocial matters and proposed the potential incorporation of a technical counsellor within the Parole Boards. The role of the counsellor would be to serve several critical functions, such as providing specialised expertise in psychosocial evaluations and ensuring that judges have access to comprehensive and relevant assessments of individuals' mental health and social backgrounds. This expertise would enhance the quality of the information considered during parole hearings, leading to more informed decision-making.

Participants were also queried regarding the role of victims in the evaluation of parole applications. From the judiciary's perspective, this approach would be contentious, as victims should have a role in the trial process but should not dominate the decision-making stage, which ought to centre on the offender and their reintegration. In this context, prison defence lawyers emphasised that increasing victim involvement in the parole application and granting process could be counterproductive, unless there is a system in place that acknowledges and provides reparation for victims.[7]

VII. THE FUTURE

The historical and political analysis of parole reforms in Chile over the past decade reveals that the functioning of parole has been influenced by crime control policies and prevailing public sentiment. This relationship underscores the complex interplay between legislative frameworks and societal attitudes towards crime and punishment. As public perceptions of safety and security evolve, they significantly impact the political landscape, leading to reforms that

[7] During the drafting of this chapter, in November 2023, Law No 21,627 was enacted (Ministerio de Justicia y Derechos Humanos 2023), instituting stricter requirements for obtaining parole and for the first time recognising the victim's role in parole proceedings. The law grants victims the right to be notified of parole applications, to present submissions to the court and to participate in communications. Art 4 mandates that Gendarmería inform the court of any parole applications from convicted individuals, which must be followed by a notification to the victim within five days. The victim, either personally or through a representative, may submit written arguments to the Parole Board during the first five days of April and October. The Parole Board may also conduct a hearing, upon request, in cases of significant concern, such as the severity of the crime or if the individual is a repeat offender. Additionally, Art 6 states that monitoring and intervention plans must aim to prevent secondary victimisation. The convicted individual is required to sign an agreement to refrain from intimidating or harassing the victim. If the victim believes this agreement has been violated, they can report the behaviour to the court responsible for executing the sentence.

may prioritise punitive measures over rehabilitative objectives. Thus, understanding the trajectory of parole reforms necessitates a critical examination of the socio-political dynamics that underpin them, highlighting the need for a balanced approach that considers both public safety and social reintegration.

This phenomenon aligns with comparative research indicating that high-profile criminal cases and societal crises often serve as catalysts for populist penal policies, which can significantly affect parole systems by aligning them with prevailing public sentiment (Freiberg et al 2018; Fitzgerald et al 2022). Carr (2023) further highlights how political interference, particularly in high-stakes cases, can undermine professional autonomy within parole decision-making processes. Similar findings have emerged from scholarship in the Global North (Beckett and Sasson 2004; Clear and Frost 2014; Tonry 2018), illustrating that societal values, political pressures and media representations are vital for understanding the evolution of parole policies.

As a result, the parole system in Chile has undergone significant alterations concerning its eligibility criteria, institutional structure and overall conceptual framework. These transformations have fluctuated between restrictive measures characteristic of a retributive and populist approach and more progressive paradigms aimed at embedding reintegration objectives within parole. Nevertheless, the prevailing paradigm at present reflects a managerial approach that prioritises the minimisation of risks posed by parolees to society. This focus is evident in the discretionary evaluation and approval processes in place, as well as in a standardised case management system that fails to accommodate individual distinctions and contextual analyses. This scenario is further complicated by the perception of incarcerated individuals, who often regard parole as merely a bureaucratic formality, thereby significantly diminishing their agency throughout the process.

The continual reforms to the parole system have resulted in increasingly stringent application restrictions and a corresponding decline in parole granting, ultimately undermining its original function as a progressive mechanism for penal compliance aimed at fostering social reintegration.

Any recommendations for reform must be framed within two critical structural aspects at the legislative and political levels. The first is the establishment of a legislative framework for sentencing execution. For years, there has been a call in Chile for a dedicated system for executing sentences, highlighting the need to unify penitentiary regulations through legislation and to create a specialised court for sentence execution, staffed by judges with exclusive responsibilities. Such measures would clearly separate judicial oversight from the support provided by parole officers, allowing the latter to adopt a therapeutic approach rather than the current corrective focus on control.

The second aspect involves developing a comprehensive penitentiary policy that positions parole as a key mechanism for enhancing the progressiveness of sentences. To achieve this, the system must be strengthened with adequate budgetary, institutional and organisational resources. An effective prison policy should include robust evaluation mechanisms, tailored intervention plans to address the diverse needs of incarcerated individuals and sustained support systems that ensure continuity upon release. Additionally, this policy must align with a variety of penalties that prioritise alternatives to incarceration. Given the influence of external factors on parole, it is essential to consider the dynamics of the penitentiary system and the implications of legislative changes to create long-term strategic planning for institutional and budgetary frameworks.

VIII. CONCLUSION

This chapter has provided a comprehensive analysis of the evolution of the parole system in Chile, highlighting the historical development, legislative reforms and socio-political dynamics that influence its current function. Drawing on insights from Southern criminology, it situates the Chilean experience within the broader context of global trends marked by increasing restrictions on parole, largely driven by populist penal policies.

The developments observed in Chile have fundamentally challenged the rehabilitative ethos of parole and raise critical questions about our expectations of the system. To understand the implications of these changes, it is essential to examine the nature and purpose of parole itself. In the Chilean context, the conception of parole is now often perceived as a discretionary benefit rather than an inherent right. This distinction has implications: if parole is framed as a right, the primary focus shifts to ensuring compliance with established criteria for its granting. In contrast, viewing parole as a privilege necessitates a thorough assessment of an individual's progress in the reintegration process and their efforts to desist from crime. This latter approach poses significant challenges, as human behaviour, despite advances in risk assessment tools, remains fundamentally unpredictable, and conduct within prison may not accurately predict behaviour upon release.

When considering the purpose of parole, it is necessary to ask whether it primarily serves a pragmatic function – such as reducing prison overcrowding – or whether it is more closely aligned with public safety objectives, namely, preventing recidivism by promoting and supporting social reintegration. Furthermore, it is essential to evaluate the extent to which these objectives align with the institutional incentives of those responsible for making parole decisions. In the Chilean case, the judiciary's institutional mission appears disconnected from either goal, as judges may perceive their role in granting parole as one of risk management rather than facilitation of reintegration. This perceived risk is compounded by a flawed assumption that parole decisions should be based on the certainty of non-recidivism. Consequently, when a parolee reoffends, it is often interpreted as an 'error' in the decision-making process, reflecting what the editors of this book have termed a 'crisis of ideas' surrounding parole, where the emphasis is increasingly placed on the system's ability to predict future recidivism.

The current perception of parole as a discretionary benefit may inadvertently undermine the very principles of reintegration that it was originally intended to uphold. This evolution highlights the need for a nuanced understanding of parole, one that balances the necessity of public safety with the goal of supporting individuals in their journey towards becoming law-abiding members of society.

From a Southern criminology perspective, the Chilean experience with parole presents both striking similarities and deep differences. Chile has notable parallels to the processes of restriction and delegitimisation observed in the Global North. While much of the Latin American literature underscores the influence of punitive populism and attributes institutional weaknesses and corruption – often linked to organised crime – as vulnerabilities to external pressures, Chile's case does not markedly differ from the trends of parole restriction in Western nations. In this sense, the dehumanisation of incarcerated populations and the logic of 'incorrigibility' used to justify permanent incarceration, as Dichter (2021) identifies, appear to be a phenomena with global resonance. The Southern criminology perspective argues that the system fails to address the deeper social inequalities that contribute to crime, such as poverty and discrimination. From this perspective, reforms to parole systems must go beyond merely being legal mechanisms; they must address the social and economic barriers faced by the most vulnerable prisoners.

The Chilean context also reflects another global trend in which parole is viewed as a privilege, and restrictive measures have been adopted in response to public pressure and media portrayals of shocking cases such as in Australia (see Moffa et al 2019; see also chapter two in this volume). This highlights the influence of media pressure and high-profile cases on parole policy, which underscores the necessity for parole systems to be resilient against populist pressures. Future reforms should rely on evidence-based decision-making rather than reacting to public sentiment, ensuring that decisions are guided by rehabilitative goals rather than populist demands.

However, significant differences and points for discussion arise from the comparative analysis. First, there is a need to challenge the Northern assumptions about parole. The critique of the Global North's dominance in setting criminological norms is pertinent to the discussion of Chile's parole system. This experience highlights the insufficiency of Northern models that often prioritise managerial control and public safety over reintegration. This context calls for approaches that address the structural factors contributing to crime, such as poverty and social exclusion, acknowledging that parole can act as a social exclusion tool.

Moreover, the distinctive social realities of the Global South, particularly concerning inequalities, must inform the development of parole policies. Addressing these deeper social inequalities is essential for reframing parole as not only a criminal justice tool but also a mechanism for achieving broader social justice goals. Future parole systems should integrate restorative justice principles, focusing on repairing the harm caused by crime, especially in contexts marked by systemic inequality.

The Chilean experience can also inform comparative studies across the Global South, examining how other countries with similar socioeconomic dynamics handle parole. This approach can help shift the focus from Northern-dominated discourses and broaden the understanding of how parole can be adapted to different cultural and structural realities.

There should be balance between public safety and reintegration. The increasing focus on risk management within the Chilean parole system has shifted the emphasis from rehabilitation to control. It is imperative to restore a balance in parole policies, ensuring that public safety does not overshadow efforts to support prisoners' reintegration into society. Future parole policies should prioritise the development of comprehensive support systems that facilitate successful reintegration for parolees, reinforcing the rehabilitative foundations of the parole system.

In conclusion, the evolution of the parole system in Chile serves as a critical case study that reflects broader global trends in penal policy. The insights drawn from this analysis emphasize the necessity for a balanced and holistic approach to parole reform – one that integrates public safety with the imperative of reintegration. By addressing the deeper social and economic barriers faced by vulnerable populations and challenging the punitive tendencies of populist policies, a more just and effective parole system that serves the interests of society can be created. The lessons learned from the Chilean experience should inform future discussions and policies, both in Chile and internationally, to foster approaches to parole that genuinely support the reintegration of individuals into society.

REFERENCES

Alvarez, P, Marangunic, A and Herrera, R (2007) 'Impacto de la Reforma Procesal Penal en la Población Penal Carcelaria del País' *Revista de Estudios Criminológicos y Penitenciarios* 11.

Annison, H and Guiney, T (2022) 'Populism, Conservatism and the Politics of Parole in England and Wales' 93(3) *The Political Quarterly* 416.

Armstrong, R and Durnescu, I (2017) 'Parole and Beyond: International Experiences of Life After Prison' in R Armstrong and I Durnescu (eds), *Parole and Beyond. International Experiences of Life Prison* (London, Palgrave Macmillan) 1–18.

Arriagada, I, Farías, J and Walker, A (2021) 'Evolución de la Población Penal en Chile desde 1991 a 2007: Aproximación empírica a los efectos de la reforma procesal penal' 16(31) *Política Criminal* Article 31 https://doi.org/10.4067/S0718-33992021000100062.

Asociación Nacional de Magistradas y Magistrados de Chile [National Association of Judges of Chile] (2020) 'Presidenta pidió el rechazo de la acusación constitucional contra Ministra Silvana Donoso' https://magistrados.cl/presidenta-pidio-.

Beckett, K and Sasson, T (2004) *The Politics of Injustice: Crime and Punishment in America* (London, SAGE).
Biblioteca del Congreso Nacional (BCN) (2012) 'Historia de la Ley No 20.587' https://bcn.cl/1tywg.
—— (2016) 'Historia de la Ley No 20.931' https://bcn.cl/2ip94.
—— (2018) 'Guía Legal sobre la Reforma Procesal Penal' www.bcn.cl/portal/leyfacil/recurso/reforma-procesal-penal.
Carr, N (2023) 'Politicisation of Parole' 70(2) *Probation Journal* 101 https://doi.org/10.1177/02645505231184543.
Carrington, K, Hogg, R and Sozzo, M (2016) 'Southern Criminology' 56(1) *British Journal of Criminology* 1 https://doi.org/10.1093/bjc/azv083.
Clear, TR and Frost, NA (2014) *The Punishment Imperative: The Rise and Failure of Volume Crime Control* (New York University Press).
Cochran, JC (2014) 'Breaches in the Wall: Imprisonment, Social Support, and Recidivism' 51(2) *Journal of Research in Crime and Delinquency* 200 https://doi.org/10.1177/0022427813497963.
Consejo de Reforma Penitenciaria (2009) 'Recomendaciones para una Nueva Política Penitenciaria' Documento de trabajo no publicado.
Dichter, TA (2021) 'Worst of the Worst: Rehabilitationist Roots of Life without Parole' 17(3) *Law, Culture and the Humanities* 529 https://doi.org/10.1177/1743872117733190.
Droppelmann, C, Vial, P, Villagra, C, Montanari, D and Faúndez, S (2023) 'Libertad condicional en Chile: análisis de una reforma en curso' in Centro de Políticas Públicas UC (ed), *Propuestas para Chile. Concurso de Políticas Públicas 2022* (Pontificia Universidad Católica de Chile) 93–129.
Eurosocial (2015) 'Ejecución de la Pena Privativa de Libertad: Una Mirada Comparada' http://eurosocial-ii.eu/es/showbiblioteca/2833.
Figueroa, U (2018) 'La libertad condicional en el sistema de justicia chileno. Funcionamiento actual y principales modificaciones al decreto Ley 321' 35 *Revista de Derecho* 63 https://doi.org/10.21703/issn0717-0599/2018.n35-04.
Fitzgerald, R, Freiberg, A, Dodd, S and Bartels, L (2022) 'Building Public Confidence in Parole Boards: Findings from a Four-Country Study' 66 *British Journal of Criminology* 1395 https://doi.org/10.1093/bjc/azab097.
Freiberg, A, Bartels, L, Fitzgerald, R and Dodd, S (2018) 'Parole, Politics and Penal Policy' 18(1) *QUT Law Review* 1 https://doi.org/10.5204/qutlr.v18i1.742.
Fundación Paz Ciudadana (2013) 'Redescubriendo la libertad condicional' https://pazciudadana.cl/biblioteca/documentos/conceptos-n-30-redescubriendo-la-libertad-condicional-2/.
Garland, D (2002) *The Culture of Control: Crime and Social Order in Contemporary Society* (Oxford, Oxford University Press) https://doi.org/10.1093/acprof:oso/9780199258024.001.0001.
Gendarmería (2013) 'La reincidencia: un desafío para la gestión del sistema penitenciario chileno y las políticas públicas. Estudio de reincidencia de individuos egresados el año 2010' (Subdirección técnica. Chile).
—— (2019) 'Reincidencia delictual en egresados/as del subsistema penitenciario cerrado chileno, año 2016' (Departamento de Estadística y Estudios Penitenciarios).
—— (2024) 'Estadística' www.gendarmeria.gob.cl.

Hochstetler, A, Delisi, M and Pratt, T (2010) 'Social Support and Feelings of Hostility Among Released Inmates' 56 *Crime & Delinquency* 588 https://doi.org/10.1177/0011128708319926.

León, M (2019) *Las moradas del castigo: Origen y trayectoria de las prisiones en el Chile republicano (1778–1965)* (Ediciones Centro de Estudios Bicentenario).

Ministerio de Justicia [Ministry of Justice] (1925) 'Decreto Ley 321, que establece la libertad condicional para las personas condenadas a penas privativas de libertad, Chile' [Decree Law 321 of Parole in Chile] https://bcn.cl/2if1g.

—— (2012) 'Ley No 20.587, modifica el régimen de Libertad Condicional y establece, en caso de multa, la pena alternativa de trabajos comunitarios, Chile' https://bcn.cl/2nd64.

Ministerio de Justicia y Derechos Humanos (2016) 'Ley No 20.931 facilita la aplicación efectiva de las penas establecidas para los delitos de robo, hurto y receptación y mejora la persecución penal en dichos delitos, Chile' https://bcn.cl/2ip94.

—— (2019) 'Ley No 21.124 que modifica el Decreto ley 321, de 1925, que establece la libertad condicional para los penados, Chile' https://bcn.cl/2f6my.

—— (2023) 'Ley No 21.627 que modifica diversos cuerpos legales para establecer mayores exigencias para la obtención de la libertad condicional, Chile' https://bcn.cl/3ggf4.

—— (2024) 'Reglamento de Establecimientos Penitenciarios, Chile' https://bcn.cl/2f58p.

Moffa, M, Stratton, G and Ruyters, M (2019) 'Parole Populism: The Politicisation of Parole in Victoria' 31(1) *Current Issues in Criminal Justice* 75 https://doi.org/10.1080/10345329.2018.1556285.

Judicial Observatory [Observatorio Judicial] (2020) 'Cuatro razones para rechazar la acusación constitucional contra Silvana Donoso' https://observatoriojudicial.org/3990-2/.

Pratt, J (2007) *Penal Populism* (London, Routledge).

Riego, C and Duce, M (2008) *Prisión Preventiva y Reforma Procesal Penal en América Latina, Evaluación y Perspectivas* (Santiago, Centro de Estudio de Justicia de las Américas).

Salinero, S (2012) '¿Por qué aumenta la población penal en chile?: un estudio criminológico longitudinal' 18(1) *Ius et Praxis* Article 1 https://doi.org/10.4067/S0718-00122012000100005.

Schaefer, L and Williamson, H (2018) 'Probation and Parole Officers' Compliance with Case Management Tools: Professional Discretion and Override' 62(14) *International Journal of Offender Therapy and Comparative Criminology* 4565.

Sepúlveda, E and Sepúlveda, P (2008) 'A 83 años del Establecimiento de la Libertad Condicional en Chile: ¿un Beneficio Desaprovechado?' *Revista de Estudios Criminológicos y Penitenciarios, Gendarmería de Chile*.

Tebar, B (2004) 'El modelo de libertad condicional español' (Doctoral thesis, Universidad Autónoma de Barcelona).

Tonry, M (2018) *Sentencing Matters* (Oxford, Oxford University Press).

Tversky, A and Kahneman, D (1973) 'Availability: A Heuristic for Judging Frequency and Probability' 5(2) *Cognitive Psychology* 207 https://doi.org/10.1016/0010-0285(73)90033-9.

Vîlcică, ER (2018) 'Revisiting Parole Decision Making: Testing for the Punitive Hypothesis in a Large US Jurisdiction' 62(5) *International Journal of Offender Therapy and Comparative Criminology* 1357 https://doi.org/10.1177/0306624X16668512.

Villagra, C and Droppelmann, C (2017) 'The Law, Practice and Experience of "Conditional Freedom" in Chile: No Man's Land' in R Armstrong and I Durnescu (eds) (2017) *Parole and Beyond. International Experiences of Life Prison* (London, Palgrave Macmillan) 191–218.

Villagra, C (2022) 'History and Transformations of the Models of Rehabilitation in the Criminal Justice System in Chile' in M Vanstone (ed), *The Palgrave Handbook of Global Rehabilitation in Criminal Justice* (London, Palgrave Macmillan) https://doi.org/10.1007/978-3-031-14375-5_5.

Wilenmann, J (2020) 'Neoliberal Politics and State Modernization in Chilean Penal Evolution' 22(3) *Punishment & Society* 259 https://doi.org/10.1177/1462474519882974.

15

What if We Better Valued Therapeutic Alliances and Working Relationships in Parole Officer Work?

ROSEMARY RICCIARDELLI AND MICHEAL P TAYLOR

I. INTRODUCTION

RELATIONSHIPS ARE FUNDAMENTAL to all correctional work, and the alliances formed among people within probation and parole spaces can affect wellness, positively or negatively. Responsivity ambience refers to the way people interact with one another and adapt to their social environments, as well as how these interactions, in turn, shape those environments (Lewis 2016; Taylor et al 2024a). In one jurisdiction, parole/probation officers (POs)[1] (n = 144) were found to have an average of at least one mental health disorder (Carleton et al 2020). Moreover, 63.2 per cent screened positive for symptoms consistent with post-traumatic stress disorder, 37.4 per cent for major depressive disorder, 33.1 per cent for general anxiety disorder, 12.4 per cent for panic disorder and 5.2 per cent for alcohol use disorder (Carleton et al 2020: 8). Norman and Ricciardelli (2022) described environmental factors as being the most stressful, such as workplace relationships affected by the agency's culture. In response, we ask: what if more was done to foster alignment between POs, their clients and the therapeutic environment?

[1] While we acknowledge the jurisdictional and functional distinctions between probation and parole, for the purposes of this chapter and from a cultural standpoint, we view the vocational roles of probation and parole officers as more similar than different. In Canada, parole officers are typically employed at the federal level, while probation officers operate within the provinces and territories. Among Canada's 13 provinces and territories, there are 14 correctional jurisdictions, including the federal system represented by the Correctional Service of Canada (CSC). Our findings are based on the experiences of parole officers employed by CSC working exclusively with adults.

Parole potentially represents an ideal process for the facilitation of moral, legal and social forms of rehabilitation (McNeill 2012). However, responsive parole work, as shaped by POs, colleagues and clients, means traversing iterative and linear processes: being attuned to what is most needed at a given moment (Norman 2013). Recognising that the mental illness experienced by practitioners is beholden to their wellness and may inhibit their capacity to craft rehabilitative interventions for those on their caseload (Maier and Ricciardelli 2022), we attend to the presupposition that conditions of employment operate in tandem with conditions of confinement (Ricciardelli and Power 2020). Unpacking this complexity, we explore in this chapter how the effort POs put into building relationships means they subsequently become shaped by those connections. In doing so, we differentiate workplace relationships in terms of therapeutic alliances, where consensus among clients and practitioners relates to bonding, versus the working alliance, referring to the distribution and effective use of human resources within the team environment.

We extend the implications and interpretations of our findings from a study of federally employed parole officers to probation officers recognizing the fact that both titles have distinct meanings in Canada despite the considerable occupational overlap among these roles. While the nuances are beyond the scope of this chapter, it is important to note that, like in other countries, parole focuses on preparing prisoners for release and supervising formerly incarcerated individuals as they reintegrate into society.

In Canada, federal parole applies to prisoners with sentences of two years or more and supports their reintegration into society. A conviction has been made and, in most cases, parole is afforded to inmates once they have served two-thirds of their custodial sentence – known as 'statutory release' – a legislative requirement that ensures community supervision to maintain continuity of the sentence until the final warrant expiry date, at which point the statutory authority to supervise the person ceases.

In contrast, probation refers specifically to a period of community supervision that does not require a conviction (eg suspending the sentence pending completion of ordered conditions), nor is it linked to a period of imprisonment – although it may accompany such judicial dispositions. That said, recognising the commonalities shared among POs, regardless of their role, we draw on international core correctional practice literature to conduct a narrative review of psychotherapy, in probation and parole, to present an aetiological approach to desistance as responsive to human needs. Next, we offer a brief discussion on the study and methods from which we draw our findings. Our results reveal how POs describe listening to their clients as essential to understanding their complex needs for crafting potential intervention strategies. Then we turn to organisational barriers thought to hinder responsivity. We show how barriers mediate programme integrity and the capacity for building stronger workplace relationships, before concluding with some directions for developing the conditions of responsivity in probation and parole work.

II. THERAPEUTIC ALLIANCES AS CORE TO CORRECTIONAL PRACTICE

Relationships are fundamental to PO work and ambient across all situations people perceive, come to believe and ultimately project onto others (Taylor et al 2024a). Reciprocity exists as people interact within their social environments where, in theory, rehabilitation ideally 'hooks' people into responsive change when the capacity to promote wellness leads them to a better life. Through understanding attributes such as acceptance, respect, support, empathy and belief – in reference to the 'good lives model' – relationships emerge as meaningful and effective for curating conditions for criminal desistance (Ward 2012; Lewis 2016). However, on that desistance journey, 'ruptures' occur as a normal process of growth which have the quality to enhance or undermine relationships and ultimately promote or hinder pathways to desistance (Lewis 2016). One interpretation of ruptures in the supervisory relationship is when POs become preoccupied by 'deficits' and risk management which can create discord that does more to foster punitivity than rehabilitation (Ward and Maruna 2007).

Despite being often attributed to Zetzel (2003), Bibring (1937) initially conceived the notion of a therapeutic alliance. An alliance applies to various therapeutic contexts. In probation and parole, it refers to the bonding between the PO and client, and is argued to lead to consensus for identifying rehabilitative goals underpinned by mutually agreeable tasks (Ward 2012; Blasko and Taxman 2018; Malhotra and Chauhan 2020). POs are to help support their clients through interpersonal relationships characterised by openness, warmth and enthusiasm (Dowden and Andrews 2004). Effective correctional practices, rooted in psychotherapy (Andrews and Kiessling 1980; Blasko and Taxman 2018), mandate tailoring casework to clients' specific needs, foundational to all evidence-informed practice (Norcross and Wampold 2018).

Dowden and Andrews (2004) identify the 'therapeutic alliance' as the fifth and final core correctional practice (CCP).[2] Our interpretation is that order of significance is important. In their original text, Dowden and Andrews highlight the quality of interpersonal relationships between staff and clients as the last – but not least – consideration. We believe the order matters, emphasising the value of establishing alliances in PO work. Therefore, we propose that 'relationship factors' should play a more central role than initially stated:

> The fifth and final component of CCP, relationship factors, is also arguably *the most important*. Essentially, this approach argues that the interpersonal influence exerted by the correctional staff member is maximized under conditions characterized by open, warm, and enthusiastic communication. An equally important consideration

[2] The five core correctional practices identified by Dowden and Andrews (2004: 204–05) and reordered according to our interpretation of significance are: (i) quality of interpersonal relationships between staff and client; (ii) use of community resources; (iii) problem solving; (iv) anticriminal modelling and reinforcement; and (v) effective use of authority.

> is the development of mutual respect and liking between the offender and correctional staff member. This approach asserts that correctional interventions will be most effective when these types of relationships exist. (Dowden and Andrews 2004: 205, emphasis added)

As some contemporaries have suggested, there is a need to reorder principles and privilege responsivity in practice (Fretz and Bogue 2023). We agree that therapeutic alliances are fundamental to all correctional practice (Ricciardelli and Perry 2016), including how staff interact with each other in the workplace environment. On this basis, Norcross and Wampold (2018: 1896) conclude that alliances 'accounts for client improvement (or lack of improvement) as much as, and probably more than, the particular treatment method'. In this sense, intervention efficacy is not limited to the aggregation of common attributes (ie general responsivity) or particular characteristics in an individual case (ie specific responsivity). Instead, treatment success relates to a constellational triad between the complexity of personal characteristics matching practitioner and client. Second, there is diversity in adherence to care ethics; and third, there are varieties in treatment selection. Thus, congruence is a major curative component of POs' work, where empathy and relatability are necessary to formulate a therapeutic alliance with clients (Lambert and Barley 2001).

Labrecque et al (2022) focused on community correctional services and conducted a meta-analytic review of 25 studies to assess officer and supervisee outcomes related to community correctional practice and training. Here, the difference between efficiency and effectiveness is fundamental. They found punitive models ineffective, while rehabilitation-focused approaches adhering to core correctional practices reduced recidivism. The authors operationalised 'relationship skills' as active listening and rapport building (Labrecque et al 2022: 9). In doing so, they recognised the risk, need and responsivity (RNR) principles as garnering the most scholarly attention to date, thus dictating most modern agency-based training programmes (Labrecque et al 2022: 3). The 'what works' correctional literature detailed in the seminal *Psychology of Criminal Conduct*, now in its 7th edition (Bonta 2023a; Bonta and Andrews 2024), values RNR principles. While 'specific responsivity' is a convention of matching stylistic preferences or unique circumstances (Labrecque et al 2022; Bonta 2023a), 'general responsivity' involves restructuring cognitions and behaviours within a milieu characterised as an 'environment conducive to learning' (Bourgon and Bonta 2014: 5).

III. DESISTANCE

While the correctional 'what works' literature beginning in the 1990s initiated with three 'core' principles (ie RNR), it quickly developed a fourth: professional discretion (Andrews et al 1990). A decade later, the framework had expanded to 18 principles organised around three themes (Polaschek 2012: 2). However, revitalising the 'lost scrolls' of what Balzarini (2023) calls the 'correctional bible' suggests we should reorder RNR by situating responsivity first (Fretz and Bogue 2023). Refraining from the term 'model' here is intentional because RNR is better conceived as a scaffolding for correctional interventions theory argued to lack explanatory depth (Ward et al 2007; Polaschek 2012; Varpio et al 2020). Following Polaschek (2012: 3), RNR fails to realise fully how reductions in 'offending' may improve the community because 'the only way to intervene effectively is through compassionate, collaborative, and dignified human service intervention'.

Bonta (2023a) has since revised the framework to 15 principles, rebranded to include 'core RNR principles and key clinical issues'. Therapeutic alliances, fitting most neatly among the responsivity principles, are thus situated among several other considerations. While the RNR framework adds complexity to core correctional practices, Andrews (2011) had long anticipated fidelity issues and programme integrity while recognising the need to manage effective support for correctional staff. Bonta was the 'disciple' of Andrews (D Evans, personal communication, 11 December 2023), who, along with several others,[3] founded of the 'Canadian School of Rehabilitation', which now forms the basis for widespread adoption of RNR (Cullen 2002; Cullen 2013; Smith 2013; Bourgon and Bonta 2014), despite ongoing implementation challenges across jurisdictions worldwide (Bonta 2023a; 2023b) – all beyond the scope of the current chapter.

Following Ward and Hudson (1998), the construction and development of core correctional practice represents a framework wherein distal factors (ie general responsivity) are proximal to therapeutic alliances (ie specific responsivity). Thus, 'theory knitting' (Kalmar and Sternberg 2008), or what the grounded theorists term 'theoretical sampling' (Charmaz 2020), requires ongoing attunement and sense-making in the field (Weick 2020). With relationship responsiveness prioritised, fidelity to core correctional practices requires resourcefulness in at least two ways. First, from an efficiency perspective, the proximal issue of resourcing means POs must perpetually enact care in highly controlled, resource-constrained environments where managerialism means that austerity privileges fiscal deficits (Deering 2011). Consequently, focus on efficiency rather than effectiveness opens a panacea for 'correctional quackery' (Gendreau et al 2002; Latessa et al 2002; Gendreau and Listwan 2018), where iatrogenesis can ensue, meaning so-called treatments exacerbate psychopathologies.

When retribution exists within an organisation, as found in correctional services governing parole, the conflation between moral blame and accountability

[3] The literature recognises the Canadian School of Rehabilitation, initially attributed to Don Andrews and Paul Gendreau, and later developed by Robert Ross, James Bonta, Robert Hoge and Stephen Wormith (Bourgon and Bonta 2014; see also Cullen 2013). However, we also wish to acknowledge Donald G Evans as an original advocate and influential figure, whose work exemplifies the maxim that true power often resides in the influential shadows. Evans's dedication to the therapeutic alliance has distinguished his career in this field (McNeill 2023).

inhibits insight for developing opportunities around organisational learning (Weick and Sutcliffe 2015; Dekker 2017; Roache and Thomson 2023). Thus, a second, albeit distal, problem is theoretical wastefulness, where novel insights and reintegration of evidence-informed practices lead to fewer conceptual developments (Ward and Hudson 1998; McNeill 2012). From this view, core to all correctional practice is how relationships are foundational to learning and represent a human resource for the common good (Ward and Maruna 2007; Ward et al 2007; Ward 2012; McNeill 2023). We reiterate how therapeutic alliances are core to correctional research, theory and practice (Lewis 2016). Therefore, a paradigm shift in correctional services requires expanding the scope beyond individual psychopathology to conceptualise therapeutic alliances as a function of relationships among workplace, organisation, and societal applications (McNeill 2012; 2016; 2023). In this way, attributing blame to locate accountability reinforces a punitive mindset that undermines potential for resilience in rehabilitative goal-setting. In practice, parole operations can create harsh conditions that strain workplace relationships and, as ruptures occur, can sometimes devolve into hostility and 'spiralling incivility' (Ricciardelli et al 2023). Put simply, environments that emphasise blame amid resource constraints hinder the ability to learn.

Responsiveness to client needs is a product of antecedent conditions experienced through working relationships among correctional workers in such an environment. As Montoya-Barthelemy et al (2022: 172–73) show when reviewing literature in the USA, the human and fiscal costs stemming from non-fatal injuries are highest in correctional work. This evidence also emerges in Canada, where well-being is an ecological issue that permeates the community organisations as a whole (Ricciardelli et al 2024b; Taylor and Ricciardelli 2023). Recognising correctional workers, including POs, is a growing area of focus related to a national public safety strategy (Oliphant 2016; USJE 2019; Ricciardelli et al 2021; 2022a; 2022b; Carbonell and Ricciardelli 2023; Cassiano and Ricciardelli 2023a; 2023b; Taylor and Ricciardelli 2023), where workplaces enculturate belief around the experience of perceptions as projections. In this view, we understand POs exemplify a 'secondary victim' (Dekker 2017) when their mental illness stems from stress injuries as a result of their occupation (Oliphant 2016).

IV. CURRENT STUDY

Our current study explores rehabilitative dynamics within Canada's national correctional service, drawing on 150 semi-structured interviews with federally employed parole officers to investigate workplace relationships and well-being (Ricciardelli et al 2022b). Data collection was facilitated through formal recruitment via internal listservs and an informal snowball sampling process, with ethics approval from Memorial University of Newfoundland (file number 20201495). Due to geographical, resource and public health restrictions during COVID-19, all interviews were conducted by phone, allowing effective rapport and disclosure (Novick 2008; Mealer and Jones 2014; Saarijarvi and Bratt 2021). Conversations, lasting 75–120 minutes, were guided by an interview script, transcribed verbatim, and analysed using NVivo to identify emergent themes. We focused on relational dynamics, job satisfaction and accountability among POs, with 130 themes initially identified and refined through a variant of interrater reliability which, in practice, was achieved through collaborative discussion among the research team (Hemmler et al 2022). A more comprehensive understanding of our broader project was detailed in a recently edited volume (Ricciardelli et al 2024a).

V. FINDINGS

We found the human service orientation that POs brought to their role, in theory, brought different relationships between clients and colleagues. We also discovered unexpected nuances in how those relationships were enacted in practice. Interviews consistently revealed that workplace relationships varied between clients and colleagues. On the one hand, POs engaged clients during the re-entry process, which involved appreciating their unique circumstances. For instance, one PO bought mittens for a client who was unprepared for the cold Canadian winter, recognising their discomfort while waiting for a bus. Navigating public transportation post-incarceration is often a source of anxiety for parolees, and the harsh winter only adds to their stress. The PO's providing warmth eased the client's discomfort and demonstrated an understanding of the importance of addressing non-criminogenic needs and how the parolee perceives their relationships in parole (Ricciardelli 2018). This approach reflects what Maslow (1958) described as 'self-actualized' care, where physiological needs are addressed within probation and parole practice.

Our findings capture these complexities in client needs and show how POs thoughtfully curated support while crafting rehabilitative interventions. However, following the positive perspectives, there was a need to re-examine barriers to forming therapeutic alliances, particularly concerning workplace dynamics. Ultimately, we reveal how these relationships influence both the integrity of parole work and the effectiveness of correctional programming.

A. Crafting Rehabilitative Interventions by Attending to a Variety of Client Needs

A variety of skills were needed to establish the bond between the PO and their client. For P124, their 'favourite aspect to the whole thing [was] interacting with people'. Thus, rapport was foundational to forming relationships characterised by a dialogue that began with listening:

> everyone has their story and I'm of a personality type myself and enjoy engaging the people and hearing their stories and, of course, in the course of my work, we're not just [listening], you need to be professional but civil and obviously it always helps to present with a friendly demeanour, there's no sense in coming across as some twit, you can say, that is counterproductive. So, the interactions with people, I guess is the short answer because if you have effective communication interaction with people, you are going to enhance your ability to do this job. (P124)

Communicating effectively, according to P124, means showing a 'professional', 'civil' and 'friendly' demeanour, and such qualities are rooted in verbal and nonverbal types of communication (Birdwhistell 1971; Bonaccio et al 2016; Taylor and Ricciardelli 2023). Developing rapport meant hearing what the client needed while demonstrating enthusiasm and focusing on establishing relationships orientated to the POs' professional capacities. Trust was established over time, while POs validated what was heard – and, when feasible, met the expressed needs of the individual under supervision. The therapeutic alliance was, therefore, rooted in a bond established through task consensus, enabling the PO and client to work effectively towards mutually beneficial goals.

Participants valued engaging with clients and forming meaningful therapeutic alliances, emphasising relationships grounded in actively listening to clients' self-expressions. As another PO described the complexity of clientele needs, they remained vigilantly attuned:

> What I always found fascinating about the job [is] ... I've had high functioning, high needs sex offenders. Or I also had for, I'd say, about 8 years, low-functioning schizophrenics. With the low-functioning schizophrenics, you have to deal with this in a much different way than you do with high-functioning sex offenders. The same as even with high-functioning sex offenders, you're going to deal with them differently than you deal with your just generalized violence guys ... The only offenders that I'm a little on edge with, are the acutely mentally ill. And that was – is more about I used to stand at the top of the range thinking, please let the voices be saying be nice to the [PO]. Please let the voices be saying it. Cause you just never know what the damn voices are saying. And it's not that they necessarily mean ill intent to you cause they don't. It's just they are so ill. And, unfortunately, sometimes they are very strong and very quick. (P31)

Here, P31's words describe specialised needs for individuals based on criminal history, mental health, positioning and lived experience, and thus an attachment and attunement to those on their caseload. Such complex dynamics made each relationship unique. Nevertheless, the bond meant responsiveness, which means attentiveness to the holistic circumstances of the person to whom the PO was assigned. The openness and warmth elucidate P31's enthusiasm for 'hearing' the client despite the psychological toll sometimes posed by psychosis. As such, hearing was a foundational skill for crafting interventions that required disrupting negative thought patterns (ie pro-social modelling/reinforcement). P12 explained that expressions were diverse, and clients sometimes struggled to interpret real-world events. Thus, central to hearing was responding in a way that supported desistance while also challenging 'distortions' that may contribute to reoffending:

> Sometimes it really honestly depends, it can actually be the offenders themselves. I would say more at max that was the case, a lot of very rigid thinkers who [are] very distorted in their thinking, very paranoid, very challenging and so you're constantly I won't say arguing with people but you're constantly in that mental battle with them, trying to pick and choose words that won't contribute to those distortions that they have. (P12)

P12's words evinced how maximum-security settings mediated communications and shaped rigid interpretations. As such, maladaptive thinking took a psychological toll on POs' ability to challenge certain cognitions. Thus, carefully negotiating where, when and which 'battles' to challenge was a problem-solving skill related to the therapeutic alliance. However, through hearing clients and validating an understanding of their needs and positioning, hearing meant responding in a manner that resonated with the client. Thus, minimally, the client needs to feel understood, and feeling understood contributes to bonding, which, ideally, progresses to lessons about which goals and tasks to work on collaboratively in the therapeutic alliance.

The timing was, therefore, key because establishing rapport to develop an alliance was time-consuming, albeit necessary for the PO to understand how to curate a response to their client's needs. Tact, POs explained, began by actively listening to learn about the client. P108 explained how relationships begin with meeting clients and getting to know them by hearing:

> I enjoy meeting with my offenders and seeing who they are because on paper they obviously can sound like monsters but then you understand what got to the point where they committed those offences. So, I like meeting up with them; seeing who they are in real life as opposed to just through a paper trail. Understanding their own history and their own life and how they got to the point where they're at today … I like meeting up with them and I like doing the post-suspension interviews where a guy has breached and kind of understanding what kind of insight a guy has into his risk factors and then like if a breach is serious I do feel revoking an offender because then I'm looking out for the safety of the public. So, I like that part of the work too like writing those reports to the parole board. They're really important and I know I do good work with my reports. So I do actually enjoy sitting down [to] write a good report and highlighting my concerns about a case and or even the way around, like highlighting how much progress a guy has made.

Palpable in P108's experience is reframing a conception about clients who sometimes can sound like 'monsters' (Carrier 2022). Despite hearing from them, it is necessary to appreciate their unique interpretations. In doing so, meeting and listening to clients informs dynamic assessment predicated on relationship factors. Once the PO appreciates the dynamics of that relationship – and the client and PO understand one another – the formation of that therapeutic alliance grounds all other occupational responsibilities (eg report writing, revocation).

B. Learning and Interpersonal Knowledge

Knowing how one interprets the world and expressing that interpretation are essential to learning how to work together. Thus, in bonding, the goal of a therapeutic alliance is to distil areas of consensus and mutual agreement through hearing and understanding one another. Dialoguing with clients meant appreciating the ongoing realities affecting their lives. For the PO, the task meant determining what was necessary for negotiating an effective alliance to gain therapeutic insights (eg referrals to community-based resources, including psychiatry). Hearing meant 'getting to know' a person and learning about them through authentic and dedicated listening. P9 described this practice of discerning and attuning to 'micro-expressions':

> We do so much through reading of expressions and micro-expressions and when some of these guys not being incredibly articulate, you do a lot of body language reading. I found I had to go from time to time, if I picked up on a tone of voice or something or if somebody didn't call who in the pass had been really needy [I had to check on them in person].

Here, P9 refers to vocalics and the nature of tone in knowing clients through expressions of 'body language'. The PO gained insights to mirror what, how and why clients communicate, thus enabling their interpretation of expressions in parole work. Such astuteness meant a firm grasp of interpersonal knowledge about the client, which helped identify their wellness or decompensation. Insights gleaned from such bonds were pivotal to enacting all other core practices. Before attuning to risk/needs for effectively brokering community support, the PO first needed to understand how cues were interpreted.

In other words, learning about clients was represented both as an art and as a science (Norcross and Wampold 2018), which meant understanding how to respond efficaciously and tailor correctional plans based on what was needed. As such, an alliance formed once understanding enabled the interpretation of nonverbals and expressions of self to effectively guide the POs' discretion. Then, collaboration for goal setting ensued to establish consensus for task agreement related to the corrective treatment plan. Accordingly, relationships were constantly in flux, meaning case planning and assessment were dynamic and included intuitive acting. From this view, POs were curators in rehabilitative processes where diversity was supported to align re-entry and reintegrative processes aimed at desistance.

> There are certain guys that I've been able to watch do that [desist] … There was one guy I had on my caseload at [institution] that I supported for day parole. He went

> out, he thoroughly messed up. Lit himself on fire. Came back in. Got more time and then ended up back on stat [statutory release] but he and I kept in touch when he was out and then when he got back out again. He got back out and then we kept in touch and he was like 'hey, I could really use your help. Like this is what's going on with me. This is what's going on in my life. How do I deal with this? I'm not getting anywhere with my PO or my PO is great or I'm trying to get a job, I'm going to school', that type of thing. We would talk fairly regularly. Once a month. He actually ended up graduating from, or getting like a substance abuse, counsellor thing. And even with like his criminal history, which was huge, he was able to get that kind of waived cause to work with vulnerable people. So, I got to go to his graduation. (P90)

In P90's words, the observation shows how desistance and successful reintegration are sometimes measured by the client returning without being mandated to seek advice. Despite revocation at one point in the reintegration journey, the PO describes the therapeutic alliance as a bond in which the client assumes responsibility to support others. A strongly developed rapport meant bonding over time, leading to a therapeutic alliance beyond the scope of the supervisory role. Despite setbacks, the relationship alludes to how 'volunteerism may reduce criminality through a gradual process of pro-social socialization' (McNeill and Maruna 2007: 232). As P90 observed, a positive orientation towards their client was a source of inspiration for the PO's own self-regard. And, for the criminalised people who leveraged their experience to overcome their 'criminal history', the client evolved into a human-service practitioner.

C. Organisational Barriers to the Therapeutic Alliance

POs noted that the challenges clients face are complicated not just by their dynamic needs, but also by how CSC operated. While we previously emphasised how building trust and a therapeutic relationship was central to effective correctional work, we now focus on how workplace culture sometimes creates administrative challenges. These challenges make it harder for POs to connect with individuals, set goals and reach agreements in case planning. For instance, P79 shared that discussing sexuality, though a normal part of the role, was stymied by a lack of gender-responsive practitioners:

> I think it may have like a reluctance or a comfort level with talking about certain offences, whether it be sex offences or some of their past history, maybe they've been sexually abused, they maybe more willing to speak with a female. They maybe more willing to talk with the male, so that's a tough one, it's hard for me to say for sure, 'cause I got some guys that are more than willing to disclose some of these details and some that aren't.

P79 speaks to how some parolees are more comfortable with women POs and others with men. The diversity of client needs was also complicated by how perpetration and victimisation sometimes overlap (Ricciardelli et al 2020). Meanwhile, the variety of these dynamics requires complexity for matching POs and clients when casework entails sex crimes (Taylor et al 2024b). One proximal factor is the discomfort that requires establishing an effective therapeutic alliance, while the systemic barrier mediated by working relationships is a distal one. Thematic analysis of the relationships among correctional co-workers revealed that resource constraints sometimes fuelled blame and incivility, which complicated the working environment.

Working relationships meant interdisciplinary and professional collaboration across a client's case management team. POs explained how they felt better equipped to provide clients with the non-material resources necessary for cultivating a therapeutic alliance if they had positive and supportive working relationships with their colleagues. P15 explains:

> Working within the programming was wonderful ... We get quite a few high-risk sex offenders and people with very complex issues, mental health and substance abuse intertwined, and yes so some more challenging cases ... I love the frontline work, so I do see myself doing this job for quite some time, though I recognize that there is like an emotional mental health toll. We'd be consulting with the mental health team that's working with the individual too, it might involve their, psychiatrist, it might involve their psychologist or their community counsellor ... we don't do those daily, it might be once a month, it might be once a week, [it] just depends on the individual's needs, we could consult on a daily basis with the halfway house staff [or] facility staff because they have eyes on the individual throughout the night and they do checks, and so if they have seen any signs of intoxication or changes in behaviour, attitude, any increases in risk for mental health, suicidal plans or tendencies or self-harming. All those things would be discussed and shared, and a plan would be created to address them.

P15's words demonstrate how relationships with colleagues underpin the capacity for rehabilitative intervention. Relationships were thus core to all correctional practices when identifying clients' needs, meaning treatment planning occurred through teamwork. While POs are proximal to developing responsivity in a particular case, supporting desistance meant recognising collective efforts. Proximal to supervision was the distribution of human resources across a case management team, where variety in professional insights involved curating care provisions in supporting sufficient complexity in the team's diversity when crafting interdisciplinary interventions.

Recognising the value of collaborative efforts across a case management team, P5 stated:

> I think of all the colleagues that I've worked with in corrections my whole career, I see so much integrity and professionalism. Nothing is slapped together ... I feel like parole officers definitely go above and beyond and it's very good quality work, so that's rewarding in that I know I've put in what I can to make a good assessment of someone's risk.

Aside from risk assessment, the PO refers to interdisciplinary working relationships among colleagues to promote desistance. The variety inputted across a case management team, informed by the therapeutic alliance, meant matching client complexity within working relationships. Thus, echoing how relationships at work are integral, P3 explained:

> I work at a great jail! So we've all helped each other and that again is just expected we just do it and we've all figured out a way to do our job without any support. We don't have clerks, we don't even [have] sentence management, at first there wasn't even any other departments here.

P3 highlights the value of positive workplace relationships, exemplified by the sentiment of working in a 'great jail' even amidst a lack of administrative support. However, organisational challenges, such as the ineffective distribution of resources across the roles in a case management team, impeded the POs' practice. Additionally, resource constraints, particularly inadequate staffing, directly affected their ability to maintain strong working alliances, underscoring how administrative demands shaped the perception and reality of the workspace. For instance, where scarcities led to POs feeling unsupported, scarcity often spiralled into stifling workplace relationships. As P19 responded, when asked what was 'the most challenging aspect of your job as a parole officer?' they said, 'the organization':

> It's big, it's bureaucratic, people are stressed … I feel [sigh] isolated from beyond. Like my direct manager. I don't feel a lot of support coming from above. I would say that that's the case in any, any position … And there's a huge disconnect between regional headquarters and national headquarters and the institution … Well, because they come up with these brilliant ideas, and then they expect us to just do it with very little consultation, from the front lines and it's patronizing almost. Like they expect miracles almost and then it's like 'ok, we'll just add that on to the list' and they hardly ever see anyone from those buildings step foot in an institution … that part's difficult.

P19 describes the disconnection experienced in the 'bureaucratic' organisation where people are 'not in touch' (Taylor and Ricciardelli 2023). As staff elevate through the chain of command, the distance in relationships means administrators, managers and practitioners become disconnected. As a result, POs felt underleveraged in organisational decision-making, where the resulting sense of isolation compromised relationship qualities enculturated by workplace and organisational structures.

D. Managerial Integrity and Workplace Relationships

The integrity of operations was seen to hinder the relational aspects of parole work. For example, P21 was asked, 'What the most challenging part of the job is? … coworkers and management', explaining:

> We've been given so much responsibility, we have all this responsibility we have absolutely no control and we're the first person to get thrown under the bus. Whether that's your co-workers doing that to you, or your manager doing that to you – so

> I will tell you in the fourteen years I have been in corrections I have respected maybe three managers out of ten. I've never wanted to be management, I don't want to be management, but sometimes when you see the shitty jobs that other managers are doing you say to yourself 'maybe I should be management'. But part of being management is towing the line for the manager above you, if I don't believe in something I can't, I can't just blindly toe the line.

Here, P21 discloses the strain of the working relationship emerging when colleagues and management fail to respect one another. The barrier to accountability is thus an overload in responsibility that expands the energy of POs who might otherwise focus on supporting their clients. Concern about being 'thrown under the bus' illustrates the enculturation of correctional service work as a liability and shows how organisational structures imbue a sense of injustice (Dekker 2017), especially when complexity, variety and diversity are ineffectively managed.

Other participants spoke about the degree their peers experience tension between their occupational roles and the employment conditions within the organisation. As expressed by P3, strain meant under-resourcing was a prevalent issue across the organisation. And further, sharing information with colleagues, where wellness was compromised, sometimes induced spiralling incivility:

> Yeah, it's hard to do, I mean you want to be supported by the people that you work with but they're all going through the same thing. I went to this training years ago where they talk about sliming each other and that is what happens when you slime someone with your problems, you dump it all over them. But they're dealing with the same things … You worry about your co-workers who aren't doing well. We've had a couple of suicides with co-workers. (P3)

P3's words elucidate the toxicity by which a lack of support compromises working relationships and, via 'sliming' – that is, the unsolicited disclosure of tolling casework (see Taylor et al 2024b) – sometimes exacerbated the hazards of correctional work at the expense of relationships among colleagues so far as to result in suicidality. As P3 suggests, preoccupation with goals and tasks, conflated with efficiency for the organisation, undermined therapeutic relationship bonding. The POs 'worry' about colleagues for whom recognition and support are lacking, contributing to the general malaise among staff. As such, the implications of compromised wellness mediated working relationships and therapeutic alliances through enculturated perceptions, projections and beliefs about workplace organisational functions.

For POs, aiming to support clients and establish alliances in such a climate took a toll, contributing to their compromised wellness. With self-care lacking, POs struggled to effectively instate boundaries pivotal to parole work in fostering their capacity to help others (Norman et al 2022). Regarding human resource limitations, P9 explained how the lack of psycholcgists on site exemplified the challenge of resource constraints:

> we have one psych nurse part time who is fabulous but that's not enough when you are dealing with a lot of cognitive functioning issues and brain injuries and so that's

> one facet that we don't have the resources to deal with twenty-five individuals who all have unique challenges … There's a much higher percentage of the diagnosed mental health issues, the schizophrenic issues and a lot of bipolar and pseudoeffective disorders … but they take a great deal of time. That's one facet but the other facet is there's a much more resource focus on indigenous offenders and that is another whole issue but it takes more time. If you have a group hearing, if you have to have a group consultation on every sort of case trying to get people organized is like herding cats. (P9)

P9's words demonstrate first a lack of resources available to provide tailored support for matching clients' complex needs with the requisite variety of professional skills. Such necessities were dynamics for ensuring interdisciplinary teams are equipped with the diversity necessary for responsive interventions. Therefore, group consultations and case conferencing were a collaborative effort to distribute resources effectively and develop responsibility in correctional plans. Consequently, POs who experience strain felt unsupported, which was mediated by working relationships that had the potential to function as a resource and support therapeutic alliances with clients or exacerbate isolation and organisational disconnect.

Setting boundaries as a form of self-protection meant negotiating the capacity to help others with the tension of untenable workloads and managerial demands:

> The caseload … it's unrealistic. Like it's really unrealistic. I could manage that stress if I had support from not just my manager but my manager, my co-workers, our assistant wardens, our wardens. If everyone was supportive and positive, I could manage that caseload better. I would say that's almost more of a stress to me than the heavy caseload because I feel like I can't go to anyone for help. Because as soon as you ask for help, well you're just shitty at your job … And then when something goes wrong, they turn around and go 'oh, well you didn't do your job well enough'. So, you don't have the support. You can't ask for help and then there's the judgement on you, if you can't keep up. So, I would say that's more stressful because I could handle a caseload like what I have if I could ask for help. (P117)

In P117's words, the 'unrealistic' caseload is a stress made unmanageable by the strained relationships in the workplace, which can present as barriers to support, compromising the working alliance and, thus, provisions available to support clients. As work relations distracted rather than supported POs' capacity for managing their workloads, concern for judgement and inferring blame were also detrimental to POs' operational integrity.

VI. DISCUSSION: INTEGRATING REHABILITATIVE KNOWLEDGE

The complex needs of clientele accessing probation and parole services around the world are associated with structural inequities that are difficult to navigate on an individual basis (Phelps 2018; Phelps and Ruhland 2022; McNeill 2023).

Nevertheless, POs were found to navigate judgement, intuition and accountability, all pertaining to soft skills, in developing a repertoire for probation and practice. These are necessary requirements in balancing the subjective and objective components of responsivity (Norcross and Wampold 2018), where evidence-based interventions mean attending to proximal and distal factors in which POs relate, operate and curate interventions to clients' sometimes complex needs. Put differently, POs work proximally in casework to understand clients by learning through hearing – not just listening. Thus, bonding arrives from establishing rapport iteratively, through which identifying mutual goals leads to consensus for correctional case planning.

A therapeutic alliance means POs are attentive to the dynamic flux in relationships to curate immediate responses based on unique needs. However, these dynamics were contingent on ambient workplace characteristics, including teamwork and how perceptions, projections and beliefs about the organisation resulted in learning (Dekker 2017; Taylor et al 2024a). Sometimes, learning was inspiration in creating a sense of wellness for POs who found value in working with clients and, at other times, learning meant recognising the issues tied to structural barriers that contributed to psychological distress. We believe there is a need to incorporate stasis by attending to both working and therapeutic alliances among all people in correctional organisations as a prerequisite for interventions to be effective and to progress service users towards the objectives of desistence and rehabilitation.

Therefore, fidelity to core correctional service practices may be reimagined across two lines of inquiry concerning resource responsivity. First, what operational conditions (ie distal factors) mediate rehabilitation and therapeutic alliance formation? Second, in which ways do the insights gained from correctional work provide for accountability in building therapeutic alliances? We suggest responsiveness pertains to the quality of workplace relationships in terms of human service in probation, parole and correctional work. One example of the distal and proximal factors in parole casework may be collaborative casework assignments according to gender expression or preference. Matching clients with POs is an organisational factor with which responsivity means allocating human resources effectively. Matching practitioners with clients to optimise choice comes at little to no fiscal cost – and communicates an understanding 'for whom' interventions should work. Differentiation between therapeutic alliances and working relationships is sparse in the literature. Our scholarship has found it productive to draw clear distinctions where working relationships are a distal factor mediating the collaborative effort of the proximal work in forming alliances.

We found the core of integral correctional practice was programme delivery, in which human needs were situated, based on the evidence of responsiveness in psychotherapy (Norcross and Wampold 2018). However, the preoccupation with individual psychotherapy as merely one component fails to address the broader implications of how structural and organisational factors shape individuals' understanding of their environment. Focusing solely on individual 'offenders' neglects deeper issues within legal, moral and social systems that urgently require reform. To elevate the social dimension of correctional agencies, we differentiate workplace relationships in two key ways. First, therapeutic alliances must prioritise collaboration that aligns with clients' dynamic needs as they perceive them. This approach fosters a bond that enhances the capacity to build consensus around general goals and specific tasks. Second, worker relationships pertain to human resource allocation, which requires effectively leveraging the strengths of interdisciplinary teams to collaborate in human service work with their clientele.

Put differently, dialogue is core to understanding where, when, how and why to use certain skills, such as role-modelling, advocacy, problem-solving or asserting authority, to guide rehabilitation (Dowden and Andrews 2004; Innes 2015). We understand responsivity as the exercise of diverse expressions in attuning and attending to human needs. Sometimes, this means pushing and pulling clients through adversity to foster interpersonal growth. Other times, it means brokering effective referrals to the community, leveraging cognitive/behavioural restructuring or being assertive in the authoritative use of discretion. What is pivotal is that organisational governance is structured in service to responsivity, providing a novel avenue to conceptualise programme effectiveness and integrity by attending to setbacks that detrimentally affect wellness, positionality, identity and re-entry into society. As such, setbacks are a part of learning, representing progress for probation and parole service users and providers alike.

VII. CONCLUSION

This chapter has contributed to a deficiency in the 'what works' correctional literature regarding responsivity principles, for which we demonstrated that staff are key stakeholders in human service. As such, our theoretical contribution remains conceptual and limited by a scarcity of scholarship on responsivity in corrections specifically, which future studies can develop. Studies focusing on analyses regarding gender, race, ethnicity, age or years of occupational tenure would greatly supplement the nuances in our findings. Future research, we suggest, may stratify samples by demographic factors, thus unpacking the various themes identified and the less salient themes with greater specificity, especially across workplace units where probation and parole operate. As such, we urge researchers to consider the diverse and complex factors that differentiate responsiveness in therapeutic and working alliances while considering what the future of the vocation might look like when these factors are better aligned.

REFERENCES

Andrews, DA (2011) 'The Principles of Effective Correctional Programs' in EJ Latessa and A Holsinger (eds), *Correctional Contexts: Contemporary and Classical Readings*, 5th edn (New York, Oxford University Press) 228–37.

Andrews, DA and Kiessling, JJ (1980) 'Program Structure and Effective Correctional Practices: A Summary of the CaVIC Research' in RR Ross and P Gendreau (eds), *Effective Correctional Treatment* (Toronto, Butterworth) 441–63.

Andrews, DA, Bonta, J and Hoge, RD (1990) 'Classification for Effective Rehabilitation' 17(1) *Criminal Justice and Behavior* 19.

Balzarini, TK (2023) 'Revitalizing the Lost Scrolls of Correctional Bible: Before the Risk–Need–Responsivity Model' in PR Magaletta, M Ternes and M Patry (eds), *The History and Future of Correctional Psychology* (Cham, Springer International Publishing) 137–63.

Birdwhistell, RL (1971) *Kinesics and Context* (Philadelphia, University of Pennsylvania Press).

Blasko, BL and Taxman, FS (2018) 'Are Supervision Practices Procedurally Fair? Development and Predictive Utility of a Procedural Justice Measure for Use in Community Corrections Settings' 45(3) *Criminal Justice and Behavior* 402.

Bonaccio, S, O'Reilly, J, O'Sullivan, SL et al (2016) 'Nonverbal Behavior and Communication in the Workplace' 42(5) *Journal of Management* 1044.

Bonta, J (2023a) 'The Risk-Need-Responsivity Model: 1990 to the Present' (Manchester, HM Inspectorate of Probation).

—— (2023b) 'Transforming Community Supervision Through Evidence-Based Practice' (Public Safety Canada)

Bonta, J and Andrews, DA (2024) *The Psychology of Criminal Conduct*, 7th edn (New York, Routledge).

Bourgon, G and Bonta, J (2014) 'Reconsidering the Responsivity Principle: A Way to Move Forward' 78(2) *Federal Probation* 3.

Carbonell, M and Ricciardelli, R (2023) 'Correctional Officer Culture in Canada: Proving Oneself for In-Group Acceptance' 103(6) *The Prison Journal* 791.

Carleton, RN, Ricciardelli, R, Taillieu, T et al (2020) 'Provincial Correctional Service Workers: The Prevalence of Mental Disorders' 17(7) *International Journal of Environmental Research and Public Health* 1.

Carrier, N (2022) 'Monstrosity, Correctional Healing, and the Limits of Penal Abolitionism' 19(1) *Crime, Media, Culture: An International Journal* 95.

Cassiano, MS and Ricciardelli, R (2023a) 'Correctional Officers' Views of Prison, Punishment, and Rehabilitation' *Handbook on Prisons and Jails* 119.

—— (2023b) 'Sources of Stress among Federal Correctional Officers in Canada' 50(8) *Criminal Justice and Behavior* 1229.

Charmaz, K (2020) '"With Constructivist Grounded Theory You Can't Hide": Social Justice Research and Critical Inquiry in the Public Sphere' 26(2) *Qualitative Inquiry* 165.

Cullen, FT (2002) 'Rehabilitation and Treatment Programs' in JQ Wilson and J Petersilia (eds), *Crime: Public Policies for Crime Control* (Oakland, CA, ICS Press).

—— (2013) 'Rehabilitation: Beyond Nothing Works' 42(1) *Crime and Justice* 299.

Deering, J (2011) *Probation Practice and the New Penology: Practitioner Reflections* (Chesterfield, Ashgate) 9–28.

Dekker, S (2017) *Just Culture: Restoring Trust and Accountability in Your Organization*, 3rd edn (Boca Raton, FL, CRC Press).

Dowden, C and Andrews, DA (2004) 'The Importance of Staff Practice in Delivering Effective Correctional Treatment: A Meta-analytic Review of Core Correctional Practice' 48(2) *International Journal of Offender Therapy and Comparative Criminology* 203.

Fretz, R and Bogue, B (2023) 'Reconfiguring Risk-Need-Responsivity (RNR) Assessment Based on the Recent Influx of Research on Trauma and Recidivism' 32(3) *Journal of Community Justice* 5.

Gendreau, P, Goggin, C, Cullen, FT et al (2002) 'The Common-Sense Revolution and Correctional Policy' *Offender Rehabilitation and Treatment: Effective Programmes and Policies to Reduce Re-offending* 359.

Gendreau, P and Listwan, SJ (2018) 'Contingency Management Programs in Corrections: Another Panacea?' 34(1) *Journal of Contemporary Criminal Justice* 35.

Hemmler, VL, Kenney, AW, Langley, SD, et al (2022) 'Beyond a Coefficient: An Interactive Process for Achieving Inter-rater Consistency in Qualitative Coding' 22(2) *Qualitative Research* 194.

Innes, C (2015) *Healing Corrections: The Future of Imprisonment* (Boston, MA, Northeastern University Press).

Kalmar, DA and Sternberg, RJ (2008) 'Theory Knitting: An Integrative Approach to Theory Development' 1(2) *Philosophical Psychology* 153.

Labrecque, RM, Viglione, J and Caudy, M (2022) 'The Impact of Community Supervision Officer Training Programs on Officer and Client Outcomes: A Systematic Review and Meta-Analysis' 40(4) *Justice Quarterly* 587.

Lambert, MJ and Barley, DE (2001) 'Research Summary on the Therapeutic Relationship and Psychotherapy Outcome' 38(4) *Psychotherapy* 357.

Latessa, EJ, Cullen, FT and Gendreau, P (2002) 'Beyond Correctional Quackery – Professionalism and the Possibility of Effective Treatment' 66 *Federal Probation* 43.

Lewis, S (2016) *Therapeutic Correctional Relationships: Theory, Research and Practice* (London, Routledge).

Malhotra, S and Chauhan, N (2020) 'The Therapeutic Alliance Between the Child, Parents and Health Professionals' in *Handbook of Clinical Neurology* (Oxford, Elsevier) 323–32.

Maslow, AH (1958) 'A Dynamic Theory of Human Motivation' in CL Stacey and M DeMartino (eds), *Understanding Human Motivation* (Howard Allen Publishers) 26–47.

McNeill, F (2012) 'Four Forms of "Offender" Rehabilitation: Towards an Interdisciplinary Perspective' 17(1) *Legal and Criminological Psychology* 18.

—— (2016) 'A Desistance Paradigm for Offender Management' 6(1) *Criminology & Criminal Justice* 39.

—— (2023) 'Beyond the Individual: Correcting Corrections' 32(7) *Journal of Community Justice* 5.

McNeill, F and Maruna, S (2007) 'Giving Up and Giving Back: Desistance, Generativity and Social Work with Offenders' in McIvor G and Raynor P (eds), *Developments in Social Work with Offenders* (London, Jessica Kingsley Publishers) 224–339.

Mealer, M and Jones, J (2014) 'Methodological and Ethical Issues Related to Qualitative Telephone Interviews on Sensitive Topics' 21(4) *Nurse Researcher* 32.

Montoya-Barthelemy, A, Gibson, BR, Lee, CD et al (2022) 'Occupational and Environmental Hazards of Correctional Settings: A Scoping Literature Review From ACOEM's Presidential Task Force on Correctional Institutions' 64(3) *Journal of Occupational and Environmental Medicine* e172.

Norcross, JC and Wampold, BE (2018) 'A New Therapy for Each Patient: Evidence-Based Relationships and Responsiveness' 74(11) *Journal of Clinical Psychology* 1889.

Norman, DA (2013) *The Design of Everyday Things* (New York, Basic Books).

Norman, M and Ricciardelli, R (2022) 'Operational and Organisational Stressors in Community Correctional Work: Insights from Probation and Parole Officers in Ontario, Canada' 69(1) *Probation Journal* 86.

Norman, M, Ricciardelli, R and Maier, K (2022) '"In This Line of Work, Boundaries Are Important": Occupational Stress and the Well-being of Community Parole Officers During the COVID-19 Pandemic' 46(4) *Canadian Journal of Sociology*.

Novick, G (2008) 'Is There a Bias Against Telephone Interviews in Qualitative Research?' 31(4) *Research in Nursing and Health* 391.

Oliphant, R (2016) 'Healthy Minds, Safe Communities: Supporting Our Public Safety Officers Through a National Strategy for Operational Stress Injuries' (Ottawam House of Commons) 1–40.

Phelps, MS (2018) 'Mass Probation and Inequality Race, Class and Gender Disparities in Supervision and Revocation' in JT Ulmer and MS Bradley (eds), *Handbook on Punishment Decisions* (New York, Routledge) 43–61.

Phelps, MS and Ruhland, EL (2022) 'Governing Marginality: Coercion and Care in Probation' 69(3) *Social Problems* 799.

Phillips, J (2016) 'Myopia and Misrecognition: The Impact of Managerialism on the Management of Compliance' 16(1) *Criminology and Criminal Justice* 40.

Polaschek, DLL (2012) 'An Appraisal of the Risk-Need-Responsivity (RNR) Model of Offender Rehabilitation and Its Application in Correctional Treatment' 17(1) *Legal and Criminological Psychology* 1.

Ricciardelli, R (2018) 'Parolee Perceptions of Case Management Practices During Reintegration' 13(6) *Victims & Offenders* 777.

Ricciardelli, R and Perry, K (2016) 'Responsivity in Practice: Prison Officer to Prisoner Communication in Canadian Provincial Prisons' 32(4) *Journal of Contemporary Criminal Justice* 401.

Ricciardelli, R and Power, NG (2020) 'How "Conditions of Confinement" Impact "Conditions of Employment": The Work-Related Well-Being of Provincial Correctional Officers in Atlantic Canada' 35(1) *Violence and Victims* 88.

Ricciardelli, R, Spencer, DC and Dodge, A (2020) '"Society Wants to See a True Victim": Police Interpretations of Victims of Sexual Violence' 16(2) *Feminist Criminology* 216.

Ricciardelli, R, Andres, E, Mitchell, MM et al (2021) 'CCWORK Protocol: A Longitudinal Study of Canadian Correctional Workers' Well-being, Organizations, Roles and Knowledge' 11(12) *BMJ Open* e052739.

Ricciardelli, R, Maier, K and Norman, M (2022a) '"You Have to Be Really Careful, in This Environment, of What You Say and What You Do": A Qualitative Examination of How Organizational Culture Shapes Parole Officers' Work and Well-being' *Probation Journal* DOI: 10.1177/02645505221127184.

Ricciardelli R, Norman M and Maier K (2022) 'The Mental Health and Well-being of Canadian Federal Parole Officers: A Qualitative Investigation' (Union of Safety and Justice Employees, USJE) 1–74.

Ricciardelli, R, Taylor, MP, Maier, K et al (2023) 'Parole Work in Canada: Tensions in Supervising People Convicted of Sex Crimes' 67(16) *International Journal of Offender Therapy and Comparative Criminology* 1699.

Ricciardelli, R, Maier, K, Norman, M et al (2024a) *Parole Work in Canada: Caseloads, Cultures, and Carceral Spaces* (Lanham, MD, Rowman & Littlefield).

Ricciardelli, R, Siqueira Cassiano, M and Foley, G (2024b) 'The Well-Being of Correctional Officers in Canada' in H Arnold, M Maycock and R Ricciardelli (eds), *Prison Officers: International Perspectives on Prison Work* (Cham, Springer International Publishing) 409–31.

Roache, D and Thomson, SB (2023) 'Naturalistic Decision-Making Method' in JM Okoko, S Tunison and KD Walker (eds), *Varieties of Qualitative Research Methods* (Cham, Springer International Publishing) 333–39.

Saarijarvi, M and Bratt, EL (2021) 'When Face-to-Face Interviews Are Not Possible: Tips and Tricks for Video, Telephone, Online Chat, and Email Interviews in Qualitative Research' 20(4) *European Journal of Cardiovascular Nursing* 392.

Smith, P (2013) 'The Psychology of Criminal Conduct' in FT Cullen and P Wilcox (eds), *The Oxford Handbook of Criminological Theory* (Oxford, Oxford University Press) 69–88.

Taylor MP and Ricciardelli R (2023) '"Not in Touch": Nonverbal Communication and Frontline Perceptions of Inter-organizational Justice in Parole Work' 28(3) *Theoretical Criminology* 382.

Taylor, MP, Ricciardelli, R and Shively, R (2024a) '"Making a Difference": Interpreting Responsivity Ambience for Parole Work' 10(20) *Heliyon* DOI: 10.1016/j.heliyon.2024.e39617.

Taylor, MP, Ricciardelli, R and Spencer, DC (2024b) 'Parole Work in Canada: The Realities of Supervising "Sex Offenders"' *Probation Journal* 0(0) DOI: 10.1177/02645505231223.

Union of Safety and Justice Employees (2019) 'Protecting Public Safety. The Challenges Facing Federal Parole Offices in Canada's Highly Stressed Criminal Justice System' (USJE) 1–47.

Varpio, L, Paradis, E, Uijtdehaage, S et al (2020) 'The Distinctions Between Theory, Theoretical Framework, and Conceptual Framework' 95(7) *Academic Medicine* 989.

Ward, T (2012) 'The Good Lives Model of Offender Rehabilitation: Basic Assumptions, Aetiological Commitments, and Practice Implications' *Offender Supervision: New Directions in Theory, Research and Practice* 41 DOI: 10.4324/9780203832974-11.

Ward, T and Hudson, SM (1998) 'The Construction and Development of Theory in the Sexual Offending Area: A Metatheoretical Framework' 10(1) *Sexual Abuse: A Journal of Research and Treatment* 47.

Ward, T and Maruna, S (2007) *Rehabilitation Beyond the Risk Paradigm* (London, Routledge).

Ward, T, Melser, J and Yates, PM (2007) 'Reconstructing the Risk–Need–Responsivity Model: A Theoretical Elaboration and Evaluation' 12(2) *Aggression and Violent Behavior* 208.

Weick, KE (2020) 'Sensemaking, Organizing, and Surpassing: A Handoff' 57(7) *Journal of Management Studies* 1420.

Weick, KE and Sutcliffe, KM (2015) *Managing the Unexpected: Sustained Performance in a Complex World* (Hoboken, NJ, Wiley & Sons).

Zetzel, ER (2003) 'Current Concepts of Transference' in CF Andrew and TL Steven (eds), *Influential Papers From the 1950s* (London, Routledge) 109–24.

16

Generative Justice: Exploring its Reintegrative Possibilities and the Implications for Parole Reform

MARY CORCORAN, BETH WEAVER AND FERGUS McNEILL

I. INTRODUCTION

THIS CHAPTER BUILDS on emerging work surrounding the burgeoning concept-praxis which we call 'Generative Justice' (GJ). Initiated by the authors, and shared with a founding network of academics and activists (some with direct experience of criminal justice systems), we have begun exploring the characteristics and contours of forms of justice that might be thought of as collaboratively 'generated' among diverse communities, and which are in turn 'generative' of solidaristic social relations. This, we argue, stands in stark contrast to perceptions and experiences of parole, particularly in the UK and the USA; experiences which, we argue, are often alienating, degrading and disintegrating in effect. Taking this as our starting point, we then proceed to elaborate what GJ is, how generativity and solidarity are connected in theory and practice, and what kinds of justice GJ represents and seeks. In so doing, we draw on empirical research conducted by one of us (Weaver) into Italian social cooperative through-the-gate structures of employment, whose origins, modus operandi and manner of relating are, we propose, expressions and examples of generative justice in practice with people serving prison sentences, people nearing release, people on day release or people who have been released. In our conclusion, we circle back to consider the implications of GJ for the future of parole through this lens.

II. PAROLE, CONDITIONALITY AND ALIENATION

Parole is conditional release from prison to the community, where the parolee serves the remainder of the sentence under supervision and subject to certain conditions, and where they therefore endure 'the purgatory of being a conditional citizen' (Vaughan 2000: 26). In contrast to Foucauldian readings of penal supervision (*cf* Robinson and McNeill 2023), McNeill (2018; 2020) argues that, at least where 'mass supervision' has become a reality (*cf* Miller 2021), conditionality of this sort

> functions less to discipline poor and marginalised people and more to disqualify them from the entitlements of ordinary citizenship. In so doing, conditionality constructs them as denizens, thus serving to limit the liabilities for the state that arise from social inequalities. (McNeill 2020: 295)

While, as McNeill (2020: 296) acknowledges, 'penal practitioners can and do provide care and assistance', there are significant constraints on their capacities to ameliorate, let alone address, the socio-structural deprivations underpinning much offending, in turn shaping both the unequal processes of criminalisation and the profoundly inadequate conditions into which many formerly imprisoned people are released (Weaver et al 2021).

Many people on post-release licences report inadequate through-the-gate transitional arrangements (Weaver et al 2021). Post-release, the effects of substandard housing provisions, the pressures of conditional welfare arrangements, social isolation and insufficient economic resources texture and constrain their daily lives. For example, in a Scottish study, post-release supervision was typically described by Weaver et al's (2021) participants as consisting of short meetings to 'check in' and report on current circumstances while simultaneously being dominated by risk-centric decision-making (see also Weaver and Barry 2014). A number of parolees referred to a pervasive sense of surveillance and monitoring (Weaver et al 2021). Ultimately, as Weaver et al (2021) observe, these deprivations and constraints further complicate capacities to comply with their release conditions and are aggravated, for some, by experiences of addictions, poor mental health, homelessness, poverty and trauma, which together degrade people's sense of social connectedness and human dignity. Indeed,

> the vulnerabilities that conditionality creates … exacerbate … structural inequalities … to symbolically degrade and disqualify, producing symbolic, political and material effects for the 'penal state' that uses both hands to push away those that it has made vulnerable and whose vulnerabilities it has itself magnified through conditionality. (McNeill 2020: 306)

In spite of these cumulative and multilayered structural and systemic disadvantages and degradations, somehow many people can and do recover from contact with the criminal justice system, and (re)gain a sense of belonging. However, this is rarely attributed, by those affected, to what happens *on parole*. Indeed, in our experience, recoveries of this sort are co-produced in and through social relations *outside of the penal system*, where relations, values and practices of solidarity and subsidiarity are more often found (Weaver 2015). Our similar observations over decades, with different projects and communities, prompted us to explore what we tentatively termed 'generative justice'.

III. GENERATIVE JUSTICE

We soon discovered that the term was already in use by political theorists in the field of ecological activism to refer to 'relations of open reciprocity, communal sharing, gift giving and voluntary collaboration [that allow] value to circulate in its unalienated forms, including labor power, political expression and interspecies ecological exchanges' (Eglash 2016: 377).

Ron Eglash's idea of generative justice as a 'transformative and sustainable reparative process' (Eglash et al 2024: 2) resonated with our own thinking and experience, as did his recognition that such processes begin with the 'bottom-up circulation of unalienated [ie uncoerced] exchanges' (ibid 373), which are not extractive in nature. Indeed, Eglash argues, just interactions are most likely to occur where value is co-produced and circulated for the common good, rather than with the aim of monetising or exploiting value from one another for personal gain. We similarly understand practices of generative justice as prefigurative and emergent, and as arising in and from (in our case) existing communities, movements and organisations involving justice-affected people. Crucially, these sites respond to justice-affected people in ways that are generative of social relations characterised by solidarity, subsidiarity, recognition, reciprocity and inclusion.

Despite their very different contexts and entirely independent development, these two visions of generative justice share common features. Both rest on a moral economy of exchange, gift relations and reciprocity, and the rights of 'value generators to create their own conditions of production' (Eglash 2016: 382). Eglash draws on dynamics of peer interaction and horizontal organisation, a rebuttal of 'top-down' hierarchical decision-making, a celebration of action from below. Self-help, social justice and sustainability are foundations for 'truly self-generating sources of value', without which there is 'no way to obtain human [and non-human] flourishing' (Eglash 2016: 251).

In the context of criminal justice, generative justice also shares some obvious similarities with reparative justice approaches (broadly defined), but it attends to the harms of criminalisation as well as crime, it is more concerned with looking towards the future than the past, it insists on the interconnections between criminal and social (in)justices, and it locates responses in ideas and practices which are often outside the conventional criminological canon or have originated outwith the criminal justice system.

In certain respects, GJ's focus on activism and practice is similar to Transformative Justice (Brown 2019), though, in our experience, GJ need not start from or assume a commitment to penal abolitionism. There are closer parallels with the Systemic Justice movement in that we connect criminal (in)justice to damaging, cumulative, intersecting iniquities arising from racial, social, gendered and economic marginalisation and disqualification (Systemic Justice 2023). Likewise, we argue that solidarity, recovery and reparation are animated by those directly affected (and allies) as they identify and respond to converging opportunities for change and action.

In this vein, we also draw on Nancy Fraser's (1998) work, because of its emphasis on the coexisting demands for the material, symbolic and political conditions that might enable social justice. These are equal recognition (of status), redistribution of material resources and representation in political decision-making. Applying Fraser's ideas to considerations of GJ more specifically, we can perhaps clarify and identify important formative thresholds where reparation and recovery (both subjective and social) can begin. Firstly, there is a need for recognition, where the intention is to address the 'hidden injuries' caused by disrespect or degradation arising from criminal stigmatisation (Fraser 1998: 4). Secondly, recognition becomes the qualifying condition for parity of participation and representation, ie equal and unburdened interaction with other citizens, particularly in decision-making about the direction of the life of a community or polity. Thirdly, the distribution of material resources must be such 'as to ensure participants' independence and voice' (Fraser 1998: 5), consistent with notions of epistemic justice (Fricker 2007) and epistemic participation (Schmidt 2019), which both connect with, yet go beyond, the framing of voice in theories of procedural justice (eg Weaver et al 2023).

Together, these three conditions proffer some foundational tests for reflecting on how or why projects may design or reflect practices around recognition, participatory parity and practical assistance as antidotes to, or in efforts to ameliorate, intersecting disqualifications and exclusions. But they also offer avenues for thinking afresh as to how, or indeed whether, parole might be either generative or just in its goals, means, norms or effects.

These three conditions also serve to highlight what 'Maloptical' (McNeill 2018; 2019) parole (ie forms of parole that misrecognise their subjects) fails to provide if and where it produces degradation in place of recognition, silencing instead of participation, and disqualification in place of material provision. We will return to questions about the complex relationships between parole and justice in our concluding discussion. In the next section, however, we discuss evidence drawn from one example of a form of in-prison and post-release support (drawing on Weaver's research on social cooperatives) that, far from being Maloptical, seems to illustrate the possibility, the practicality and the promise of more generative approaches.

IV. RE-ENTRY VIA SOCIAL COOPERATIVES IN ITALY

A. Methods

As part of a wider study of 'work integration social cooperatives' in different European countries, one of us (Weaver) conducted 40 semi-structured interviews in Italy: 22 were with prisoners or former prisoners and 18 were with professionals. In the main, the professionals occupied various roles in two different types of social cooperatives (discussed below) in Northern Italy, and from groups with other relevant roles – ie a magistrate, an academic, staff of non-governmental organisations (NGOs) and a cooperative consultant. Weaver also spent time in and around the different workshops to get a feel for and sense of the cooperative culture.

In terms of the demographics of 'worker' participants (ie imprisoned or formerly imprisoned people), six were female and 16 were male, and the average age of the worker participants was 41. The youngest participant was 22 and the eldest 65. Of these participants, eight worked inside the prison; eight were on alternative sanctions (meaning they worked outwith the prison but returned to the prison at the end of the working day); and six were former prisoners who were no longer subject to criminal justice sanctions but still worked for the cooperative. The majority ($n = 18$) were either serving or had served what we (in the UK) would classify as a long-term sentence, eg more than five years for convictions of robbery (five), drug-related offences (seven) or homicide (six), with others mentioning property or violent offences. Sixteen of the 22 participants had served more than one prison sentence. These baseline demographic data broadly reflect the overall portrait of prisoner and former prisoner employees in participating cooperatives. The types of work the cooperatives provided are consistent with other work integration social cooperatives in the region and include recycling, agriculture, textiles, warehousing and some specific projects – making dental moulds, archiving digital records and glass engraving.

The aim of the research was to examine the ways in which social cooperative structures of employment can support social integration and desistance from crime. The research explored the legislative and policy contexts that enabled the development and implementation of social cooperatives and explored how the cooperatives variously enabled or constrained the social integration and desistance of their members.

Data were analysed using Braun and Clarke's (2019) method of Reflexive Thematic Analysis. This involved familiarisation with the data, which was achieved by repeatedly replaying the audio recordings while reading the transcripts, identifying patterns occurring within and across the interviews, and taking preliminary notes to document these analytic observations. The next iterative stage involved generating and refining initial codes, which, once 'completed' and clustered, informed the development and definition of core themes in response to the research aims and objectives. The findings presented here briefly outline the structure of the cooperatives and existing research into their impacts. We highlight primarily workers' experiences of participating in the various social cooperatives, and both workers' and professionals' understandings of social cooperatives in supporting the social reintegration of imprisoned and formerly imprisoned workers.

B. Social Cooperative Structures and Impacts

In different countries, there is a range of different cooperative structures – and even not-for-profit organisational structures – that provide high-quality, paid employment for those distanced from the labour market, including justice-involved people, those anticipating release and those recently released from prison. The Italian social cooperatives we focus on here provide not only employment, but also resettlement services for those both in prison and in the community. Though space prohibits a fuller analysis of the social and cultural contexts in which they arose, in brief, these 'social solidarity cooperatives' (as they were initially known) emerged from civil society *before* they were subsequently institutionalised in Law 381/1991. Specifically, according to this law (Article 1), social cooperatives are created to:

> pursue the general interest of the community in promoting personal growth, and in integrating people into society by providing social, welfare and educational services and carrying out different activities for the purposes of providing employment for disadvantaged people. (Borzaga and Depredi 2012: 39)

The law identifies two types of social cooperatives: social cooperatives supplying social services (A-type) and social cooperatives integrating disadvantaged people into work (B-type). In this latter case, at least 30 per cent of employees must be disadvantaged workers, a category which includes imprisoned people and those formerly imprisoned. The law also frames social cooperatives as collective organisations that invest in and engage with the local community, and represent the interests of different groups of stakeholders; in this sense, there is a co-productive element to cooperatives. The decision-making process of social cooperatives is also democratically driven – on the principle of 'one member, one vote' (ibid). Not all those participating in the cooperative are, however, members; rules of membership diverge, but tend to be the choice of the worker and come with a nominal fee.

While we also have insufficient space here to elaborate the economic dimension of social cooperatives, evidence confirms their resilience in withstanding economic and pandemic crises (Tortia and Troisi 2021) and suggests that social cooperatives have a beneficial impact on local economic and social development (Montrone et al 2024) because of the collaborative relationships that they establish with public services and private enterprises, and with each other – sometimes in the form of consortia (Borzaga and Tortia 2009).

As Borzaga and Depredi (2012: 46) observe, the collaborative relationships enhance collective action, 'foster social cohesion' and encourage altruistic behaviour, and this is reinforced by the horizontal mechanisms of governance and influence that structure the cooperative approach. As we go on to discuss, and as Borzaga and Depredi observe, influence between cooperatives and community is bidirectional to the extent that:

> networking relationships and external ties can influence the internal equilibrium of the [cooperative], because internal norms develop in connection with the social

> values prevalent in the community of reference ... Therefore, adherence to general community ideals influences the social norms within the network and the behaviour of all parties. (Borzaga and Depredi 2012: 46)

While this can contribute to attitudinal change – be it towards parolees, or perceptions of collective agency and social cohesion (Pestoff 2009) – it is through this mutual engagement, exchange and social recognition that social cooperatives, for example, can support not only desistance from crime, but also the more elusive objective of social re/integration (*cf* Rubio Arnal and McNeill 2024).

If prefigurative politics is 'the deliberate experimental implementation of desired future social relations and practices in the here-and-now' (Raekstad and Gradin 2020: 10), then the emergence of these social cooperatives from civil society in response to an unmet need prior to their subsequent institutionalisation in Italian law (Borzaga et al 2017) is an important example of this. They are deliberately and intentionally committed to a more horizontal, egalitarian, inclusive and democratic approach that privileges cooperation between equals, highlights reciprocity and mutualism, and promotes a political notion of solidarity (Hunt and Benford 2004), claiming the need to empower citizens and local communities, and enabling them to claim and enforce their rights. There is, therefore, significant overlap with social movement praxis here.

V. EXPERIENCES OF SOCIAL COOPERATIVES: WORKERS' VIEWS

Across many workers' accounts, work, family and the home are cited as intrinsic and interdependent elements of the change process, and for many, as essential conditions of social integration. While the emphasis on these elements is reportedly something of a cultural norm in Northern Italy, the significance of employment in workers' accounts also reflects, at least partly, the social welfare and penal context. To come out of prison on alternative sanction, one *must* have a job, but also, for those who do not meet the eligibility criteria for social security (INPS-IT 2024), participation in paid work is the only real means outside of criminal activity or illicit alternatives of gaining an adequate income to meet subsistence needs.

For many workers, both in and outside of prison, obtaining an income was a key incentive for wanting to work. The fact that the cooperative is almost the sole provider of work in prisons was cited by imprisoned people as a major incentive for working for it. In this regard, initial motives were both individual and instrumental. While this remained the main, initial incentive for some, often and over time, people's motivations for staying involved and the perceived outcomes and benefits expanded to include more personal and relational concerns. Personal outcomes included the acquisition, development or maintenance of work skills and a sense of accomplishment. The relational aspects included the relational context of work (eg feeling part of something, developing a sense of belonging and togetherness), as well as the relationality that participation in work and in specific work contexts heralded (eg being closer to or providing for one's family).

> At first, I decided to work for the co-op just to have the chance to go outside prison to stay closer to my family but after starting work for the co-op – I really started enjoying the cooperative environment and culture ... to be a member of the co-op makes me feel part of a group, of a family. (Worker, Male, Age 36_1)
>
> To be working alongside others is really important and working together makes you feel connected to something. Before I felt so isolated. There is a sense of togetherness among the women working in here. (Worker, Female, Age 32_6)
>
> Working means that I can provide for my family. (Worker, Female, Age 42_3)
>
> Working on the outside, you can interact in a way that you can't in prison and you can have different conversations compared to those you have in prison. (Worker, Male, Age 22_9)
>
> The best part is the opportunity to see your family at lunch break in a different environment from the prison ... for us, this brings a very different outlook because it improves the dynamics with our families. (Worker, Male, Age 34_19)

And indeed, as one professional put it:

> [P]roviding a job is not the only thing, but through work, we put the person at the centre of our relations inside the co-op. The social relationships within the cooperative and the feelings that develop among people who belong to the co-op are the most important part of the rehabilitative journey. (Professional_1)

What also emerged was a symbolic or communicative aspect to work, in terms of what it signifies or demonstrates to oneself and to others about one's capacity to live differently. The social recognition of this change that some participants experienced mattered greatly to them.

> I had the need to show myself that I was able to work and so it is that I am. (Worker, Male, Age 33_18)
>
> To show that I am able to change my behaviour and that I can behave responsibly and reliably ... It is a way of showing I have changed ... It shows that when I am released, I can be trusted, I am reliable. (Worker, Male, Age 45_4)
>
> Work, in general, is central to rehabilitation – not just for the money. It is a way of proving you have changed, that you can take responsibility and that gets recognised by the officers and the co-op, so you feel good. (Worker, Female, Age 41_7)
>
> I am different. I have to show to my family that I am a different person and I have noticed that they are looking at me with different eyes. (Worker, Male, Age 43_10)

More negative comments related to the level of pay, although this varies between cooperatives. Some mirror pay rates in the private sector; in others, pay can be up to €200 less per month. Overall and otherwise, self-reported job satisfaction was high.

For some, particularly those working in prison, the cooperative context of the work was of no consequence; it was the only option available to them, and it was the opportunity to work and to earn an income that was of significance to them. But working for a cooperative in prison is a different experience to working for one in the community; it is more difficult to experience the cooperative culture in a 'secondary' and secure environment, where there is limited or no interaction with others outside the prison.

More generally, the cooperative values of self-help, self-responsibility, democracy, equality, equity and solidarity and the ethical values of honesty, openness, social responsibility and caring for others shape both the cooperative culture *and* how it is experienced.

> The ethics of the co-op is one of inclusion; it is to move towards, to develop, active citizenship. It is a way of acting – or being. (Professional_2)

Crick (2002: 2) argues that active citizenship represents a focus on 'the rights to be exercised as well as agreed responsibilities'. Although the concept of responsibility appears in participants' accounts (in relation to the symbolic meaning of work), in the main, the idea of 'responsibility' *as a value* was more frequently expressed by those working outside of the prison – by former prisoners and by professional employees. What emerged strongly was a feeling of solidarity, which very clearly meant sharing a common or mutual responsibility through reciprocity. Reciprocity, in turn, implies *inter*-dependence and therefore on a sense of shared solidarity (Donati 2009):

> In the cooperative, we all have to cooperate with each other and so the way we relate to and interact with each other is different – the whole experience is different. It is a matter of responsibility. We are all part of something that together is collectively owned. A boss [in a private firm] can instruct you to do something but, whatever way, the final product belongs to him or to her. You produce it for them. It is not yours. In a co-op the final product is yours, so you are invested in the whole process. A cooperative depends on cooperation. It cannot function any other way, so unlike the private sector, there is a chain of responsibility rather than a chain of command … so, if I make a mistake, there is no sanction or punishment – we work together, all of us, to find the solution. We work together through the good and bad things. (Worker, Female, Age 40_5)

In addition to references to shared responsibilities, experiences of solidarity were often expressed in reference to feeling 'at home' or being part of a 'family', terms that imply a sense of mutual respect, support and trust and a sense of belonging and togetherness.

> I feel at home here and, for me, this is my home. (Worker, Male, Age 43_10)

> To be a member of the co-op makes me feel part of a group, of a family. (Worker, Male, Age 36_1)

> I have a high level of satisfaction but – that depends also on the people I am working with [and their] level of satisfaction and the shared levels of trust required of working cooperatively. This is where the meaning of it is for me. (Worker, Female, Age 40_5) [insert added]

> I have a really good relationship with … the other workers. It is a very collaborative culture and when new workers come in, we help them. So there is a sense of solidarity there … we collaborate and help each other with the work that we have to do. (Worker, Female, Age 32_6).

The impacts of the social cooperatives were also discussed in terms of how their interaction with others within the cooperative, whether workers or professionals, made them feel accepted, respected and valued.

> I feel that here I am a person. I don't feel discriminated [against] here and this is very important for me. (Worker, Female, Age Not Given_2)

> [Name of professional] said to me [when I arrived] 'thank you for coming here' and this made me [feel] very happy because I thought I was the one that should be thanking them, rather than the co-op thanking me. I won't ever forget this in my life. (Worker, Male, Age 43_10)

> I have discovered here that people here are very sensitive and kind and I feel respected here. (Worker, Male, Aged 33_18)

Individualised support, underpinned by mutual respect, was a key element of the cooperative experience, as was the protected and protective environment that cooperatives provided.

> I have been helped by the right people here. I have always found people ready to listen to me … I think the most important thing that co-ops are able to do is listen to people and to give them answers. If they don't understand you, they go on asking you until they are able to understand you and give you answers. (Worker, Male, Aged 46_20)

One of the key values and principles of cooperatives is democratic member control. As noted above, this means 'one member, one vote', and it reflects the co-ownership of the cooperative from which the sense of shared responsibility is intended to derive. Not all workers are members. While some felt that they had a say in the operation of the cooperative and were heard, others believed they were restricted to expressing their views on specific work-related issues rather than the governance of the cooperative.

> I can influence the work we do and … and I can give my opinion. (Worker, Female, Age 32_6).

Notwithstanding this, while some felt their membership provided them with the opportunity to have an equal say, others felt that this aspect of ownership was less meaningful than the autonomy they enjoyed in their work.

> I am free to organise or manage my own work … I am very independent. I am much more free here than I could be in the private sector. (Worker, Male, Age 54_21)

> I think we have the opportunity to play a decisive role in very few cases. (Worker, Male, Age 54_21)

> There is no real means of influencing the overall operation and development of the co-op because it is the management that decide everything, even though we are

> members. We participate in the annual meeting but we don't have any significant opportunity to influence things otherwise (Worker, Male, Aged 65_22)

This dynamic was considered to relate to the size of cooperative, which suggests that the expression and experience of cooperative principles *in practice* risked being diluted in larger organisations.

> The co-op now is bigger than it was before and this has significantly altered the dynamics … I have my own idea of what works in cooperatives and for me it relates to their size. A small co-op is better like this one at the beginning … In a smaller environment, you can really take care of people; in a larger co-op you start changing your … philosophy. (Worker, Male, Age 54_21)

VI. THE ROLE OF THE COOPERATIVE IN SUPPORTING SOCIAL RE/INTEGRATION

The Italian social cooperatives involved in Weaver's study are all affiliated to or provide NGO facilities (as well as A-type cooperatives). These serve three aims: (i) they provide support to prisoners and formers prisoners; (ii) they provide support to communities; and (iii) they offer the opportunity to workers and members to volunteer in the community as a means of providing structure, reinforcing cooperative values, developing new social relationships and supporting social or community integration.

Another key contribution that workers identified was the opportunity that the cooperatives offered in terms of learning new or remembering old norms of interaction; they offered a process of (re)adjustment and (re)socialisation, a means of (re)building a life and opportunities to (re)learn how to interact differently than the relational norms they had become accustomed to after years in prison.

> Work is central to resocialisation into the outside world and this means that you need this re-education of the outside world while you are in prison … I mean in terms of being in the world and building a life. (Worker, Female, Aged 41_7)

> You need to pass through the co-op to start being reintegrated into society. The co-op is the right mechanism for coming out of prison because you need to start down a different path … [it] helps you learn how to cope with the demands of work … and how to manage social relationships. (Worker, Male, Aged 43_10)

> The most important fact is the capacity to feel, to be part of a group, a sort of family. In this way they start to rebuild or build positive relationships. (Professional_2)

As noted already, work and family were almost without exception proposed as the key ingredients of integration – the spaces or spheres from which one feels variously included or excluded. As such, the cooperatives also provided support to the families of imprisoned workers and facilitated family mediation, and they created the space for family contact to occur in more natural and private environments for those on day release, thus enabling family reintegration.

Cooperatives provide work as well as supporting access to 'mainstream' employment, drawing on their networks of professional relationships. Cooperators, those employed by the cooperative in professional roles, appear to be skilled collaborators and negotiators.

> I think the co-op is able to help you because the manager has a good relationship with the private sector so they can help you find the best opportunity … acting as a guarantor for you … and this makes a huge difference. (Worker, Male, Age 46_20)

'Worker' participants also discussed the idea of integration and what it meant to them in terms of not feeling or being seen to be different; not feeling stigmatised and marginalised, but just the same as anyone else. People felt they were integrated when they had work and were a part of a family, community and/or social network. Being normal meant 'being' and 'doing' in the same way as others around them; it was about *mutual* identification, social recognition, acceptance and belonging, which gave people a sense of self-respect and social worth.

> Working for the co-op has given me a sense of what it is to be normal and to take responsibility … [it] has taught me how to live normally, within the rhythm of life. (Worker, Male, Age 35_11)

> I feel that I am well accepted by people for what I am, as a normal person and not as a former prisoner. This is a very important element to improve your self-confidence … people from the area, not only from the coop, treat me as a normal person. (Worker, Male, Age 46_20)

In the context of this chapter, we do not have space to explore public attitudes to people with convictions in Italy in any depth. But most participants – professionals and workers – reported that there is a significant stigma attached to imprisoned and formerly imprisoned people, and, in terms of supporting reintegration, this can be a considerable challenge. However, the different cooperatives, to differing degrees, engaged with and invested in the local communities in which they are embedded. Various strategies for enhancing community cooperation and support included holding social events for workers, professionals and communities to participate in. Cooperatives developed community-facing features, eg running a café or shop; engaging in and/running charitable initiatives and services that benefitted people in the local community; providing social services to meet local unmet need; and providing work for people from the community. Often, the people who worked for the cooperative – besides the 'workers' – also came from the local community. Thus, there were strong local community relationships that were carefully maintained by the cooperatives.

Of course, the question of the impacts of cooperatives on reoffending is complex; participation in the cooperative might trigger change or it might provide opportunities to consolidate a process of change that has already begun. Evidence about reconviction is harder to assess. A significant challenge encountered during this research was the absence of mechanisms for monitoring people after their release from prison in Italy; recidivism rates are not routinely collected or calculated. Moreover, the cooperatives do not maintain follow-up data on the people that formerly worked with and for them.

However, according to the professional participants, this varied from person to person. What seemed clear, however, was that, in the main, involvement with the cooperatives gave people real and sustainable opportunities to live differently and this generated a perception of low rates of recidivism:

> Recidivism rate is very low. There was only one case that the man ... resumed his old criminal lifestyle. (Professional_1)
>
> The recidivism rate is very low. (Professional_2)
>
> Very low, not significant. (Professional_3)
>
> In [our] experience, the recidivism rate is very low: 2–3%. (Professional_4)
>
> I don't have a percentage in my mind but it is well known that the employment opportunities provided by the cooperative help to stop recidivism. (Professional_6)
>
> We don't have an absolute percentage ... we can see that of the people we work with in the cooperative, 70% of people don't commit crime again, while the percentage is the other way round in the case of people that aren't involved in the co-op. (Professional_8)
>
> We had statistics from 1987 to 2004 ... and we can say that very few of them recidivated: 68% of people that we engaged with here were reintegrated; 14 % were recidivists and the remaining percentage is ... people we lost [track of]. (Professional_13)

This was borne out by workers' perceptions of the difference that the cooperative has made to them.

> I did not have the opportunity to change before – like now, with the cooperative work. I am ready for change now and there are positive things happening with my family and with my work. I have a better balance. (Worker_Male_Age 45_1)
>
> Yes, I have stopped offending. I am going home to Tunisia and I would like to get married and start a family. I have learnt so much about what is really important ... I am not concerned because things are different now. I am different now ... working for the coop has given me a sense of what it is to be normal and to take responsibility and I want to hold on to that and take the chance I have been given. (Worker_Male_Aged 35_6).

VII. CONCLUSIONS: SOCIAL COOPERATIVES, GENERATIVE JUSTICE AND PAROLE REFORM

The examples above suggest that Italian social cooperatives are prolific sites of generativity enacted for, by and with justice-affected people. We also hypothesise that such generative practices are intentionally designed to foster solidaristic social relationships as well as providing vital frames for personal re-evaluation based on self-worth, dignity and a sense of place in the community. In this sense, generative practices may be seen as the building blocks of solidarity, while solidarity is in turn formative of more sustained forms of justice. Solidarity building, it follows, is both a condition and an outcome of generative justice.

A. Generating Solidarity

Further, as the work of the wider Generative Justice network shows, these kind of practices and experiences occur in many countries and domains of criminal justice practice and civil society, mainly in community-led projects, but also in anti-poverty, equality, sustainability, environmental and social movements (McNeill et al forthcoming, 2026). That said, we also recognise the hyper-local or situated nature of these projects, which raises possible practical issues about the potential, plausibility and desirability of 'scaling-up' to meet mass demand, or whether and to what extent their dynamics can be reproduced within state agencies or structures like parole systems. Here, we alight on three characteristics that problematise that prospect.

Firstly, the capacity of cooperatives to generate solidarity is shaped by structures or practices that facilitate ways of being-in-relation through which to build collaboration, based on grounded acts of self-responsibility, mutual aid, democracy, equality and solidarity. These 'fraternal' values inform modes of relating which generate the kinds of relational goods on which desired outcomes depend. Trust, reciprocity, shared responsibility and cooperation are both the premise and the promise of relational goods, and as such they underpin GJ principles, practices and projects.

A second proposition is that deliberative and commonplace (micro)practices involving acceptance and recognition can generate more sustained, solidaristic social relations (which we argue are productive and just preconditions to establishing structures for building justice better; see below). As Donati (2011) elaborates, notions of reciprocity or mutual exchange are central to social relations – they are the 'engine', or, in his words, 'the generating mechanism of social relations'. It is the practice of reciprocity that generates and regenerates the bond of the relationship, motivated by the maintenance of the emergent relational goods. Critically, this reciprocal orientation is also the source of collective intentionality in larger groups, where those groups are premised on social relations that are characterised by solidarity. Reciprocity and mutuality are not, however, common features of parole systems; rather, these systems tend to *act upon* parolees in order to secure their compliance and, with it, a presumed reduction in – or at least containment of – their riskiness (Corcoran and Grotz 2016).

Thirdly, the unidirectional exercise of supervisory power over an individual violates another precondition and product of solidarity: subsidiarity

(Donati 2011). Subsidiarity is facilitated by moving resources to support the other without making them passive or dependent, but in such a way that it allows and assists them to do what is required in accordance with their priorities and concerns. Risk-focused parole supervision, by contrast, is more likely to produce passivity or resistance precisely because it imposes prescribed priorities and agendas on parolees (Werth 2023), depriving individuals of capability to shape the conditions of their own flourishing (Sen 1999: 87–90).

By contrast, subsidiarity both requires and consolidates solidarity – which is about sharing a common or mutual responsibility through reciprocity – and which, as we have emphasised, implies interdependence and trust. Subsidiarity is also connected with the notion of 'responsibility' *as a value* – as an interactive norm, rather than always being instrumentally and narrowly conceived in relation to one's offence. In generative justice settings (*cf* McNeill et al forthcoming), group members tend to develop an interlinked sense of self-responsibility *and* mutual responsibility born out of shared oppression, lived experience, interdependence and reciprocity. As Gitterman (2006: 93) observed, when 'group members become involved with one another, they develop helping relationships, and become invested in each other', out of which a sense of belonging, community and 'we-ness' is co-produced (Weaver 2015). This 'we-in-relation' is key to solidaristic subjectivities.

In sum, cultures of solidarity like those produced in the cooperatives discussed above emerge where people share a common or mutual responsibility through reciprocity, which implies interdependence. What we extrapolate from this is that the cultural and relational environment of GJ spaces, places and practices seems to produce the very resources through which recovery and integration – perhaps even desistance – can be enabled, and in so doing, allows generative justice to be expressed and practised.

B. Generating Justice

As constituent parts of the criminal justice apparatus, parole systems purportedly balance fairness for individuals against multilayered risks and protections. Although this alone does not preclude state agencies from generative capacity, it amplifies questions as to the form/s and conditions of justice they enable and/or frustrate by virtue of their function. These questions are inseparable from the penal purposes of reintegrative justice(s) they represent. Indeed, working within traditional discourses of criminal justice in modern liberal democracies, the legal philosopher Antje du Bois-Pedain described reintegration as the core social function of punishment and argued that 'there is reintegrative momentum inherent in punishment … Far from threatening or challenging an offender's membership in the community, punishment reasserts or reinforces it' (du Bois Pedain 2017: 203). In other words, the point of punishment is supposedly to create pathways to reintegration. Yet the contemporary policy and practice of what we have termed 'Maloptical' parole frustrates that purpose. The example of the social cooperatives we have discussed above – and, we suspect, of generative justice approaches more generally – at least suggests the possibility of developing other models of re-entry support that can generate reintegrative momentum through the practice of mutuality, reciprocity, subsidiarity and solidarity.

In our view, the generation (or regeneration) of solidarity is both a condition of justice and a product of it. Recognising this places a primary emphasis on creating certain conditions in which people can thrive; conditions that facilitate human flourishing and growth, and which recognise the human dignity of the other. What is being generated is the sense and experience of solidarity and belonging, from which other relational and material goods are generated. The principle of subsidiarity describes how we go about doing that.

Clearly, the notions of justice in play here extend far beyond the retributive and risk logics dominating our criminal justice systems. Indeed, though epistemic, social, distributive and relational justice – the theories of justice underpinning our concept of generative justice (see McNeill et al forthcoming, 2026) – might seem far from criminal justice, the links are not difficult to make in theory or in practice (as we hope we have illustrated above).

In GJ, the development of greater belonging and solidarity brings us closer to justice as a value and norm, rather than as a system or process: it helps us identify and make our individual contributions, it helps us form or reform the right relations with one another, and it brings us closer to discerning and enhancing our collective good. By contrast, the kind of justice that seeks compliance, docility and machine-like integration seems more concerned with stability and security – and with preserving the status quo – than with differentiated justice and with individual, relational and collective flourishing. As such, the justice in GJ is, first and foremost, a way of 'doing justice' that is generative in effect and relational in character.

We suspect that pursuing GJ in the context of re-entry into society probably means looking beyond the problems and potentialities of the system itself, and in all likelihood means decentring the system from what we understand as post-release reintegration. This is not necessarily to deny the necessity or value of professionalised and state-sanctioned systems of parole supervision. However, it is to insist that the primacy of social relations in both reintegration and justice processes necessitates forms of grassroots and civic engagement (Corcoran et al 2018). While these forms of horizontal engagement were once key parts of many Western probation systems, in late modernity, they have withered away as systems, and services have residualised around risk management and other core statutory functions (Maguire et al 2019). (Indeed, we wonder whether contemporary staff working in the parole systems we know best (ie in the UK) still feel able to claim social [re]integration as their goal.)

We argue, therefore, that there is an urgent need for social innovation in systems and practices of parole that goes beyond parole system reforms, as the gap between the scale of the challenges and the scale of the available solutions continues to widen. Our existing models are failing or have become stagnant, and the internal systems reforms (focused, for example, on release timing or decision-making processes) are, at best, ameliorative rather than transformative. This is perhaps partly what has driven recent calls in the USA for probation and parole abolition (Loopoo et al 2022). Indeed, there are regions of the world where far greater effort is being put into collaborations between the state and civil society to support reintegration. Singapore's 'Yellow Ribbon Project' is one interesting example. So, while ours is certainly a call to utopian methods (Levitas 2013; Wright 2013), and for the development of sustainable alternatives that utopian theories require, there are many examples (small and large) in many places, like the example we discuss above, that indicate the prefigurative, 'adjacent possible' (Loader and Sparks 2012; 2022) is much closer than we think.

In the final analysis, we argue that transformative change depends centrally on the recognition that the generation of relations of solidarity (and thus of just social relations) must lie at the heart of our efforts. Crime itself can be understood as a source, a sign and a symptom of *relational* problems. When we harm one another and find ourselves in conflict, relationships suffer – and *relational work needs to be done*. Acknowledging that the pre-history of criminalised harms is also often one of failed relationships between the state and its citizens, it follows that the relationality involved is not simply interpersonal or interactional in nature; rather, generative practices are also integral to and concerned with responses to the effects of systemic and penal harms. Indeed, attempts at healing and recovery from various social and systemic harms are often undermined by the dehabilitating (Scott 2016), degrading (Cottam 2018: 21–48) and 'anti-social' (Carlen 1998) effects of penal and rehabilitative systems. More constructively, embedded within our orientation is the consciousness and the experience that, despite this damaging context, in particular places and projects, practices of recognition, acceptance, inclusion and solidarity with others are being developed with and by justice-affected people to a significant, if often invisible, degree.

REFERENCES

Borzaga, C and Depedri, S (2012) 'The Emergence, Institutionalisation and Challenges of Social Enterprises: The Italian Experience' 75 *Revista de Economía Pública, Social y Cooperativa* 34 www.redalyc.org/articulo.oa?id=17425798003.

Borzaga, C and Tortia, E (2009) 'Social Enterprises and Local Economic Development' in A Noya (ed) *The Changing Boundaries of Social Enterprises* (Geneva, OECD) 195–228.

Borzaga, C, Poledrini, S and Galera, G (2017) 'Social Enterprise in Italy: Typology, Diffusion and Characteristics', ICSEM Working Papers 44 (Liege, The International Comparative Social Enterprise Models (ICSEM) Project).

Braun, V and Clarke, V (2019) 'Reflecting on Reflexive Thematic Analysis' 11(4) *Qualitative Research in Sport, Exercise and Health* 589.

Brown, M (2019) 'Transformative Justice and New Abolition in the United States' in P Carlen and L Ayres Franca (eds), *Justice Alternatives* (London, Routledge) 73–87.

Carlen, P (1998) *Sledgehammer: Women's Imprisonment at the Millennium* (Basingstoke, Palgrave Macmillan).

Corcoran, MS and Grotz, J (2016) 'Deconstructing the Panacea: The Benefits Fallacy in Volunteer Recruitment in Criminal Justice' in A Hucklesby and MS Corcoran (eds), *The Voluntary Sector in Criminal Justice* (Basingstoke, Palgrave Macmillan) 93–116.

Corcoran, MS, Williams, K, Prince, K and Maguire, M (2018) 'The Penal Voluntary Sector in England and Wales: Adaptation to Unsettlement and Austerity' 89(1) *Political Quarterly* 187.

Cottam, H (2018) *Radical Help: How We Can Remake the Relationships Between Us and Revolutionise the Welfare State* (London, Virago Press).

Crick, B (2002) 'Education for Citizenship: The Citizenship Order' 55 *Parliamentary Affairs* 488.

Donati, P (2009) 'What Does "Subsidiarity" Mean? The Relational Perspective' 12(2) *Journal of Markets and Morality* 211.

—— (2011) *Relational Sociology: A New Paradigm for the Social Services* (London, Routledge).

du Bois-Pedain, A (2017) 'Punishment as an Inclusionary Practice: Sentencing in a Liberal Constitutional State' in A du Bois-Pedain and A Hart (eds), *Criminal Law and the Authority of the State* (Oxford, Hart Publishing) 199–228.

Eglash, R (2016) 'Of Marx and Makers: An Historical Perspective on Generative Justice' 13(1) *Revista Teknokultura* 245 10.5209/rev_TK2016.v13.n1.52096

Eglash, R, Robinson, KP, Bennett, A, Robert, L and Garvin, M (2024) 'Computational Reparations as Generative Justice: Decolonial Transitions to Unalienated Circular Value Flow' 11(1) *Big Data & Society* https://doi.org/10.1177/20539517231221732.

Fraser, N (1998) *Social Justice in the Age of Identity Politics: Redistribution, Recognition, Participation* (Berlin, Wissenschaftszentrum Berlin für Sozialforschung) www.ssoar.info/ssoar/handle/document/12624.

—— (2005) 'Reframing Justice in a Globalizing World' 39 *Anales de la Cátedra Francisco Suárez* 89.

Fricker, M (2007) *Epistemic Injustice: Power and the Ethics of Knowing* (Oxford, Oxford University Press).

Gitterman, A (2006) 'Building Mutual Support in Groups' 28(3/4) *Social Work with Groups* 91.

Hunt, SA and Benford, RD (2004) 'Collective Identity, Solidarity, and Commitment' in DA Snow, SA Soule and H Kriesi (eds), *The Blackwell Companion to Social Movements* (Oxford, Blackwell) 433–58.

INPS-IT The Italian Social Security System (2024) 'Portale Inps – Social Security Benefits and Deductions (2024: np)' www.inps.it/it/en/previdenza/benefici-previdenziali-e-detrazioni.html.

Levitas, R (2013) *Utopia as Method: The Imaginary Reconstitution of Society* (Basingstoke, Palgrave Macmillan).

Loader, I and Sparks, R (2012) 'Beyond Lamentation: Towards a Democratic Egalitarian Politics of Crime and Justice' in T Newburn and J Peay (eds), *Policing: Politics, Culture and Control* (Oxford, Hart Publishing) 11–41.

—— (2022) 'Reasonable Hopes: Social Theory, Critique, and Reconstruction in Contemporary Criminology' in A Liebling, J Shapland, R Sparks and J Tankebe (eds), *Crime, Justice, and Social Order: Essays in Honour of AE Bottoms* (Cambridge, Cambridge University Press) 100–26.

Lopoo, E, Schiraldi, V and Ittner, T (2023) 'How Little Supervision Can We Have?' 6 *Annual Review of Criminology* 23.

Maguire, M, Williams, K and Corcoran, MS (2019) '"Penal Drift" and the Voluntary Sector' 58(3) *The Howard Journal of Crime and Justice* 430.

McNeill, F (2018) *Pervasive Punishment: Making Sense of Mass Supervision* (Bingley, Emerald Publishing).

—— (2019) 'Mass Supervision, Misrecognition and the "Malopticon"' 21(2) *Punishment and Society* 207.

—— (2020) 'Penal and Welfare Conditionality: Discipline or Degradation' 54 *Social Policy and Administration* 295.

McNeill, F, Corcoran, MS and Weaver, B (forthcoming, 2026) *Generative Justice: Theory, Practice, Prospects* (Bristol, Bristol University Press).

Miller, RJ (2021) *Halfway Home: Race, Punishment, and the Afterlife of Mass Incarceration* (New York, Little Brown & Co).

Montrone, A, Searing, EAM and Poledrini, S (2024) 'How Did the Pandemic Crisis Affects the Financial, Economic and Social Performance of Social Enterprises? Insights from Italian Social Cooperatives' (Nonprofit Policy Forum) www.degruyter.com/document/doi/10.1515/npf-2023-0106/html.

Pestoff, V (2009) 'Towards a Paradigm of Democratic Participation: Citizen Participation and Co-Production of Personal Social Services in Sweden' 80(2) *Annals of Public and Cooperative Economics* 163.

Raekstad, P and Gradin, SS (2020) *Prefigurative Politics: Building Tomorrow Today* (Cambridge, Polity Press).

Robinson, G and McNeill, F (2023) 'Punishment in the Community: Evolution, Expansion, and Moderation' in A Liebling, S Maruna and L McAra (eds), *The Oxford Handbook of Criminology*, 7th edn (Oxford, Oxford University Press).

Rubio Arnal, A and McNeill, F (2024) 'Exploring Social Re/habilitation and Developing a New Conceptualisation of Re/integration' in F Coppola and A Martufi (eds), *Social Rehabilitation and Criminal Justice* (London, Routledge) 251–67.

Schmidt, K (2019) 'Epistemic Justice and Epistemic Participation' (PhD diss, Washington University in St Louis) https://openscholarship.wustl.edu/art_sci_etds/1787.

Scott, D (2016) *Prisons: Places of Harm and Dehabilitation* (London, OpenDemocracy).

Sen, A (1999) *Development as Freedom* (Oxford, Oxford University Press).

Systemic Justice (2023) 'Surfacing Systemic (In)justices: A Community View' https://systemicjustice.ngo/wp-content/uploads/2022/09/SystemicJusticeACommunityView.pdf.

Tortia, E and Troisi, R (2021) 'The Resilience and Adaptative Strategies of Italian Cooperatives during the COVID-19 Pandemic' 15(4) *Foresight and STI Governance* 78.

Vaughan, B (2000) 'Punishment and Conditional Citizenship' 2(1) *Punishment and Society* 23.

Weaver, B (2015) *Offending and Desistance: The Importance of Social Relations* (London, Routledge).

Weaver, B and Barry, M (2014) 'Managing High Risk Offenders in the Community: Compliance, Cooperation and Consent in a Culture of Concern' 11(3) *European Journal of Probation* 303.

Weaver, B, Piacentini, L, Moodie, K and Barry, M (2021) 'Exploring and Explaining Non-Compliance with Community Supervision' 61(2) *British Journal of Criminology* 434.

Weaver, B, McCulloch, T and Vaswani, N (2023) 'Envisioning Social Justice with Criminalised Young Adults' 64(3) *British Journal of Criminology* 675.

Werth, R (2023) 'More Than Monsters: Penal Imaginaries and the Specter of the Dangerous Sex Offender' 25(4) *Punishment and Society* 977.

Index

www.ingramcontent.com/pod-product-compliance
Ingram Content Group UK Ltd.
Pitfield, Milton Keynes, MK11 3LW, UK
UKHW020845290926
15470UKWH00004B/1565